PEREGRINE BOOKS
Y71

ESSAYS IN
SOCIOLOGY AND SOCIAL
PHILOSOPHY

MORRIS GINSBERG

MORRIS GINSBERG

ESSAYS IN SOCIOLOGY AND SOCIAL PHILOSOPHY

Penguin Books

Penguin Books Ltd, Harmondsworth, Middlesex, England
Penguin Books Inc., 3300 Clipper Mill Road, Baltimore, Md 21211, U.S.A.
Penguin Books Australia Ltd, Ringwood, Victoria, Australia

—

Essays in Sociology and Social Philosophy Volume 1, *On the Diversity of Morals,*
first published by William Heinemann Ltd 1956
Essays in Sociology and Social Philosophy Volume 2, *Reason and Unreason in Society,*
first published for the London School of Economics by Longmans, Green & Co. 1947
published by William Heinemann Ltd 1956
Essays in Sociology and Social Philosophy Volume 3, *Evolution and Progress,*
first published by William Heinemann Ltd 1961

—

This selection first published in Peregrine Books 1968
Copyright © Morris Ginsberg, 1968

—

Made and printed in Great Britain
by Hazell Watson & Viney Ltd
Aylesbury, Bucks
Set in Linotype Georgian

Contents

1. The Problems and Methods of Sociology   7
2. The Individual and Society   56
3. The Idea of Progress: a Revaluation   71
4. Social Change   129
5. National Character   162
6. Antisemitism   190
7. The Life and Work of Edward Westermarck   209
8. On the Diversity of Morals   235
9. Reason and Experience in Ethics   271
10. Psychoanalysis and Ethics   315
11. The Nature of Responsibility   342
12. Ethical Relativity and Political Theory   362
    Index   379

[1]

The Problems and Methods
of Sociology*

INTRODUCTION

SOCIOLOGY may be defined as the study of society, that is, of
the web or tissue of human interactions and interrelations. It is
concerned with all that happens to human beings in virtue of
their relations to each other. It differs from some of the special
social sciences, such as economics or jurisprudence, in stressing
the interdependence of social facts and the necessity of viewing
them in relation to each other, and from others, such as history, in
trying to go beyond the description or classification of particular
facts to the establishment of laws or generalizations.

Since social relationships are infinitely varied and subtle, sociologists have concentrated their attention on those relations which
have come to assume a definite form or outline in societies, that
is groups possessed of recognizable structure, and institutions, that
is established forms or modes of relationship between men or
groups. Sociology is also sometimes described as the study of social
institutions, the term 'institutions' being regarded as including
societies in this case. It must be remembered, however, that behind societies there is always Society, and that the conditions
under which definite forms of grouping emerge out of unorgan-
ized human relationships is an essential problem of sociology.

The principal problems of sociology may be set out under the
following headings:

(*a*) *Social structure*. This is concerned with the principal forms
of social organization, i.e. types of groups, associations and
institutions and the complexes of these which constitute societies.

* First published in *The Study of Society*, eds. F. C. Bartlett and others
(London: Kegan Paul, 1939).

7

The study of social structure should clearly include certain parts of what is usually called demography, namely, the distribution of the population, its quantity and quality, in so far as these affect or are affected by social relations.

(*b*) *Social function and social control.* An account of the way the structures work, are regulated and sustained. This requires a study of law, morals and religion, manners and conventions and of other forms of social control.

(*c*) *Social change.* The study of short- and long-range trends in the life of societies, including the problems of development, arrest and decay of societies and, eventually, of the development of mankind as a whole.

These groups of problems have not been dealt with equally fully by sociologists, nor can it be claimed that sociology in its present condition is a systematic body of knowledge in which these problems are considered from a common point of view. The reasons for the diversity of approach can only be understood in the light of the history of sociological thought. Broadly it may be said that sociology has had a fourfold origin in political philosophy, the philosophy of history, biological theories of evolution, and the movements for social and political reform which found it necessary to undertake surveys of social conditions. The different current conceptions of sociology and the unequal development of its branches appear to be due to the fact that one or other of these aspects of social problems has received particular emphasis in different countries and at different times.

The same reasons account for the varying importance attached by sociologists to the philosophical and more strictly scientific sides of their subject respectively. Those who have come to sociology from the philosophy of history have been mainly interested in problems of social change, and have searched for dynamic laws of human development. This was the guiding idea in the sociology of Comte, and it retains its place in more recent French sociology. Durkheim and his school no doubt considered the attempt to deal with humanity as a single whole over-ambitious, and therefore laid stress on the detailed study of specific societies.

Yet the comparative method is for Durkheim the method *par excellence* of sociology, and the laws formulated are regarded as having general validity.

In England the main interest has been in studies of human development, although here the influence of biological theories of evolution made itself strongly felt and directed attention to a general study of genetic factors in the life of social groups. On this side, sociology may be said to have arisen by way of reaction against the comprehensive schemes of development suggested in the philosophies of history of the eighteenth and nineteenth centuries.

At the present time there is a great deal of scepticism regarding the possibility of a 'world history' or a 'world sociology'. Such scepticism is due in part to the difficulty of handling a vast accumulation of historical and anthropological data, in part to the prevailing view of the 'relativity' of historical and sociological research, and also to the fact that the notion of development appears to have lost its impetus. Yet the belief in the unity of mankind persists, and efforts at comprehensive syntheses are widely welcomed. Perhaps the most important empirical contributions towards synthesis will come from studies of 'culture contact', but it would seem that the time is hardly ripe for all-inclusive schemes of human development, and that the discussion of the relevant problems will remain for the present on the methodological and philosophical level rather than on that of exact science.

The influence of philosophy on sociology can also be traced through its connexion with political science. Among the Greeks the systematic study of political life was a branch of general philosophy. In modern times the inquiry into human affairs again began with the criticism of political authority and was not primarily an investigation of facts, but rather an evaluation of them in the light of an ideal conception of society based on the 'law of nature', or later on other ethical theories. Sociology may be conceived as a development of political science in that it includes within its scope the study not only of governmental institutions but of other social institutions, such as marriage and the family, caste and class, forms of property, and economic organization. But just as in the case of political science it is not always easy to keep apart the ethical discussion of the ends of political organization from the account of actual forms of government, so in the handling of other social institutions ethical analysis and factual study are often interwoven. It must, indeed, be admitted that in a great many sociological treatises the study of actual facts receives but slight attention.

The line of demarcation has proved very difficult to draw. Durkheim, who began by insisting on the desirability of distinguishing sociology from philosophy and on the importance of treating social facts *'comme des choses'*, has ended by converting sociology into a kind of philosophy, deriving moral and religious values and even the categories of thought from society. In England, Hobhouse endeavoured in the scientific part of his work, to avoid the use of terms with an ethical colouring, and to differentiate clearly between social science and social philosophy, although some of his critics have held that he did not succeed in doing so (21).* Probably a great deal of the opposition shown towards sociology as a branch of learning is due to the fact that for the philosophers it is not philosophical enough, and for empirically-minded scientists not scientific enough.

The study of contemporary social conditions has in the main been inspired by direct interest in practical reform, and in general it has not been guided by any comprehensive theory of society as a whole. Except in America it has not usually been conducted by sociologists, but by students of the special social sciences, such as economists, statisticians, public health officials and the like. With the emergence of planning on a big scale there is, however, likely to be a growing demand for broader theoretical investigations. In this way sociology may acquire a more reliable basis than it has hitherto possessed.

The desire to free sociology from the charge of vagueness and all-comprehensiveness has led some of the German sociologists to

* For such references see end of essay.

treat it as having its own special and distinct field of inquiry. Thus L. von Wiese has elaborated a 'relational' sociology, the object of which is to analyse and classify social processes, and to show how social structures arise through the action of the elementary social processes of association and dissociation. The treatment of the social processes and relationships is behaviouristic, the inward aspects being relegated to psychology. A. Vierkandt, on the other hand, regards sociology as being concerned with the analysis of fundamental social relationships, such as leadership, respect, submission, struggle and power. The method followed in his treatise, *Gesellschaftslehre* (38), is described as 'phenomenological' in the sense given to this term by E. Husserl (18). To what extent this method really goes beyond psychological introspection or inductive generalization cannot here be discussed. Outside Germany it does not appear to have found many followers.

On the whole it may be granted that one of the functions of sociology is to disentangle the social factor in human life, but it may be doubted whether an abstract discussion of social relationships, or a phenomenological analysis of them without constant reference to the varied contents within which they are manifested, is as fruitful as the defenders of the 'specialist' view of sociology maintain. Further, it is clearly also the function of sociology to study the relations between the social and other factors in human life. The degree and type of influence which these exert can be determined only by inductive methods, and the problem may receive a different answer with regard to different societies and different periods. It seems evident, therefore, that sociology cannot thrive without constant contact with numerous special studies, such as economic history, law, morals, and religion, and that its function is not only to interpret social relationships, but to study their interconnexions.

To illustrate the nature of sociological research I have selected for brief discussion a few topics falling within the three divisions distinguished above, and have added some comments on problems of method.

SOCIAL STRUCTURE

A. POPULATION

1. Quantitative aspects.

The quantitative aspects of population have generally been studied from an economic point of view. Sociologists have not yet treated the subject systematically, although it is clear that it must be the starting point of any adequate morphology of human societies. Numerous attempts have, however, been made to correlate various social phenomena with the volume and density of population. Among the most important of these is Durkheim's theory that an increase in the density of population is the main cause of social differentiation, and that 'civilization', which consists according to him in an intensification of contacts, is thus essentially connected with an increasing density of population (6).

Durkheim's treatise is of interest methodologically as illustrating the difficulties of inductive generalization in sociology. In seeking to establish his law concerning the transition from the 'mechanical' to the 'organic' types of society, he studies the character of the legal systems of a small number of selected societies (the ancient Hebrews, the early Romans, and Christian societies since the fourteenth century. His aim is to demonstrate the growing importance of the contractual, as contrasted with the repressive, elements in law and to connect this change with the growing importance of the division of labour in densely populated societies. A much more comprehensive survey of legal systems would, however, have been desirable, as well as some attention to apparently negative instances of densely populated areas, like China, where the organic type of society has not yet emerged. Durkheim's guiding hypothesis is nevertheless recognized as valuable, and it has suggested fruitful inquiries, among them C. Bougle's study of the relation between the size and mobility of population and the spread of democratic ideas (3).

Another example may be given from the numerous studies of

the bearing of demographic factors upon war (33). Several writers have suggested that there is a definite connexion between 'over-population' and war. A psychological version of this theory is given by F. Carli, who argues that periods of rapid expansion in population are followed by an increase in imperialistic attitudes, which encourage expansionist tendencies, rivalries, and eventually war. In the case of the War of 1914–18, his theory is that the great increase in European population during the nineteenth century led to a disturbance of equilibrium, economic, political, and psychological, and that this was ultimately responsible for the war. The general thesis is disputed by many authorities,* and the relationship, if it exists, is evidently very complex.

Another aspect of the case is ably presented by A. and E. Kulischer in their work, *Kriegs- und Wanderzüge: Weltgeschichte als Völkerbewegung* (20). These authors regard war as a species of migration, and they have brought together a vast amount of data relating to (i) the military campaigns and migrations of the barbaric peoples (seventh to tenth centuries), (ii) the period of absolutism, and (iii) the world movements of the nineteenth and twentieth centuries. In their view changes in the direction of migration, of which war is only one, constitute an essential or decisive factor in world history.

A comparative study of types of expansion, and the conditions determining them, seems to be greatly needed. Is A. J. Toynbee right in saying that geographical expansion is a symptom not of social growth but of social disintegration, and that 'militarism has been by far the commonest cause of the breakdown of civilizations ... on record up to the present date'?†

2. *Qualitative aspects.*

The problem of the bearing of the quality of the population upon social life and change has been approached in a variety of ways, which may be briefly exemplified. First, there are the explanations by historians of social processes in terms of supposed racial or national characteristics. Secondly, numerous statistical

* Cf. Carr-Saunders (4), pp. 305 ff.   † Cf. (37), iii, p. 150.

studies have been made by the so-called 'anthropo-sociologists' (Ammon, Lapouge, and others) of selective migration and other forms of social selection (33). Thirdly, investigations of social mobility and theories of the 'circulation of elites' may be mentioned. In this category is Pareto's theory that the different types of social structure and civilization are determined by the proportions in which certain types of individuals are found in the population (26). Of the same type is Pirenne's extremely well-documented analysis of the social origins of the men who were responsible for the growth of early capitalism in Europe.

These and other contributions to the subject belong, of course, to very different levels of scientific precision, but they all raise problems of fundamental importance to social psychology. Are social changes definitely correlated with changes in genetic characters, or at least with changes in the distribution of these characters in the population? That the quality of the population must count is *prima facie* probable, but the relations between the inborn characters and the social environment are exceedingly subtle, and may well be such as to render possible great social changes without any real alteration of genetic type.

In the first place, the social environment may exert an influence by encouraging some qualities and inhibiting others. Thus an authoritarian political system may cause individuals of independent mind to emigrate, and so affect the general quality of the stock; but far more commonly it will simply have the effect of compelling such individuals to exercise their qualities in non-political spheres of activity. Further, the social environment may influence the form in which individual capacities and tendencies are realized, without in any way changing the hereditary endowment. The desire for the approbation of his fellows may lead a savage to collect skulls, a financier to collect millions, and a scientist to collect specimens. In short, the same hereditary element may have very different effects according to the mode of expression encouraged by the social atmosphere.

Finally, great caution must clearly be exercised whenever resort is had to supposedly 'inborn' qualities in explaining social behaviour. Rules prohibiting sexual relations between near kin have often, for example, been attributed to an inborn aversion to incestuous relationship, without ascertaining whether there is any independent evidence of the existence of such an inborn tendency. Acquisitiveness, again, is sometimes regarded as an inborn trait, but comparative studies suggest that it varies greatly in intensity among different peoples, and anthropologists have argued that among some primitive peoples its intensification is due to contact with Europeans and the fresh economic incentives which they bring with them. Similarly the emotions of shame and jealousy may have an innate basis, yet the forms of their expression are now known to vary widely with social conditions. An adequate social psychology should account for these variations as well as for the relatively constant elements, and for this extensive sociological studies are required.

B. SOCIAL STRUCTURE

A full account of social structure would involve a review of the whole field of comparative social institutions, which cannot, of course, be attempted here. Attention will therefore be confined to the principal conceptions which have been found useful in classifying the main types of social groups and institutions.

We may begin with the distinction drawn by F. Tönnies (36) between community and association, which has played an important role in German sociology.* Community is a form of grouping arising spontaneously or naturally, resting on an accord of feeling and on a type of will, called by Tönnies *Wesenswille*, which is deeply rooted in the entire personality. Association, on the other hand, is artificially formed, reflective or deliberate, resting on a type of will which he calls the *Kurwille*, a deliberate decision consciously adopting means to attain given ends. Community is organic, spontaneous, creative; association is mechanical, artificial, and held together by ties which belong, to use Bosanquet's phrase, 'to the world of claims and counterclaims', the world of

* For MacIver's somewhat different use of the same terms, see page 17.

rivalries, bargainings, compromises. In the history of civilization Tönnies thinks that there has, on the whole, been a movement from community to association, from the type of solidarity exemplified in the intimate life of the family, the kindred, the village or the small city, to the type of union seen in contractual associations or in the large city where, despite spatial contiguity, individuals do not really share in a common life.

In his later work the distinction between the communal and associational is combined by Tönnies with two other criteria to provide a more complex classification. These are the presence of a common determinate will enabling the group to act as a whole, and the question of whether the relationship is one of equal fellowship or of domination. This yields three types of relationship, which he designates *Soziale Verhältnisse*, *Samtschaften*, and *Körperschaften*, each of which may be either communal or associational. Thus the parent-child relationship is communal, i.e. based on deep-seated instincts and feelings, but authoritarian in character; the *Verhältnis* of brothers, friends, or comrades is again communal, but based on fellowship or equality; while in the communal relationship of marriage, subordination and fellowship are intermingled. Associational relationships are exemplified in the relation of master and servant, or master and apprentice, which historically has tended to pass from the communal form of the Middle Ages to the associational form of modern times. The most general form of the associational relationship is the contractual, e.g. between creditor and debtor, or employer and employed, which binds individuals in a specific way while in other respects they may remain strangers or even be enemies.

In the *Verhältnisse* there is no common determinate or unitary will, though the members are aware of their mutual relations. At the opposite end of the scale is the *Körperschaft*, which can act as a unity, whereas the *Samtschaft* is intermediate between these two. The members of a *Samtschaft* are bound by common feelings, attitudes, and desires, but it cannot act as a whole until it is organized into a definite corporate body. Examples of communal

Samtschaften are the medieval estate or the Indian castes; modern social classes are more associational in character.

The *Körperschaft*, as we have mentioned, is characterized by its capacity of acting as an organized whole. The contrast between the communal and the associational type can be seen by comparing the medieval guild with the modern joint-stock company. That the contrast admits of degrees will be realized when an employers' association is compared with a trade union. The former is thoroughly associational, that is, deliberately designed to serve business ends only, leaving the members no more bound to one another than are the shareholders of a joint-stock company; but the latter has many elements of community, serving numerous social ends and providing varied opportunities for fellowship.

It will be seen that, for Tönnies, what essentially distinguishes community from association is the fact that the former embraces all the ends of man,* while the latter serves particular ends. This distinction, in itself fairly clear, is, however, combined by him with others more disputable, between, for example, the instinctive and the reflective, the spontaneous and the deliberate, and the mechanical and the creative. It is interesting to note that it is these latter distinctions which were seized upon by the numerous movements in German thought and politics which have for their slogan 'Back to Community'. They served as the vehicle of a protest against the mechanization of modern civilization and the individualism or atomism of modern societies, which are ascribed to an over-valuation of reason and a neglect of feeling, intuition, or instinct. Hence the emphasis on 'soul' and 'blood', and the demand for intimate and devoted group life, expressed in the youth movements and more recently in National Socialism. In this way the notion of community was turned to uses foreign to Tönnies's thought, and given a sentimental connotation rendering it unsuitable for scientific application.

As used by R. M. MacIver, the distinction between community and association is based on the range or inclusiveness of the relationships which bind the members to one another. 'Wherever any

* *'nimmt den ganzen Menschen in Anspruch'* (*Einleitung*, p. 100).

group, small or large, live together in such a way that they share not this or that particular interest, but the basic conditions of a common life, we call that group a community. The mark of a community is that one's life may be lived wholly within it, that all one's social relationships may be found within it.' Associations, on the other hand, exist for specific purposes. MacIver adds another category, which corresponds roughly to Tönnies's *Samtschaften* and which he calls 'spontaneous configurations', which may be enduring, as in the case of the social classes, or temporary, as in the case of crowds. They are different from associations in that they are not formally set up. The term 'group' is used by MacIver to stand for a 'collection of social beings who enter into distinctive social relationships with one another'. Associations are groups expressly organized for special purposes. A community is a group occupying a given locality and serving wide and inclusive interests. There are also looser configurations of people, responsive to like and common interests, but not expressly organized to fulfil specific functions.

For MacIver there are, then, three main types of groupings: (i) inclusive territorial unities; (ii) interest-conscious unities without definite organizatons (caste, class, crowd); and (iii) interest-conscious unities with definite organizations, which may be either primary (face-to-face) or large-scale. Apparently he does not apply this latter distinction to the two other forms of grouping. In his classification MacIver also makes use of the distinction he draws between interests and attitudes; communities and classes, in his view, reveal more directly social attitudes, while associations, being definitely functional, stand in closer relation to social interests. Further, MacIver holds that in the course of social evolution, with increasing diversification of interests, groupings which in early society had a communal quality tend to become more associational in character, although he does not think that this necessarily involves a loss of unity.

Von Wiese (42) employs what he calls 'social distance' as the criterion for classifying social wholes. By this is meant the degree of nearness or immediacy binding the members. He thinks that it is not in accordance with ordinary usage to designate all collectivities as groups; for instance, states or churches would not be appropriately designated groups. He suggests a threefold classification, into *Massen, Gruppen,* and *Abstrakte Kollektiva.* In crowds (*Massen*) the relations between the members are immediate and personal; in groups the relations are indirect, i.e. mediated by an organization; 'abstract collectivities' are thought of as impersonal, as the bearers of values more enduring than the particular individuals who enter into them.

Crowds are either 'concrete' or 'abstract'. They consist of an indefinite number of people without any organization, held together by a common affect and vague notions of unity, the concrete type being temporary, the abstract type, e.g. 'the public', more enduring in character. Groups are formations having recognizable identity and unity. They are characterized by: (i) relative permanence and continuity; (ii) an organization based on the division of functions among the members; (iii) an idea of the group existing in the minds of the members; (iv) the emergence of traditions and habits; and (v) relations to other groups. Among the 'abstract collectivities' are included the State, the Church, estates (*Stände*), social classes, the economic system, and the 'collective system of the mental life', namely the arts and sciences, with their auxiliary services.

Although the term '*abstrakte Kollektiva*' is awkward, especially in its English rendering, it is clear that von Wiese has made a valuable contribution by pointing to the existence within the community of complexes, such as the economic system or the arts and sciences, which are not associations, or even compounded of associations. Further, a mere enumeration of associations concerned with specific purposes conceals the fact that in actual life interests are interwoven and that this interweaving is represented in structures going beyond particular associations.

To provide for these structures MacIver has suggested, in the latest edition of his work *Society* (21), the term 'institutional complexes' or 'functional systems'. It is easy to see that societies may be usefully distinguished by the different ways in which, for example, Church and State and the economic organizations are related and adjusted to each other, that is, by different types of institutional complex, and to bring out the nature of these functional connexions is an important part of sociological study.

A review of the various classifications proposed, including a number not mentioned above, and a direct study of the facts classified, reveal that among the criteria which have been found helpful in analysing and classifying social structures are the range or inclusiveness of the social relationships; the personal or impersonal nature of the bond; the capacity of acting as a determinate whole; the degree to which members are conscious of the whole, or of symbols representing the whole; duration or relative permanence; whether membership is automatic or voluntary; and whether the group is 'open' or 'closed'. The data do not lend themselves readily to dichotomous classification, but for the sake of clarity they have been set out in diagrammatic form below.

The diagram does not, however, illustrate all distinctions of importance. It omits, for example, the presence or absence of the

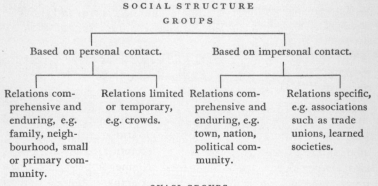

SOCIAL STRUCTURE
GROUPS

Based on personal contact. Based on impersonal contact.

Relations comprehensive and enduring, e.g. family, neighbourhood, small or primary community.

Relations limited or temporary, e.g. crowds.

Relations comprehensive and enduring, e.g. town, nation, political community.

Relations specific, e.g. associations such as trade unions, learned societies.

QUASI-GROUPS
E.g. social classes, 'the public', or 'sets' of people having common interests such as sport or social reform.

FUNCTIONAL SYSTEMS OR COMPLEXES
E.g. the capitalist system, the feudal system, or the most inclusive complexes, 'culture areas' or civilizations.

principle of subordination and hierarchical organization. Further, the distinction between groups and 'quasi-groups', the need of which is seen in the fact that Tönnies was obliged to invent the term 'Samtschaft' and MacIver 'loose configurations', is naturally difficult to draw with any precision. It is arguable, for example, that nationalities or nations may not be organized groups, but are really Samtschaften.

The classification of 'culture areas', or complexes of entire civilizations, is still in its infancy. Gobineau enumerated nine distinct civilizations, Spengler eight. Toynbee (37) draws up a list of twenty-one 'societies'. These he classifies in various ways, so as to range them in a continuous series. At the one extreme are societies which do not appear to be related to any others, either earlier or later than themselves. At the other extreme are societies so intimately related that the question arises whether they are really distinct. Between them are societies standing in various degrees of relationship. Thus they may be 'affiliated' through having derived their religion from a universal Church, or the relation may consist in the fact that the later society has been precipitated by a Völkerwanderung which accompanied the fall of the earlier society. The classification of societies, and especially the distinctions drawn between the various modes of 'affiliation', are made by Toynbee to yield a whole philosophy of civilization. The twenty-one societies are held to be comparable and to provide material for an analysis of the factors at work in the genesis and growth of civilizations.

Toynbee does not apply his method to the simpler societies, but several attempts have been made by ethnologists to work out schemes of culture areas. Recently Montandon (24) has enumerated twelve. Unlike the complexes differentiated by historians and archaeologists, the ethnologists' schemes appear to contain units based not on complexes of traits actually found, but on hypothetical and disputed reconstructions of contacts and migrations.

The problems which emerge from the foregoing considerations may now be summarized:

(a) Under what conditions do the various modes of grouping which have been distinguished arise; e.g. what determines the emergence of nations? In particular, what determines the transition from quasi-groups or *Samtschaften* to definitely organized groups such as associations?

(b) How are the different groups and quasi-groups related to the functional systems, or to the community as a whole? Associations of employers or of workers, for example, have stood in very different relations to the political organization in different societies. Thus in Rome the corporations were not a part of the political machine, whereas in medieval cities they frequently formed the units for electoral purposes, and in contemporary examples of the corporate state they are again becoming integral parts of the political structure. Similarly the relations between religious organizations and social and political institutions vary greatly in different societies. The study of functional interconnexion is therefore a necessary complement to the detailed study of specific associations and institutions.

(c) Are there any regularities in the changes which associations and institutions undergo, and, again, are these changes functionally interconnected? For instance, are changes in the institution of property correlated with changes in family organization, and are changes in class structure functionally connected with changes in the economic and political structure?

It will be observed that in the study of the more advanced societies, at least, the functional and the comparative methods are complementary. For it is only by means of comparative study that we may hope to be able to distinguish between mere concomitance and functional interconnexion.

SOCIAL CONTROL

In developed societies we find several types of norms regulating and controlling behaviour, such as those of law, morals, religion, convention, and fashion. The most important problems arising in this connexion are:

(a) What are the characteristics distinguishing these norms from each other?

(b) Under what conditions, social, economic, and political, do the various norms arise and become differentiated?

(c) What influences are exerted by the various forms of social rules upon one another; e.g. to what extent is law affected in its historical evolution by changes in moral outlook?

(d) In relation to law in particular, there arises the important question of how it is related to ideal justice, and whether there are any valid methods for studying this relationship.

Broadly speaking, these problems constitute the domain of comparative jurisprudence, of comparative morals and religion, and of social philosophy. There is available a vast body of descriptive and analytic material, but it must be confessed that despite the numerous comparative studies that have been made, especially during the last century, the task of comprehensive synthesis remains unachieved. Here the questions involved can only be discussed in very general terms, and with the restricted object of indicating a sociological mode of approach.

With regard to legal rules, it seems to be widely agreed that wherever there are limitations upon the will of individuals which are more than casual devices, and are determined in a constant manner, we have rules which are legal in their essence. In politically organized societies, i.e. in states, these rules are formally promulgated and enforced by explicit sanctions; but even here law is not in the main state-created. It is only as a result of a very long process of development that the State has come to take over, to an increasing extent, the administration of justice and the creation of the law, and to claim, at least in theory, supreme power over other associations which originally possessed their own law. It would seem that, historically, the need for reducing law to unity and system comes to be felt when the inner order of associations breaks down, or when, owing to changes in the distribution of power, a clash occurs between different associations and their spheres must be delimited. If a developed sociology of law were in existence it would show how changes occurring in the power of the various groups and social classes are reflected in changes in current views as to what is 'fit' or 'decent', and more slowly in changes in the norms of the law.*

An interesting historical generalization regarding the emergence of juridical rules, which seems to rest on a wide inductive comparison, is that juridical rules arise and become systematized when the central power which is to become the State must, in order to keep down its rival, the oligarchic nobility, come to an accord with the plebeians. Here both military and economic factors are clearly important, since military power is essential to centralization, while it is only when the people have attained a certain degree of wealth and coherence that they become of importance to the emergent monarchies.†

In developed systems it is usually easy to assign a given norm to the sphere of law, religion, morality, convention, or fashion, but there seems little agreement among students as to wherein precisely the difference lies, or as to why norms with apparently identical content are placed by different societies in different groups. The problems here raised have been much obscured by the tendency to confuse questions of sociological fact with philosophical or ethical considerations of what ought to be. For example, law is sometimes described as heteronomous and morality as autonomous. This distinction, however, ignores the fact that even in highly developed forms of morality the rules are in large measure heteronomous, since they come to the individual from the group and are maintained to a great extent by external sanctions. The most one can say is that moral rules tend to rely more on internal sanctions, i.e. upon a recognition by the individual of the 'intrinsic' worth of certain acts, and of the intrinsic rightness of certain rules.

A similar objection holds, I think, in the case of the view that law is 'the minimum of morality'. This formula may be of service in defining what law ought to be, in the sense of restricting legal regulation to those acts the performance or omission of

* Cf. Ehrlich (7), ch. 4.   † Cf. Hubert (17), pp. 132 ff.

which is so essential to the good of society that they cannot safely be left to individual choice or discretion. But clearly it does not describe law as it is, or has been. For on the one hand law is not always in conformity with moral standards, and on the other its sphere is often much wider in fact than the minimum indicated; in many societies legal sanctions are provided for religious and moral injunctions. To anyone who consults the literature on the subject it must, indeed, be obvious that no brief formula can describe the very complicated relations between the different types of social norms. This situation is due partly to the absence of any agreement among lawyers as to the nature of law, and partly to the fact that non-legal norms have not yet been systematically surveyed. Meanwhile the following suggestions are tentatively formulated:

(i) We may follow Ehrlich in saying that the 'legal norm regulates a matter which, at least in the opinion of the group within which it has its origin, is of great importance, of basic significance.'* What is regarded as of basic importance is a matter which will differ very widely in different societies. Thus in patriarchal societies, where social order is closely linked with the order of the family, the injunction, 'Thou shalt honour thy father and thy mother', is likely to be a legal proposition, while in other societies such an injunction may be relegated to morals, or even to etiquette. It has also been observed that what is regarded as of basic importance by the group within which the law originates may not seem to be of such importance to the community as a whole (no ethical evaluation being here attached to the term 'importance').

(ii) Form and precision are essential attributes of law. By comparison with the body of law, the accepted morality of modern communities is vague, uncertain in its application, and unsystematic. This, however, has not always been the case. In the later Middle Ages, for example, when casuistry flourished, positive morality did tend to approximate to law in elaborateness and precision. From the fourteenth century onwards, as Sidgwick tells

* (7), pp. 167-8.

us (31), 'ecclesiastical writers worked out a quasi-legal body of rules applied to the detail of life through the agency of the confessional, and their authority was not seriously disputed before the Reformation.'

(iii) One aspect of the lack of definiteness of moral systems is that with regard to moral rules the correspondence between rights and duties is less precise than in the case of law. Thus if there is a general duty of beneficence, this does not involve a specific right on the part of any given individual to claim assistance. On this ground some authorities have described the essential distinction between law and morals as consisting in the fact that the former is imperative-attributive, while the latter is imperative only. This distinction seems, however, to ignore the fact that we certainly admit moral claims which have as yet no legal force. The point would rather appear to be that in the case of morals there are general rights and duties, the exact application of which is left in varying degrees to the individual.

(iv) The various classes of norms appeal to different feelings. In the main the violation of a legal rule evokes different feelings from those experienced when a moral rule is broken, a *faux pas* committed, or an act of indecency witnessed. Here there is clearly much work for social psychology to undertake. To social psychology belongs also the analysis of the sense of community and group solidarity, and of the psychological bases of custom, authority, and obedience.*

The psychology of the moral life has been much further developed than the psychology of law, owing to the fact that it has long formed a part of the philosophical handling of ethical problems. Indeed there are ethical thinkers who regard ethics as consisting essentially in the history of moral development and the psychological analysis of moral approval and disapproval. To me, however, it seems clear that the psychology and sociology of morals must be definitely distinguished from ethics proper. Ethics must, of course, start with moral judgements as data, but in dealing with them its method should be critical in the Kant-

* For a brief account of social conventions, cf. (11).

ian sense. In other words, it should seek to elicit the assumptions latent in the judgements, the categories they employ, and in the light of this critical work to discover whether any fundamental principles can be formulated whereby actual morality could be made more coherent and systematic.

In the present chapter we are concerned only with the psychology and sociology of morals, and the main trends of study will be briefly indicated.

On the psychological side, the English moralists of the eighteenth century devoted much attention to the analysis of moral approval and disapproval. The 'moral sense' school, best represented perhaps by Hutcheson, regarded approbation and disapprobation as 'simple ideas which cannot be further explained'. Hume considered approval to be more like a feeling, consisting in a specific or peculiar kind of pleasure, generalized and made disinterested by sympathy.

Adam Smith departs entirely from the notion that approval and disapproval are simple entities. Our approval of tenderness or humanity, for example, is qualitatively different, he holds, from our approval of daring or magnanimity. Approval is, in short, a perception of the agreement of our feeling with the feeling of others, made possible by our power of sympathetic identification. Similarly disapproval is a perception of disagreement or difference between the feeling of the agent and the feeling of the onlooker, when on entering sympathetically into the situation of the agent we find that we cannot share his feelings.

This perception of agreement or disagreement makes possible a further judgement of propriety or impropriety, that is, a recognition of the appropriateness or fitness of the feeling to its object. In the case of virtue or excellence this judgement of propriety is further complicated by admiration, i.e. approval heightened by surprise or wonder. Moreover, we judge not only of the propriety or impropriety of acts, but also of their merit or demerit, and these notions are connected by Adam Smith with two special emotions, namely gratitude and resentment. That act has merit or deserves reward which is the approved object of gratitude; that act has demerit or deserves punishment which is the approved object of resentment, 'approval' in both cases signifying the realization that either we or an impartial spectator would, if placed in the given situation, experience gratitude or resentment.

The above analysis relates to the judgements formed by the individual concerning the propriety and merit of the acts of others. Adam Smith notes that, in fact, our moral criticisms are at first directed upon others, and that it is only gradually that we learn to apply them to ourselves. We find that others are ready enough to judge us, and thus come gradually, and with difficulty, to see ourselves as others see us. To do this we have to place ourselves at a certain distance from ourselves, and invent the impartial spectator, 'the man within the breast', to judge our own conduct. The inner spectator is aided by general rules, however, in the absence of which impartiality is difficult to attain, and the regard for general rules is what we call the 'sense of duty'.

Among recent writers those who stand nearest to Adam Smith are E. Westermarck and S. Alexander, although both lay greater stress on the part played by social factors in the development of moral sentiments. Westermarck's theory of the moral emotions closely resembles Adam Smith's account of merit and demerit. Westermarck believes that they are species of what he designates the 'retributive' emotions, typified by resentment and gratitude. These are not as such moral, but they can become moral when they are disinterested and impartial. Disinterestedness is made possible by the power of sympathy, which enables the individual to experience emotions on behalf of others.

The impartiality and generality of the moral judgement are due to the fact that it expresses emotions felt by society at large, and not by any given individuals. What the moral judgement expresses is not the emotions felt by the individual, but rather the tendency of certain acts to call forth emotions in the community. Like Adam Smith, Westermarck admits here an element of reflectiveness or reason, and he contends that on the whole moral judgements have gradually become more enlightened in the course of moral development. It should be noted that Wester-marck uses his analysis of morals as the basis of his comparative study of social institutions, and considers that the analysis is largely confirmed by the results of his research (39, 40).

Alexander (1) follows Adam Smith even more closely than does Westermarck. The foundation of the moral judgement he asserts, is gregariousness, which in man is transmuted into a conscious social interest. Under this impulsion we become interested in one another's actions, and by its aid the elementary impulses of resentment and gratitude grow into approbation and disapprobation. Men come to discover what will arouse the resentment of others and what others can be induced to sympathize with, and these discoveries, at least in so far as they relate to the simplest conditions of a common life, assume the character of invariable rules. Conscience is 'nothing but the mass of loyalties which gather round ends which have been found experimentally in the course of time to satisfy the passions of men as adjusted on one another in submission to the social sense, and which is accordingly consulted as occasions arise as a short compendium and convenient *vade mecum* of conduct.'

Alexander will not concede that the harmonizing agent is reason, although he holds with Hume that reason is concerned not only with the finding of the means necessary for satisfying the passions, but also with the cool comparison of different ends and the balancing of their attractions. No doubt he means that right and wrong cannot be ascertained by reference to *a priori* rules, but only by an experimental attempt to harmonize or adjust the desires or wills of the individual concerned, and that this attempt is made under the impetus of the social impulse. It follows that if an individual feels that a particular mode of adjustment is wrong, presumably all he can do is to work on the sympathies of others until his wishes are fulfilled.

Alexander's attitude towards the part played by reason appears, indeed, somewhat inconsistent. Mere sociality, and even the best of good will, are surely not enough to solve the difficult problems of social adjustment. Alexander himself admits that the business of morality is to discover a system which 'satisfies objectively' the impulse of sociality. To determine these objective conditions is surely the task of reason, although it may be true that in practice reason has not yet been given much scope in securing social adjustment. According to Alexander there are 'wise' and 'foolish' adjustments, and in the end reason is brought back in the form of the 'wise man', or *phronimos*. The wise man has to consider not only what people actually desire, but what they might desire if they had his insight. In order to be consistent, however, Alexander would have to say that the conclusions reached by the wise man are not morally good, or right, until he has succeeded in inducing others to accept them, and that until there is social approval there can be no moral goodness.

Yet perhaps, as Alexander suggests, the function of the great moralists is to enlarge the contents of human nature by revealing impulses hitherto unsuspected, or by increasing or arousing sensitiveness to claims hitherto neglected. In this contribution, he contends, rather than in any claim to authority, lies their importance. But it would appear that in the end morality has little to contribute to the difficult problems of human adjustment beyond the maxim 'that ye love one another', for what is morally good only emerges when the conflicts have in fact been resolved. This would be a depressing conclusion, if true, and indeed the actual moral codes known to history, even if they incorporate elements of reason, certainly cannot be held to have been dominated by reason. If, however, as Alexander believes, morality consists in an adjustment of wills, reason may yet come to be of increasing importance in determining the objective conditions of harmonious adjustment; and, if so, ethics would necessarily be more closely related to psychology and sociology than it has been hitherto. Alexander's own discussion is of interest to the sociologist chiefly because it suggests that in order to understand the nature of morality we may usefully begin by inquiring how changes in social adjustment are actually brought about, and especially by examining changes in the sensitivity of the community. Studies of this kind have hardly yet been systematically attempted.

That the roots of morality are to be found in the social instincts is a view which has also been propounded with great power by H. Bergson (2). Here, however, the view appears in a distinctive form due to Bergson's theory of the relations between instinct, intuition, and intelligence, and to the distinction that he draws between two types of morality, the 'closed' and the 'open'. In the morality of 'closed' groups, the rules obtaining are imposed by the pressure of social habits. Obligation is then not, as Kant thought, a matter of reason, but a form of necessity analogous to instinct. In the social animals the adjustment of individual behaviour to the requirements of the group is, according to Bergson, automatically assured by the hereditary structure. Man is also a social animal, but being possessed of intelligence he has a measure of self-dependence and the power of initiative, which necessitate a subtler power of constraint. This is supplied by the feeling of obligation, the form which necessity takes in free beings capable of reflection. Rules arise out of the structure of the group, and each has its own constraint due to habit; the specific obligations are, however, always held together by a respect for custom as such, which binds the individual to his group and expresses his sense of solidarity with it.

By contrast 'open' morality is not group morality, but is found in exceptional individuals: sages, mystics, prophets, and saints, whom it inspires with a love going beyond the group to humanity, and indeed to love absolute, which is God. Closed morality acts through pressure, open morality through suasion, aspiration, enthusiasm. The former is static or fixed, the latter always in the making, always in movement. In Bergson's view the two moralities differ qualitatively, and from the one to the other there is no direct road. It is a mistake, he thinks, to suppose that we can pass from the love of family, group, or nation to a love for humanity as a whole. Group morality is limited in its nature, and is indeed infected with hate and fear of the stranger. The higher morality is open only to the few who can transcend the limitations of group life, and who by their example exercise a fascination over others. Between the *âme close* and the *âme ouverte* there is the *âme qui s'ouvre*. Here the two moralities intermingle and are projected on an intermediate plane, in which justice is transformed by benevolence, and benevolence by justice.

Bergson's discussion has the merit that it seeks to account not only for the aspects of morality which are expressed in formed habits and the acceptance of imposed rules, but also for those forms of approval which we employ when we describe acts as noble, magnificent, heroic, sublime. But his distinction between the two types of morality is clearly too sharply drawn. In the first place, he exaggerates the immobility or fixity of the morality of what he calls the closed groups. In our own time, for example, very different and conflicting views are held regarding the major problems of social life, such as war and the use of force in general, property, or sex, and a detailed study of the thought of former ages reveals similar conflicts of opinion and attitude. Morality, in so far as it finds expression in the ideas of any social group, is always in the making, although the rate of movement may differ from age to age and people to people. In the second place, Bergson appears to be too ready to appeal to the mystical powers of the great moral innovators. There is no reason for regarding such innovators as supra-social, and their teachings are certainly not effective unless they become the vehicle of large and massive forces. For the sociologist the important problem is to show under what conditions the aspirations of the few can become the habits of the many, and in particular to explain why it is that in so many instances great moral ideas remain ineffective for ages and then suddenly inspire revolutionary fervour. If there are indeed two types of morality, as Bergson thinks, then it is the fields in which they overlap that are of fundamental interest to the sociologist.

It will be seen from the above brief survey that moral psychology has shown morality as moving between the poles of obligation and approval, pressure and aspiration, right and good. This duality has been variously accounted for. It has been ascribed to a conflict between impulse and reason, between the social and other impulses, or between free intelligence and automatic habits. Perhaps a more fundamental explanation is to be found in the fact that morality is an attempt to introduce order in the life at once of the individual and of the group, and that correspondence between the two is achieved, if at all, only with great difficulty. Moral rules arise out of the needs of the social structure, they embody an adjustment of human relations to the requirements of the group. The adjustment is, however, for the most part crude and unsystematic, and the individual, in submitting to the requirements of the larger order of the group, may often fail to satisfy his inmost needs.

Moreover, as communities become more complex, stratified groups arise within them which give rise to a division and conflict of loyalties. Obligation then ceases to be a simple reflection of the pressure of formed habits and group-suggestion, and the sense of duty becomes more complex than the mere acceptance of a rule because it is a rule. Perhaps the preoccupation of modern ethics with the notion of right and duty, in contrast with the Greek thinkers' emphasis on the notion of the good, is due to the fact that in modern conditions the view that in accepting the moral law the individual will find his own fulfilment has lost its *prima facie* plausibility. The difficulty is brought home to the reflective individual by the diversity of moral standards which he finds prevailing among the different groups within his own community, by glaring contradictions between private and public morality, and by the huge discrepancy between the ethical teaching of the spiritual religions and the moral principles which actually guide even enlightened men. Although for a great many people morality may still be conventional and authoritarian, a growing number of individuals are finding that even *Sittlichkeit* is not enough in a world of conflicting loyalties and allegiances.

In psychoanalytic literature Adam Smith's inner spectator, 'the man within the breast', reappears in the form of the 'super-ego', to which are attributed the functions of self-observation, moral censure, and repression. But while for Adam Smith it is

33

the social group that provides the mirror in which the individual gradually comes to see himself, in psychoanalytic theory it is the father who provides the model for the super-ego. Without questioning the importance of the part played by early infantile experiences in the formation of character, it may nevertheless be suggested that psychoanalysts have tended to treat the family too much in isolation from the wider social group, and in particular to neglect the pervasive influences exerted by the group upon the family. Freud himself notes that in the course of the individual's development the super-ego comes under the influence of persons, such as teachers, who are in the nature of substitutes for the father, and he even suggests that the super-ego of the child is modelled not so much on the pattern of the parents as on the super-ego of the parents, which they derive from *their* parents, and which thus becomes the bearer of the social tradition. But surely this suggestion implies that the authority exercised by the parents is itself socially conditioned, and leads us back to an inquiry into the origins of social norms, of which those regulating life within the family form only a part.*

The account given by Freud of the process whereby the external authority of the father is turned into an inner authority gives rise to a more radical criticism. The process is explained by self-identification with the father, but it is clear that in the course of this identification the father, and the later father substitutes, are idealized and given attributes which make them worthy of love. What is the root of this idealization? Why have men to persuade themselves that the people they obey are not only powerful, but wise and just? Is there not here a basic value judgement, of which no account is taken in the psychoanalytic theory of morals? Must we not value wisdom and justice, if we have to attribute these virtues to our leaders in order to justify our obedience to them? Probably this aspect of the problem tends to be neglected by psychoanalysts because they are more directly concerned with the repressive and authoritarian elements in morals than with the source of primary approvals and disapprovals.

* Cf. Fromm (9).

34

In the sociological study of morals perhaps the most interesting problem concerns the variability of moral judgements. Contrary to widely held views, comparative studies reveal a considerable uniformity in the moral judgements regarding the fundamental social relationships. If we compare the list of *prima facie* duties drawn up by W. D. Ross* with the duties enumerated in comparative studies such as Westermarck's, the resemblance is striking. The duties of fidelity, reparation, requital, equitable distribution, beneficence, and non-maleficence or non-injury, are insisted on very widely in the primitive world, and even the duty of self-improvement is anticipated on the primitive level in the notions of self-regard and self-respect.† Westermarck himself concludes that 'when we study the moral rules laid down by the customs of savage peoples we find that they in a very large measure resemble the rules of civilized nations.'‡

The chief difference lies, of course, in the range of persons to whom the rules are held to be applicable, a range which has expanded in the course of history with the expansion of the social units and the accompanying widening of the altruistic sentiments. Other variations are traceable to differences in the general level of knowledge, to changes in religious beliefs, to the unequal complexity of social and political circumstances, to the degree of clarity with which the ends of life are apprehended, to the dominance of partial interests, or to confusions arising out of the difficulty of defining the relations between the collective good and the component parts. Above all, with growing social differentiation hierarchical orders emerge, each with its own morality. Thus military groups, for example, inculcate codes of honour and superiority, while economic differentiation generates a class morality enjoining obedience and submission on the one side and restraint and considerateness towards 'inferiors' on the other.

The problem of the relative significance of economic, political, intellectual, and religious factors in the shaping of morality is not one that lends itself to summary treatment, and in any case it may be doubted whether sociology has yet developed methods refined

* (29), p. 21.   † (40), ii, p. 143.   ‡ (39), p. 197.

enough for its solution. It would be very difficult, for example, to estimate the comparative influence of economic, religious, and specifically moral factors in the changes of attitude reflected in the abolition of slavery, or the partial humanization of the criminal law. Hobhouse's elaborate survey shows a certain parallelism of ethical development with the general development of thought,* and of both with social development (16), but the connexion which he claims to establish is not very close or direct, and he recognizes that social change frequently governs, rather than obeys, the moral conscience (14).

The association between morals and religion seems to be closest in the case of the spiritual religions and the 'middle' civilizations, where religion provides sanctions for both moral and legal injunctions. Westermarck thinks that the 'moral ideas of uncivilized men are more affected by magic than by religion, and that the religious influence has reached its greatest extension at certain stages of culture which, though comparatively advanced, do not include the highest stage.'† The question of the definition of ligion, however, enters here. It is arguable that what has occurred in the higher stages has been, not a lessening of the influence of religion, but a change in the character of that influence, in other words, that both religion and morals have come to rest increasingly on inward experience and less on authority. In this way it is possible for the religions to provide a body of moral convictions at the very time when their formal doctrines are losing in importance. For further discussion of the complicated problems involved the works of Hobhouse and Westermarck may be referred to, as well as the rather different approach to the subject made by Carveth Read (27).

SOCIAL CHANGE

Of the large number of topics which fall under the head of social change, I shall here consider only the problem of social development or evolution.

* (15), pt. II, ch. 8.   † (40) ii, p. 747.

As is well known, the notion of development was familiar to philosophers long before the emergence of the biological theory of evolution, and in the opinion of many it has, indeed, a clearer relevance to the growth of mind and society than to the process of biological change. Since sociological theory has been profoundly influenced by the conceptions of evolution as current in biology and in philosophical speculation directly bearing on biology, however, it is useful to consider social evolution in the light of these conceptions. Three trends of theory may be distinguished, all of which have affected, as they may have been affected by, the study of social change.

First, evolution has been used to describe the process of differentiation of species from a common stock or common stocks, that is, in Darwin's phrase, the process of 'descent with modification'. Secondly, biologists have used the term evolution to describe not merely the process of differentiation or diversification of species but also the fact that in the course of organic evolution there has occurred a movement from 'lower' to 'higher' levels of life. It will be seen that this can be readily linked with the notion of progress in sociology, though difficulties at once arise regarding the interpretation of the terms 'higher' and 'lower', which may require different definitions in biology and in sociology. Thirdly, the conception of evolution has been generalized and applied to the whole range of the natural world. Thus in theories of 'emergent evolution' the attempt is made to map out successive orders of integration, exemplified in the series, say, of atom, molecule, colloidal unit, cell, and multicellular organisms of increasing complexity. This has an obvious bearing on sociology in that societies may come to be regarded as constituting the 'next' level in development, and all known societies may be arranged in a series of ascending levels, whether 'emergent' or not.

The theory that similarities of form or structure can be explained by descent from a common source was applied to social phenomena before the appearance of Darwin's *Origin of Species*. It was used, for example, in relation to language by Sir William Jones a quarter of a century before Darwin was born. Darwin himself used the case of language to illustrate the principles of 'genealogical classification'. Comparative philologists have classified the large number of languages found in the world into families or stocks, and recently there seems to be a tendency to establish connexions between groups of languages which had formerly been regarded as remote from each other. Their derivation from a common source is indeed not improbable.*

With regard to other aspects of human culture the notion of evolution was clearly enunciated by Tylor:

To the ethnographer the bow and arrow is a species, the habit of flattening children's skulls is a species, the practice of reckoning numbers by tens is a species. The geographical distribution of these things and their transmission from region to region have to be studied as the naturalist studies the geography of his botanical and zoological species.

By means of numerous illustrations Tylor goes on to show that the idea of evolution is more easily verifiable in the study of culture than in biology, and there can be no question that the combination of morphological classification with the study of geographical distribution has played an important part in the development of ethnology and archaeology since Tylor's time.

It is, however, regrettable that sociologists have not paid more attention to the evidence for linguistic evolution, which raises in an interesting form all the major problems connected with the nature of social change, and also serves to bring out important differences between biological and social evolution. Thus it is clear that linguistic changes do not depend upon changes in the inherited structure of the people who create or adopt them, that the kinship or affinity of languages has nothing to do with continuity of descent in the biological sense, and that the survival of particular languages in the struggle for existence is determined by quite other factors than those important in the biological sphere. Other relevant problems concern the role of cumulative individual

* (23), p. 85.

variations in social change, the influence of unconscious factors, the contribution of great personalities, and the nature of convergent evolution. The material for the solution of these problems is far more abundant in relation to language than to any other cultural elements.

While the idea of evolution in the sense of descent with modification can thus be applied fruitfully to the study of parts of culture which can be shown to have undergone a process of diversification from a common source, the same idea has proved even more suggestive when interpreted in the second of the senses distinguished above, and applied to societies taken as constituting unitary systems or wholes. Here the biological analogy is the classification of living things on the basis of level of organization or integration. Despite the charge of anthropocentrism, few biologists would deny that in some sense vertebrates are of higher organization than invertebrates, and mammals of higher organization than other vertebrates.

The criteria of advance have been variously defined. Some have found the criterion in increasing complexity, but perhaps the most satisfactory criterion is the degree of independence of a particular environment. Adaptation to the environment is not sufficient, for the lower organisms may be just as well adapted to their environment as the higher are to theirs. What is important is rather increasing plasticity and adaptability to varying environments, with consequently increasing self-dependence. This is achieved, as Spencer saw, by an increasing specialization of the parts of the organism, accompanied by an increasing integration. The integration is traceable not only in bodily structure and function, but also in the growth of mental powers, that is, of the ability to bring different actions and experiences to bear upon one another and so form them into systems. In dealing with the higher levels comparative psychology is therefore of the greatest importance, and it becomes possible to use as a criterion of advance the degree to which control of the conditions of life is consciously guided or directed.

The extension of the concept of evolution, conceived as a change in the level of organization, to the field of sociology is readily intelligible. Whether or not all life is social in character, it is clear that mental and social development come to be increasingly interconnected. Moreover, beyond a certain point further organization is achieved not so much by changes in the organic structure, as by the building up of structures of a different kind, namely the systems of relationships between individuals which we call social structures. In the case of human societies the most significant change which occurs is the replacement of the mechanism of genetic transmission by that of social heritage or tradition. The new mechanism makes possible cooperation on an ever-increasing scale, and above all it immeasurably increases the power of 'interlearning',* i.e. of learning from the experience of others, whether near or distant in time or space. It is clearly this change which makes human development distinctively social development. The development or fulfilment of human potentialities through tradition, mutual stimulus, selection, and cooperation proceeds chiefly by means of those changes in the relations between individuals which constitute social structure.

Social development is thus social in two senses of the word. First, it operates through changes in social structure and especially in tradition, and not in the main through a modification of genetic type. Secondly, it has consisted in an extension of the cooperative elements in human relations. The first point raises the difficult question of the influence of 'racial' and more general genetic factors on human development, and cannot be discussed here, but in my opinion there are good grounds for asserting that the course of history has been on the whole independent of germinal change.†

With regard to the second point, an enormous movement of unification is apparent throughout most of human history. It is exhibited in the increase in size of political aggregates, in the growth of political and economic interdependence, and possibly, despite cultural diversity, in an underlying assimilation or con-

* This point is treated with great thoroughness by Spiller (35).
† Cf. (4), concluding chapter, and (13), ch. 3.

vergence in science, art, religion, and culture generally. Although some interdependence has always existed, there can be no doubt that it has grown enormously in the course of history. It is interesting to note in this connexion that, according to Toynbee's recent survey, the 'unrelated civilizations' are in a minority of six out of twenty-one, that these belong to the infancy of civilization, and that the present conditions of mutual influence preclude the possibility of unrelated civilizations ever emerging again.*

It might, however, be urged that in thus insisting on unification we have ignored the element of force, pressure, and conflict, which perhaps has also increased, and that this element must be included in the conception of social development, since it has certainly played a large part in extending the area of social organization.

The problem may be approached in two ways. In the first place, an attempt might be made to show that, taking the history of humanity as a whole, the cooperative principle has been gaining ground over the principle of conflict. Even if the general movement from force to persuasion reflects no more than a change of tactics on the part of dominant groups, the fact that the change had to be made indicates a wider diffusion of knowledge and the power of self-direction among the masses of men. It might be argued, again, that the empires created and maintained by war have eventually perished by war,† and that enduring success has only been achieved when conquerors have managed to transmute force into authority, and to secure some measure of inward unification by winning the consent, or at least the acquiescence, of the governed.

If this attempt to estimate the net gains of the cooperative principle in humanity be deemed impracticable, it might be contended, in the second place, that we could still arrange human societies on a scale from the same point of view, by maintaining that those communities have achieved a higher organization which have secured order and efficiency in large areas with a

* (37), i, pp. 184 ff. † Cf. Toynbee (37), and Gordon Childe (5), p. 265.

minimum of coercion, and have thus provided greater opportunities for the fulfilment or realization of human capacities. Further, even if such a line of development were only one among many others it would retain its importance as an indication of the possibilities open to mankind. If the biological analogy is to be pursued we ought not, indeed, to expect evolution along a single line, still less should we expect all evolution to be progressive. Evolution, Julian Huxley tells us,

is a series of blind alleys, some extremely short, leading to species and genera that undergo no further development or even become extinct, others longer, to be reckoned in millions of years, which yet come up in the end against their terminal blank wall. Only along one single line is progress and its future possibility being continued – the line of man.*

Perhaps progressive evolution, as judged by the criteria above indicated, including the criterion of free cooperation, is likewise only one of many types apparent in the history of mankind, and yet the societies that are moving in this line may in the long run show greater vitality than others, and more promise of further development.

On the view here briefly indicated progressive social evolution has consisted in: (i) a growing command over the conditions of life, achieved by increasing knowledge of nature, including mind and society; (ii) the growth of cooperation, partly by an increase in the size of communities, partly by the organization of the relations between communities; (iii) a change in the character of cooperation in the direction of freedom, and the emergence into the consciousness of men of the sense of their unity and of the need for reconciling the requirements of order and liberty on a world scale.

Taking mankind as a whole, development in one direction has clearly often been accompanied by loss and retrogression in another. Thus increase in the scale of organization has often been

* (19), p. 98.

42

achieved on the principle of subordination and has meant a loss of freedom; increasing power over nature, and even collective efficiency, may result in stultifying and thwarting the deepest needs of individuals. Yet on the balance there may often have been a net gain, and no doubt some communities will have come nearer than others to satisfying the joint requirements of development and in this sense may be further along the road of progressive evolution.

Two of the criteria of development referred to above, namely increasing control over the conditions of life and the growth of cooperation, may be readily expressed in terms which a biologist might use without committing himself to any particular ethical theory. Doubt may, however, arise regarding the third, which might be thought to introduce distinctively ethical categories. If, however, development is understood as consisting in a process whereby a full realization or fulfilment of human capacities is gradually attained, that society might be regarded as most developed which evokes the most spontaneous devotion to common ends among its members and releases the greatest fund of intelligent energy. It might, indeed, be urged that the societies which have developed furthest in such directions will have greater vitality as compared with societies which are based on subordination and deny scope for initiative to the bulk of their members.

Whether or not this form of argument would satisfy a biologist, it is clear that ethical and biological criteria of development cannot be assumed to coincide without careful examination. Increase in power over nature, including human nature and social organization itself, may be used in the service of bad ends, and even intelligent and free cooperation within a community may be ethically bad in so far as it ignores or overrides the just claims of other communities. Clearly not all development, and not even all social development, is good. The most one can say is that on the assumptions of a rationalist theory of ethics there could be no ultimate fissure between the requirements of ethics and the requirements of a scientific sociology. This must not blind us to the fact that the development which has occurred in history has, on any theory of ethics, been decidedly uneven, although perhaps, taking mankind as a whole, a substantial advance has nevertheless been made.

The difficulties in the way of general progress arise partly from the fact that development, as judged by the criteria defined above, has been unequal, and advance in one direction has often constituted a hindrance to advance in another. Thus with respect to the growth of the power of conscious control, our control over inorganic nature infinitely surpasses our control over life, mind, and society; and since the former type of control may be used for purposes of destruction, there is the danger that before mankind has acquired sufficient knowledge of the causes of social change, and sufficient moral wisdom to apply it aright the whole social structure may be wrecked, and the work of organizing mankind have to be begun all over again.

Further, if progress is to move more securely, it must now be on a world-wide scale. As a result of improvements in technical power, the communities of the world have become closely interdependent, and, unless their interaction is rationally controlled, a clash between them may lead to irretrievable disaster. Self-contained development is increasingly difficult and precarious. Autarchy necessitates stringent autocratic discipline, and this, besides severely limiting the individuality of the component members of the group, frequently fosters enmities with other groups and in turn demands a greater degree of militarization within.

The chances of 'limited' progress are therefore slighter than they have ever been before, and increase in the scope of organization grows ever more vital as a component of development, while at the same time infinitely complicating the problem of reconciling order with freedom. The element of hope in the situation is that the problem has at last begun to be faced on a world scale, and that the conception of a self-directed humanity has emerged, at least in theory. It is sometimes urged that the forces making for disruption are inherently discrepant and must eventually bring about their own defeat. But this optimistic estimate ignores what Renouvier has described as the 'terrible solidarity of evil', the fact that greed and deceit, violence and war, breed and support each other. A theory of social dynamics must take this 'solidarity' into consideration.

The place of the theory of social development in wider evolutionary theories can only be briefly mentioned here. In Hobhouse's work the evolution of society is considered as a phase in the evolution of mind. He argues that 'orthogenic evolution' can be made intelligible only by assuming the presence within the system of reality of a conational force, which by a series of syntheses grows in scope and articulateness and becomes at last conscious of its efforts in the growth of humanity.

In the philosophy of holism, societies are not regarded as constituting a new type of whole: 'the society or group is organic without being a whole.'* In dialectical materialism, society appears as a sort of 'emergent' or qualitatively new entity. This is hinted at also by C. Lloyd Morgan (25), and developed further by W. M. Wheeler (41).

In a different form the notion that societies constitute qualitatively new wholes had been used by sociologists long before the rise of the philosophy of emergent evolution. It was implied by Wundt, for example, in his theory of creative synthesis in relation to the general will of groups, by Durkheim in his theory that social facts are *sui generis*, and by many others who conceive of a group mind as different from the sum of its parts. On general grounds, however, we should expect to be able to explain social phenomena in terms of laws governing (i) the human mind, (ii) the interactions of human beings with one another, and (iii) the consequences of such actions. From the point of view of methodology, therefore, the question of whether there are irreducible social laws must not be prejudged in the interest of general theories of emergent evolution, or in order to secure an independent status for sociology, but should only be decided *ambulando* as our knowledge of social phenomena grows.

* Cf. Smuts (32), p. 339.

METHOD

A. TYPES OF GENERALIZATION IN THE SOCIAL SCIENCES *

A survey of sociological work shows that the generalizations which have so far been attempted may be classified under the following heads:

(i) Empirical associations, or correlations, of varying degrees of definiteness between concrete social phenomena. Thus it may be shown that in certain areas urban divorce rates are approximately double the rural rates, or that the marriage rate varies with variations in the volume of trade, or that crime rates are higher in towns than in the country.

(ii) Generalizations formulating the conditions under which institutions or other social formations arise. For example, the development of capitalism may be held to be associated with the existence of large accessible markets, a sufficient specialization of the industrial arts to make indirect methods of production profitable, the existence of a class of workers who find it difficult to earn an independent livelihood, and perhaps also the dominance of a certain mentality, which is expressed in the desire and the capacity to apply accumulated wealth to profit-making, besides other factors.

(iii) Generalizations asserting that changes in given institutions are regularly associated with changes in other institutions. For instance, the extension of public order in the simpler societies and in the early civilizations may be linked with an extension of stratification according to the principle of social and economic subordination; or social and cultural changes may be alleged, as by followers of historical materialism, to be invariably associated with changes in class structure.

(iv) Generalizations asserting rhythmical recurrences or phasesequences of various kinds. Examples are the attempts to distinguish the 'stages' of economic development which have been

* For a fuller discussion, see (10), 1.

made by Bücher, Schmoller, and many others, and the view that economic development passes through phases of expansion and contraction, or from phases of aristocratic control, from above, to phases of democratic control, from below.

(v) Generalizations describing the main trends in the evolution of humanity as a whole. Examples are Comte's law of the three stages; the Marxist theory of a movement from an undifferentiated or classless society through various forms of class differentiation to a classless society again; Hobhouse's attempt to correlate social development with mental development; as well as many other schemes of social evolution which do not stress the notion of recurrence or repetition of given sequences, but are concerned rather with the trends that can be disentangled in human culture as a whole.

(vi) Laws stating the implications of assumptions regarding human behaviour, but leaving to further inquiry the problem of how far the assumptions correspond to fact, and to what extent deviations can be explained by reference to 'disturbing' factors. Examples are the laws formulated in economic theory.

It will perhaps be generally agreed that sociological investigations should be carried out in accordance with what Mill called the 'Inverse Deductive Method'. In other words, inductive generalizations, whether reached by statistical methods or by the comparative method, should be further verified by deduction from more ultimate laws. Mill himself thought that these laws would be furnished by psychology and by the new science for which he proposed the name of 'ethology', and which corresponds to a considerable extent to what is now called social psychology. Possibly, however, there may be sociological laws *sui generis,* and some may think that the laws of biology are also of importance in dealing with the evolution of societies.

If, now, we look back at the types of generalization enumerated above, it will be seen that the degree to which they satisfy the requirements of the Inverse Deductive Method varies greatly from case to case. Thus most of the investigations falling under the first head remain on the empirical level. It will, however, be observed

47

that statistical associations are held to be 'intelligible' when an interpretation of the relationship can be given in terms of motives assumed to be normally operative in popular psychology. For instance, the alleged relation between increase in the crime rate and economic crises is held to be intelligible if economic factors can be shown to result in a loss of morale; a fall in the birth rate is regarded as explained if appeal can be made to generally operative motives, such as the desire to maintain a certain standard of living. The psychological factors are as a rule stated only in general terms, although it is often felt that they ought to be more accurately investigated by a scientific psychology.

In historical generalizations, also, further explanation is sometimes attempted in psychological terms. Thus Pirenne's generalization that in the history of European capitalism there has occurred a regular alternation between periods of economic freedom and of economic control, and a similar alternation between periods of energetic innovation and periods of conservatism and stabilization, is explained by him in psychological terms. The 'new men' who introduce a new phase are marked by audacity and independence, while their descendants are anxious rather to preserve what has been won, and are inclined to support any authority capable of giving them the necessary security. Here again the psychology employed is of the popular variety, as in the description of the *parvenu*.

The more ambitious generalizations formulating long-range trends in the history of humanity are usually supported by inductions from data reached by the comparative method, but in most cases they are linked deductively with wider theories of development. Only a few examples can be given here. Spencer's law of a transition from militant to industrial types of society is reached explicitly by the inverse deductive method, that is by the comparison of a number of societies, supported by a deductive analysis of the nature of compulsory and voluntary organizations. The whole argument is further connected by him with his general law of evolution, on the assumption that increasing differentiation of functions must eventually limit the scope of governmental organs and encourage voluntary and contractual cooperation over ever wider fields of social life (34).

Durkheim's law of a movement from 'mechanical' types of society, which are based on the similarities between men, to 'organic' types, based on the division of labour, is established inductively, and chiefly by means of a comparison of the legal systems which prevail in societies of the two types. The explanation of the law appears to be in biological terms, since he finds the cause of the development in the increasing density of population, which according to him necessitates increasing specialization and division of labour. The explanation is not teleological. Civilization, which depends on an intensification of social life, is not an end foreseen; not a function of the division of labour, but merely its 'contre-coup'.*

Hobhouse's sociological theories are based on a wide induction of facts derived from anthropology and history. He traces the development of the human mind in the spheres of cognition, of control over natural forces, of ethico-religious belief and practice, and of imaginative creation. As a result he attempts to establish a correlation between mental advance and the growth of the social fabric, as judged by the scale of organization, efficiency in control and direction, cooperation in the satisfaction of mutual needs, and the scope afforded for personal development. The correlation is rough and indirect, and there is in particular a lag in the accommodation of social to ethical developments. Yet in Hobhouse's view it is sufficiently clear to justify the hypothesis that the underlying force of historical evolution is to be found in the growing power of the mind, gradually obtaining a firmer grasp over the conditions of its development, but as yet not completely in control.

The argument is on the whole inductive, but since Hobhouse's sociological studies are part of a wider philosophical system, they are no doubt influenced by another hypothesis which he had come to accept, concerning the part played by mental forces in the whole process of evolution. This hypothesis, in turn, is formulated by

* (6), p. 308.

Hobhouse on the basis of both a wide empirical survey and a metaphysical analysis of the logical requirements of systematic explanation, and he attaches great importance to the fact that these two lines of investigation lead to similar conclusions.

Of the main types of generalization enumerated above, those of the sixth group alone are reached deductively. There seem to be great differences of opinion regarding the way in which, in the case of economic theory, the transition is effected from deductive theory to the empirical facts. According to some authorities, the laws of economics are analytic propositions bringing out the implications of certain assumptions regarding human behaviour. In so far as these assumptions correspond to fact the implications will be taken to hold good in fact, in the absence of disturbing factors. Other authorities, however, regard economic laws as hypotheses which have to be tested or verified by the facts. To the latter authorities induction and deduction are integral parts of one set of logical operations; to the former induction has no verificatory function, the business of empirical studies being merely to reveal the fields within which theories otherwise established may be correctly applied, or to suggest new problems for deduction (22,28).

B. THE COMPARATIVE METHOD

It will be clear from the above discussion that in a great deal of sociological work appeal has to be made to the comparative method, and some account of it is therefore appropriate.

In essentials this method is an application of a general rule of inductive logic : to vary the circumstances of a phemonenon with the object of eliminating variable and inessential factors, and so arriving at what is essential and constant. What is peculiar to the method is the use of data derived from different regions or different times. Reference to the types of regularity distinguished above will show that the use of comparative data is of varying importance. When a phenomenon under investigation exhibits sufficient individual variations within the same society, or at the same period of time, it may be possible to establish real connexions without going outside that society or period. In the statistical study of crime, for example, differences of economic status, of education, of type of family life, of psychological make-up, and of hereditary disposition within the same society afford sufficient variation of circumstances to render possible some estimate of the relative significance of the different factors involved in criminal behaviour.

Yet even in the investigation of problems of this kind comparative studies may be of great importance, and are in some cases unavoidable. A study of the causes of suicide, for example, may be conducted within a particular group by noting its incidence in different economic grades, social classes, and religious denominations, and in relation to various psychopathic traits. But if the study were confined to a particular group certain empirical associations might easily be given undue importance. Thus a lower incidence of suicide among Catholics might turn out to be connected with the fact that in the particular locality studied Catholics lived mostly in rural areas, and in order to carry the inquiry further it would then be necessary to find areas in which religious denominations were differently distributed.

As soon as we move from the study of phenomena presenting individual variations to that of complex social formations or institutions, the importance of comparative studies becomes obvious. If, for example, we wish to know the conditions under which slavery, or serfdom, or any other forms of economic organization arise, it is necessary to study their history in different societies. The problem of the extent to which a phenomenon like the rise of nationalism is conditioned by the need for economic or political unification, by the growth of the middle classes, or by war, or the problem of the limits set to national assimilation by racial heterogeneity or differences in religion, obviously requires wide comparative study for its solution. In short, as soon as sociology passes from the descriptive to the analytic level, the comparative method is essential alike for tracing genetic connexions and for establishing any other mode of causal relationship.

It is important to note that the comparative method is not as such committed to any particular theory of social evolution, still less to evolution along a single line. Its primary object is to provide a social morphology, or a classification of the forms of social relationships, with a view to facilitating causal analysis. This includes analysis of the causes which explain why one form succeeds another, but we cannot assume at the outset of the inquiry that the laws of social change are necessarily evolutionary in character. It is true that in some of the earlier expositions of the comparative method the belief in regular or unilinear evolution was implied, but this belief is not essential to the method, nor has it in fact been held by the more important thinkers.

Even the arch-evolutionist Herbert Spencer did not believe that every people necessarily passed through the same stages in regular and progressive order, and he insists that 'it is only by taking into consideration the entire assemblage of societies that the law of evolution can be shown to be at work in society.'* There is hardly a trace of the notion of automatic development in Tylor's work. As early as 1865 Tylor explained that the similarities in institutions or beliefs which can be found in different parts of the world may be variously accounted for, sometimes by the like working of men's minds under like conditions, sometimes by common descent, sometimes by borrowing direct or indirect.

Similarly Freeman (8), using historical material, carefully explains that likenesses may be due to direct transmission, independent invention and like circumstances, or common descent, and that the comparative method is not committed to any of these explanations *ab initio.* The notion of automatic or unilinear evolution is also entirely foreign to the use made of the method by such writers as Sidgwick, in his *Development of European Polity* (30), or more recently H. Sée and Sombart, in their studies of the rise of capitalism and of the different forms of land-ownership, or Lord Bryce, in his study of democracy. It is to be observed, further, that the method can be and has been used without reference to any evolutionary theory whatever, as by Westermarck and Durkheim.

In applying the comparative method, one should certainly not

* (34), iii, pp. 598 ff.

start with hypothetical first stages and then deduce subsequent development. In the absence of direct evidence of historical genesis, reconstructions of early stages should only be made, if at all, not at the beginning, but at the end of an inquiry. In other words, when we already know something of the nature of institutions, and of the conditions under which they came into being, we may be able to infer which institutions are likely to have existed in the circumstances in which prehistoric primitive man lived. Such reconstructions should be inferences from theories and facts otherwise established, and not the foundation on which sociological theory is made to rest.

REFERENCES

1. Alexander, S., *Beauty and other Forms of Value* (London: Macmillan, 1933)
2. Bergson, H., *Les Deux Sources de la Morale et de la Religion* (Paris: Alcan, 1932)
3. Bouglé, C., *Les Idées Égalitaires* (Paris: Baillière, 1889)
4. Carr-Saunders, A. M., *The Population Problem* (London: Oxford University Press, 1922)
5. Childe, V. Gordon, *Man Makes Himself* (London: Watts, 1936)
6. Durkheim, E., *De la Division du Travail Social*, 5th ed. (Paris: Alcan, 1926)
7. Ehrlich, E., *Fudamental Principles of the Sociology of Law* (Cambridge, Mass.: Harvard University Press, 1936)
8. Freeman, E. A., *Comparative Politics* (London: Macmillan, 1873)
9. Fromm, E., 'Autorität und Familie', *Schriften des Instituts für Sozialforschung*, 1936, V, 76–135
10. Ginsberg, M., 'Causality in the social sciences,' *Proc. Aristotelian Soc.*, 1934–5, XXXV, 253–70.
11. Ginsberg, M., 'Conventions, social', *Ency. Soc. Sci.*, ed. E. R. A. Seligman, 1931, IV, 351–3
12. Ginsberg, M., 'Recent tendencies in sociology', *Economica*, 1933, XIII, 22–39
13. Ginsberg, M., *Sociology* (London: Thornton Butterworth, 1934)
14. Hobhouse, L. T., 'Comparative ethics', *Ency. Brit.*, 14th ed., 1929, VI, 156–64

15. Hobhouse, L. T., *Morals in Evolution,* 3rd ed. (London: Chapman & Hall, 1915)
16. Hobhouse, L. T., *Social Development* (London: Allen & Unwin, 1924)
17. Hubert, R., 'Croyance morale et règle juridique', *IIe Annuaire de l'Institut International de Philosophie du Droit,* 1936, 125–44
18. Husserl, E., 'Phenomenology', *Ency. Brit.,* 14th ed., 1929, XVII, 699–702
19. Huxley, J. S., 'Natural selection and evolutionary progress', *Rep. Brit. Ass. Adv. Sci.,* Blackpool Meeting, 1936, Presidential Address (sect. D), 81–100
20. Kulischer, A., and Kulischer, E., *Kriegs- und Wanderzüge: Weltgeschichte als Völkerbewegung* (Berlin: de Gruyter, 1932)
21. MacIver, R. M., *Society* (New York: Farrar & Rinehart, 1937)
22. Marshall, A., *Principles of Economics,* 7th ed. (London: Macmillan, 1916)
23. Meillet, A., *Les Langues dans l'Europe Nouvelle* (Paris: Payot, 1918)
24. Montandon, G., *Traité d'Ethnologie Culturelle* (Paris: Payot, 1934)
25. Morgan, C. Lloyd, *Emergent Evolution* (London: Williams & Norgate, 1923)
26. Pareto, V., *The Mind and Society* (London: Cape, 1935)
27. Read, Carveth, *Natural and Social Morals* (London: Black, 1909)
28. Robbins, L., *Nature and Significance of Economic Science* (London: Macmillan, 1935)
29. Ross, W. D., *The Right and the Good* (London: Oxford University Press, 1930)
30. Sidgwick, H., *Development of European Polity* (London: Macmillan, 1903)
31. Sidgwick, H., *The Elements of Politics,* 2nd ed. (London, Macmillan, 1897)
32. Smuts, J. C., *Holism and Evolution* (London: Macmillan, 1926)
33. Sorokin, P., *Contemporary Sociological Theories* (London: Harper, 1928)
34. Spencer, H., *Principles of Sociology,* 3rd ed. (London: Williams & Norgate, 1897–1906)
35. Spiller, G. G., *The Origin and Nature of Man* (London: Williams & Norgate, 1931)
36. Tönnies, F., *Einführung in die Soziologie* (Stuttgart: Enke, 1931)
37. Toynbee, A. J., *A Study of History* (London: Oxford University Press, 1934)
38. Vierkandt, A., *Gesellschaftslehre,* 2nd ed. (Stuttgart: Enke, 1928)
39. Westermarck, E., *Ethical Relativity* (London: Kegan Paul, 1932)
40. Westermarck, E., *Origin and Development of Moral Ideas* (London: Macmillan, 1906)

41. Wheeler, W. M., *Emergent Evolution and the Development of Societies* (New York: Morton, 1928)
42. Wiese, L. von, *Allgemeine Soziologie* (Munich: Duncker & Humblot, 1924, I; 1929, II)

SUGGESTIONS FOR GENERAL READING

Hecker, J. F., *Russian Sociology* (London: Chapman & Hall, 1934)

Ogburn, W. F., and Goldenweiser, A. (eds.), *The Social Sciences and their Interrelations* (London: Allen & Unwin)

Les Sciences Sociales en France: Enseignement et Recherches, Centre d'Études de Politique Étrangère (Paris: Hatmann)

The Social Sciences: Their Relations in Theory and Teaching (London: Le Play House, 1936)

Thurnwald, R. (ed.), *Soziologie von Heute* (Leipzig: Hirschfeld, 1932)

[2]

The Individual and Society*

I T is fashionable nowadays to say that the old antithesis between the individual and society is outworn. Nevertheless, the frequency with which this repudiation of the antithesis is repeated shows that it is far from discarded. Its continuing influence can be seen in the current arguments as to the place of psychology in the explanation of social phenomena, in the new antithesis between culture and personality, or between individual and social character. It can be seen above all in political discussions, where it appears in the form of a contrast between the good of individuals and the good of the state. We are told repeatedly that the ultimate source of conflict in the world today is to be found in the struggle between two opposed ideals, that which attaches supreme value to the individual and that which subordinates his good to that of the community. While originally the term individualism seems to have been coined in explicit opposition to socialism, the revival of individualism in our own time is often directly intended to express opposition to 'totalitarianism'. In both cases there is an underlying assumption that the opposed terms between them exhaust the possibilities, and that no midway is open.

The problems raised are eminently suited for an international symposium. By this I do not mean that social and political theories follow national lines, but rather that the issues involved and the terms employed to express them differ widely from country to country and age to age, and therefore call for comparative study. Everywhere in the modern world there is to be traced a double movement – on the one hand, a breakdown of the older social structure and with it a liberation of the individual; on the other, an enormous increase in collective powers and a process in

* First published in *Bulletin international des sciences sociales* (U.N.E.S.C.O.), vol VI, no. 1, 1954.

which the community takes on functions previously left to the individual, the family or some other body. The movement may be described in another way as consisting in a transition from the conception of personal rights inhering in individuals and limiting the law, to a conception of rights as defining social relations and of law as based on rights so defined. The problem has been how to base liberty on law and law on liberty. But the steps taken to solve it, or to hinder its solution, have differed very widely, under different historical conditions. Inevitably, therefore, words like 'liberalism', 'individualism', 'democracy', 'socialism', 'collectivism', have had and still have very different meanings.

In this discussion I propose to confine attention to the antithesis between society and the individual. To this end it is necessary to distinguish the different senses in which the term individualism has been used. In Englsh the word appears, according to the Oxford Dictionary, to have been used for the first time by Henry Reeve in his translation of de Tocqueville's *De la démocratie en Amérique*, in 1840. Reeve explains that he takes the term directly from the French, in the absence of an exact English equivalent. De Tocqueville used it to express an attitude of mind which leads each member of the community to 'draw apart from his fellow-creatures and to leave society at large to itself'. 'Individualism', he says, 'is of democratic origin and threatens to spread in the same ratio as the equality of conditions.'* In this sense the term stands for a feeling or attitude and hardly for a coherent theory. It is used in a somewhat similar sense by many German writers when they claim that individualism is a trait which forms part of the German national character. Under this term, and under the parallel terms 'particularism' or 'subjectivism', are included a number of traits or qualities such as a tendency to turn inwards, a desire for independence or for freedom from external constraint, distinctiveness in self-expression, passing into self-will and self-absorption.†

* vol. I, bk. II, ch. 2.
† Cf. my essay on 'German views of German mentality', *Reason and Unreason in Society*, ch. VIII.

As a theory individualism appears in three forms which may be designated, political, sociological and methodological. The most influential has been the political. In essentials this is the theory that the good of the state consists in the well-being and free initiative of its members and that this is best secured by each individual pursuing his own good in his own way, with a minimum of state interference. Sociological individualism is the theory that society is to be conceived as an aggregate of individuals whose relations to each other are purely external. It is best understood by contrast with those forms of the organic theory which consider society as in some sense a new whole, other than its interrelated members. Methodological individualism need not, though in fact it often does, commit itself in advance to any theory of the nature of society or of the ends of political action. It insists that in studying social phenomena it is best to begin with individual actions and to consider social wholes as complexes of social relationships, arising out of the behaviour of individuals in so far as this is directed towards or away from other individuals. Historically, these three forms of individualism have often been interwoven. Those who wish to confine state intervention to the minimum required in order to allow individuals to pursue their own good in their own way, are apt to consider society as an aggregate of self-determining individuals, who remain self-determining despite their relations to others, and on the metaphysical side such thinkers are often upholders of atomism. The methodological individualists sometimes repudiate atomistic views, but they seem to think that there is a necessary connexion between their methodological assumptions and political individualism. Even a cursory glance at the history of social thought is, however, sufficient to show that the association between these forms of individualism is far from complete. Sociological individualism has been held concurrently with state absolutism, as e.g. by Hobbes. On the other hand, those who have claimed wide powers for the state have not necessarily committed themselves to a 'holistic' methodology or to any view of the structure of society which merges the individual in the social whole, as can easily be seen by comparing the views of such liberal thinkers as Green and Hobhouse.

In methodological individualism the antithesis between society and the individual is reflected in the contrast between the 'holistic' approach and the 'compositive'. In the former, societies are supposed to be studied as wholes; in the latter, they are constructed out of 'intelligible' elements. But in attacking 'holism' the critics are attacking a man of straw. I do not know of any sociologists who in fact study modern societies as wholes. I suppose the nearest example would be found in the work of Durkheim and his followers. But even in their case, despite a good deal of talk about *la societé*, the actual procedure consists of a study of variations in and between groups of social facts, e.g., between the rate of suicide and religious affiliation or family structure. The characteristics of the group such as the degree of integration or of social control are inferred as likely to account for the observed variations. When Halbwachs* replaces the generalization reached by Durkheim by a more comprehensive generalization which relates the proportion of suicides to the urban and rural *genre de vie*, he does so, I take it, because he thinks that religious organization and family life are both affected by the degree of complexity characteristic of life in town and country. Whether in this he succeeds or not, I will not here inquire. But I can see no objection in principle to assigning such characteristics as complexity or 'complication' to groups, providing they are sufficiently clearly defined. To assign characteristics to groups is by no means the same as to consider them as entities which exist independently of the individuals which compose them. I doubt therefore whether the French sociologists can properly be regarded as subscribing to the 'realist' or 'essentialist' tradition in philosophy. In the case of thinkers like Hobhouse such an attribution is too absurd to be even considered.

The 'individualist' approach has been most fully expounded by Professor Hayek in various writings. His basic contention is 'that there is no other way towards an understanding of social

* *Les causes du suicide.*

phenomena but through our understanding of individual actions directed towards other people and guided by their expected behaviour.'* 'What we do in the social sciences is to classify types of individual behaviour which we can understand.'† What he means by 'understanding' is not clear. We are said to 'understand' other people's action by the analogy of our own minds. The business of social science is to develop a classification of types of 'intelligible' behaviour and to construct models which reproduce the patterns of social relations which we find in the world around us. Thus in economics, we are told, we classify acts of choice made necessary by the scarcity of means available for our ends. We then see that a given means can be useful for one or many ends, a given end can be achieved by several means, different means may be wanted for a given end, etc. We then have a sort of logic of choice which we can use in interpreting the situations with which we have to deal.

Whether this is an adequate account of economic analysis I am not competent to judge. There are certainly some economists who recognize the limitations of the individualist approach. Thus, e.g., Professor Frank H. Knight points out that 'the individual is not a datum and social policy ought not to treat him as such.' The productive capacity and the tastes of the individual depend on the level of the group of which he is a member. The society which acts as a unit in internal and external policy is, he maintains, a complex of institutions, traditions, knowledge or belief and common interest groupings rather than an organization of individuals. So again he argues that international rivalry cannot be understood without taking into account the inequalities between states and regions and their differences in level of culture. 'The social game is played for stakes which involve the major values of life ... and it goes on continuously, generation after generation, with players constantly dropping out and being replaced.'‡

* *Individualism: True and False*, p. 8.
† 'The facts of the social sciences', *Ethics*, Vol. LIV, October 1943, p. 8.
‡ *Freedom and Reform*, pp. 383-4.

Whatever may be the case in economics, I can think of no example of sociological investigation conducted on the model advocated by Professor Hayek. The nearest approach to is to be found, I suppose, in the *verstehende Soziologie* of Max Weber and his recent followers. But it is very doubtful whether the account that Max Weber gives of his methodology corresponds at all closely to the methods which he himself employed in actual investigations. His studies of capitalism or of stratification or of slavery in the ancient world come nowhere near an analysis of the intentions of the individuals concerned. If sociology is defined as the understanding or interpretation of social behaviour in the sense of indicating the *Sinn* or intention of the agent, then the bulk of his work is not sociological.

Whatever be our views about Max Weber's work, it is easy to see that, in general, sociological investigations do not follow the procedure outlined by him. Consider as an example the problem of the sources of inequality in the distribution of property. In trying to account for it we have to investigate at least the following: (i) variations in law and custom, such as the rules governing inheritance, e.g., primogeniture, legitim, free bequest; (ii) class endogamy, since if children of the rich were to marry children of the poor there would be greater equality than when the children of the rich marry the rich; (iii) size of family and differential fertility; (iv) inequality of saving, itself dependent on magnitude of income; (v) chance or luck in investments; (vi) differences in skill and foresight whose causation again is complicated, both individual and social factors being involved.

It will be seen that in the main we are not in such an investigation concerned with the intentions of individuals, but rather with structural relations and their bearing on individuals, and so it will be if we take any other example of a massive social phenomenon. It may be added that according to the methodological individualists institutions are considered as the result of the combined effects of individual actions. But these effects cannot be 'understood' in the sense required by the theory, since they are supposed to function without a designing mind. The fundamental laws of sociology would on this view, it seems to me, be the laws governing the interactions of individual minds, and if these laws are to enable us to understand social phenomena, the understanding in question would differ entirely from the sort of understanding which consists in grasping intuitively the intentions of individual agents.

It is interesting to note that those who consider that the aim of the social sciences is to classify types of individual behaviour which we can 'understand' make no use of psychology. In order to 'understand' it is not necessary, we are told, to delve deeply into human motives. We operate with motives familiar to us in our own actions and interpret other people's actions by analogy. An action is directly 'intelligible' if it corresponds to what we would do in similar circumstances. But more than that seems to be claimed. It appears that we can, 'in principle', derive from the knowledge of our own minds an exhaustive classification of all the possible forms of intelligible behaviour. It would be interesting to inquire what we would know of the possible forms of, let us say, the relationship of love or hate, if the sole basis of our information was what we knew of our own mind. I suspect that there is here a confusion between the use of 'intelligible' in the sense of being referable to conscious use of means to attain given ends, unaffected by emotion or other sources of deviation, and 'intelligible' in the sense of being referable to any motive familiar in our own experience. In the case of the former we might conceivably arrive at deductive classifications; in the case of the latter we should go wildly wrong if all we had to go on was what we believed ourselves to understand of the processes of our own mind.

The sharp separation of the social sciences from psychology which is implied in these views is a mistake. There are branches of sociology, e.g. criminology, in which psychological analysis is indispensable. In the study of religion or morals as social forces, it would be absurd to ignore the contributions of psychology. Much light can be thrown on the actual working of institutions, including economic institutions, by psychological analysis. It is entirely arbitrary to confine 'understanding' to what can be learnt by unaided and untrained introspection.

It appears to be a basic assumption of *verstehende Soziologie* and *verstehende Psychologie* that what we know within our minds is somehow more intelligible than what is outwardly observed. But this is to confuse the familiar with the intelligible. There is no inner sense establishing connexions between inner facts by direct intuition. Such connexions are in fact empirical generalizations, of no greater validity than the similar generalizations relating to outward facts. I may imagine that I understand the behaviour of a person striking another in anger. But this only means that such behaviour is familiar in my experience of myself. The connexion between anger and its stimuli is not a necessary connexion and is in fact difficult to establish even empirically, as is evident from the experimental investigations of the relation between frustration and aggression. Such generalizations as 'the unfortunate envies the rich', 'he who is disgraced tends to depreciate superior values'* are not really more 'intelligible' than, say, that syphilis produces general paralysis. We imagine that we 'see' the connexion in the former case, but there is no logical necessity about it. Anyone to whom certain foods are 'taboo' will experience disgust at the sight of the food. Nevertheless the disgust is induced by traditions and is not directly intelligible to anyone brought up in a different tradition. To understand the connexion in this case a sociology of 'taboo' is required.

It is true that in certain branches of social inquiry it is legitimate to take the individual and his motives as a datum. We need have no quarrel for example with economists who wish to proceed in this way. But in comparative sociology and psychology the individual cannot be taken as a constant. The problem is to determine in what ways the tendencies inherent in the human mind affect the relations between individuals, and conversely how the social relations react upon the mind, developing or modifying its inherent tendencies. It is at this point that we come up against the central difficulty in social theory. The psychological

* Jaspers.

terms that we use to describe the community, such as will, mind, purpose, well-being, are drawn from the life of the individual, and this leads us to think of the group as simply an aggregate of its component members and to interpret the common will or the social purpose as the sum or product of particular wills. In reaction from this exaggerated individualism we tend to move to the opposite pole and to erect society into a new kind of whole which stands outside individuals or in which they are merged. Years of controversy have shown neither of these extreme views is tenable.*

Despite differences in formulation, it emerges from these controversies that individuals must be considered as both self-determining and interdependent. Genetically every individual is unique. It is true that the basis of his constitution is inherited from the ancestral stock. Nevertheless the combination of genes with which he starts is, as combination, peculiar to him. Moreover, as he develops he responds selectively to his environment and therefore no two individuals can ever have strictly the same environment. These conclusions are, I think, strongly confirmed by the numerous investigations into the part played by hereditary and environmental factors in the shaping of behaviour. Furthermore, the relations of the individual to other individuals in his environment are far more subtle and intimate than those involved in merely organic growth. For they enter his very being and constitute the content and substance of the self. To understand them we need a theory of internal relations. The character of an individual is moulded by the relations in which he stands to others, while conversely the relations are the outcome of the character of the members entering into them. Love, hate, respect, pride, vanity, are as processes or dispositions parts of the self, but necessarily have reference to others whether as objects of satisfaction, or as evoking response. The self thus consists largely of relations to others. Yet in this respect again, each individual is unique and in a measure self-determining, since the combination of social

* Cf. MacIver, *Community*, and the works of L. T. Hobhouse, especially *Social Development* and *The Metaphysical Theory of the State*.

relations into which he enters is as peculiar to him as the combination of genes with which he starts.

The problem of the degree of self-determination of the individual is complicated by the fact that he is a member of a variety of groups. Groups may be considered as complexes of relations having a certain consistency and permanence, defined in institutions. These groups may be conceived as circles some of which fall within, while others cut across, each other. Thus the individual is a member of his family, his neighbourhood, his professional association, his church, his nation, his state, his linguistic or culture area. The relations in which he stands to these various groupings vary in depth and pervasiveness and his character is variously affected by them. The groupings themselves are not fixed but are subject to constant motion and transformation. The greater the variety of the groupings and of the degree of the mobility of individuals within them, the greater the opportunities of selective response, and consequently the greater the possible variety of individual character. Though the individual consists largely of his social relations, there is thus a core of individuality in each person which is uniquely his own and which is, in the last resort, unshareable and incommunicable.

It follows from these considerations that none of the terms which have so far been used to describe societies can be adequate. The question whether society is a sum of its parts or not is meaningless. Subtle, internal relations involving mental references are not additive. You cannot add the love of A for B to the love of B for A, or substract either from their hatred of C. Nor is the effort of, say, the family life on its members commensurable with the effect upon them of, say, their church or state. Individuals are in fact enmeshed in a network of relations varying in scope and intensity, partly supporting, partly neutralizing and partly conflicting with, each other. To this complex of relationships there seems to be no analogy in the world of physical objects, not even of organisms. The analogy with the individual mind is closer. But the theory of a group mind has not stood the test of criticism. Minds in relation to each other do not constitute a mind in the sense in which each individual has a mind. Societies have a mental organization but they are not minds. They are relational complexes of a peculiar kind, with characteristics of their own.

This view has important ethical implications. There is a sense in which we may properly speak of a social or common good, distinguishable in thought though not separate in reality from the good of individuals. The reference is then to a form or pattern of life considered good as a form or pattern. In this sense, for example, we may speak of one type of family life as better than another. This seems to imply that we can attribute goodness or badness to the relations between individuals and not only to the individuals entering into them. But strictly it is the life of the members in their relations to one another that is good or bad and not the individuals apart from the relations or the relations apart from the members. When the good of the community is said to be opposed to the good of the individual, it will be found either that a sectional good is parading in the guise of the good of the whole community, or that the good has been falsely conceived to lie in ends which will not make life better for anyone, or that certain individuals claim the power to decide what is best for the rest of society. Clashes of interest there are, of course, in plenty, and there is the difficulty of grading or choosing between different values or unavoidable evils. But the issues thus involved are only obscured if interpreted in the form of a clash between the good of individuals and the good of the community, supposed in some mysterious way to be different from theirs.

Political individualism seems to me to have been definitely overcome in English liberal and liberal-socialist thought. The strength of individualism lay in its resolve to reduce coercion to a minimum, in its profound respect for personal liberty. But a succession of thinkers from J. S. Mill to T. H. Green, L. T. Hobhouse, J. A Hobson, Lord Lindsay, Ernest Barker and others have shown that personal liberty and state control are not necessarily opposed. 'There are', as Hobhouse has said, 'many enemies of liberty besides the state and it is in fact by the state that we have fought them.'* The power of the state has been extended in English legislation with the object of securing greater equality in personal rights, particularly in the economic sphere, and of organizing public resources for common objects such as education, health, unemployment insurance. Neither of these extensions of state power involves any loss of personal liberty. Nor is there any substance in the charge so often levelled against the socialist trend in liberal thought that it sacrifices liberty for equality. What social liberals are concerned to maintain is that freedom itself is subject to the principle of equality; in other words, if any are to be free, all should be. It follows as a corollary that since freedom can never be absolute, the freedom of each is limited by equal claims of others. It is plain that whenever there are great inequalities of power, freedom cannot be general. Hence to secure freedom for all, it is necessary that all should be equally protected against the abuse of power, and that the power of the state should be employed to reduce or remove arbitrary inequalities and to ensure that the common resources should be used not for personal ends but for the general well-being.†

I must now try to bring together the main points in this discussion. In methodological individualism the antithesis between the individual and society reappears in the emphasis laid on the inner or mental character of social facts, from which it is deduced that they can only be known 'from the inside'. I have tried to show that most sociological investigations do not proceed on this model. They are concerned with structural relations in their bearing on individuals or groups. In so far as they deal with the 'meaning' of social processes they do not confine themselves to 'understanding' in the sense of what can be known by looking

* *Elements of Social Justice*, p. 83.

† Cf. E. F. Carritt, *Ethical and Political Thinking*, p. 168: 'Those who think that liberty and equality are incompatible have probably assumed that institutions of their own time and country with regard to property and inheritance are eternally founded in the nature of things and are no limitation to the freedom of those who suffer by them. . . . Within the sacred system *laissez faire* is divinely guided to maximum liberty, but if we do not enforce just that system providence will lead us to servitude.'

within the mind. They try to disentangle the 'functions' served, not necessarily consciously, by social institutions, or else they call psychology to their aid, including the psychology of the unconscious. Psychology, however, cannot claim ultimacy or primacy in sociological explanation. Institutions are the products of minds, but conversely minds are shaped by institutions. From this point of view comparative psychology and comparative sociology are interrelated and neither can claim independent validity.

Coming to the theory of society, we must reject alike the view that society is an aggregate of individuals related externally to each other and the view that it is a mystical 'whole' independent of the individuals composing it. The character of the individual requires for its explanation a theory of 'internal relations'. The social structures embodying these relations cannot be interpreted by analogies drawn from physical objects or living organisms. But though they are mind-created and mind-sustained, they are not minds. They are rather mental structures with characteristics of their own. Languages, institutions, legal systems, the arts have their forms or patterns which the individual inherits and to which he has to accommodate himself. He grows by assimilating them and has to use them even in his most 'creative' moments. Looked at in this way, individuals can be seen to be at once self-determining and interdependent, though in what degree, depends upon the type of social structure and the relation of the individual to it.

As far as political and economic individualism is concerned, English experience has shown that the attempt to find a principle determining clearly the sphere of state activity has broken down. The principle that coercion should only be used to limit coercion has had to be widened to include forms of coercion made possible by inequalities of power arising from inequalities in possessions. It was realized that individuals were not really, in a competitive system, 'free and equal' to accept or reject a bargain. This has led to legislation qualifying and defining the freedom of contract, the conditions of work and the remuneration of workers. Similarly the principle: 'To every man full liberty provided he does not interfere with the like liberty of another' has not proved workable. For the 'like' liberty we must substitute 'any one of a system of liberties' and this implies some conception of a common good or general well-being, whose definition cannot be left entirely to each individual. Furthermore, as Lord Lindsay has pointed out, in treating all human relations in terms of contract the individualists ignored the amount of government and organization which is not contractual and which is involved in modern industry.* The lessons thus provided by English experience and thought are, I think, permanent contributions to political theory and they are not in the least shaken by recent restatements of the individualist position.

Turning now to the relations between the different forms of individualist doctrine, it must be repeated that the association between them is far from complete. A believer in the group-mind need not be a totalitarian. Bosanquet,† for example, regarded the state as an embodiment of the general will, but he restricted the action of the state, in so far as it used compulsion, to the 'hindering of hindrances of freedom'. On the other hand, the theory of a general will *may* be used to justify totalitarianism, as when communist writers maintain that it is the function of the Communist party, or rather its leaders, to interpret the general will, in other words, to tell the workers what they ought to will or what they would will if they understood their 'true' interests.

Similarly those who refuse to accept methodological individualism as the principal method of sociological investigation are not committed to a holistic view of society or to a totalitarian view of political action. They are well aware of the complexity of human relations and of the dangers of concentrated power. But they deny that the only choice open to us is between a 'spontaneous' competitive order on the one hand, and a system of all-pervading control on the other. It is odd that those who attack what they call 'scientism' should feel able to predict with certainty that any form of socialism must necessarily lead to cultural

* Cf. 'Individualism', *Encyclopaedia of Social Sciences*, vol. IV, p. 679.
† *The Philosophical Theory of the State.*

and political totalitarianism. There are many alternatives between spontaneous mutual adjustment and total planning, many different ways of apportioning control between centralized and non-centralized organs. These matters cannot be settled by purely methodological arguments. 'Scientism', it may be added, is not peculiar to planners. It was the empiricist philosophers who came nearest to assimilating the methods of the social sciences to those of the natural sciences, and it was they who were the strongest supporters of political and economic individualism. In any event, 'logicism' is no improvement on 'scientism'. A socialized liberalism must refuse to put its trust in the hidden hand of mutual adjustment. But it lays no claim to omniscience. On the contrary it insists that only experience can show what sort of control and what sort of authority are likely to be conducive to, or destructive of, liberty on the whole. The answer to questions of this sort does not depend on a general 'logic of liberty' but on quite special knowledge of the conditions of successful planning, personal and collective, political and extra-political.

The Idea of Progress:
a Revaluation

I. THE FORMS OF THE BELIEF IN PROGRESS *

IN 1851 a very competent historian of the idea of progress testified to its wide influence. 'From the beginning of this century', he writes, 'the idea of progress has in effect established itself in such a way that in principle it is no longer contested by anyone and the only question that remains to be pursued is that concerning the conditions in which it is realized.'†

In this there was some exaggeration. None of the writers whom M. Javary discusses (Turgot, Condorcet, Herder, Kant) in fact succeeded in formulating a law or principle of progress and he himself in the course of a very searching examination concludes that there is no such law but that man has a duty to promote progress. It was not until the latter half of the nineteenth century that the attempt was made to define the idea of progress with some precision and to link it with scientific and philosophical theories of development. The popularity of the idea was due in great measure to the buoyant hopefulness inspired by the triumphs of applied science. On the scientific side the idea was later given powerful impetus by its association with the biological theory of evolution. The culminating point was reached towards the end of the century. No law of progress had in fact been scientifically established. But the general idea harmonized with notions of development that had become current in science and philosophy, and it provided an inspiring justification for

---

* This essay gives, in extended form, the substance of the Chairman's Address delivered at the First Annual General Meeting of the British Sociological Association on 22 March 1952.

† A. Javary, *De l'Ideé de Progrès*, 1851, p. 74.

movements of social and political reform. Despite its vagueness, it thus became part of the general mental outlook and for many it provided the basis for a working faith of great vitality.

In the twentieth century the mood is more cautious. The concept of unilinear or automatic progress is subjected to searching criticism and there is growing scepticism of any deductive arguments claiming to deduce progress from more general philosophical theories of development or from the biological theory of evolution. It comes to be realized that before a theory of progress can be safely established a wider survey of the steadily accumulating data of archaeology and history will have to be made. The search for a general law is not abandoned. Nevertheless attention comes to be concentrated on the study of specific lines of progress and on the elaboration of methods for investigating the relations between them.

Looking back on the movement as a whole we can see that the idea of progress has passed through three stages. In the first, progress was an ethical ideal towards which humanity was considered to be moving, but it was not clear whether what was claimed was that in the past humanity had in fact progressed, or only that it was sure to do so in the future. The survey of the past was in any case rapid and perfunctory. In the second phase, attempts were made to define the notion of progress more clearly and to formulate and establish general laws of progress. Though supported by an appeal to the data of history and, later, of comparative sociology, the basic conceptions were derived from more general philosophical theories or from the biological theory of evolution. In the third phase, it comes to be realized that if progress has occurred, it is neither simple nor continuous, that advance in one direction is frequently accompanied by retrogression in another, that the question of value must be clearly distinguished from the question of fact and that the criteria of general progress are still to seek. Accordingly, attention is increasingly concentrated on the conditions of advance and deterioration and on the possibility of gaining control over them. Furthermore, modern psychological theories raise in a more acute form the ancient problem of the relation between knowledge and virtue, and expose the *naïveté* of the assumption which earlier theories had taken for granted that intellectual advance will be necessarily reflected in improved human relations. Thus both on the philosophical side, concerned with the goals, and on the scientific side, concerned with the conditions, of progress, modern theories tend to be more modest in their claims and more tentative and exploratory in their approach.

The core of the theory of progress which persisted through all these phases was the belief that mankind has moved, is moving and will move in a direction which satisfies ethical requirements. But this general belief was interpreted in many different ways, often incompatible with each other. On the one hand, progress was sometimes considered to be certain and inevitable. Thus, for example, de Tocqueville, for whom progress consisted in the movement towards equality, urged that it was a providential fact, possessing all the characteristics of a Divine decree: 'it is universal, it is durable, it eludes all human interference.'* From a totally different point of view, Spencer concluded that 'The ultimate development of the ideal man is logically certain – as certain as any conclusion in which we place the most implicit faith.' Elsewhere he explains that though progress is a necessity, it is not to be assumed that it is either regular or uniform, and that it is only by taking into consideration 'the entire assemblage of societies' that the law of evolution can be shown to be at work in humanity.†

On the other hand, it is easy to show that at no time during the two hundred years in which the idea of progress has been influential in Western thought has the fatalistic interpretation been universal or even general. Even Condorcet qualifies his strong faith in the happiness and perfectibility of mankind by the requirement that men will make the right use of the forces which the growth of knowledge will put at their disposal. Among later writers Renouvier subjected all forms of predestinarian or

* Preface to Part 1, *De la démocratie en Amérique*, 1835-40.
† *The Principles of Sociology*, vol. III, p. 598 seq.

necessitarian views of progress to a devastating analysis. He urged that neither from the religious nor from the scientific points of view can progress be shown to be assured. He protests vigorously against those who base their optimistic hopes for the future of man on a quasi-religious faith, which comes near turning progress into a sort of god. To a deeper religious insight the final end of humanity presents itself as not necessarily attainable in this world, and as dependent on Divine aid. Nor can science afford proof of inevitable or assured progress. It is no doubt true, he argues, that good acts tend to support one another, to be cumulative in their effects, and thus to grow in strength and influence. But this is not enough to guarantee future progress. For evil too has its own 'solidarity'. Error and vice are in their own way cumulative and tend to produce further error and vice in individuals as well as in nations. There is no assurance that the forces making for disruption or deterioration must cancel each other out and thus bring about their own defeat. Progress is possible and has actually occurred during certain periods in the history of many peoples. But we are not justified in ascribing to it universality, continuity or necessity.* As far as English thought is concerned, it may be doubted whether the necessitarian interpretations were ever taken seriously. It is interesting to note that Bagehot, who approaches the problem from the point of view of the biological theory of evolution, and might have been expected to favour such interpretations, quite clearly rejects them. Progress, he thinks, is not the rule in the history of mankind, but rare and exceptional, and depends on an uncommon combination of energy and balance of mind, hard to attain and harder to keep.†

The question whether progress is necessary or contingent is closely connected with another, namely that of the relation between the idea of progress and that of Providence. In some of the early formulations and again in some recent theories the two concepts are often linked. Kant's view of history as the gradual moralization of man is at the same time a theory of history as the

---

* *Essais de Critique Générale*, 1864.
† *Physics and Politics*, 1872.

working out of a Divine purpose. Lessing's famous essay on *The Education of the Human Race* * represents history as a progressive series of religions through which God educates the human mind. In the later stages, however, man passes from a state of tutelage to a stage of independent thought. Education in other words becomes *self-education*; and this is not far removed from the concept of the development of mankind in accordance with the laws of mental life. Herder works out the connexion between Providence and Progress in another way.† God is the ultimate source of law both in the physical world and the world of history. But having designed the world, He remains inactive, and development proceeds in accordance with inevitable laws. History is a process whereby man is slowly educated for humanity (*Erziehung zur Humanität*), that is, a process through which the qualities of *Menschlichkeit* are elicited and extended to the whole of mankind. In this way the path was prepared for the view that history is not the expression of a predetermined plan, but the result of laws immanent in historical life itself. But this conception of the self-development of humanity may in its turn easily be given a religious colouring. For the reason which slowly reveals itself in history may be conceived as the reason of God, regarded not as a transcendent being guiding the destinies of mankind in accordance with a preconceived plan, but as immanent in the world and expressing itself in it.

The movement of thought here briefly sketched may be said to pass through three stages. It begins with the Christian conception of the world as a preparation for the Kingdom of God, moves to the idea that history is an education of mankind in accordance with a predetermined plan, and passes into the thought of the self-development of mankind as an expression of Divine immanence. In the first stage, the emphasis is on Providence, while the notion of Progress may be implicit but is hardly articulate. In the second stage, the two concepts are linked, while in the third lip-service is paid to the notion of Providence, but the difficulties of

* 1780.

† *Ideas of the Philosophy of the History of Humanity*, 1784.

reconciling it with the notion of immanent development tend to push it into the background and slowly to undermine belief in it.

Professor Bury seems to me to be right in thinking that the fundamental assumptions underlying the belief in Providence and the belief in Progress are incongruous and that the latter could not take a firm hold over men's minds while the former was indisputably in the ascendant.* The idea of progress was hardly likely to obtain wide credence until attention was shifted from the kingdom to come to the kingdom of this world, and until the notion of laws was extended from the sphere of nature to the sphere of man. It was thus essentially linked with the growth of modern science, with the spread of the rationalist outlook and with the struggle for political and religious liberty. It is true that nowadays theologians often claim that the root of the modern belief in progress is to be found in the Judeo-Christian conception of history as moving towards a Messianic age. The belief in the moral perfectibility and indefinite progress of mankind is then represented as a secularized version of the Christian faith in the life of the world to come as the goal of human effort. It would, however, be as easy and as misleading to represent the modern interpretations of the Christian philosophy of history as theological versions of secular utopias. Christian theologians seem to have become deeply interested in the idea of progress only after it became a dominant element in Western thought. The Catholic Church has on occasion explicitly repudiated it, and Protestant writers find great difficulty in coming to terms with it. It is interesting to note, in this connexion, that the concept of history as a forward movement and not an endless repetition or recurrence has arisen not only in the Judeo-Christian tradition, but also, and, it would seem, independently, in Zoroastrianism.† In the case of the latter, however, it bore no fruit. Is not this failure connected with the fact that the Zoroastrian idea was not fertilized by con-

* *The Idea of Progress*, p. 21.

† Cf. N. Söderblom, art. 'Ages of the world', *Encyclopaedia of Religion and Ethics*, vol. I, p. 210.

tact with rationalist thought and simulated by the sense of man's power to mould his fate, due to the triumphs of applied science? It is thus probable that in the absence of such contact the germs of the idea of progress in Christian thought would have remained undeveloped and would never have emerged from the soil of resignation and other-worldliness in which they were embedded.

It remains to be added that nowadays Christian authorities are by no means agreed in their attitude to the belief in progress. Dean Inge, following F. H. Bradley, finds the general theory of progress incompatible with Christianity and he complains that it 'has distorted Christianity almost beyond recognition'.* Christianity, it seems, gives no ground for the assumption that given time man must become perfect. Edwyn Bevan in an essay which strikes me, as a layman, as very profound, says

that we should beware of supposing that it is possible for us to trace any approximation in the course of history to the Kingdom of God. The idea of a progressive approximation came in only with the general idea of evolution in the nineteenth century. . . . The early Church had no thought of such approximation. . . . It is only the heavenly hope that is essential to Christianity . . . there can be no assurance that things upon earth will grow any better before the end of history comes.†

In a similar vein Dr C. H. Dodd writes:

The doctrine of progress which until recently seemed to provide a scheme of interpretation, and of interpretation in a Christian sense, has worn somewhat thin. . . . There are indeed considerations which encourage the hope that the evils of society are, in the long run, self-destructive, and the good self-preservative. But it is a long way from this to the assurance that history will justify itself by the final victory of the good within the span allotted to human life on this planet. Nor is it clear that the Christian faith intends to give such an assurance.‡

* *The Idea of Progress* (Romanes Lecture), p. 21.
† *The Kingdom of God and History* (1938, Oxford Conference Series), p. 66.
‡ *History and the Gospel*, p. 180.

Professor Baillie on the other hand thinks, if I understand him rightly, that progress in his sense, i.e. the evangelization of mankind, must be taken by Christians as assured and that 'during the interim period between the inauguration of the Christian era and the end of earthly history human life and society will be more and more conformed to the mind of Christ.' His survey of the empirical facts of history, however, provides no arguments which would appeal to the non-Christian and no doubt it is not his intention to do so. He would perhaps agree with Niebuhr* that the Christian interpretations of history are not a fruit of empirical observation but of 'revelations' of the character and purposes of God. The philosophies which base themselves on a study of the facts of history are rejected because they fail to give us the comfort they propose to administer, because they do not give us any ground 'for the retention of some kind of optimistic outlook on future earthly history'.† The non-theologian may tentatively suggest that perhaps there are no grounds either for optimism or for pessimism, that the facts justify neither complacency nor despair.

The culminating point in the history of the belief in progress was reached towards the end of the nineteenth century. Its high priests and incense bearers were, as Bury says, all rationalists. It owed its wide prevalence to the optimism inspired by the triumphs of applied science, made visible in the striking advances made in the technical conveniences of life, and, on the theoretical side, by the deeply ramified influences exerted by the ideas of development and evolution on all branches of thought and inquiry. In the beginning of the twentieth century, however, there were signs that the belief had been seriously weakened and in the interval between the two wars there was a widespread impression that it was about to be relegated to the realm of exploded myths. Professor Bury's survey which appeared in 1920 suggested that though the belief still occupied a commanding position, it carried the seeds of its own destruction within itself and that it would in all probability fall a victim to its own denial of finality. Dean Inge,

* *Faith and History*, p. 156 † Baillie, *The Belief in Progress*, p. 188.

in his Romanes Lecture published in the same year, dismisses it as a 'superstition' and thinks 'it is nearly worn out.' *

In more recent times the belief in progress has been further weakened by the growing recognition that advances in technical knowledge are by no means sufficient to ensure social and moral progress, and the fear that the use of scientific knowledge for destructive purposes may outpace and arrest the growth of its powers for good. On the theoretical side, the sceptical attitude to progress is reinforced by the revival of cyclical theories of civilization by such writers as Spengler and Pareto, by the movements in modern psychology which emphasize the irrational elements in human nature, and, on the side of theology, by a reformulation of the doctrine of original sin. This stresses the finitude and limitations inherent in the nature of man and dismisses as intolerable *hubris* the claim that he can ever become master of his fate.

Despite these many-sided attacks the idea of progress retains its vitality. It is so deeply rooted in the modern mind that its critics never entirely reject it and consciously or unconsciously leave a loophole for escape. A few examples may be given. Thus Professor Bury comes very near self-contradiction when he declares that the notion of progress itself suggests that 'its value as a doctrine is only relative, corresponding to a certain not very advanced stage of civilization; just as Providence, in its day, was an idea of relative value, corresponding to a stage somewhat less advanced.'† Dean Inge's criticism is really directed against the application of the idea of progress to reality as a whole. But he leaves open the possibility of progress in spheres within reality, and suggests that 'there may be an immanent teleology which is shaping the life of the human race towards some completed development which has not yet been reached.' And he sees some ground for this belief in what he calls 'the climbing instinct of man', the persistence of a discontent with things as they are and of a hope for better things, which must be assumed to serve some

* Inge, op. cit., p. 29.   † Bury, op. cit., p. 352.

function.* Professor Toynbee, who strongly upholds a cyclic theory of civilizations, ends by suggesting that 'the breakdowns and disintegrations of civilizations might be the stepping stones to higher things on the religious plane' and even goes so far as to say that the next stage in this advance may lead to a new species of society 'embodied in a single world-wide and enduring representative in the shape of the Christian Church.'†

The latest critic, Professor Baillie, dismisses theories of progress as 'secularized and distorted versions of the Christian hope' and he appears to favour a pluralistic view of history according to which there could be no such thing as general progress, but at most progress within disparate and separate traditions. Yet he follows Toynbee in holding that a religious impulse may be carried over from one civilization to another, and ends by formulating a theory of progress as consisting in the evangelization of mankind.‡ In all these cases, it would seem that the idea of progress is sufficiently alive to make its critics hesitate in rejecting it outright, though it must be confessed that their acceptance of it is half-hearted and, in all probability, incompatible with their fundamental presuppositions.

For more positive formulations of the theory of progress in contemporary thought we must look elsewhere. They fall, I think, mainly into three groups. The first is Marxism, which appears to be the only form of the nineteenth-century philosophies of history that has remained influential. Despite the frequent rejection by Marxists of the 'bourgeois' concept of progress, they retain the belief of the early rationalists that man can make himself. They look forward confidently to an age when the 'true realm of freedom will blossom out of the realm of necessity in the fully developed Communist Society of the future.' There are next non-Marxist sociological theories of social development, of which the most important is that of Hobhouse. This is noteworthy for its rejection of all forms of determined or automatic progress, for the clarity with which it distinguishes between evolution and

* Inge, op. cit., p. 25 seq.   † *Civilization on Trial*, p. 240.
‡ Baillie, op. cit., ch. V.

progress, and for the elaboration of a method for studying the relation between ethical development and the different aspects of social development. The third is due to the rise of a generalized theory of evolution extended to include the field of human history and seeking to avoid the errors and contradictions inherent in the earlier applications of evolutionary theory to sociology. On this view, sometimes linked with Marxism, social evolution, which is considered to include the emergence of morality, is to be regarded as the last of a series of ascending levels of 'emergent' or 'creative' evolution, each level having its own laws. It is maintained that on the basis of such a theory a definition of progress can be given in scientific terms.*

It emerges from this brief survey that theories of progress fall into two main groups, namely those which regard progress as the work of Providence and those which consider it as the unfolding of man's powers in accordance with laws immanent in his nature. According to the one, man makes himself; according to the other, 'it is He hath made us and not we ourselves.' Both may, however, take a determinist or non-determinist form, or alternate uneasily between the two. Thus Kant's theory of progress is determinist. He sees history as a process in which Providence utilizes the conflicting passions of men to bring out the potentialities of their rational nature and to lead them to a goal which, left to themselves, they would not seek. This sort of Providential teleology is again appealed to in recent theological versions of the theory of progress and, like Kant's, they lay stress on the intractable elements in human nature. On the whole, however, these recent theories are, despite occasional lapses, non-determinist, though they do not succeed in overcoming the difficulties which have of old beset the efforts of theologians to reconcile freedom with predestination.†

The theories of the second group do not escape these difficulties and they too frequently hover between determinism and

* Cf. J. S. Huxley, *Evolutionary Ethics* (Romanes Lecture), 1943.

† E.g. Dr E. W. Barnes, in an interesting discussion, speaks of the 'progress to which we seem committed by a Power beyond ourselves' (*Religion amid Turmoil*, 1949).

non-determinism. The hesitation is ultimately to be traced to the difficulty of connecting the long-range trends and patterns of history with the efforts of individuals, and the unproved assumption that sociological laws must be the same in kind as the laws of the natural sciences. The problem must therefore remain unresolved until we know a good deal more than we do of the nature of human interactions. There is, however, nothing in the concept of development, interpreted as the unfolding of man's rational nature, which necessarily commits us to determinism. The laws of development may well be laws of the will, or of wills in interrelation, and we need not assume at the outset that these are subject to a blind fate.

In dealing with the issues raised in this rapid review of the various forms of the theory of progress, I propose to begin by considering the way in which they were handled by the writers of the eighteenth century. Their contribution remains of abiding value as expressions of the rationalist spirit and by virtue of the moral drive which inspired them. I shall pass next to the criticisms directed against them by Comte and to his own efforts to establish a law of progress on a scientific basis. Though in this he failed, he has much to tell us which is still of importance, especially in the analysis he offers of the difficulties standing in the way of progress. I shall then deal with the influence of the theories of development due to Hegel and Marx on the idea of progress, and with the impact of the biological theory of evolution. Finally I shall try to show that while, so far, no general law of progress has been discovered, it is possible to point to certain trends in the history of mankind which, in the light of a rational ethic, may be adjudged progressive and that further progress, if not assured, is a possible end of rational endeavour.

II. THEORIES OF PERFECTIBILITY

To the thinkers of the eighteenth century progress meant in the first place human perfectibility. This is formulated most clearly by Condorcet:

The human species can be improved, firstly, by new discoveries in the arts and sciences and, consequently, in the means of well-being and common prosperity, secondly, by progress in the principles of conduct and moral practice and thirdly by the improvement of human faculty. This may be the result of improvements in the instruments which increase the intensity or change the direction of the use of our faculties or perhaps also of a change in the innate organization itself.

The principal agent of improvement in all these directions was reason. Condorcet believed there were indefinite possibilities of improving the inborn constitution of man. But leaving this, which would involve the inheritance of acquired characters, aside, the advance of knowledge was assured by the cumulative efforts of generations, by improvements in method and by a wider diffusion of educational opportunity. Progress in knowledge would be reflected not merely in increasing command over the forces of nature but also in the improvement of human relations.

Men could not become enlightened upon the nature and development of their moral sentiments, upon the principles of morality and their natural motives for conforming their conduct to their interests, either as individuals or as members of society, without making an advance in moral practice not less real than in moral science itself.

The main condition of moral progress was intellectual progress and the removal of the barriers that stand in its way. 'Les méchants', said Cabanis, Condorcet's literary executor, 'ne sont que de mauvais raisonneurs.' * There was nothing intractable in human nature, putting a limit to moral amelioration. By rational effort man could achieve a social order based on freedom, equality and justice. Man had the power to make himself.

A second basic element in the eighteenth-century theory of progress was the belief in the unity of mankind. Condorcet sets out to trace the 'advance of the human species towards truth and happiness'. Turgot, Kant and Herder are all concerned with the nature and possibilities of 'universal history'. There was, of course, an intimate connexion between the belief in perfectibility and the belief in the unity of mankind. The rational faculty was the same

* Cf. Picavet, *Les Idéologues*, p. 596.

in all men. It followed, according to Condorcet, that there was no people, however lowly in the scale of development, which was for ever condemned not to exercise its reason, and, sooner or later, the distinction between advanced and retrograde peoples would disappear. From another point of view Kant argued that the moralization and rationalization of man, which was the *telos* of history, could only be achieved through the cooperation of all mankind. It will be seen that the belief in the unity of mankind was based on the fundamental rationality of man and the ethical obligations that this carries with it.

Thirdly, implicit in perfectibility was the concept of development. This, however, was as yet vague and variously interpreted. To begin with, the belief in perfectibility did not always imply that in the past men had moved steadily towards perfection, but only that they would do so in the future. Condorcet did indeed think that a study of the past showed that there had been a movement in the direction which he thought to be desirable. But there were many others who emphasized the fact that hitherto improvement had been blocked by pernicious institutions and that these must be removed before progress could be assured. One of the most telling criticisms that Comte made of these earlier views of progress was that their conclusions did not follow from their premises. If it was really the case that social institutions had in the past been mainly hurtful and destructive, it would follow that retrogression and not progress was the law of history. *'Ainsi conçue, l'étude du passé ne présente plus, à vrai dire, qu'une sorte de miracle perpétuel, ou l'on s'est même interdit d'abord la resource vulgaire de la Providence.'* *

Next, despite the belief in the unity of mankind, the process of advance was not always conceived as single or unitary. Herder, for example, thought that the culture of humanity was made up of a succession of unequal and broken curves, having different maxima and minima. Each individual and each people could be happy in their own way and there was no single or unique state of perfection to which the whole human race was tending.

* *Cours*, vol. VI, p. 189.

Finally, different answers were given to the question whether the process of development depended on the free choice of men or whether it went on, so to say, over their heads. For Kant progress was the work of Providence. In the course of history man was being slowly moralized. But this was not due to any desire on the part of individuals, but to a power above them which uses the passions of men to promote ends in which as individuals they have little or no interest.

If we ask [he says], by what means this continuous progress towards the better can be maintained or accelerated, we see at once that this does not depend on what we do (as for example on the education we give to the young) but on what human nature does in us and with us, to lead us on to a path, which, left to ourselves, we would not easily choose. It is only from it, or rather from Providence (which alone possesses the highest wisdom required to this end), that we can expect success in a process which goes on primarily in the whole and through it in the parts.*

Herder contrives to combine a belief in Providence with both freedom and determinism. Human events are determined by the native endowment of men and their external environment. Yet evils sooner or later correct themselves and men are led to seek reason and justice. The writers of the French Enlightenment are often philosophically determinist in outlook.† But at the same time, they stress the power of man, by the use of reason, to control his future development. The connexion between the notions of progress and of development is thus left obscure. Above all, though the advance of knowledge is considered to be the main factor in progress, the eighteenth-century writers do little, as M. Javary warns us, to study its conditions. Kant, in his own way, reminds us that the laws of the movement of civilization had not yet been discovered, that the science of man still awaited its Kepler and its Newton.

In the main the inspiration of the eighteenth-century theories

* *Kants Werke*, Cassirer, vol. VI, p. 395.
† Cf. R. Hubert, *Les Sciences Sociales dans l'Encylopédie*, p. 186.

of progress was ethical in character. Liberty and equality were worthy ideals for reasonable men. The transition was easily made to the conclusion that humanity had in fact been moving, or at any rate would in the future move, towards them and that progress consisted in this movement. We may again quote Condorcet: 'Our hopes for the future of mankind can be reduced to three important points: the destruction of inequality between nations, the progress of equality within nations and finally the perfecting of man [*le perfectionnement de l'homme*].' By equality of nations he means equality of right, that is the freedom to the independent exercise of their reason. Inequality within each nation he attributes to three causes: inequality of wealth, inequality of position between those who can transmit assured means of subsistence to their family and those whose means are limited to their own life, and, finally, inequality of education. These inequalities would perhaps never completely disappear, but they could and would be progressively reduced by various methods such as insurance schemes and, in the case of education, by improvements in methods which would make it possible to give the mass of the people the instruction they needed and remove all differences save those resting on the distinction between talent, genius and common sense. Improvement in knowledge would lead to improvement in morals, for there was a natural link between truth, virtue and happiness. Distinctions of rights between the sexes had no justification and would disappear. Above all, war would be condemned as the greatest crime against humanity.

In view of what has happened since Condorcet wrote and despite the set-backs, we may agree with the verdict of P. Janet that there was nothing utopian in these prophecies.* It remains that these predictions were based on hopes for the future rather than on inferences from the history of the past. Condorcet himself shows that he is by no means certain of the triumph of light and reason or that there is a necessary connexion between intellectual progress and social or moral progress. New errors may still arise or ancient ones revive; there will always remain a certain

* *Histoire de la Science Politique*, vol. II, p. 735.

disproportion between what man knows, what he desires to know and what he thinks he needs to know. There will be progress but only on condition that we know how to use the forces at our command.*

In the nineteenth and twentieth centuries larger claims have frequently been made and as frequently controverted. The work of Bury stops with Herbert Spencer and I know of no survey of the field which carries it further. To make such a survey would mean to write the history of the social sciences in relation to developments in the natural sciences and philosophy. Here I can only follow up certain lines of inquiry which have a direct bearing on the basic ideas of the eighteenth-century thinkers.

III. COMTE

We may begin with the work of Comte. As in the case of his predecessors his approach was ethical. He was, as Mill says, a 'morality intoxicated man'; 'every question with him is one of morality, and no motive but that of morality is permitted.† But his conception of justice is not theirs. He has no love for 'the rights of man' which for him belong to the metaphysical age and are the watchwords of anarchy. Nor does he believe in unlimited perfectibility. Progress follows natural laws, and it is only when these have been discovered that a scientific politics, aware both of the limits and possibilities of development, will enable men to direct or accelerate desirable trends of change. His claims to have discovered the fundamental laws of social development would not now be conceded by anyone, and it would not be profitable to examine them again. But there are certain features of his work which are still of interest, especially his account of human nature, his analysis of the difficulties which stand in the way of progress and of the relations between intellectual and social development.

Development is for Comte the process whereby the distinctively human qualities are gradually unfolded. Progress is the development of order. But not any kind of order. Comte is sometimes

* *Esquisse.*　　　† *Auguste Comte and Positivism*, p. 140.

accused of empty tautology because he occasionally speaks of progress as the aim of development. But he makes it quite clear that not all development is progressive, but only that which carries with it improvement. The criteria are to be found in the growing power of altruism over egoism brought about by a fusion of intelligence and sympathy. His fundamental law is formulated by him thus:

Le type fondamental de l'évolution humaine, aussi bien individuelle que collective, y est, en effet, scientifiquement représenté comme consistant toujours dans l'ascendant croissant de notre humanité sur notre animalité, d'après la double suprématie de l'intelligence sur les penchants, et de l'instinct sympathique sur l'instinct personnel.*

Comte's account of human nature is certainly not open to the charge of excessive intellectualism. He rejects the definition of man as a rational animal as meaningless and he anticipates modern psychology in stressing the continuity between the minds of animals and of men. The preponderating power in human behaviour belongs not to the intellect but to the instincts and the emotions. Left to itself, the intellect would waste itself in idle curiosity and would achieve but little. It has no energy of its own and is moved to action only by the instincts. Among these the egoistic or self-regarding are more powerful than the social or other-regarding. It is, he remarks, 'a deplorable coincidence' that in respect of the faculty most important for human development man is so poorly endowed.† Primarily it is the egoistic impulses which force man to work, to increase his knowledge and to co-operate with others. Slowly and with difficulty the intellect and the social impulses come to support each other. The division of labour brings home to men their need of and dependence upon one another. The intellect develops through the stimulus of social contact and is given steadiness by the larger aims thus set before it. Reciprocally the altruistic tendencies are strengthened by the greater command which the intellect gives man over his passions and the increasing insight which it makes possible into the needs

* *Cours*, vol. VI, p. 721.   † *Cours*, vol. IV, p. 388.

of others. In this way the subjective conditions are provided for progress. But these conditions are recognized as precarious and uncertain in their operation. The intellect cannot of itself prescribe the ends of action. It is the servant and not the master of the passions. If it is to be used in the service of humanity it must overcome its inherently anarchic and egoistic tendencies and this can only be achieved if it comes increasingly under the sway of the altruistic emotions. Comte thinks that an historical survey shows that the altruistic tendencies have in fact grown in strength and that they have the capacity for 'indefinite extension'. In this he may well have been right. It is interesting to note that Dr Westermarck from an entirely different point of view and on the basis of a very extensive comparative study comes to much the same conclusion. Nevertheless, our confidence in an optimistic sociology is shaken when we find it wedded to a pessimistic psychology. Comte's analysis provides no sort of assurance that the intellect has sufficient strength to ensure the triumph of the benevolent over the egoistic impulses.

Among the factors hindering progress the most important is what Comte calls 'intellectual anarchy' or the absence of any agreement on the fundamental principles which might serve to guide political action. In language which would be highly appropriate today he complains that except on occasions of emergency, when there is a temporary coalition (in which each party usually hopes to have its own way), it is becoming increasingly difficult to induce even a small number of minds to adhere to a plain and explicit profession of political faith. The result is a mental condition of 'half conviction and half will', in which, in Guizot's phrase, men 'will feebly, but desire immensely' and in which, in consequence, they become the ready victims of political quackery and illusion. Ultimately this anarchy is to be traced to two factors, namely, the persistence of modes of thinking from the metaphysical and theological stages of mental development, and, secondly, to the 'dispersive' effect of the division of labour in the domain of science itself. As mischievous survivals from the earlier ways of thought Comte instances his pet aversions, the 'rights of man' and the 'sovereignty of the people'. Nowadays we could supply better examples, such as the widespread tendency to reify abstractions, e.g. 'capitalism', or the confusions of thought and the passions engendered through the personification of collective entities, e.g. nations.

The evils arising from excessive specialization are now even greater than they were in Comte's time. I can best sum them up in the words of Whitehead:

The dangers arising from this aspect of professionalism are great, particularly in our democratic societies. The directive force of reason is weakened. The leading intellects lack balance. They see this set of circumstances, or that set, but not both sets together. The task of co-ordination is left to those who lack either the force or the character to succeed in some definite career. In short, the specialized functions of the community are performed better and more progressively but the generalised direction lacks vision. The progressiveness in detail only adds to the danger produced by the feebleness of co-ordination.*

For the removal of these dangers Comte looked to the development of 'positive philosophy'. This would give a *vue d'ensemble* and would also provide an ethic. The root of the trouble lay in the fact that the social sciences had not yet reached the positive stage. He doubted whether the unification required would be achieved by those who come from the natural sciences; these were too specialized and apt to over-simplify as soon as they leave their own domain. What was needed was a new system of education which would break down the isolation between the various studies and make for better balance between them and general knowledge. The unification hoped for did not involve the reduction of the laws of nature to a single principle. The laws governing the various groups of phenomena were irreducible. But he thought that a 'subjective unity' could be reached by employing similar methods throughout. If the methods of positive science were used in dealing with social phenomena the prevailing anarchy would be progressively reduced. Experience shows that men are agreed only upon such subjects as have been reduced to positive science,

* *Science and the Modern World*, p. 276.

while on other subjects widely divergent views continue to be held.

It is clear that the problems raised by Comte have not been resolved. The division of labour within the sphere of science has been carried much further than in his day and has made it more difficult to arrive at intellectual unity, in the form of a common world-conception. The gaps between the natural sciences and the social sciences remain and many would say are unbridgeable. If the social sciences are to be judged by the degree of agreement among their exponents they would be seen to be very far from having reached the positive stage. Surveying recent developments in psychology, Professor Flugel, a friendly witness, says: 'In their aggressive sectarianism the various schools are apt to remind us painfully of the no less disconcerting growth of militant nationalism just at a period when the world was palpably in need of greater unity.' * He adds, however, that there are indications that the great period of schisms is past and that during the last twenty years the tendency towards *rapprochement* has been at least as great as that towards division. Similar remarks would probably apply to anthropology and sociology. Some philosophical students of the history of science would give a less favourable verdict. Professor C. D. Broad, for example, writing in 1925, concludes that 'there are not the beginnings of a scientific psychology, whether of individuals or of communities.'†

These judgements need not be further scrutinized here. The fact that they can be put forward by competent authorities brings home to us, however, how far Comte's hopes for a positive science of human relations are from being realized and still more how far such knowledge as has been achieved in this domain is from providing the basis for the *'vue d'ensemble'*, which he thought necessary for unity of thought and social effort. Comte's enthusiams blinded him to the difficulties. In mitigation it has to be remembered that even in the sphere of inorganic nature the fundamental discoveries date only from the time of Galileo and Newton. In the biological sciences the crucial developments are

* *Rationalist Annual*, 1947, p. 13.
† *The Mind and its Place in Nature*, p. 664.

even more recent, and progress in them is now very rapid. There is nothing to preclude the hope that in the next hundred years or so equal progress may be made in the sphere of mind and society.

There remains the question whether the social sciences can provide the basis for a unified ethic. Comte had no doubt of the answer. He passes readily from the indicative to the imperative mood. His fundamental law that in the course of history the altruistic tendencies gradually predominate over the selfish is not only a statement of fact but a guide to action. The function of a positivist ethic is to systematize this spontaneous process and to turn into a conscious aim that which has been working itself out unconsciously in the course of man's struggle with the forces of nature. Positive science with its emphasis on the profound connexions between individuals in society would be far more likely to promote a social morality than theological ethics which stresses personal salvation or metaphysical ethics which can yield no common standard. Avoiding absolutism, it would be far more practical and adaptable to changing circumstances.

Modern positivists would not be so sanguine. They would refuse to turn statements of fact into statements of what ought to be. The ultimate rules of ethics, they would say, express wishes or volitions and, as such, can be neither true nor false. I do not share this view, but even if it were admitted much would remain for a science of ethics to do. Such a science would be concerned, I suggest, with the following: (i) the classification of rules of action into primary and derivative. This would, among other things, facilitate the inquiry into the variability of moral rules, since differences of opinion depend to some extent on confusions between primary and derived rules; (ii) the logical discussion of their mutual implications and consistency; (iii) the discovery of their psychological or sociological origins and conditions; (iv) a study of the ways in which people in fact deal with conflicting claims. If such a science existed, it would be of value as a guide to policy, whether or not it could take the place of philosophical ethics. Political differences sometimes turn on differences of view regarding the basic values of life. But at least as frequently they turn on different interpretations of the facts, or of the consequences likely to follow, or of the relations between means and ends. It is thus reasonable to hope with Comte that the growth of positive knowledge in the sphere of human relations would help in reducing the area of disagreement or at least in giving fuller insight into what the disagreement is about. That the social sciences can be used by rival politicians in defence of contradictory policies is a sure sign of their immaturity.

We can now deal with Comte's central problem, that of the relation between intellectual development and general social development. As is well known, he thought he had discovered the law governing the intellectual history of man. This was the law, namely, that human thought passes through three stages, the theological, the metaphysical and the positive. The virtues and defects of this generalization are well known and need not be discussed here again. What is more important is the parallelism that he traces between the stages of intellectual development and the stages of social and political development. He maintains that there is a definite correlation between the theological stage and militarism; between the metaphysical stage and the social period which he calls the juristic and in which a defensive military organization takes the place of the earlier offensive military organization, and finally between the positive stage of thought and the phase of industrialism and the cessation of war. Of this connexion he offers but very poor evidence and in any case his prophecies were quickly belied by events. He did not foresee the clashes that would result from the intensification of nationalism, and his concentration on the elite nations of Europe blinded him to the possible consequences of the industrialization of the non-Western communities. Yet on a long view, the association which he alleges between industry and peace may prove to be sound. Industrialization is now rapidly bringing about the economic unification of the world, and this may well necessitate political unification. The association with the positive spirit presents greater difficulties. No one would now take seriously Comte's proposal of a spiritual world-authority consisting of positivist scientists. The problem is whether a scientific humanism can fill the spiritual vacuum which the technological changes due to science help to create.

On this there are several things to be said. To begin with, it was part of Comte's teaching that the movement towards positivism is not simultaneous in the different domains of activity and that the rate of advance is unequal. The social sciences were the last to reach the positive stage and Comte thought that he had himself secured their foundations. We can see now that they are still in their infancy and that in any case their effect on the mentality of the mass of the people is very slight. Our deeper mental habits go back millions of years to the ages of myth and make-believe, and they offer tremendous inertial resistance to the relatively recent efforts at critical reflection. If the teaching of the psychology of the unconscious is to be accepted, and, I think, in essentials it must be, it would follow that the educational systems so far developed have hardly begun to tackle the forces that stand in the way of rational behaviour. Wars and other forms of group-conflicts may not be directly caused by unconscious drives and archaic modes of thought and belief but they are certainly made easier by them and in turn encourage them.

The problem is complicated by the unequal rate of change. It is a commonplace that the advance of the physical sciences has created problems with which the social sciences are ill equipped to deal. In this connexion the time-span between changes is all-important. Whitehead has drawn attention to the enormous acceleration in the rate of social changes in recent history. In prehistoric times the time-span depended on changes in the physical configuration of the earth and was of the order of a million years. Changes due to alterations in climatic conditions were of the order of five thousand years. When technologies emerge in the pre-scientific age the average time-span for social change was about five hundred years. Whitehead thinks that no radical advance was made in technology between A.D. 100

94

and A.D. 1400. The structure of society begins to be seriously affected by technological changes after A.D. 1700 and since then their impact on society has been greatly accelerated and intensified. We do not know to what extent the outward changes brought about by applied science have modified the underlying mental habits formed during long ages of slow change. We are only beginning to realize that the assumptions about human nature on which the social sciences rest may require radical revision. There is no ground for despairing of reason while so much remains to be done to deepen our knowledge of the factors making for unreason in belief and action.

It is sometimes thought that radical improvements cannot be achieved until methods have been discovered for changing the innate basis of the emotional constitution of men. Comte, though not a Lamarckian, thought that to some extent the moral and physical improvements achieved by one generation could be transmitted through the hereditary structure to the next. In this he would not have the support of modern biology. It would seem that changes in innate constitution can only come about through mutation and selection. There is, however, now wide agreement among biologically minded sociologists that in the main social changes are independent of changes in germinal structure. Vast changes in the way of living have in fact been brought about, for better or worse, without alteration of racial type or innate faculty. The problem is thus in the main one for sociology and not for genetics. The same hereditary factors may have the most contrary effects according to the direction given to them and the ways they are adjusted to one another.

Several points of interest emerge, I think, from this brief survey of Comte's work. Society to-day suffers to an even greater extent than in his day from what he called 'intellectual anarchy', the absence of any commonly accepted world-view which might serve as a basis for a political philosophy. It is still true that 'modern society has not yet got its morals.' On the other hand his remedy is worse than the disease. We are hardly likely to entrust final authority to a group of omniscient priests, who, though not possessed of temporal power, would yet dominate the spiritual life of men, especially if the units of communal organization were as small as Comte thinks desirable. Again Comte was right in taking the extension of altruism as an essential element in human progress. Were he writing to-day he could point to the great efforts made since his time to banish disease and poverty, ignorance and neglect over ever wider areas of the world. What he did not succeed in proving is that this growth of altruism is the key to all history and that 'universal love' is the goal to which mankind is moving in accordance with an ineluctable law of human nature. Moreover, his reaction against the Revolution led him to erect a false antithesis between liberty and equality and thus to obscure the part played by the search for justice in the history of mankind.

Finally, as we have seen, his views of human nature hardly justify his optimistic faith in the power of the intellect to advance morality. Ultimately for him morals are an affair of the 'heart' and not of the 'head'. All the intellect can do is to provide information as to the means needed for the satisfaction of wants. But in this respect it ministers to the egoistic impulses as well as to the altruistic, and the former are much the stronger. The subjective conditions are thus not necessarily favourable to the growth of altruism. Nor is there any certainty that positive knowledge of the objective conditions of social life will be used for good; the social sciences like other sciences can be used as instruments of oppression and destruction. Comte's fundamental law is therefore ethical rather than sociological. It indicates the goal to which humanity ought to be moving; it does not describe the course which humanity has in fact steadily followed and which it must necessarily continue to follow in the future.

IV. HEGEL AND MARX

It is beyond my province to follow up the various ways in which the concept of development is interpreted by the German Idealists. But a brief reference must be made to Hegel's philosophy of history in so far as it bears upon the problem of progress. It has certain similarities to Comte's theory. Both see in history a process whereby mind reaches self-consciousness. In political theory both reject the doctrine of natural rights and, though both interpret progress as a movement towards the realization of freedom, their view of freedom is decidedly anti-liberal. The differences, of course, are no less fundamental. Hegel's view of the whole of reality as a process whereby the Absolute Mind attains to self-consciousness would have been rejected by Comte in common with all other 'metaphysical' theories. Here we are only concerned with the problem of historical progress. As is well known, Hegel conceives of history as the story of the expansion of the consciousness of freedom.

The Orientals have not attained the knowledge that Spirit – Man *as such* – is free; and because they do not know this, they are not free. They only know that *one is free* (i.e. the despot). The consciousness of freedom first rose among the Greeks and therefore they were free; but they, and the Romans likewise, knew only that *some* are free – not man as such. . . . The German nations, under the influence of Christianity, were the first to attain the consciousness that man, as man, is free: that it is the freedom of spirit which constitutes its essence.*

The trouble with all this is that what Hegel understood by freedom remains one of the mysteries of philosophy. If by freedom is meant submission to the General Will and if the best interpreters of the general will are the government officials of the type that Hegel knew in the Germany of 1830, then the oligarchic bureaucracies that have sprung up since his time might well be regarded as exemplifying his formula of expanding freedom. Those who think that the subjective opinions and desires of the many, which Hegel dismisses as mere contingency, as the contemptible caprice of those who think 'they know better', should play an important part in freedom, will look in another direction for progress in history. Yet even on a democratic interpretation the expansion of freedom cannot be taken as the key to all history. It represents one line of development and a progressive

* *Lectures on the Philosophy of History*, Introduction.

one. But there have been and obviously still are currents moving in an opposite direction, and there can be no certainty of the outcome. We may indeed find some encouragement in the fact that many of the totalitarian forms of government have not proved viable, and that in all cases they arose in areas which had no strong tradition of free government. But this does not prove that the movement towards freedom is irreversible, or that the expansion of freedom is the general law of social development.

Both Kant and Hegel regarded the rationalization and moralization of man, which for them constitute the significance of history, as a process through which the passions of men are utilized to produce results which they do not desire or foresee. But while Kant is frankly theistic and teleological there are endless arguments as to whether in Hegel's view the guiding power, 'the cunning of reason', is to be conceived as immanent in men or as transcendent or both. If man is slowly rationalized in the course of history one would expect the influence of man's reason to be on the increase and to become more important in the later phases. But this inference does not seem to be drawn either by Kant or Hegel; the process of history is something that goes on over men's heads throughout. There are similar ambiguities in the Marxist position. For Marx too the movement towards freedom is what gives significance to human history, and great stress is laid on the connexion between freedom and rationality. His followers, in their flight from anything that savours of theology, are anxious to avoid the use of teleological terminology and are thus led to stress the automatic or necessary character of social development. Popular exponents of Marxism lay stress alternately on the scientific certainty and inevitability of communism and on the need for vigorous individual effort. The ambiguity is 'ideologically' convenient. Widespread belief in the inevitability of communism is one way of weakening resistance to it, and it is comforting to believe both that salvation lies in your own hands and that 'history is on your side'.

Deterministic interpretations of Marxist doctrine now exert a profound influence extending far beyond its formal adherents.

This can be seen in the wide-spread acceptance of the view that war between 'capitalism' and 'communism' is inevitable, that economic systems are inevitably moving towards collectivism and that any form of socialism must inevitably lead to cultural and political totalitarianism. For none of these beliefs is there any scientific warrant. It has not been proved that the main causes of war are economic, that the cultural and economic pattern of societies is uniquely determined by the character of the economic organization or that socialism cannot develop in a variety of forms. Whether Marx himself took a strictly deterministic view of social change I will not venture to decide. He certainly speaks of the laws of capitalist production as 'tendencies which work out with an iron necessity towards an inevitable goal',* and he asserts that a society cannot overleap the natural phases of evolution or shuffle them out of the world by decrees, though it can shorten and lessen the birth pangs. On the other hand it is easy, as has often been done by exegetists, to cite passages in the opposite sense. There is equal ambiguity about the way in which the economic factors are related to the rest. Engels, as is well known, stressed the reciprocal or organic nature of the relationship. But from many passages in Marx it would seem that the only process which can be said properly to show independent development is the economic. Other changes have no continuity of their own, but merely reflect the basic economic changes: 'Morals, religion, metaphysics and other ideologies and the forms of consciousness corresponding to them here no longer retain a look of independence. *They have no history, they have no development. . . .*' Those who are not in the Marxist fold will be inclined to say, I think, that if the concept of development is not properly applicable to the history of thought it would be more sensible to banish it altogether from sociology. Whatever interpretation be adopted, and however highly we value the contribution made by Marx to the method of historical investigation, it seems safe to conclude in the light of modern research that Marx did not succeed in revealing 'the economic law of

* *Das Kapital*, Preface to first German edition.

motion of modern society', still less, as Engels claims for him, in discovering the true mainspring of history.

V. EVOLUTION AND PROGRESS

I now turn to the impact of evolutionary theories on the idea of progress. The terminology used in discussions of this problem is still confusing despite repeated attempts at clarification. The term 'evolution' is sometimes used to describe any form of orderly change. In biology it stands for a particular type of orderly change, namely that whereby new specific forms have arisen by a process of differentiation from the old. Whether the diversification of species is a concept which can be properly applied to changes in the inorganic realm I will not venture to inquire. The term 'development' is, of course, much older than that of evolution and independent of it. Development is a process whereby that which exists 'potentially' becomes actual. Biologists use the word in discribing ontogeny or the emergence of the adult organism out of the germ. The characters of the adult exist potentially in the germ plasm in the sense that, if the life history is known, we can predict that a particular type of organism will arise under specifiable conditions. In this case the potentialities are inferred from the end results. The term 'potentialities', however, has a meaning when these are not known. A man may try to find out what he is capable of by experimenting, and we may learn something of his capacities from his past attainments. There seems to be no difficulty in using this notion of the realization of potentialities with reference to groups large or small. Thus the theories of social development so far considered may be expressed in the form that human development consists in the unfolding of man's powers, individual and collective, and the use of such powers in dealing with nature and with himself. Similarly, I take it, the term 'evolution' could be used in sociology in a sense analogous to that given to it in biology, if new elements of culture can be shown to arise from the old by a process of diversification. Neither development nor evolution is the same as progress. Progress is development or evolution in a direction which satisfies rational criteria of value. Whether the study of evolution can of itself provide us with standards of value is open to argument, but until there is agreement on such standards we obviously cannot tell from the mere fact that a thing has evolved whether it has progressed or not.

The notion of evolution in the sense of the diversification of species has been fruitfully applied in at least two realms of culture, namely, in the history of language and of tools. Languages have been classified into families or stocks and their similarities and differences have been studied with the aid of a theory which can be appropriately described as 'descent with modification'. The tendency of recent comparative philology has been, I understand, to establish connexions between linguistic stocks which had formerly been regarded as remote from each other, and their derivation from a common source seems not unlikely.* The resemblance to biological theory was noted by Darwin but it is interesting to find that the theory that similarities of structure can be accounted for by descent from a common source was used by Sir William Jones a quarter of a century before Darwin was born. In the case of tools a similar approach has also proved fruitful. As Tylor pointed out, 'The geographical distribution of these things and their transmission from region to region have to be studied as the naturalist studies the geography of his botanical and zoological species.' Tylor added that evolution in this sense is in fact more easily verifiable in the study of culture than in biology. Marx made a similar point when he called for a history of tools which would be to social organs what Darwinism was to organs of animal species, and he thought that such a history of human technology ought to be easier to write than the history of 'natural technology'.† Furthermore, not only is the concept of evolution in the sense of diversification of species fruitful in the study of linguistic and technological change but the biological theory of the agencies at work in the evolution of living things

* Cf. Meillet, *Les Langues dans l'Europe Nouvelle*, p. 85.
† *Das Kapital*, ch. XIII.

has close analogies in the cultural realm. Languages, for example, evolve through variation, heredity and selection, though, needless to say, the terms have a different meaning from that which they have in biology. Linguistic history also provides examples of 'orthogenic' or oriented evolution, and raises in an interesting manner the problem of convergent and parallel evolution as against derivation from a common source.

In other realms of culture the concept of evolution in the sense here used has not proved so fertile. This is due, I think, to the difficulty in arriving at a workable social morphology. Let anyone compare the great natural classifications discussed by Darwin in the fourteenth chapter of the *Origin of Species* with what passes for morphology in sociological treatises and he will realize the gulf that separates them. Hobhouse tried hard to achieve a morphology, but with doubtful success. He operates in fact with very broad classifications such as his classification of societies into those based on kinship, authority and citizenship. In this the intention is to discover the principles which hold society together or the leading forces which at successive stages give specific character to the social union. Such classifications are rather more suitable for a theory of development than of evolution in the sense above referred to. Thus a society based on citizenship may be said to be more developed than those based on kinship or authority in the sense that it retains the element of mutuality and cooperativeness characteristic of the former, combines it with the extension of scale and regularity of order achieved by the authoritarian states, and adds a measure of freedom to the constituent parts and an elasticity to the whole, which are peculiarly its own. To prove development in this sense, it is not necessary to show that societies everywhere begin with the system of kinship, pass on to that of authority and end with that of citizenship, but only that a survey of history shows that the first is the characteristic mode of the lower and earlier stages of culture, the second of the advance towards civilization, and examples of the third on a large scale are found in the modern world. Hobhouse's work shows, I think, the value of an approach of this kind for the theory of progress. The idea of evolution, on the other hand, in the sense of diversification of species, valuable as it has proved in dealing with some elements of culture, may well turn out to be of lesser importance in this connexion, and in some cases may not be applicable at all, as e.g. in dealing with art.

Recently some biologists have claimed that the concept of progress can be fruitfully used in biology and even that from evolutionary theory an ethic can be derived. Various criteria have been proposed. Evolution is said to be progressive when it produces types that are more dominant or more varied and abundant; or have more control over and greater independence from the environment; or have the ability to cope with a greater variety of environments; or develop powers of awareness which enable them to respond with greater plasticity and discrimination to their environment. That such criteria are useful in describing certain lines of evolution is beyond doubt. Whether they provide the basis for an ethic is quite another question. It is clear that progress in the sense defined is not a universal law of evolution and, if it were, it is difficult to see how ethical problems could arise at all. As biologists tell us again and again, the history of life provides examples not only of 'progress' but of retrogression, degeneration and decay.

Clearly this is equally true of human history. In social change as in biological change many trends, often of long range, can be traced. Among these we have to choose, but the ground of the choice cannot be deduced from the trends; a value judgement has to be made. Consider, for example, the trend towards individualization. It is possible to trace along some evolutionary lines an increase in the range and variety of reactions and consequently in the ability of the individual organism to act as an independent unit. If, however, you maintain that it is *right* to encourage individual diversity and originality you are making an ethical judgement which surely cannot be deduced from the fact that such trends have been shown to exist. If you add that individualization is a prerequisite for the best types of society, that involves a conception of what societies are the best. If you add that societies which encourage freedom and diversity are likely to have greater survival power than societies based on other principles, you have not only to establish this probability, but you are adopting survival as the ultimate criterion of right and good. This will not do, for, as biologists have often pointed out, survival may be achieved by the most diverse and contradictory ways, by progress as well as retrogression, by reduction of needs and by greater fitness to satisfy them, by the extermination of others or by cooperation with them, by parasitism and friendly symbiosis. In short, sheer survival affords no criterion. The quality of life must be considered, and this clearly requires an independent value judgement. The verdict of T. H. Huxley thus stands that from the facts of evolution no ethic of evolution can be derived.

In the generalized theories of evolution the diversification of species is taken to be only one aspect of a more general process occurring not only in the animate world but also in the inanimate. Evolution is used to describe the emergence of a series of levels of reality, each obeying its own laws, but constituting an 'advance' on the preceding member of the series. The laws describe the mode of relatedness or the governing principles peculiar or specific to each level. The laws of the 'higher' levels do not displace the laws of the 'lower', but add something new or qualitatively distinct of their own. Stated thus the theory would include the various forms of 'emergent' evolution and some forms of 'dialectical' materialism. I cannot pretend to discuss these very ambitious theories on their own ground. I can only comment briefly on the bearing they have on the problem of social progress. Some exponents of the theory have suggested that the formation of societies might be considered as constituting a new level of organization or integration, linked with the levels preceding it but following organizing principles of its own. The hierarchy of levels might, for example, as Lloyd Morgan suggested, be the following: atom, molecule, colloidal unit, cell, multicellular organism, society of organisms. These are in an order of advance from 'lower' to 'higher' as judged by increasing differentiation and complexity of organization.

This theory is philosophically attractive in that it brings the various spheres of the inorganic world and the world of living things under one comprehensive scheme of interpretation. There is however, considerable danger of converting the continuity of processes which it traces into a metaphysical principle which in some way 'brings' these processes about. Not to mention Lloyd Morgan's 'nisus' or Smuts's trend towards holism, it is not uncommon to find biologists speaking, for example, of 'Evolution becoming self-conscious' in human societies. This is a crypto-teleology in which Evolution takes the place of the Absolute of the Idealist philosophers. It comes, perhaps unintentionally, to be conceived as a unitary agency which remains the same through its varied manifestations, strives to express itself in the various levels of organization, and culminates in human society.

These metaphysical doubts might perhaps be dispelled by more careful formulations in which the personification of abstractions might be avoided. Yet the ambiguities are not to be dismissed too lightly, above all, because they suggest that there is a natural law of progress, for which in fact no proof has been given. The really important thing in the generalized theory of evolution, it seems to me, lies in its insistence on the qualitative distinctness of the different levels of organization. From the point of view of sociology, therefore, the laws governing social organization and social development have to be ascertained by direct study of the facts and not be deduced from what is known of the laws of preceding levels. But so far as I can see, no laws of social development, and consequently of progress, have as yet been discovered. Hence you cannot say on the grounds of general evolutionary theory that human society is moving inevitably to collectivism, as Needham claims,* or that the progress of man requires the maintenance of class distinctions, as Bateson suggested,† or that

* *Integrative Levels* (Herbert Spencer Lecture), 1937.

† *Biological Fact and the Structure of Society* (Herbert Spencer Lecture), 1912.

authoritarianism or totalitarianism is wrong, as one of the most recent exponents of the biological theory of evolution maintains.* All such assertions assume that the laws of social change are already known and they all imply ethical judgements which may or may not be valid, but which, as we have seen, cannot be deduced from general evolutionary theory.

VI. TRENDS OF SOCIAL CHANGE

Our survey shows that the nineteenth-century thinkers have not succeeded in discovering any general law of social progress. It may, however, be the case that along certain lines progress has occurred and that, in exploring them, possibilities of further progress may be discerned which might henceforth serve as a goal of human effort. The biological analogy is on this point instructive. From the most recent surveys it appears that as judged by biological criteria it cannot be shown that overall progress, or progress towards any definite goal, is characteristic of evolution or inherent in it. 'There is progress, but it is of many different sorts and each sort occurs separately in many different lines.'† In social development the situation seems more hopeful. For here there are strong tendencies towards convergence and the unification of mankind is one of the clearest trends in human history. The prospects for unified advance towards a common goal are therefore far from being excluded by the known facts.

We may begin with certain trends which exhibit advance, leaving aside for the moment the question whether this advance satisfies ethical criteria. The clearest and most easily verifiable is that of knowledge, especially of science. The rate of advance is, of course, unequal for different periods of time and different branches of knowledge, but that there has been advance no one, save perhaps extreme relativists, would deny. The criteria of advance are not in dispute. A science is more developed in so far as it serves to explain phenomena unknown before or hitherto

* G. G. Simpson, *The Meaning of Evolution*, 1950.
† Cf. G. G. Simpson, op. cit., p. 343 seq.

unexplained. Advance is estimated not by reference to final truth or even agreement with first principles taken as beyond doubt, but rather by the range and comprehensiveness of the experiences covered and the degree to which the different experiences can be made to support one another. Advance, in other words, involves increasing systematization of experience, whereby the probability of the partial systems entering into it, as modified by their inter-connexion, is progressively increased, though without reaching certainty. In the natural sciences there are well recognized standards, which would be challenged only by those who hold that all knowledge is conditioned by the social configuration of its time and place and can be judged by no universally applicable principles. In other branches of knowledge there may be no generally accepted criteria of significance or importance, and theories can gain adherents which in more developed sciences would be quickly exposed as without foundation. The extent to which this can happen is a fair measure of the position of a branch of knowledge on a general scale of development.

Apart from the sheer accumulation of experience, advance in knowledge has been due mainly to improvements in method. The most important of these have occurred in two directions. First there has been a growth of detachment, that is in distinguishing between subjective and objective factors of belief and of making allowance for the emotional factors affecting belief. A glance at the different sciences will show that they advance in proportion as they gain in objectivity, the difficulties of detachment being greatest in the sciences dealing directly with man. Secondly, advance has depended on the ways in which purely deductive thinking has been balanced by observation and experiment. These have differed at different times in the history of thought and in the different sciences. By all accounts the success of modern science has been due to the steady pursuit of observation and experiment, the provision of instruments extending the range and improving the accuracy of observation, and the development of new methods of analysis which made it possible to deal with continuous processes in conceptional terms, and to trace order in the midst of change and qualitative diversity. The balancing of the experiential and conceptual modes of inquiry has been achieved with the greatest success by the physical sciences. It becomes more precarious as we approach the sciences of life and mind. This anyone can see who considers the part played by mathematics in the different sciences and notes the frenzied efforts made from time to time by the social sciences to elaborate conceptual schemes which have very little connexion with empirical investigation. It may be added that in part the advance of knowledge has consisted in the attention given to the method of method itself, to scrutiny of the processes by which data are obtained and analysed, and recently to a study of the various ways in which allowance can be made for the subjective factors, personal or social, which might affect the results. In this respect again the social sciences are at a disadvantage, for their methodology is still uncertain and objectivity is more difficult to attain than in any other branch of inquiry.

The development of knowledge is most easily seen in the growing power of man over the forces of nature. The points of advance are well marked, though in this as in other developments there is no law of automatic progress. The growth of thought in the early Oriental civilizations was not, for example, reflected in equal advances in the industrial arts. The reason for this discrepancy is partly to be found in the nature of the dialectical interest in its early forms which diverted attention from practical applications and partly in the slave system which diminished the need of mechanical aids or substitutes. In the modern period industrial advance comes to be directly connected with the growth of applied science. In this phase the rate of change is enormously accelerated and the process becomes increasingly conscious, deliberate and disciplined. In this respect modern technology differs fundamentally from the technology of the pre-scientific ages, though it arises from and is continuous with it.

When we come to social organization, that is the efforts of men to regulate their relations to each other, significant long-range trends are much more difficult to establish than is the case in dealing with the growth of knowledge of and control over the environment. The many attempts that have been made to formulate regular stages in the history of institutions are now seen to have been often vitiated by the inveterate tendency to assume a single line of evolution. Yet, if we are searching not for laws of development but for the light that history may throw on the possibilities open to mankind, certain lines of change can be easily seen to be of great importance. Here I want to draw attention to two significant trends, firstly, the growing power of articulate thought in the shaping of legal systems and especially the emergence of the concept of law as an instrument of social policy; and, secondly, the unification of mankind. Recent comparative studies have shown that in the lower societies custom is not perhaps so rigid as was once thought. Nevertheless, when changes do occur, they are largely unconscious. When differentiated organs of government emerge, e.g. chiefs and councils, their decisions in particular cases necessarily involve interpretations of custom, and in this way substantially new customs may occasionally emerge. As the scale of organization extends and governmental authorities have to deal with a variety of customs, their decisions have to be generalized and codified. Maine pointed out that many societies never pass beyond what he called the era of codes. But a small number of progressive societies pass from the mere declaration of the law to law-making, using for this purpose, as he explains, legal fictions, equity and legislation. In the case of some societies there is a further development in which more or less systematic efforts are made to base legislation on some conception of general well-being, and, what is equally important, to disentangle the unconscious or half-conscious assumptions underlying the law and the 'ideologies' which are used in its defence. This movement from the unreflective custom to declaration, systematization and codification of law, thence to deliberate legislation and the critical scrutiny of the ethical basis of the law, unquestionably constitutes growth in self-direction and the rational ordering of life.

The growing power of reason in the history of law has been

discussed by Max Weber from another point of view. With the aid of a comparative study of the various legal systems of the world, Weber seeks to show that law passes from what he calls a charismatic phase, in which the law is derived from the revelations of prophets, to a phase in which law is an empirical creation by a special class of legal advisers; further to a stage in which law is imposed by strong authorities, secular or theocratic; and finally to a phase in which the law is systematized and rationalized by a body of experts. Weber is primarily interested in what he calls formal or functional rationalization, that is to say the generalization and systematization of legal rules and techniques, and he shows that this is not always directed to securing the 'material' rationalization of the law. It is easy to see that technical expertise may be used both to promote and to defeat social ideals. Nevertheless, it seems to me that Weber pays insufficient attention to the role of ideals in the shaping of the law and in particular to the fact that students of legal systems have come to realize that legal decisions rest on unconscious assumptions of an ethical and political nature, and that if legislation is to be rational these assumptions must be made explicit and examined.* That the recognition of this need has passed from the philosophers to judges and administrators is surely an important factor in the movement towards the rational shaping of public policy.

The most important trend for the purpose of our discussion is that towards the unity of mankind. We have seen that this was one of the root ideas in the early theories of progress. They all made use of the 'happy artifice of Condorcet' of treating the successive peoples who pass the torch as if they were a single people running the race. It is necessary in dealing with this conception to distinguish between unity of origin or descent, unity in the sense of interconnexion and interdependence and unity of aim or purpose. We may leave aside the question of the genetic or biological unity of the human species as of doubtful significance in this context. With regard to interconnexion and interdependence recent archaeological work has brought out the essential

* See especially W. Friedmann, *Introduction to Legal Theory*, ch. XXIII.

unity and continuity of the civilizations of the ancient East, and we learn from Professor Childe's account that the links between these centres of civilization and the European barbarisms of prehistory are also more or less definitely established.* Cultural interaction is the lesson taught by the whole of history and prehistory. During the last four hundred years this interdependence has been enormously intensified and accelerated owing to the ebullient energy of the European peoples, and is now world-wide.

It is often argued that the unification so far achieved is relatively external or superficial, that there is no such thing as civilization but only civilizations. The weakness of the position can be seen from the fact that there is no agreement about the number of such distinct civilizations in time or in space. To take but one example, Spengler thought that what he calls Oriental Christianity (*arabisch-magische*) and Western Christianity (from about A.D. 900) were totally different religions. From another point of view Alfred Weber has argued that when a religion is transplanted to another social setting it becomes an entirely different religion. In this sense there would not be one Christianity but several, not one Buddhism or Muhammadanism but several. Arguments of this sort turn a partial truth into a violent paradox.

The motives inspiring this 'pluralist' interpretation of civilization are complex. There is in the first place the reaction against what may be called the cultural imperialism of the West, the tendency to set up Western or European-American civilization as a standard and to identify its development with the development of humanity. This is clearly a healthy reaction. The European peoples have not recognized sufficiently what they owe to other civilizations or the extent to which contact with them is likely to affect them in their future development. There is, in the second place, the 'relativist' view of history, fortified by the revival of Comte's doctrine of the social consensus in the shape of what is now called 'functionalism'. This leads to an over-emphasis of the uniqueness or individuality of the different societies. But the notion of individuality in this context is extremely vague.

* Cf. V. Gordon Childe, *The Most Ancient East.*

What is a distinguishable unit from the point of view of political structure may be but a fraction of a more inclusive unit considered economically or culturally. Functionalist theories are generally non-historical, and their application to history would present great difficulties. Admittedly development is not unilinear. There are different traditions, each to a large extent following its own line. But they never have been completely independent, and radical changes have frequently been due to contacts, friendly or otherwise, between them. The effects of contact must differ greatly in different spheres of culture, leading to genuine assimilation in some and to mere syncretism in others. Thus at one time any society will contain elements borrowed from others which it has integrated with its own, and also other elements which have not been and never may be fully absorbed. In short, cultures have their specific character and follow their own course, but in various ways and degrees they have always acted upon one another and the interconnexion has itself grown or developed in the course of history. Neither in time nor space can we say where one society or civilization leaves off and another begins. The multilinear character of development does not exclude an underlying unity and continuity. In this as in other cases development involves both diversification or differentiation as well as integration.

VII. UNITY OF AIM

Today, I suppose, the peoples of the world would generally be considered as falling into five or six groups, namely: (1) East Asia; (2) India and Indonesia; (3) Islam; (4) Russia and its satellites; (5) the 'Western' world, and a sixth group which seems to be emerging in the African world. It is easy to see that none of these either does or can develop independently of the rest. For better or worse mankind is rapidly becoming one in the sense at least of the interdependence and interconnexion of its parts. Is it also attaining unity in the deeper sense of unity of aim or purpose? There are some who think that this is only possible on the basis of religious unity. This appears to be the central tenet of Professor Toynbee's theory of the rise and fall of civilizations. 'What may happen is that Christianity may be left as the spiritual heir of all the other higher religions . . .: while the Christian Church as an institution may be left as the social heir of all the other churches and civilizations.'* In Professor Toynbee's opinion this view is supported by the results of his very elaborate survey of the relations between civilizations and the higher religions. At bottom, however, it rests on his conviction that Christianity approximates more closely to final religious truth than any other religion. This raises the problem of the reality or possibility of progress in religion in its acutest form. That there has been such progress is a view held not only by theologians.

Whitehead, for example, tells us that religion 'is the one element in human experience which persistently shows an upward trend. It fades and then recurs. But when it renews its force, it recurs with an added richness and purity of content. The fact of religious vision and its history of persistent expansion is our one ground for optimism.'† Whether, however, it is Whitehead's view that Christianity is the fullest expression of this vision is not clear. Elsewhere he says that both Christianity and Buddhism, 'the two catholic religions of civilization', are – if we are to judge by the comparison of their position now with what it has been – in decay. 'They have lost their ancient hold upon the world.'‡ I cannot be sure that I have understood what Whitehead took to be the criteria of the persistently upward trend in religious experience. So far as I can see, the advance consists mainly in increased ethical insight. This in his opinion justifies the inference that 'there is a rightness permanently inherent in the nature of things' and leads to the conception of God as 'the completed ideal harmony' and of his purpose as 'the attainment of value in the temporal world.' What Whitehead means by 'rightness in the nature of things' is extremely difficult to gather. In *Science and the Modern World* he suggests that the order we find in nature is 'never force – it presents itself as the one harmonious adjustment of complex

---

* *Civilization on Trial*, p. 240. † *Science and the Modern World*, p. 268.
‡ *Religion in the Making*, p. 44.

detail. Evil is the brute motive force of fragmentary purpose disregarding the eternal vision.'* The religious experience, it seems, does not include a direct intuition of a personal God. Yet Whitehead thinks himself justified in speaking of God as 'wise' and as 'pursuing a purpose'. The nearest approach to a definition of 'what men call God – the supreme God of rationalized religion' – is that he is 'the actual but non-temporal entity whereby the indeterminateness of mere creativity is transmuted into a determinate freedom'.† How near this is to Christian doctrine or to that of any other world-religion is beyond my power to determine.

I have made this brief reference to Whitehead not, of course, with any intention of estimating his contribution to the philosophy of religion, but merely in order to illustrate the difficulty of laying down criteria of religious advance or of applying them to the higher religions of the world. In dealing with this problem Professor Toynbee is far more daring. Civilizations in his view move in recurring cycles of birth, death, birth. The movement of religion, on the other hand, he suggests may be 'on a single continuous upward line'.‡ As to the nature of the advance Professor Toynbee leaves us in no doubt. The other religions are measured by the yardstick of Christianity. They are the forerunners of Christianity, partially foreshadowing its truths. How can such a view be made convincing to non-Christians? They will find it difficult to believe, for example, that we know enough of the 'true purpose of life on Earth' to say that it consists not in the establishment of the best possible human society in this world but rather in preparation of souls for another life,§ or 'that the Christian soul can attain, while still on earth, a greater measure of man's greatest good than can be attained by any pagan soul in this earthly stage of its existence.'* Is there any ground for believing that if a universal religion were to arise on the ruins of Western civilization, it would retain these beliefs in any form, or that it would necessarily link its interpretation of the significance

---

* p. 268.   † Whitehead, op. cit., p. 90.
‡ Toynbee, op. cit., p. 236.   § p. 250.   * p. 251.

of suffering and of love with the distinctive dogmas of Christianity? These are highly speculative matters on which the decisive voice is not that of empirical evidence. On the facts I do not see that Professor Toynbee has shown that Christianity is gaining ground in the world either in the sense of winning new adherents or in the sense that the Christians are becoming more Christian. His forecast of future trends is therefore precarious.

On the whole, unilinear advance is as unlikely in religion as in other spheres of culture. The great religions each follow their own course, though not without mutual influence. In each it is possible to make out points of advance as well as of stagnation and retrogression. To obtain an estimate we should have to consider, first, the direct experiences of the seers and prophets. These are hardly commensurable. There are, secondly, the interpretations given of these experiences and their embodiment in the general system of thought. These are presumably subject to tests of logical coherence and, unless an extreme relativistic view is adopted, it may prove possible to evaluate the contribution made by the religions of the world to knowledge. Thirdly, we should have to consider how far the institutions created by the religions succeed in providing their adherents with the spiritual opportunities to live the kind of life which is closest to their ideal. Fourth, there are the influences exerted by the religions and their institutions upon the political and economic life of the community and on the relations between communities. It may well be the case that in respect of insight into the nature of things and of man's place in the world the religions have made contributions of increasing importance. On the institutional side, whether within the churches themselves or in their relations to other institutions, the issue would be far more doubtful. Gains and losses would be very difficult to balance and some would say impossible.

I do not share this view. It is both legitimate and possible to inquire what part was played by the Christian churches in the spread of education, in the abolition of slavery, the emancipation of women or the control of war. Similarly the role of the caste system and its relation to Hinduism or the impact of Confucianism at different times on Chinese society lend themselves to investigation. The studies so far made of the social record of the religions of the world make it abundantly clear that development has not proceeded along a single line and they do not reveal a persistently upward trend. The religions of the world may in the future learn more from each other than they have in the past,* but I cannot see any ground for believing that any one of them, however modified by its contact with the others, is likely to provide a basis acceptable to all for the spiritual unification of mankind.

The problem of religious progress leads directly to that of moral progress. If there is any aspect of their teaching in which the higher religions tend to converge it is to be found in the emphasis they all lay on moral universalism, and the best ascertained general trend in their development is their gradual moralization. Can we find in the history of morals indications of a movement towards unity of aim or purpose? It is clear that in morals as in religion, development does not follow a single rectilineal course. There are distinct traditions each growing in its own way. In each, however, lines of advance can be traced and there are marked tendencies towards convergence. Crucial contributions are made in the ethical teaching of the world-religions. They all set up an ideal of life going far beyond the traditional or conventional morality and beyond the occasional intuitions reported from earlier phases. They all discover the golden rule.†

---

* In Whitehead's view 'the decay of Christianity and Buddhism, as determinative influences in modern thought, is partly due to the fact that each religion has unduly sheltered itself from the other' (*Religion in the Making*, p. 146).

† Compare the following:

CONFUCIUS : When asked: Is there a maxim which one may observe as a rule of conduct for life? the master replied: Is not this to be found in the word SHU, i.e. to act to others as one would act towards oneself, or as this is translated by his disciple Tseng Tze: 'to love others with the heart with which one loves oneself'.

BRAHMANISM: Good people do not injure living beings; in joy and sorrow, pleasure and pain, one should act towards others as one would have them

They all, though with varying limitations, inculcate the duty of not injuring others. And this is extended to include self-sacrifice to prevent injury to another. They all teach universal kindliness and good will. They all, though in different ways, come to recognize the intrinsic value of virtuous conduct and the importance of sincerity and inward acceptance as against outward show and external constraint. These are no mean achievements. Indeed, their early formulation has led some students, for example, Buckle, to doubt the reality of moral progress. This view, however, will not stand inspection. The principles formulated by the ancient religions and philosophies were conceived in terms of personal salvation or personal goodness and took little account of social relations. Though they single out elements essential to all morality, they are clearly inadequate when applied to the conditions prevailing in large-scale complex societies. Personal benevolence may have to be checked in the interests of social order. Love and good will cannot in themselves suffice to remove the sources of conflict or help us in defining the limits of compulsion. To put yourself in the place of the other is no doubt an excellent maxim and increasing sensitiveness to the claims of others is unquestionably an important element in moral progress, yet by themselves such maxims give no indication how conflicting claims are to be reconciled. The insistence on inwardness and the values of the good will may lead to a separation between law and morals and leave both at the mercy of a rough empiricism and the blind forces of tradition. In complex societies the problem is to find the way to curb power and to reduce the conflicts that arise from inequalities of power. It becomes necessary to examine existing institutions in the light of moral principles and above all to discover the criteria of just law. I do not see how anyone can deny that considered from this point of view real progress

---

act towards oneself (*Mbh.* 13, 113, 9, quoted E. W. Hopkins, *The Ethics of India,* p. 138).

HEBREW: What is hateful to you, do not do to your fellow creature (Hillel, *Sab.* 31a).

CHRISTIAN: Do to men what you wish men to do to you (Matt. vii, 12).

has been made in many societies. Despite the enormous increase in the scale and complexity of modern societies, there is now deeper knowledge of the relations between freedom and equality, between the needs of personality and the needs of the social order; and we can point to many experiments designed to give this deepened insight practical expression.

It is sometimes said that in dealing with the social troubles of the modern world we must abandon what is called the 'moralistic' outlook. But this implies a very narrow interpretation of morality, which makes the difference between good and bad a matter of unerring intuition or sacrosanct tradition, and explains all the ills of the world as rooted in human sinfulness. By others the rejection of 'moralism' is justified on the ground that ends do not permit of rational investigation, while the problem of means is one for science and not for ethics. But in fact ends and means interpenetrate and effective valuation must take into consideration the various ways in which they affect each other. In so far as modern ethical thought has made any real progress it is to be found, I think, in the recognition that conceptual analysis has to be combined with an empirical study of the conditions and consequences of action, that ideals have to be related to the possibilities which social life offers. From this point of view the efforts of legal theorists to disentangle the principles underlying the law, the utterances of judges in dealing with conflicting interests, and the methods used by courts of arbitration in settling industrial or international disputes are of at least as much interest to the moralist as the conceptual analysis of the philosophers. In morals as in other spheres, it has come to be recognized that principles have to be tested not only by their inner consistency but by their relevance to particular situations and their power to solve definite problems. In this sense modern ethical thought has made considerable advance even if the solutions offered continually raise fresh questions. The case for moral progress rests above all on the persistence of the quest for justice in the history of mankind, spurred on by the sense of injustice. Of this quest we can say with greater confidence than of the religious quest that it persistently shows upward trends. This does not mean that the movement is not fitful or irregular or that it is not liable to be diverted or checked. But it does mean that, despite retrogressions, there is some continuity of advance, that men learn from their failures something of the direction in which future advance is to be sought.

This brings us back to the problem of the goals and criteria of progress. I believe that the eighteenth-century thinkers were right in regarding progress as a movement towards 'reason and justice' and in laying stress on equality as the core of justice. Condorcet, as we have seen, looked forward to a condition of mankind in which inequalities based on differences of sex, wealth and educational opportunity or political grouping would be progressively reduced. His hopes were based on his belief in equality as a principle which all possessed of reason must ultimately recognize as valid. His treatment of the historical development of equality as an ideal and of its application in practice was slight. Among later writers the problem is handled most fully by Engels in the *Anti-Dühring*.* Engels traces the historical conditions which in Western societies favoured the generalization of the idea of political and social equality, and the emergence of the notion of human rights reaching out beyond particular states. In his view the extension or diffusion of the idea is causally linked with changes in economic structure. Those who are not committed to theories of economic determinism will assign more importance than he does to the sense of injustice, the reaction against glaring inequalities which can and does, on occasion, overleap the boundaries of class and race.

In any event the vitality of the idea of equality and its correlate, freedom, is by no means exhausted. It is spreading to the farthest corners of the earth and is everywhere contributing to the mental emancipation of peoples. In practice, of course, equality of rights is far from being universally assured. Yet in many states considerable progress has been made in equalizing the conditions of well-being and it would be truer now than it

* Ch. X.

was in the days of Marx that the idea of equality is taken for granted by the general public, and indeed 'already possesses the fixity of a popular prejudice'. Of special interest in this connexion is the amazing speed with which the idea of the emancipation of women is now spreading in the Oriental world. The most recent example is that of China where the marriage law promulgated in 1950 reverses an age-long tradition of subjection and may well turn out to be one of the most important changes brought about by the revolution. In the relations between states the principle of equality is recognized as an ideal for international law to follow. The disparity between the small and the 'great' powers and among the great powers themselves makes the application of the principle precarious, and it is often derided as meaningless. But despite the sceptics, I believe that in the relations between states, as in other human relations, there is force in the notion of equality before the law and of equality in the right of making the law. The world has at any rate reached the point where the problems involved can be discussed in practical terms. In judging the possibilities of a solution we should take into consideration not only the failures that have occurred but also the successes of human effort in solving partial problems of the same nature, e.g. in securing equitable relations within states. The rationalization of the common law of England took about a thousand years and is far from being fully achieved. The rationalization of world law may well not take so long.

My argument implies that equality and freedom are ideals which can be rationally defended and that progress consists in the movement towards them. It has nothing to do with either metaphysical or theological theories of the *telos* of history. I do not believe that history is a process in which men are moralized despite themselves. Nor do I believe that in any other form the laws of overall human development have been established, from which the future of mankind can be inferred with any certainty. We know of no general law of progress. The verdict of Renouvier stands that 'The true law lies in the equal possibility of progress or regress for societies as for individuals.' All that I am concerned to maintain is that as judged by rational criteria certain trends can be traced in the history of mankind which can be adjudged progressive and that by examining the conditions of success and failure, we can, if we choose, move farther in the direction indicated by them. It will be said that this empties the idea of progress of any real content. With this I cannot agree. If progress consists in the growth of rationality, we ought not to expect it to follow predetermined lines. It is in the nature of reason to throw out efforts, to search for alternative possibilities, to seek to understand itself, and the conditions in which it has to work. What the theory of human progress, as I understand it, asserts is (a) that there has been development in the efforts of men to gain knowledge and to organize human relations; (b) that within this development we can trace certain elements which are either themselves progressive or show the possibilities of progress, as judged by ethical criteria; and (c) that to turn these possibilities into actualities is to follow in the line of progress. The theory is not, I think, compatible with relativist interpretations of knowledge or morality. It takes for granted the unity of the human reason and the possibility of a rational ethic.

It will be urged at this point that the world is now hopelessly divided into two hostile groups differing radically and irreconcilably in their ethical outlook. But is it really the case that the communists and their opponents differ in the conception they have of the ultimate ends of social life? In theory at least it is not true, as is sometimes alleged, that the communists deny the value of individual personality. On the contrary they claim, as socialists have always done, that they aim at the liberation of the individual. Nor is it true that in theory the communists have a different view of the relations between ends and means than the bourgeois philosophers. Both sides realize in their own way that means and ends are interdependent and must therefore, in any final valuation, be considered together. In so far as there is an ethical difference it is one of moral temper rather than of ethical theory. The liberal mind is characterized by an abhorrence of fanaticism, a greater readiness to count the cost in terms of human happiness and human lives, a profounder awareness of the corroding and demoralizing effects of violence both on those who employ it and those who suffer from it. By contrast, the totalitarian, in whatever camp he may be found, is single-minded and fanatical, moved to desperation by the inertia of the masses and the dilatory habits which he associates with the liberal spirit. Above all the totalitarian ignores the distance between the final end he sets himself, which, though in fact vague and cloudy, is to him vivid and compelling, and the means which are needed to bring it about. The result is that the means turn into ends, power is sought for its own sake and, as usual, grows by what it feeds on. The final end then tends to be pushed farther and farther into the future, whilst it is represented at the same time as just round the corner, given sufficiently thorough and drastic action. It thus serves to provide an 'ideology' which relegates the universal morality admitted in theory to the millennium and erects an interim ethics based on the class struggle from which all ordinary moral standards have disappeared. This dual morality is highly convenient; the interim ethics can be used to defend the actions of the revolutionaries, while the universal ethic of the classless age can be appealed to in condemning the actions of their opponents. The substance of morality is thus destroyed in the supposed service of an apocalyptic good, and the barriers against arbitrary power are broken down in the name of freedom.

The fact that both sides in the present conflict can speak in the name of morals may be thought to strengthen the arguments of those who reject what they describe as the 'moralistic' approach in politics and may even lead some to doubt whether there are any universally valid moral principles at all. The ambiguities involved are no doubt partly due to the vagueness of the ideals and principles to which appeal is made. But they arise, I think, to a greater extent from confusions between questions of fact and questions of values and from ignorance and distortion of the relevant facts. It is important to remember that ideological distortions are well-nigh as common and as difficult to dispel in the realm of fact as in the realm of values. Pseudo-science can be as confusing as pseudo-ethics. Both are involved, for example, in the claims of the doctrinaires that a market economy is essential for social progress or that without a violent revolution there can be no 'real' freedom or equality.

The problem remains whether, even if we had deeper insight into the fundamental principles of morals and a better grasp of the forces at work in society, advancing knowledge would necessarily be turned to greater social good. This, as we have seen, was the assumption on which the early theories of progress were based. Nowadays no one would claim that there is any law which ensures that virtue and enlightenment will go together. Yet there is some correlation between intellectual and moral development and there is a good deal to support the hope that in 'ethics good, as in science truth will prevail.'* For good includes tolerance, spontaneity, flexibility in the search for new values, and these are qualities which may prove decisive in the struggle with types of society which rely on fanaticism, rigidity of organization and the suppression of individual variety. At the lowest we can say that there is no ground for suggesting any permanent disharmony between social justice and social efficiency. The choice therefore lies with ourselves.

The view that man can by taking thought direct in some measure the course of his future development is sometimes dismissed as mere 'scientism', based on the belief that the human mind can as it were 'pull itself up by its own bootstraps'.† The case is argued elaborately, but it fails to carry conviction. It is admitted that we can do something to discover the principles of human interactions and that we can make use of the knowledge thus gained to secure the conditions favourable to the growth of civilization. But this, which is all that those who believe in the possibility of conscious direction of social change need, is then strangely identified with the view that the social process can only be known 'from the inside', presumably by each individual

* Hobhouse, *Social Development*, p. 339.

† F. A. Hayek, 'Scientism and the study of society', *Economica*, February 1944, p. 31.

for himself. Two quite different distinctions are here confused, namely, that between centralized and non-centralized control of social forces, and that between the kind of knowledge obtained by the natural sciences and the kind of knowledge which, in Hayek's view, is alone open to the social sciences. I cannot see why those who believe in what he calls 'a conscious social purpose' need commit themselves to centralized or total planning or to the theory that the methods and assumptions used in the social sciences must be completely assimilated to those used in the natural sciences. In any case the contrast between individualism and collectivism is drawn much too sharply by Hayek. There are many 'collectivists' who are well aware of the limitations of our knowledge and of the difficulties that hinder the growth of an enlightened common will. Humility of mind is no monopoly of individualists, nor is the *hubris* of the specialist confined to the collectivists.

I have assumed throughout that a rational ethic is possible and the case for progress, as I understand it, stands or falls with this assumption. By a rational ethic I mean an ethic that is based on a knowledge of human needs and potentialities and of the principles of justice, that is the principles designed to exclude arbitrary power and to secure an equitable distribution of the conditions of well-being. Such an ethic does not imply a fixed code or one uniform for all peoples. As our knowledge of, and sensitiveness towards, human needs grow and greater control is achieved over the conditions of development, the system of rights and duties must, on any theory of human progress, undergo change. There will thus in all probability never be a universal code of morals, though the history of moral development suggests the possibility of agreement on what may be called a minimum code, of the kind now trying to find legal expression, in a list of human rights. The rationalist will not, of course, attempt to construct a code *de novo*. His procedure is to start with existing rules, to eliminate palpable inconsistencies and to generalize and systematize those that have proved their worth. He has above all to distinguish between those conditions of well-being which can be secured only by collective effort and may require coercive sanction and those which are best left to the individual. This is the basis of the distinction between the sphere of law and the sphere of morals and, in this sense, the differentiation of law from morals is in the line of progress. This differentiation, however, does not imply independence. The ultimate basis of law is ethical and it is highly important for a rationalist ethics to keep in close touch with legal developments, especially as law is rapidly becoming an active and articulate agent of social change.

From the point of view of our discussion, the philosophical controversies regarding the nature of the ultimate premises of ethics – interesting as they are in themselves – are of no great relevance. Whether these premises come from cognition or from feeling or from both, there remains enough work for rational investigation. The links between the ultimate premises and the rules derived from them have to be scrutinized and validated, and above all, the relation between the ultimate or intrinsic ends and the conditions needed for their attainment has to be discovered and evaluated. For this task, it is clear, moral philosophy needs the cooperation of the social sciences.

We scarcely need to be reminded that knowledge alone will not suffice. The optimism of the early theories of progress which assumed that intellectual development was the chief or sole determinant of social progress is dead and beyond hope of resurrection. It is only too obvious that knowledge can be used for evil purposes and that the situation is made more serious when to the power over nature is added power over the minds of men. Yet it is a futile thing to rail against science and technology. If they can be used as instruments of oppression and destruction they can also be used to promote freedom and well-being; if they facilitate the concentration of power they can also show us how to prevent its abuse. The moral neutrality or indifference of the sciences leaves the path open to progress or regress. The choice is ours. It remains that if knowledge is not a sufficient, it is a necessary, condition of progress. It can give no assurance of ultimate success, but it can point to the possibilities open to men and thus help to provide the will with the opportunity to choose among them. Knowledge offers no apocalyptic visions, but it can do something to help man to make his own history before the end is reached.

BIBLIOGRAPHY

Baillie, J., 1951, *The Belief in Progress*

Bateson, W., 1912, *Biological Fact and the Structure of Society* (Herbert Spencer Lecture)

Becker, C. L., 1932, *The Heavenly City of the Eighteenth-Century Philosophers*

Broad, C.D., 1925, *The Mind and its Place in Nature*

Buckle, H. T., 1857–61, *Introduction to the History of Civilization in England*, new and rev. ed. with annotations and an Introduction by J. M. Robertson.

Bury, J. B., 1920, *The Idea of Progress*

Childe, V. Gordon, 1951, *Social Evolution*

Childe, V. Gordon, 1929, *The Most Ancient East*

Cohen, Morris R., 1947, *The Meaning of Human History*

Collingwood, R. G., 1946, *The Idea of History*

Comte, A., 1830–42, *Cours de Philosophie Positive*, 2nd ed., 1864

Condorcet, M. J. N. C. de, 1795, *Esquisse d'un tableau historique des progrès de l'esprit humain*, English trans., London, 1795.

Dawson, C., 1929, *Progress and Religion*

Delvaille, J., 1910, *Essai sur l'histoire de l'idée de progrès jusqu'à la fin du 18ème siècle*

Dodd, C. H., 1938, *History and the Gospel*

Engels, F., 1885, *Anti-Dühring*

Flint, R., 1893, *The Philosophy of History*

Frazer, Sir James George, 1927, 'Condorcet on human progress', in *The Gorgon's Head and other Literary Pieces*, p. 369

Ginsberg, M., 1947, *Reason and Unreason in Society*

Hazard, P., 1946, *La Pensée européenne au 18ème siècle*

Hegel, G. W. F., 1857, *Lectures on the Philosophy of History*, trans. J. Sibree

Herder, J. G. von, 1784–91, *Ideen zur Philosophie der Geschichte der Menschheit*, trans. T. O. Churchill, 2nd. ed., 1803

Hobhouse, L. T., 1906, *Morals in Evolution*, 7th ed. with Introduction by M. Ginsberg, 1951

Hobhouse, L. T., 1924, *Social Development*

Hobhouse, L. T., *Development and Purpose*, rev. ed., 1927

Hubert, R., 1923, *Les Sciences Sociales dans l'Encyclopédie*

Huxley, J. S., 1943, *Evolutionary Ethics* (Romanes Lecture)

Huxley, T. H., 1893–4, *Evolution and Ethics*, vol. IX of *Collected Essays*

Inge, W. R., 1920, *The Idea of Progress* (Romanes Lecture)

Janet, P., 1872, *Histoire de la Science Politique*

Javary, A., 1851, *De l'Idée de Progrès*

Kant, I., 1784, *Idee zur einer allgemeinen Geschichte in weltbürgerlicher Absicht*, Cassirer IV, trans. Hastie, *Kant's Principles of Politics*

Kant, I., 1793, *Über den Gemeinspruch: Das mag in der Theorie richtig sein*, Cassirer VI, trans. Hastie, op. cit.

Lessing, G. E., 1777–80, *The Education of the Human Race*, trans. F. W. Robertson

Lotze, H., 1856–64, *Mikrokosmos*, English trans. 1885

Marvin, F. S. (ed.), 1921, *Progress and History*

Marx, K., *Das Kapital*, vol. I, 1867; vol. II, 1885; vol. III, 1894 – English trans., vol. I, London, 1886; vols. II and III, Chicago, 1909

Mill, J. S., 1866, *Auguste Comte and Positivism*

Morley, J., 1886, Essays on Condorcet and Turgot in *Miscellanies*, vol. II

Needham, J., 1937, *Integrative Levels* (Herbert Spencer Lecture)

Niebuhr, R., 1949, *Faith and History*

Pareto, V., *The Mind and Society*, English trans. 1935

Picavet, Fr., 1891, *Les Idéologues*

Proudhon, P. J., 1853, *Philosophie du Progrés*

Renouvier, C. B., 1853–64, *Essais de Critique Générale*

Simpson, G. G., 1950, *The Meaning of Evolution*

Sorel, G., 1908, *Les Illusions du Progrès*

Sorokin, P. A., 1947, *Society, Culture and Personality*

Spencer, H., 1876–96, *The Principles of Sociology*

Spengler, O., 1920–22, *Des Untergang des Abendlandes*, trans. C. F. Atkinson, *The Decline of the West*, 1926–8

Tocqueville, Alexis de, 1835–40, *De la démocratie en Amérique*

Toynbee, A. J., 1948, *Civilization on Trial*

Turgot, A. N. J., 1913–23, *Œuvres, avec biographie et notes par G. Schelle*

Voltaire, F., 1756, *Essai sur les Mœurs et l'Esprit des Nations*

Weber, A., 1951, *Prinzipien der Geschichts- und Kultur-Soziologie*

Weber, L., 1913, *Le Rhythme du Progrès*

Whitehead, A. N., 1926, *Science and the Modern World*

Whitehead, A. N., 1926, *Religion in the Making*

Windelband, W., *An Introduction to Philosophy*, English trans. 1921

[4]

Social Change*

I

By social change I understand a change in social structure, e.g. the size of a society, the composition or balance of its parts or the type of its organization. Examples of such changes are the contraction in the size of the family, or rather the domestic unit, which has occurred and is occurring in many societies, the breaking up of the domainal economy with the rise of cities, the transition from 'estates' to social classes or, to go back to earlier stages, the growth of a system of publicly administered justice replacing former personal or group retaliation. The term social change must also include changes in attitudes or beliefs, in so far as they sustain institutions and change with them. The field of inquiry is thus very wide. Here I am concerned with certain fundamental problems involved in all sociological and historical analysis, but requiring reformulation from time to time in the light of current thought. I have in mind such questions as the following: is it true that in the last resort changes are to be traced back to desires or purposes or, perhaps, unconscious drives in individual minds? If the real agents are always individuals, what significance is to be attached to the phrase 'social forces'? Are these concatenations of individual desires or volitions as modified by interaction? Or is causal agency to be ascribed to changes in social structure conceived as bringing about other changes? Finally, there is the problem of teleology. Changes occur in societies which look *as if* they were designed, but in fact have not been designed or foreseen. How do such functional changes occur, and how are they related to consciously directed changes?

These questions in their turn suggest others of an epistemological kind, such as the nature of historical and sociological

* The Herbert Spencer Lecture, delivered at Oxford on 27 February 1958.

explanation and, in particular, the question as to the significance of the causal relationship as used in the social sciences. In their early stages the social sciences had to make a case for the view that social phenomena were subject to laws, and this easily led them to assume that the laws they were in search of were akin to the laws of the natural sciences. This, I take it, is what is meant by the 'positivist' or 'naturalistic' trend in the social sciences. In reaction against this trend there have been recurrent movements of thought stressing the independence or autarchy of history, or else maintaining more generally that the natural sciences and the sciences of culture differ radically in aim and method. In Germany this movement found powerful expression towards the end of the last century and the beginning of this century in the work of such writers as Windelband, Rickert, Dilthey, Troeltsch. In this country the problem was very fully discussed by Collingwood and is now again being taken up vigorously both by philosophers and by the social scientists themselves.

The movement has many strains difficult to disentangle. It has suffered greatly, I think, from the use of vague terms like positivism, naturalism, determinism and, in particular, from the tendency of methodologists to tell historians and social scientists *de haut en bas* what it is that they are supposed to be doing rather than to inquire what in fact they actually do. In many treatises on historiography the number of examples of actual historical investigations is often very small. In Rickert's *Kulturwissenschaft und Naturwissenschaft* the only example discussed at all fully is based on a comparison between von Baer's study of the development of the chick in the egg with Ranke's work on the Popes of the sixteenth and seventeenth centuries, designed to illustrate the difference between the study of repeatable and unique events. The impression conveyed is that we can safely assume without further inquiry that the sciences of culture do not in fact deal with recurrent events. Perhaps a case can be made for this, but it is certainly not obvious. The use of terms like 'naturalists', 'determinists', again, makes for much unreal polemics. Men of straw are thus erected which it is easy to knock down. The

French sociologists, e.g. Comte and Durkheim, are often said to favour a 'naturalistic' approach. But if this means that in the view of these sociologists social facts are similar in nature to the facts dealt with by the physical sciences, the claim will not stand a minute's investigation. Comte's classification of the sciences implies that there are different levels of being, each level having its own laws. It is, he thought, 'materialism' to interpret the laws of the higher levels in terms of the lower. The dynamic agencies to which Comte appeals in his analysis of social development are the instinctive and emotional drives, egoistic and altruistic, guided or directed by the intellectual faculties. His fundamental laws of social change are laws of mental evolution, though he did not think that these were psychological laws, if by this was meant laws that could be reached by introspection. They certainly were not laws of 'nature' if this means the laws of physics or biology. The use of the term 'naturalist' in reference to Durkheim is equally inapt. When he bids social investigators to treat social facts *comme des choses*, he is far from asserting that they are 'material'. He is rather warning them against the idea that the nature of social facts can be ascertained by looking within, or that the functions of social institutions are necessarily identical with the ideas we have of their ends or purposes. His view of 'collective representations' implies a conception of society as spiritual or mental in character, though the laws governing them cannot be reached by introspective psychology. His theory has much in common with theories of emergent evolution, societies constituting in his view a new level of being with laws of their own, not reducible to the laws of biology or of individual psychology. I think, further, that neither Comte nor Durkheim can be fairly regarded as determinists. Consistently or not, they are both moralists believing that social changes can and ought to be directed or guided by moral ideals.

To take another example, Spencer is often included among the 'determinists'. Yet he carefully explains that his theory that institutions evolve in conformity with general laws does not imply that the human will is not an important factor in social evolution.

The institutions of a people and the character of its members act and react on each other. A change in the character of the members will tend to be reflected in a change in the institutions, while conversely changes in institutions will sooner or later affect the character of the members. Since changes in the character of individuals can only affect institutions in so far as they are expressed in action, it follows that the voluntary acts of individuals are an important factor in bringing about changes in the structure of societies.*

Whether they are determinists or not, historians and social scientists alike certainly use the language of causality. Thus historians of populations ask whether there was a causal connexion in the nineteenth century between the rate of population growth and fluctuations in economic prosperity, and what it was that happened in 1880 to break the connexion.† A historian of English civilization is found to be asserting, for example, that the *effect* of the Norman Conquest was to bring England back to the orbit of Latin culture and to remove the chance of England developing an Anglo-Saxon life of its own, or playing a part as a member of a Scandinavian Empire. Bertrand Russell, sceptical though he may be of the value of the concept of causation to the physical sciences, has no hesitation in using it in his study of social dynamics, and he even ventures to assign the 'causes' of such a complex entity as the decay of liberalism.‡ Negative assertions are of interest in this connexion as, for example, when it is argued that overpopulation is not a cause of migration, or of war;§ or when it is concluded that the rise of the rate of crime in a given area is not connected with the racial composition of the area.

In approaching the problems of the nature of social causation, I should like to begin by putting forward certain preliminary observations.

(1) Firstly, in dealing with social changes historians and social

* Cf. *The Study of Society*, pp. 411-13.

† Cf. T. H. Marshall, 'Revision in economic history', *The Economic History Review*, vol. V, 1935.

‡ *Power*, p. 122.   § Carr-Saunders, *The Population Problem*, p. 188.

scientists have to face the same sort of problems and are in search of the same sorts of explanation. When, for example, a historian asserts that the rise in population rate in England from 1760 onwards was due mainly to a fall in the death rate, brought about by improvements in medical science and practice, and to better living conditions attributable to rising production, he is not doing anything different from what the demographer attempts to do in explaining a contemporary rise in population among peoples now in the early stages of industrialization. It is true that the historian is not interested in establishing generalizations about the rise of populations, but in determining what happened in the period under review. But in so far as he is able to specify the conditions involved, his statement is capable of being generalized, or at least of suggesting explanations of population increases in similar circumstances elsewhere.

(2) It seems to me that, as used in history and in the social sciences, causality is not taken to consist in regularity of succession. Historians quite frequently believe that they have established a real connexion between events in a particular case without claiming to have established a generalization. Likewise in the social sciences and in practical life, regularity of succession, so far from being identical with causation, rather suggests a search for causes. If we find, for example, that changes in the marriage rate are associated with changes in the volume of trade we do not forthwith assert a causal relation, but proceed to look for factors mediating the connexion. Of course, the regular recurrence of a succession is important in the discovery of causal connexions; it is one of the signs by which we judge that the causal relation is present; but the relation itself does not consist in the regular repetition of a succession. On the contrary, whether an event occurs rarely, frequently or constantly depends on the complex of the conditions which link it to its cause and the rarity, frequency or constancy of these conditions.

(3) Historians are apt to consider that the facts of history are in essence psychological facts.* The reaction against 'naturalism'

* Cf. M. Bloch, *The Historian's Craft*, p. 194.

among the German philosophers referred to above was in part due to the importance they attached to mental causes. Troeltsch, for example, argued that in the historical sphere nearly everything passes through the medium of consciousness and turns upon the interaction of conscious efforts, in which, however, unconscious elements may be absorbed. Historians, of course, are frequently engaged in searching out motives, and this not only in diplomatic or political or military history, but also in dealing with massive large-scale movements. For example in discussing the 'causes' of the Arab expansion in the seventh century, Fisher is mainly concerned to disentangle motives. Was the expansion due, he asks, to a desire to extend the faith? If this is unlikely in view of the fact that in the early stages the conquerors do not appear to have been anxious to make converts, can it be that the motive was just plunder, and that finding victory easy they were led to extend their operations and to make their empire 'as other states have made them', blindly? This is the explanation finally adopted, though it is added that religion gave the movement cohesion and an impetus which it otherwise would have lacked.* In this, as in other examples which could readily be multiplied, historians rely on implicit or unstated generalizations about the motives of behaviour. This, however, does not mean that in their view history is applied psychology. The psychology is that of daily life, using maxims widely accepted though far from being scientifically tested, or else appealing to a sort of insight into human nature, akin to that of the artist or of great statesmen endowed with the power of knowing and understanding men. As Bloch has pointed out, historians are not nearly as careful in checking their psychological assumptions as they are in ascertaining whether or not a particular event has taken place, though it does not follow that they are necessarily wrong in the attributions they make.

In so far as mental factors play a part in social change, social causation is in important respects different from natural causation. It is easy to see, for example, that motives are not measurable in terms of identical units, and that their comparable strength

* *History of Europe*, ch. XII.

cannot be stated in general terms. Thus economic motives may prevail over religious motives, or national sentiments may prove more powerful than economic interests, but, equally, they may not, and we cannot tell how many 'units' of the one will prevail over how many units of the other. Again, as has frequently been noted, in dealing with motives there is no law of the composition of forces, since some of the motives may be deprived of any effect on action through the act of choice. In group action we are nowhere near a knowledge of the various ways in which motives may be compounded, say in situations of conflict, cooperation or compromise. The processes of interaction are very complex and the results very different from the transformation of energy in the physical world.

(4) By cause, I understand a set of factors jointly sufficient and necessary to the production of the effect. In practical life we are usually not interested in stating all the conditions making up the set, but single out those which are, so to say, decisive. In some investigations, for example, in medicine, a distinction is sometimes drawn between proximate, exciting and predisposing causes, or between 'true' causes and auxiliary. Thus in dealing with tuberculosis, the cause is the tubercle bacillus and the conditions those which favour infection, or lower resistance to infection. Which conditions are taken as decisive depends to a large extent on the perspective of the inquiry. Strictly the cause includes the entire set of conditions. But in practice many conditions are not specified either because, being commonly present, they are taken for granted, or because the phenomena are so complex that many of the conditions remain undetermined and may even be undeterminable.

These are all familiar points. I mention them because they are of special relevance in considering the causal role of desires, volitions or unconscious mental drives in the analysis of social changes. I take it that no one seriously doubts that mental factors are part-conditions or cause-factors in social change. But what is sometimes forgotten is that they require the presence of other factors to be effective. Mental processes do not occur in a vacuum.

They imply a change in the situation, internal or external, which acts as a stimulus. These changes in the situation must be considered as cause-factors, since upon them depends which of the many possible reactions shall occur and in what form. We are not entitled to relegate the situational factors to the rank of auxiliary or precipitating. The weight to be attached to the different cause-factors must clearly depend upon the nature of the available evidence, in each case.

A case in point is the hypothesis offered by some psychoanalysts of the causes of war. They draw a distinction between the economic and political factors, which they tend to consider as secondary, and the psychological factor, which they regard as 'fundamental'. But it is very hard to see on what grounds greater weight is attached to repressed aggression than to, say, differences in the level of economic development between countries, which tend to encourage expansionist tendencies and frictions connected therewith. In regard to motivation it is abundantly clear that very similar motives will express themselves very differently in different social structures. It has, for example, been repeatedly shown that while economic rivalries between states are apt to generate frictions conducive to war, similar clashes of economic interest between localities within a state produce no such effect. The intensity of the competitive motive may be the same in the two cases, but the behaviour is different as we move from one form of political organization to another. As far as the psychoanalytic hypothesis is concerned, we need to know how societies differ from one another in respect of the amount and intensity of repression to which they subject their members and whether there is an ascertainable relation between such repression and intergroup conflict. For example, is there any difference in amount or intensity of unconscious tension between, say, the Scandinavian peoples and the people of the Netherlands? If such differences exist, are they in any way related to the fact that the Norwegians and the Swedes managed to settle their disputes by peaceful negotiations while the Belgians and the Dutch fought a war? Or again, can it be shown that the decline in the intensity of wars in the eighteenth and nineteenth centuries, as compared with the fifteenth and sixteenth, and the marked increase in the twentieth, were correlated with a corresponding rise and decline of inner tensions in the individuals concerned? If such inner tensions are cause-factors of war, it has to be shown with what other cause-factors they have to be linked to issue in war, and it is quite arbitrary to dismiss these other factors as secondary. The problem is to show in what ways economic and political factors intertwine to produce conditions of tension or to arouse latent tensions. Similar considerations apply to the study of the rise of nationalist movements. Like wars, they no doubt originate 'in the minds of men', and a psychological analysis of nationalist sentiments is therefore necessary and important. But reference to basic social impulses or to the need of stability and security or devotion to a cause or being greater than ourselves will not account for the different forms of nationalism or for its formidable strength in modern times.

(5) In many investigations it is natural to take the individual and his motives as a datum. Yet even in economics, as F. H. Knight has shown,* this has its limitations. The theory of market competition starts with the individual's tastes and wants and productive capacity. But the tastes and wants are socially conditioned and productive capacity involves not only personal qualities as developed in a given environment, but external agents and materials owned, recognized and protected by the existing legal order. The family, the state and even larger units are important not only as interest groups but in helping to shape the individual as a functioning unit. In any case economists would hardly regard their discipline as a branch of psychology. They are concerned not with the play of motives as such but with results of given psychological conditions as they operate upon numbers of men in their dealings with one another when the means available for the satisfaction of needs are scarce. In other social sciences the main concern is not with the intentions of individuals, but with structural relations in their bearing on individuals. But we

* *Freedom and Reform*, p. 383.

know very little of the way changes in motivation come about, or why certain mental forces come into play at certain periods, or certain types of character dominate the social scene at certain times and not at others. It seems that the social sciences, including psychology, have not been historical enough, and history has not kept close enough touch with the social sciences. The result is that our knowledge of the ever-changing tensions between individual personality and the collective life, which might furnish the basis for a theory of social dynamics, is still in its infancy.

II

With these general considerations in mind, I should like to bring out, in the light of examples drawn from different fields of inquiry, the kind of explanations that have in fact been offered of social changes and, in particular, the sort of factors to which causal agency has been attributed by competent authorities.

(1) We may begin with a case in which a social change is attributed mainly to desires and decisions of individuals. I refer to the rise of the small family system in Western countries in the latter part of the nineteenth century. There is general agreement that this has been brought about in the main by voluntary restriction of births. The evidence shows that the decline in the birth rate is not to be accounted for by changes in the amount of marriage or age at marriage, nor by an increase in involuntary sterility or spontaneous abortion. On the other hand, there is positive evidence in favour of the view that the decline is due to increasing practice of birth control. Firstly, the decline becomes more marked with the spread of propaganda in favour of birth control. Secondly, that the decline varies with the knowledge of the use of contraceptives is evidenced by the negative correlation between social status and fertility and by differences in fertility between urban and rural areas, differences which are much reduced in areas where the rural population is suburbanized. These differences suggest strongly that the decline is associated with the spread of the knowledge of contraceptives from the upper social levels to the lower, and from town to country.

There is negative evidence in support of this, for it appears that among women who do not use contraceptives the number of pregnancies is about the same in all classes.* There are further cases such as those examined by Methorst in Holland dealing with the variations in the intervals between births which do not permit of any explanation other than that of deliberate control.† Granted, however, that the decline in the size of the family is to be attributed mainly to voluntary decisions, the question remains why these come into play during the last part of the nineteenth century. The problem is to account for the changes of attitude to the bearing and rearing of children which made these decisions possible. The answer is found in numerous interlocking changes in the social and economic structure. Among these may be mentioned the establishment of compulsory education which removed children from the labour market and made the rearing of large families more costly; the provision of educational facilities for women, which contributed greatly to raising the status of women; the wider opportunities for the employment of women outside the home; the increase in social mobility which facilitated the spread of influences first felt by the upper economic grades to the lower, and strengthened the desire of parents to help their children to rise in the social scale by giving them a better education than they had themselves; the immense increase in leisure and of amusements outside the home. These and no doubt other factors connected with changes in the economic structure constituted strong inducements for the restriction of births. To these must be added changes of moral and religious outlook, and the fact that, for various reasons, the movement for the emancipation of women came in many countries to be associated with propaganda in favour of birth control. The factors vary from country to country. But everywhere the changing structure of the family seems to be conditioned by changes in the economic and social structure and the changes in mode of life associated with them, which have come about in recent decades.

(2) In the case just briefly examined a change in the social

* Pearl. † Cf. Carr-Saunders, *World Population*, p. 104.

system seems to have come about as a result of decisions, however motivated, to bring about a particular result. In this as in other cases the consequences resulting from individual acts go far beyond what is directly aimed at. As an example of a somewhat different kind, consider the changes that took place in rural society in England between the years 1300 and 1500. In 1300 the majority of countrymen were graded as villeins. By 1500 only a small minority were servile and the system of demesne agriculture, in which most of the work done on the lord's land was done by tenants in villeinage, was all but extinct. How did this happen? It seems that without any formal break the practice of leasing land for life or for a term of years spread rapidly during the thirteenth century, replacing the elaborate arrangements of tenure and service. Contemporaneously the practice of commutation became more frequent. Eventually the lawyers took a hand in giving the villein greater protection through the recognition of 'copyhold' tenure.* Here we have a tremendous change effected through countless transactions between individuals, each pursuing, as he no doubt thought, his own ends. Were these individual acts the sole cause of the change? Clearly not, for they would not have occurred, had not the circumstances favoured the transition from an arrangement based primarily on a natural economy to one based increasingly on commercial and contractual relations. The causes are the motivated acts, but the motives are shaped by the change in the conditions. There is no ground for dismissing these changes in the conditions as merely secondary or subsidiary.

(3) These examples suggest a further group of cause-factors which may be described as structural changes and structural strains. By structural changes I mean changes in the parts of a structure due to changes in other parts or to a change in the balance of forces. By strains I mean tensions set up in a society by a lack of equilibrium between its parts. The two are closely related. Thus the domain economy was made impossible in Europe in the eleventh and twelfth centuries by the rise of the towns. The urban population could not feed itself and had therefore to

* J. Clapham, *A Concise Economic History of Britain*, ch. IV.

140

obtain the means of subsistence by purchase from the rural areas. This meant that the domains no longer restricted their production to meet their own needs. As production became remunerative, the idea of working for profit began to exercise people's minds. On the other hand, the landowners, restricted to customary revenues, found it difficult to satisfy their growing needs. In this way the moral and economic foundations of the domainal system were shaken by the growth of cities and the change in the relations between town and country. With variations this transformation of the social structure occurred everywhere in Europe in much the same way, as Pirenne has shown. In the Russia of the eighteenth and nineteenth centuries similar factors brought about the decline of the relatively self-contained natural economy of the estates. The landowners wanted things that the estates could not produce, the growth of towns and urban industries increased the supply of such goods, while at the same time a market was created for any agricultural surplus the estates might offer and new channels were being opened for international exchange.*

Closely connected with the interactions between the different parts of the social structure are what I have called structural strains. By this I mean tensions set up within a society by changes in size, by clashes between the forces making for centralization and the spirit of local independence, by the failure of changes in different parts of the structure to keep pace, or by the fact, now illustrated vividly in the movement for European unity, that units which have developed to meet certain requirements, e.g. political, are not suited for others, e.g. economic. These strains set up disturbances, latent or overt, which sooner or later find expression in movements for change. Societies differ greatly in plasticity. They may be too rigid to meet changing conditions, or expand to a size which threatens inner cohesion, or adopt principles of organization which sap the vitality of their members, or fail to make the corrections in the structure as a whole, necessitated by changes in the parts. The major sources of social change are, it seems to me, conditions generating these strains or

* Cf. G. T. Robinson, *Rural Russia under the Old Regime*, p. 55 seq.

'contradictions', and the efforts made to overcome them. The Marxists have concentrated on the contradictions that arise between the forces of production and the relations of production. But it seems clear that the sources of strain are many and varied, and indeed hardly reducible to system.

(4) Changes of social structure can of course also be brought about by external influences due to contact with other societies, peaceful or warlike. The changes brought about by conquest may be very drastic indeed. The Norman Conquest, for example, was accompanied by a complete upheaval of political institutions and the whole organization of the state. On the cultural side its importance is immense. Not only did it link England again with Latin culture; it was responsible for the making of the English language. On the political side it created the conditions which were to shape the course of change for centuries, and largely determined the particular form which the struggle for popular freedom was to take in England.* The role of war in the consolidation and expansion of states was emphasized by Spencer. Diffusion and borrowing are processes occurring again and again in the history of culture. Imitation, conscious or unconscious, has been used to explain changes in constitutions and legal systems.

(5) We may next consider the contribution of outstanding individuals or groups of individuals. Their importance has been exaggerated as frequently as it has been underestimated. An interesting example is provided by the accounts given of the industrialization of Japan from 1868 to 1938. The impression is sometimes conveyed that this process was initiated and sustained by a powerful oligarchy sharing a common and clearly defined end and commanding the disciplined obedience of a docile people. Recent work shows that the activities of the politicians at most accelerated a process which was latent in the whole conjuncture of forces at work. Without minimizing the great contributions made by the big concerns in association with the government in developing new sources of power and long-distance transport and providing credit facilities, it remains that the expansion of in-

* Cf. Pirenne, *History of Europe*, p. 254.

dustry during this period owes much to the enterprise and energy of millions of small business men, farmers and workers. As to the relative importance of the various cause-factors, however, opinions differ widely. According to some authorities nearly every industry started between 1870 and 1900 did so on the initiative of the government, and mostly in factories opened and operated by the government and sold to private enterprise, when they had got over their initial difficulties.* Professor William W. Lockwood, on the other hand, takes a very different view. He argues that some of the basic industries, e.g. coal and electric power, were developed mainly through private investment and enterprise, and that in respect of a very wide range of industry, both large and small scale, there was little direct or active intervention on the part of the State.† The difficulties of dynamic analysis are evidently formidable in this, as in other instances of growth.

The part played by the 'great man' in social change has been discussed *ad nauseam* by historians and philosophers. Spencer argued that the great man had first to be made before he could remake society.‡ Others say that, however made, he is rarely the arbiter of events. Bismarck, who by all accounts must be reckoned as having exercised an enormous influence on the political events of the nineteenth century, remarked: 'The statesman can do nothing for himself. He can only lie in wait and listen until amid the march of events he can hear the footsteps of God. Then he leaps forward and grasps the hem of His garment. That is all he can do.' In the case of the founders of the great religions it may be noted that, whatever view be taken of the originality and novelty of their contributions, they rarely succeeded in imposing their ideas upon large masses of men in their own lifetime. By the time their influence comes to be widely felt their teaching has been profoundly transformed and has assimilated many elements quite foreign to its original spirit. It is what 'history' has made of them rather than, or more than, what they actually were

* Cf. Arthur Lewis, *The Theory of Economic Growth*, p. 350.
† *The Economic Development of Japan*, pp. 571–92.
‡ *The Study of Society*, p. 35.

that counts in the long run. Nevertheless, it is foolish to deny the great importance of men of genius whether as innovators or as the vehicles of large and massive forces.

It is unfortunate that so little is known as yet of the genetic basis of genius or exceptional ability. Are they to be thought of as mutations? If so, under what conditions do they occur? Or are they due to 'accidental' combinations of genes carried in the stock? Is the proportion of exceptional ability produced by a given stock constant over long periods of time? If so, are we to account for the apparent variations in their distribution over time by differences in the opportunity offered for their development or expression? Is it possible that there are always the same qualities present in a population, but that some of them remain dormant, unknown even to their possessors, awaiting the stimulus of exceptional circumstances? In more general terms, the question may be raised whether social changes are affected by changes in inborn characteristics, for example in qualities making for leadership, innovation or conservatism, or whether social changes are, as seems likely, in the main, independent of genetic changes. Only a comparative sociology giving the life history of different types of society accompanied by a genetic analysis of mental characteristics and of the action of selection can supply an answer to these complicated questions.

An interesting variant of the problems thus raised is suggested by the various hypotheses that have been put forward of the part played by 'new men' in effecting social changes. To give but one example, Pirenne's study of a thousand years of European capitalism led him to the conclusion that we can trace with a 'truly astonishing regularity' an alternation between periods of economic freedom and economic control, and a similar alternation between periods of energetic innovation and periods of conservatism and stabilization. The explanation suggested is that each phase is introduced by 'new men' who make their way by audacity and independence. Their descendants, on the other hand, lose the impetus of the early phases, are anxious to preserve what has been won and are inclined, therefore, to give their support to any

authority, however stringent, capable of giving them the necessary security. This explanation is confirmed by an analysis of the social origins of the men who were influential in initiating the new phases, supported by an appeal to a sort of common sense psychology of the mentality of the *'parvenu'* turned respectable.*
Somewhat similar views are put forward by Pareto in the analysis he gives of political and other social cultural changes with the aid of his theory of residues and derivations. Pareto's discussion is of special interest in that it raises the problem of the relations between individual psychology and sociology in an illuminating manner. He is far from suggesting that the course of events is completely determined by what goes on in the minds of particular 'speculators'. Their policy is the resultant of a complex set of forces and an indefinite number of acts, leading collectively to results which individually they do not foresee, even though they may have a clearer conception of their own ends than the masses have of theirs. In this, as in other contexts, Pareto is anxious to replace the notion of a one-sided causality by that of mutual dependence among the factors involved.

(6) Social changes are often due to a confluence or collocation of elements derived from different sources but converging at a given point. Examples will readily suggest themselves to historians. Thus the institutions of feudalism were the product of many different lines of development, some of them coming from widely different places. Among these were the Germanic *comitatus*, the Roman *patrocinium*, combined with the system of *precaria*, the deliberate efforts of the French monarchs to remodel these institutions, the association of military service with tenure and of landholding with jurisdiction. All these played their part in different European countries shaped by local conditions and varying greatly with them.†

Another striking example is to be found in the great social

---

* *Les périodes de l'histoire sociale du capitalisme.* Bulletin de la classe des lettres et des sciences morales et politiques, 1914, no. 5.

† For a brief discussion, see T. F. T. Plucknett, *A Concise History of the Common Law.*

and industrial changes in England in the 'age of invention'. These changes have been traced back to a remarkable conjunction of circumstances. There was the stimulus derived from the Continent, whether by direct importation of machines or by the immigration of skilled artisans, itself the result of long social and religious disturbances. There was the drift of able natives and immigrants to the towns in the north, which were relatively free from the restrictions of the corporations and guilds. There were the social ferments tending to dissolve traditions opposed to change. There was the rise of experimental and applied science and the interest shown in applying these to the 'useful arts'. Finally, there were the economic factors making for an expansion in the demand for English goods and an increase in purchasing power, these in their turn being due to complex collocations of causes.* Another example from our own time is provided by the Russian Revolution. In this case, too, there was a very complicated combination of circumstances. There were first the prolongation of the war of 1914 and the inability of the Czarist regime to sustain a large-scale war. There were the land-hunger of the peasantry and the presence together of a depressed peasantry with a relatively advanced proletariat. There was the fact that in Russia capitalist industry had developed as a result of foreign pressure and under the patronage of the state, with the result that a proletariat had been created without an independent class of bourgeois entrepreneurs. There was the further fact that the Russian intelligentsia did not possess social roots in the commercial bourgeoisie and was not committed to any deep-seated bourgeois allegiance. To all this must be added the existence of a small and determined group of men, able to seize power and, above all, the 'accident' of the great personality of Lenin.

(7) The notion of collocation or concurrence raises the question of the fortuitous or accidental in social change. Cournot, who was among the first to deal with this problem, attributes fortuitous events in history to the concurrence, or intersection at a given

* Cf. W. Bowden, *Industrial Society in England towards the End of the Eighteenth Century.*

point, of several series of causes and effects which are mutually independent.* He argues that were there no facts of this kind there would be no history but only science: while on the other hand, if all facts were of this kind, there would equally be no history but only annals. The real task of history is in fact to deal with this commingling of the fortuitous with the necessary and to distinguish between them. It is interesting to note that in Cournot's view the fortuitous or accidental is most commonly to be met with in political changes but is not so frequent or important in the history of science, philosophy or religion. It is perhaps for this reason that he thought political history to be of all departments of history the most superficial and the one least likely to reveal the most deep-rooted forces at work in social change. Cournot's discussion is rich in suggestion, though the application to particular cases presents insurmountable difficulties. Much in the French Revolution was according to him 'inevitable'. Yet he speaks of it as a 'grand accident' and he claims that in the long run its effect was rather to retard normal trends of change, particularly in the economic field.† Another striking example is the case of the Norman Conquest to which I referred above.

Without the Bastard's conquest [he says], and without the feudal squabbles which followed it for four centuries, that fruitful hybrid, the English type, which gives it its real value and which, by approximating to the French type in some ways, is the secret and deeply rooted source of antagonism between the two peoples, would never have come into being. The Saxon of Great Britain would have resembled the Dutch or the Dane.‡

Who can tell what was accidental in all this? According to Pirenne, at any rate, the incidents which led immediately to the conquest were indeed fortuitous, yet the orientation of the island to the Continent 'responded so profoundly to the natural circumstances that it must have been accomplished sooner or later'.§

* *Considerations sur la marche des idées*, 1872, vol. I, p. 1 seq.

† ibid., vol. II, pp. 246 and 295.

‡ *De l'enchaînement des idées fondamentales dans les sciences et dans l'histoire*, new ed., 1911, p. 672.

§ *History of Europe*, p. 248.

We may take another example from the social effects of epidemics, which must, I suppose, be considered 'fortuitous' on Cournot's tests. The repercussions of the Black Death on the economic structure of European countries have been brought out by historians. Another of its consequences was the letting loose of a wave of superstitious terror. This expressed itself in many German towns, for example, in barbarous attacks on Jews in the belief that the plague was a malignant device for the confusion of Catholics. The savage attack led to an exodus to Poland where, under Casimir the Great, the Jews found protection. In this way a series of events originating in the Far East was an important factor in the formation of an East European Jewry, which in the centuries to come was to develop distinctive characteristics of its own and to play an important role in the history of the entire Jewish people.

(8) An important factor in social change is the emergence of a common purpose. This term is unfortunately highly ambiguous. It may stand for an end or object thought to be desirable for the community as a whole or for every member of it. It may also stand for a common process of willing, the reaching of a decision by members of a group after joint deliberation and discussion in the course of which the desires of each are modified and adjusted to meet the desires of others. It is clear that a common purpose in this latter sense is only possible in highly integrated small communities. In the larger communities 'what is will is not general and what is general is not will'. What we find is rather a number of partial general wills, varying greatly in clearness of conception, unity of aim and knowledge of conditions. The larger the community and the wider the diversity of the groups within it, the greater is the difficulty of forming a truly common will.

Nevertheless, it is true, I think, that in communities of long standing, at any rate in the democratic world, a general will does develop both in the sense that there are more objects commonly willed and that the process of willing becomes more common in the sense that increasing numbers share, more or less consciously, in its formation. The same point may be put by saying that there is a gradual extension of the sphere of public responsibility, involving an extension of public supervision. The history of education, of public health, of the relief of the poor and more lately of the regulations of the economic system will bear this out. In all these cases a common purpose has slowly emerged and the main stages in its growth have been or can be indicated by historians. On the other hand, we have as yet no detailed psychological analysis of the processes involved in changes of group mentality. Lassalle used to speak of the accursed wantlessness of the poor. But we do not know at what point submerged needs become articulate, or under what conditions the sense of injustice and the dawning of an ideal of what justice might be rouse men to action. We know little of the factors which separate ideals and practice, or of the extent to which ideals are infected by group or sectional interests. Even at advanced levels the direct effect of social theory on practice is a matter of dispute. Common or concerted purposes no doubt operate, but in reference to large communities we ought perhaps to speak of drift or tendency rather than of settled or articulate will. The community consists of many 'publics' converging at some points and diverging at others and their mental texture varies from case to case. There are thus different levels of purposiveness in collective action. It used to be said that the function of democratic government is to express the general will. It is perhaps more to the point to say that its business is to do what it can to bring a general will into being.

III

I propose now to bring together the main conclusions suggested by my survey and then to discuss their bearing on the problem of teleology.

(1) Firstly, then, it seems to me to follow from the examples I have tried to analyse that the causal relationship has much the same significance in the social sciences as in the natural sciences. It is best described perhaps as a relation of immediacy or

continuity in transition. A cause is an assemblage of factors which, in interaction with each other, undergo a change of character and are continued into the effect. In practical life and in the scientific studies arising out of practical needs we are always in search of such continuities. We assume that one difference implies another and that changes do not occur in isolation, but are linked without gaps in time or space with other changes.

(2) Secondly, despite this fundamental similarity there are obviously important differences between social and physical causation. To begin with, owing to their greater complexity social facts are more variable and less likely to be repeated in identical fashion than physical events. Because of this, and the ensuing difficulty of isolating cause-factors, causal relationships in the social sciences cannot be stated in the form of uniform sequences or connexions between specific events, but in the form of changes of pattern within a series of interlinked events. Next, the fact that social causation involves the action of mental factors, such as desires, volitions, carries with it important qualifications. For the relation between the conditions in the physical and social environment and the mental acts they stimulate differs greatly from the relations between purely physical conditions and their effects. Individuals 'respond' rather than react to their environment and they do so selectively; and though in many investigations, such as those that lend themselves to statistical treatment, individual variations may be assumed to cancel out or neutralize each other, in other cases the variations may be all important. Again, the presence of mental factors affects the 'intelligibility' of the causal relationship. In the physical world the causal relationship is not a necessary relationship in the sense of logical entailment. What events are causally connected can only be discovered by experience, and we cannot construct the effect by combining what we know of the constituent elements. Up to a point the factual nature of the causal relationship holds also of mental or psycho-physical events. It is true that in voluntary activity we have direct experience of a causal connexion. But this is not to say that we 'understand' it. As Hume pointed out, we do

not know why we can control our outward bodily movements, but not our visceral activities or our pains. We establish the connexion or absence of connexion by experience and try to define the relationship more closely by varying the conditions and eliminating the irrelevant. Similarly we know empirically that memory is strengthened by repetition, but the scientific explanation of this is still to seek. Nevertheless, it remains that in so far as behaviour becomes more rational a good deal of it becomes intelligible in the sense that the various stages in a chain of acts are logically connected.

(3) Next we may note that the methods used in the search for causal connexions in the social sciences follow well-known rules of inductive procedure also followed in other sciences. It is assumed that (a) nothing is the cause of a phenomenon in the absence of which it nevertheless occurs, or in the presence of which it nevertheless fails to occur; and (b) that nothing is the cause of a phenomenon which varies when it is constant, or varies in no proportionate manner with it. The examples cited can readily be analysed to show that these are in fact the rules implicit in social investigations, but one or two examples may be given in further illustration. Consider the way in which historians have dealt with the problem of the increase of pauperism in rural England in the early part of the nineteenth century. This has been attributed to the adoption by the Poor Law administration of the practice of using the rates to supplement insufficient wages. That this was an important causal factor was shown by citing (1) instances of areas or parishes which had decided to change over to a policy of granting relief only when a full task of work was exacted, with the result that pauperism diminished; (2) instances of significant differences in pauperization within the same parishes as between 'non-settled' labourers who could not get relief from the parish and, therefore, had to maintain themselves by their labour, and the settled labourers who could rely on relief in supplementation of their wages; (3) instances of parishes which had never adopted the practice of relieving able-bodied men out of the workhouse, in which the pauperization which occurred

elsewhere did not happen. It seems, also more generally, that in areas where the system was not adopted, e.g. in Scotland and the North of England, the agricultural labourer did not suffer the same degradation, though there too times were often very hard.* This sort of reasoning designed to show that the effect occurred when the alleged cause was present and did not occur when it was absent was supplemented by arguments designed to exclude alternative explanations; such as the rise in the price of corn, which must have affected all the areas in the same way and could not therefore account for the differences in degree of pauperization as between different parishes, or for variations within the same parishes, following upon the abandonment of the poor law practice in question.

Another example may be taken from the historical analysis of the rise of the population which occurred in England from 1760 onwards. The rise has been attributed to technical improvements in industry and agriculture in this period. The case of Ireland appears at first sight to provide a negative instance; for in this case a great increase occurred in the absence of any marked improvement either in industry or agriculture. This and other similar instances suggest that the causation is more complex and that the rise in the population is to be looked upon as one phase of a change in the entire pattern of living associated with the industrial and agricultural revolution. Significant in this change of pattern is the fall in the death rate. But this reduction of mortality was made possible by improvements in the standard of living attributable to the new mechanical inventions, to changes in agriculture such as the introduction of root crops, which, by supplying winter food for cattle, increased the supply of fresh meat, and above all by improvements in medical science and practice, which lessened the dangers of infection and in many ways strengthened resistance to disease. The chain of causation is evidently very intricate; the medical improvements

* *The Poor Law Commissioners' Report*, 1834, and e.g. Trevelyan, *History of England*, p. 612. For a full analysis of this example, see W. H. B. Joseph, *An Introduction to Logic*, ch. XX.

led directly to the increase by reducing mortality but the increased population could not have been maintained without the agricultural and industrial changes. This type of explanation is not invalidated by the case of Ireland. There, it is true, there was no marked industrial development and the improvement in health conditions was not so great as in England. The decisive factor seems to have been the absence of a potato famine in the eighteenth century. As Trevelyan points out, 'The potato is the easiest method of supporting life at a very low standard – until a year comes when the crop completely fails.'* An examination of these and similar problems will show the vital connexion between historical studies of particular events and the more general investigations undertaken by social scientists. Both history and the social sciences, in so far as they are in search of causes, rely upon a comparison of instances designed to eliminate irrelevant concomitants and to disentangle common factors. The conclusions reached rarely achieve a high degree of certainty. This is due in the main to the greater complexity of social facts, their greater variability, and the difficulty of isolating one factor at a time and of making sure that a change in one factor has not been accompanied by changes in a great many others. In varying degrees these difficulties are common to history and the social sciences, and they account in large measure for the differences in universality, certainty and precision as between them and the natural sciences.

(4) Philosophers like Rickert, Troeltsch and Dilthey have argued, as we have seen, that in history and the sciences of culture our concern is not with general laws but with the interpretation of concrete occurrences. These being complex and unique can only be grasped, they say, by a sort of sympathetic insight or imagination. The subjects of inquiry are therefore, according to them, not repeatable elements but individual wholes (*Historische Totalitäten*). It will be seen that there is a certain ambiguity in the use of the term individual whole which sometimes stands for concrete particulars or events like the Renaissance or the

* *History of England*, p. 603, footnote.

Industrial Revolution, and sometimes for type concepts, like capitalism, feudalism, revolution, proletariat, which refer to clusters of events or forms of grouping of which there are many instances. Despite the criticism to which concepts of both these kinds have been subjected historians and social scientists continue to use them. They are undoubtedly helpful as first steps in synthesis, providing they can be freed from the emotional overtones with which they tend to be charged and providing that they do not discourage further analysis. Thus, the term 'the Industrial Revolution', for example, will no doubt survive; but no historian would nowadays pretend to grasp the movement thus designated in its entirety. Before a synthesis is attempted the movement has to be broken up into a number of concurrent series of changes, e.g. the rise of new towns, the improvements in transport, the growth of the population and the changes in the age structure of the population, the increasing division of labour and specialization of occupations, the removal of legislative impediments to enterprise, the rise of experimental and applied sciences, and the greater readiness to use them in agriculture and industry, the moral and intellectual changes tending to break down opposition to change, and so forth. To understand the meaning of these changes and their interconnexions we require detailed studies and the help of economics, politics, demography and other social sciences. To establish interconnexions is a particularly tricky matter. As Bloch has pointed out in another context, we have no right to reject them with closed minds. 'We simply must not postulate such connexions in advance. Certainly the tides are related to the successive phases of the moon. In order to know this, however, it was first necessary to determine the periods of the tides and those of the moon, quite apart from one another.'* In general, then, effective synthesis must wait upon prior analysis. Nevertheless, in some cases, a stroke of imagination may suggest a synthesis which then serves to stimulate and guide analytic inquiry. In both analysis and synthesis generalizations, psychological or sociological, are implicit and until these

* *The Historian's Craft*, p. 185.

are disentangled and tested further there is no real extension of systematic knowledge*

(5) There is another aspect of social causation to which I should like to draw attention, namely its cumulative and frequently circular character. It is easy to give examples. Thus in the history of antisemitism we find that persecution and restrictive laws and practices of various kinds encouraged the tendency of the Jews towards isolation, and isolation in turn encouraged further discrimination. Similarly, White prejudice causes discrimination against Negroes and keeps down their standard of living, and the low standards in turn stimulate antipathy.† Other examples are the following: population patterns with low birth rates and low death rates are in part causes and in part consequences of higher standards of living; the inventions which furthered the Industrial Revolution were at once causes and effects of the growing division of labour and specialization of functions.‡ Again, changes in the system of education lead to changes in economic and political structure and these in turn modify the system of education. In all these cases the 'cause' does not disappear when the 'effect' is produced but continues and is modified by its effects. The circular character of social causation may be very important from a practical point of view. When the circle is 'vicious' it may be necessary or advisable to intervene at various points simultaneously, so as to break the connexions and arrest the cumulative action and reaction of causes and effects.

(6) I come now to the problem of teleology. The causes leading to social changes so far enumerated all include as factors desires and purposive acts of men stimulated and shaped in various ways by factors in the physical and social environment. It follows that in one sense social changes are teleological, since they depend on acts initiated to bring about a preconceived end; though we should have to add the qualification that the clarity with which

* See M. R. Cohen, *Reason and Nature*, bk. III, ch. I, for a valuable discussion.

† Cf. especially Myrdal, *An American Dilemma*, ch. III.

‡ Cf. Ashton, *The Industrial Revolution*, p. 15.

the ends are foreseen varies from case to case. But purposive or, more generally, conative action is only one kind of teleology. There is also in addition the functional teleology of living organisms, which certainly does not depend on conscious contrivance on the part of the minds animating them. Such functional teleology may be described as teleology below consciousness. Is there also a functional teleology above consciousness, a pattern or scheme emerging out of the linked action of innumerable separate minds but not as such designed by any of them?

To deal with this question we need some further definition of teleology. For my purpose here I should like to adopt the definition suggested by Dr Broad.* A system is teleological (a) if the arrangement of its parts is such as might have been expected *if* it had been constructed by an intelligent being to fulfil a certain purpose, and (b) if the hypothesis of design helps us in further investigation, e.g. to discover hitherto unnoticed parts or hitherto unnoticed relations, which in their turn are found to accord with the hypothesis. It seems to me that, judged by these requirements, the use of teleology is justified in the biological sciences. In physiology, for example, the assumption that organs serve certain functions has led to important investigations and discoveries, e.g. in researches concerning the functions of the thyroid, the parathyroids, the suprarenal bodies and many organs of the invertebrates.† Is the use of teleological categories equally justified in dealing with the long-range trends of social change? I am not here concerned with theological theories of the 'ways of Providence'. These would come under the category of conscious teleology, since they would refer changes to the mind of God. Whether they would satisfy Dr Broad's second requirement may be doubted. It does not seem to have been shown that the assumption of providential guidance has led to any historical researches or discoveries. If I understand Dr Butterfield aright, he does not think that the historian as such would be led to find the 'hand of God in secular history unless he has first found that he has an

* *The Mind and its Place in Nature*, p. 81.
† Cf. L. Cuenot, in *Science et Loi*, p. 131.

156

assurance of it in his personal experience.'* For similar reasons the metaphysical theories of an absolute mind, utilizing the passions of men in the realization of a purpose which is not their purpose, are not helpful. I am not aware that they have suggested fruitful historical investigations or led to the discovery of new social relations congruent with the hypothesis. Our concern here is not with the notion of a single overriding principle governing the historical process to which few, if any, would commit themselves, but with the much more limited problem of the nature of the patterns that are discernible in social and cultural history which are not attributable to conscious design. The form or structure of languages, for example, is certainly not the product of conscious design, and is there before anyone is aware of it. Again, the changes that languages undergo are not random but have 'direction'. We learn that changes at particular points often give rise to chains of supplementary changes, so as to correct the 'disturbances', and that these tendencies may spread over centuries or even millennia.† Very little, however, seems to be known about the origin of the variations or of the nature of the selective forces which make for their survival or elimination. In this case explanation in terms of conscious contrivance breaks down, and a problem arises akin to that which biologists have to face in dealing with the origins of species. I believe, however, that a functional approach has been found to be empirically useful by linguists, and, since language is certainly not a purely physical phenomenon, the appeal to what I have called supra-conscious teleology may in this case be justified.

In dealing with other spheres of social or cultural change the issue is more doubtful. Of any set of changes it is easy to say that they were designed to bring about the results which we find they actually have brought about. But it does not follow that this gives us a clue to a closer understanding of the processes involved or enables us to predict their future course. I give one example from among the many that might be offered to illustrate this point. In commenting on the emancipation of the serfs in Russia

* *Christianity and History*, p. 107.   † Cf. Sapir, *Language*, p. 195.

in 1861, Professor E. H. Carr remarks: 'The historical function of the reform, as of the enclosures in English history, was to drive from the land into the towns and factories the labour necessary for the industrialization of the national economy.'* Apart from the question whether the agricultural workers were in fact 'driven' by the enclosures, about which there are differences of opinion,† does it help us to understand the enclosures to say that this was their function?

Good examples of the use of teleology other than that of consciously purposive acts of individual minds are to be found in the work of Durkheim. To explain a social fact it is necessary, according to him, to discover its efficient cause, i.e. the social facts which precede it, and to indicate its function, or the social needs which it meets. 'Functionalists' nowadays are generally non-historical, but Durkheim uses functional teleology to account for important historical trends. Thus, for example, he tries to show that the cause of the growing division of labour which we observe historically is to be found in an increase of the density of the population and that its function is to bring about the kind of solidarity which he calls organic. He is concerned to show that, as is also the case in physiology, it is not enough to indicate the function. Functions do not bring about their own fulfilment. A satisfactory explanation must give an account of the mechanism by which the end is achieved. In other words, both the final and the efficient cause must be given.

The question will be raised how it comes about that the means are present for the fulfilment of the functions. In biological theory the answer is found in the hypothesis that structure and function are both shaped by natural selection. Durkheim's explanation of the conjunction of mechanism and function in the growth of the division of labour is somewhat similar. An increase in the density of population sharpens the struggle for existence. In such circumstances of intensified struggle the group could not survive in a given area, unless there existed sufficient

* *A History of Soviet Russia*, vol. II, p. 10.
† Cf. Ashton, *The Eighteenth Century*, p. 47.

individual differences in capacity to make economic differentiation possible. The explanation is, it seems to me, at best incomplete. Selection can only operate on what is given and is not itself a source of variation. It follows that individual differences in aptitude and interest presupposed in the division of labour still remain to be accounted for. So far the difficulty is akin to that which, as I understand, evolutionary theory has so far not succeeded in resolving. Durkheim's attitude to the problem thus raised is not clear. In a somewhat cryptic footnote* he speaks of a possible reconciliation of mechanical and teleological theories of life. He suggests that where the cause does not cease to exist with the production of the effect, as is often the case in social change, there would be a backward reaction of the effect on the cause. Thus, for example, division of labour leads to increase of production both in quantity and quality, and this increase in turn provides the energy required and the means to make possible further differentiation. The general philosophical problem of the relations between mechanism and teleology is, however, not further pursued by Durkheim either in this context or, so far as I know, elsewhere.

Durkheim's analysis of the social functions of the division of labour has attracted a good deal of attention, but it is very doubtful whether he has succeeded in making out his case. It is true, as Comte before him pointed out, that the division of labour serves to make men realize their dependence on one another. It does not follow that by itself division of labour would suffice to bring about an organic type of society in Durkheim's sense of the word. For the term organic is used by Durkheim to describe a system in which the parts not only perform special functions while at the same time complementing each other, but do so without loss of individuality. The term thus comes to have ethical implications rooted in Durkheim's respect for the values of the individual. He recognizes that these values are not necessarily served by mere differentiation of functions and that the division of labour may work so as to defeat them. If the division of labour

* *Règles de la méthode sociologique*, p. 118.

is to make possible organic societies in the ethical sense, it must conform to the ideals of equality and liberty. But since ideals are not necessarily involved in the division of labour, they cannot be said to constitute its function.

Whether or not we recognize the operation of teleology below or above consciousness there is no reason for doubting the importance of conscious purposes. Idealist philosophers and their Marxist variants are fond of emphasizing the blindness of social processes. But they vastly overstate their case. Legal systems, educational institutions and economic structures do not make themselves. It is true that decisions often lead to consequences other than those intended, and that institutions that have come into being to serve certain ends come in the course of their growth to serve others. But, generally, there is no great mystery about this, and nothing is gained by referring such transformations to 'hidden inner laws'* or to reasons 'lying deeper in the roots of things'.† Primogeniture, for example, originated to meet a particular feudal requirement. But it became part of the land law and affected the class structure of England. This no doubt was not foreseen, but the processes involved in the change have been or can be traced by historians.‡ To take another well-known example. The Crusades originated in religious motives. But they led to the development of Italian maritime commerce and the establishment of the colossal empire of Venice and Genoa in the Levant.§ Here again no illumination is shed on the process involved by reference to hidden purposes of nature. The position of Marxists is especially ambiguous in this context. Engels, for example, tells us that though 'nothing occurs without conscious intent or willed end', the results that follow from the interactions of wills are not willed and resemble the operations we find in the 'unconscious natural world'. At the same time the human will is not helpless in the face of these forces.

The forces operating in society work exactly like the forces operating in nature; blindly, violently, destructively, so long as we do not

* Engels.　　† Bosanquet.　　‡ Trevelyan, *History of England*, p. 191.
§ Pirenne, *History of Europe*, p. 196.

understand them and fail to take them into account. But when once we have recognized them and understood how they work, their direction and their effects, the gradual subjection of them to our will and the use of them for the attainment of our aims depends entirely upon ourselves.*

We may well ask whether it is seriously maintained that this self-affirmation of the human will has to wait until the dialectical laws of social change have been finally discovered. Surely the process of self-affirmation goes on all the time, with variations in clarity and vigour, in the efforts that men make to solve the problems of social organization as they arise. History, we have been told, is the 'register of the crimes, follies and misfortunes of mankind'. It is also the register of much else, heroic self-sacrifice, flashes of insight, patient contriving and persistence of effort. Neither register discloses a single pattern, both point rather to a series of groping efforts of men slowly becoming aware of their common needs and the possibilities of harmonious cooperation. The results of their efforts are embodied in social structures which, in turn, react upon the individual concerned, creating new situations and generating new wants and strains which in their turn stimulate new efforts. Social forces thus consist of the energies of men in conscious or unconscious interaction. The individual will may be often powerless, largely because it is thwarted or unaided by other wills, though on occasions, when opposing forces are equally balanced, the contribution of one or more determined men may be decisive. Slowly the interrelations enter into consciousness, making a common purpose possible. That conscious purpose plays an increasingly important part in the shaping of events seems to me beyond doubt. But it is limited by the nature of the will and the conditions in which it has to work, including the consequences of its own action. Social processes are thus neither fatally predetermined nor free from limiting conditions. But the greater the knowledge of the limiting conditions, the larger is the scope offered to conscious direction and control.

* *Anti-Dühring*, English translation, p. 307.

5

National Character*

I. THE PROBLEM AND ITS DIFFICULTIES

IN popular thought and in serious historical and political studies the existence of national characteristics and even of national character, in the sense of a coherent group of traits exhibiting some measure of permanence and continuity, is undoubtedly frequently taken for granted. An American statesman in speaking recently of the trend of the war predicted a German defeat by internal collapse, because as he said 'the Germans will not take it.' The novelist Conrad, when asked in 1914 what England would do, felt confident in asserting that if England did come into the war then, no matter who might want to make peace at the end of six months at the cost of right and justice, England would keep on fighting for years and, if necessary, alone. In both these instances it is clear that to Germany and England is attributed sufficient continuity of character to justify prediction of their probable behaviour in given circumstances. On the other hand, when we turn to the attempts that have been made to subject national characteristics to scientific analysis the results are generally so indefinite as to raise a doubt whether the characteristics in question exist at all. It is therefore of importance at the outset to bring out the difficulties which such studies of necessity encounter.

There is, to begin with, the obvious difficulty in avoiding personal bias in observation and interpretation. The greater part of the books on the subject are *livres de circonstance*, written under the influence of particular political situations and with a view to future policy. The numerous accounts of English national character written by Germans since the beginning of the nineteenth

* Inaugural address to the Social Psychology Section of the British Psychological Society delivered at Nottingham, 17 April 1941.

century may be cited in illustration.* The earlier writers saw in the slow and organic growth of England and its sturdy independence a model for Germany's struggle and reconstruction. Later and under the influence of the new racial theories stress was laid on the ruling qualities of the Germanic peoples and England is depicted as the noblest people of Germanic race. Later still, with the emergence of the theory of *Realpolitik*, there is a strong tendency to depict English character as essentially materialistic, as persistently striving for power and profit and hiding its selfish sentiments under a cloak of ethical and religious humanitarianism. This tendency was naturally encouraged during the war of 1914–18 and is clearly seen even in writers who claim, not without reason, to be capable of viewing the problem with some coolness and fairmindedness. Thus Levin Schucking seeks to show that hypocrisy is deeply rooted in English character. It is not, he thinks, to be explained as a defence mechanism against a too stringent Puritanism, because the trait is most marked in the non-Puritan sections of the English public and can be traced back to the pre-Puritan period (2).† The best-known work on England written after the war of 1914–18, while praising the sanity, virility and spiritual balance of the English, is yet at bottom dominated by the belief that the ruling quality of the English mind is the lust for power and that this constitutes a great danger to the world, unless it is checked and controlled by the resistance of something like an equal opponent ((3), p. 506). English and French writers in dealing with the psychology of peoples other than their own show, I think, greater powers of detachment, a keener awareness of the difficulties of entering sympathetically into the minds of others, and a greater readiness to make allowance for national and personal prejudices. To give one example, Fouillée's work (4) on the psychology of peoples is generously conceived and executed, inspired by the belief that the qualities of a people are as a rule more deeply hidden than its vices and absurdities, and that the

---

* An interesting discussion of these accounts will be found in Kantorowicz, Hermann, *The Spirit of British Policy*, 1931, Introduction, pp. 35-51.

† For such references see end of essay.

lesson of comparative psychology is to inculcate at once justice and sympathy. His study of the character of the Germans, in particular, is extraordinarily fair-minded, though he cannot altogether avoid being disturbed by their growing militarism and chauvinism. A survey of the works dealing with national characteristics suggests, I think, that the errors due to bias can be to a large extent corrected by a comparison of the views that writers of different nations have of other nations than their own, while occasionally the picture they paint of other nations may also serve to reveal something of the mentality of their own. In this branch of social science as in others impartiality is very much a matter of degree, and in a measure the personal equation can be allowed for by paying attention to the historical conditions likely to affect the results of the inquiry.

Another set of difficulties arise from the great complexity of national groups and the fact that they differ widely in inner unity and homogeneity. There appears to be no generally accepted definition of nation, but for the present purpose we may say that a nation is a group of people, inhabiting or associated with a given territory, who regard themselves as a unity and have the will to give expression to that unity in political independence or at least in a measure of cultural autonomy. It is obvious that this definition would cover groups differing widely from one another in inner cohesion and complexity of structure. We cannot assume that all peoples who call themselves nations have a distinctive character, still less that this character is natural or native or equally diffused in all portions of the people.* A differential or comparative psychology of nations would have to establish a serviceable classification of types of nationhood. Such a classification would have to take into account (a) the type of political unity, e.g. whether federal or centralized, (b) degree of social differentiation and type of class structure, attention being given in particular to

* Cf. Nietzsche's remark: 'That which is at present called a nation in Europe, and is really rather a *res facta* than *nata* (indeed, sometimes confusingly similar to a *res facta et picta*) is in every case something evolving, young, easily displaced' ((5), p. 208).

the emergence of the middle classes, (c) degree of cultural homo-geneity, with special reference to language and religion, (d) age or rather stage of maturity or growth.

Politically complex nations often have sub-nations within them, as is, for example, the case in Great Britain, and the question arises whether there is a national character common to them all. Again, in most European countries there are important local dif-ferences both of temperament and character. The Picardian differs from the Gascon, the Norman from the Savoyard, and we cannot be sure that behind these divergencies there is an under-lying identity of character.* The age of the nation or its degree of maturation becomes especially important in comparative studies. The traits attributed by Tacitus to the Germanic tribes have often been regarded as specifically German; but according to modern ethnologists these traits are common to many primitive peoples. There may be differences also in speed or rate of maturation, and it has been argued, for example, that the German people has matured very slowly and that it is only in recent times that its own nature has been able to express itself over against the numerous foreign influences to which it has been for long sub-jected (cf. (7), p. 39). The degree of social differentiation is especially important in dealing with the non-industrial peoples. Most of the characteristics attributed to the Poles, for example, appear to refer only to the Polish nobility, while of the bulk of the population we know little or nothing. In the more differentiated peoples it is perhaps an open question whether class characteristics are not at least as important as the national characteristics, and it is arguable that in some cases members of the upper classes have more in common with their opposite numbers in other nations than with the lower classes in their own. It is clear that a

---

* An interesting attempt is made by Halbwachs (6) to calculate the 'dis-persion' of suicides in the various regions of several European countries. He shows that in this respect there is greater uniformity in England than in other countries, the tendency to suicide being more evenly distributed in the counties of England than in the departments and provinces of France, Italy and Germany.

comparative differential psychology would have to take into account these considerations. Meanwhile, attention is most usefully confined to nations of long standing and in comparative studies to peoples of similar levels of cultural development. It must be confessed that most studies of national characteristics have so far been very general in nature and have hardly even begun to deal with the problems suggested by the above considerations.

There is still another sort of difficulty which arises out of the lack of a generally accepted theory of the structure of individual character. Fouillée's work is based on the old theory of the temperaments. Thus he regards the Spaniard as *bilieux-nerveux*, the German as *flegmatique*, the Frenchman as *sanguin-nerveux*, while he also finds important differences in sympathy, strength of will and in intelligence ((4), pp. 144, 254, 456). McDougall bases his account on assumed differences in the intensity of the basic instincts, e.g. gregariousness, assertiveness, submissiveness, and in temperamental traits like the tendency to introversion or extroversion (8, 9). Others work with the concept of types as when Madariaga regards the Englishman as the 'man of action', the Frenchman as the 'man of thought', and the Spaniard as the 'man of passion, (10). Whatever the starting-point of the inquiry, the problem is complicated further by our ignorance of the relative importance played by hereditary and environmental factors in the formation of character. Temperament is often regarded as the innate element in character and, in so far as national characteristics are held to be constant, this constancy is attributed to the persistence of temperamental traits. But there seems to be little agreement as to what is to be included under temperament, and the study of its hereditary basis appears to be still in its infancy. Again, it seems to me very doubtful whether differences in behaviour among different peoples can be safely attributed to differences in instinctive endowment. The French are held to be more sociable than the Germans, and this is explained by McDougall, for example, as based on a difference in the intensity of the gregarious instinct. But it may well be that the difference is rather in the way gregariousness or sociality expresses itself in the two nations. The French meet to talk, to exchange ideas; the Germans to drink, to make music, to go on excursions. Further, those who are not satisfied with enumerating single traits of different peoples and wish to show how these traits unite to form distinctive characters conceived as systems must find the problem of the relative importance of hereditary endowment and environmental influences still more difficult, since very little appears to be known with regard to the genetic basis of the organizing principles of character and personality. In view of all these uncertainties in the theory of individual character, it is not surprising that the psychology of peoples has found no secure foundation and that the bulk of it consists of divination rather than observation, intuitive impressions rather than scientific analysis and interpretation. Despite all these difficulties and obscurities it seems to me to be a mistake to dismiss the whole theory of national character as an 'illusion' (11). The dangers arising out of bias and the intrusion of value judgements are not peculiar to this branch of study but beset all social studies in varying degree and can be to a great extent watched and guarded against. The difficulties of comparative study can only be removed gradually as our knowledge of the different nations grows and is supplemented by more detailed study of the character of groups within the nations. The problem of the genetic elements in national character has been, as we shall see later, much obscured by the assumption that national characteristics are racially determined. This has led to much futile argument. In all probability it would be much better to defer discussion of the part played by genetic factors until a better technique of record and observation has been developed and the relations between individual and social psychology have come to be more clearly defined.

II. THE DEFINITION OF NATIONAL CHARACTER

I propose now to inquire what exactly is understood by national character. Strictly speaking, I suppose, only persons can be said to have character and, if we follow Stout in saying that 'Character exists only in so far as unity and continuity of conscious life exists and manifests itself in systematic consistency of conduct' ((12), p. 653), then nations cannot be said to possess character. Nevertheless, nations like other groups behave in distinctive ways and if their behaviour shows some unity and continuity we may perhaps speak of a group character without committing ourselves to any theory of a group mind or group personality. In practice there seem to be two senses in which the term is used. It may, first, be used to indicate differences in the distribution of certain traits or perhaps of types in different groups, as when we say that the Germans are more docile than the English or that the French are on the whole more articulate than the English, or that the Irish temperamentally dislike regimentation. This could perhaps be called common character, and it is clear that a scientific study of it would involve a statistical examination of the frequency with which traits are distributed in different groups. But, secondly, group character is also used to indicate the behaviour patterns of the group as a whole, that is the nature of its organization as embodied in its institutions, its collective achievements and its public policy. It is then assumed that the institutions in the long run depend upon the character of the component individuals as shaped by their interactions. Clearly there is a very subtle and complex relation between institutions and the character of the individuals sustaining them, since on the one hand men make their institutions but, on the other, the institutions make the men. Hence it seems misleading to say, for example, with Madariaga that it is not English education which explains the Englishman, but the Englishman English education, or that the Reformation and the Roman Catholic Church are not to be considered as causes but as effects of national character. The relation is one of reciprocal interaction rather than of causality. The situation is complicated by the fact that institutions may not reflect the character of all the members but perhaps only of powerful sections, and that, once formed, they tend by unconscious processes to select the type that suits them. In this way many qualities in a population may remain dormant or repressed until a change of circumstances brings them into play, while again the reaction against a type that has become unduly dominant may sometimes be an important cause of change. It is thus possible for great and revolutionary changes to take place in the institutions of a nation without a parallel change in the underlying qualities of the mass of the nation. It follows that at any one moment of time we cannot safely infer the character of a people from its institutions or public policy, and that for this purpose it is necessary to know the history of the institutions and the portions of the people that have been dominant in shaping them. A great deal of what foreign writers have to say about English character is based on their impression of public school mentality. But the public school tradition dates only from the middle of the nineteenth century and few of the 'Prep.' schools which are an integral part of the system date further back than 1870. In dealing with the psychological basis of religion in England the class structure of the country becomes of great importance, since it is generally agreed that, on the whole, Anglicanism has been the religion of the gentry and of the villages, while Nonconformity is more characteristic of the middle classes and the towns. The range of variation in character has to be taken into account. Most continental observers find English character homogeneous throughout the different classes and they attribute this to the lesser rigidity of the class structure of England as compared with, say, that of Germany. But this is hardly more than a subjective impression and more accurate methods of observation and record would no doubt reveal both local and class differences. The transition from the institutions of a people to its underlying character thus raises many difficult problems.

Similar difficulties arise when the literature, the science and philosophy of a people are taken as a basis for the psychology of people. Fouillée thought ((4), p. 547) that a nation expresses itself above all in its elite, its representative men: 'If you leave out of consideration the elite of France there is no more France; France is reduced to the level of those peoples who have no history.'

'There is no national poet of any great nation', it has been said, 'who is so completely representative of his own people as Shakespeare is representative of the English', and it has even been argued that his acceptance by the world is due not so much to the greatness of his genius as to its English quality ((13), ch. VI). On the other hand, of Dürer and Bach a German writer has said that they are representative rather of Protestantism than of Germany.[14] It is difficult to see how at the present stage of our knowledge such problems can be resolved. In any case, the study of national traits as revealed in its 'representative' men must be supplemented by a study of the mentality of the people at large, especially as revealed in proverbs, folk lore and especially in wit and humour.* There is here clearly an enormous field of study.

The bulk of the more popular works on the psychology of peoples is concerned with national character in the first of the two senses distinguished above, namely the wide prevalence of certain traits in the group. They abound in rough generalizations and often exaggerate both the permanence of the characteristics and their wide diffusion. The English have been described since Froissart as 'taking their pleasures sadly' and their gravity has been contrasted with the gaiety of the French. But already Emerson noted that their 'brows were no sadder than their neighbours of northern climates', and as compared with Americans he thought them cheerful and contented. The experience of the war of 1914–18 belied the traditional opinions about the psychology of peoples. Clémenceau remarks: 'The Englishman was noted for his calm, but English soldiers tended to be more hysterical than others, the Americans were supposed to be so quick and they were so slow. The French were supposed to be gay and they were solemn' (quoted in (11), p. 39). The Chinese are reputed to be impassive and reserved in the expression of their emotions, and even a careful anthropologist like the late Professor Seligman felt justified in describing them as introvert. He found, however, on closer inquiry that what he took to be an inborn trait of the

* Cf. Baldwin's remark: 'Understand English humour, and you have gone a long way to understanding the Englishman' ((15), p. 22).

Chinese was rather a mode of behaviour set up as a standard for the governing and literary classes and never adopted by more than a small proportion of the population ((16), p. 86). So again the tradition of the Austrian as charming, easygoing and kindly was shaken by the brutalities committed after the triumph of the Nazis. Examples could easily be multiplied of similarly crude generalizations and especially of the danger of predicting the future behaviour of peoples on the basis of what is supposed to be their permanent and even innate character. Yet even when allowance is made for local and class differences and for the effects of changing circumstances there is often some truth in the generalizations reached by careful observers, and it would, I think, be a mistake to deny the existence of national traits in the case of nations of long standing merely on the ground that so far they have not lent themselves to exact analysis or quantitative measurement. Better results may be expected when more is known of the genetics of character and when a more reliable technique has been elaborated for observing and recording group differences in behaviour.

The indirect method of studying national characteristics by an analysis of the psychological basis of the collective achievements of peoples has undoubtedly proved more fruitful than the direct method based on the observation of individual behaviour. As an example I want to consider briefly some of the views that have been put forward regarding the character of the English and the Germans. With regard to two qualities of the English mentality there is universal consensus among observers both English and foreign, namely, its empiricism and individualism. Apart from the contributions made by English thinkers to empiricism regarded as a philosophical theory, the empirical habit of mind is seen in all spheres of English life. English law and English politics are based on the empirical method of dealing with particular problems as and when they arise. There is a disinclination to formulate general principles and piecemeal enactments are preferred. Even when, as has frequently been the case, legislation is undertaken after special inquiry, the inquiry is deliberately limited in scope and little attention is given to the requirements of general theory or systematic connexion.*

English international policy is especially characterized by its tentative, piecemeal method. It avoids legal rigidity and has no faith in general solutions or long-range planning. An acute French observer has seen in this trait one of the standing difficulties of Franco-British collaboration. In contrast with the habit of the English diplomatists to confine themselves to the immediate and particular, the French mind reaches out for the general and has a longing for clear-cut and logically consistent solutions. That there is a certain consistency in British foreign policy over long periods of time is due in the main to the geographical and economic situation of Britain and certainly not to the existence of deep-laid plans pursued year in and year out with Machiavellian cunning. If the British Empire was not exactly built up in a fit of absence of mind neither was it the result of a deliberate policy carefully planned beforehand and applied methodically by successive governments. The early French colonial acquisitions were also fortuitous and occasional and not the results of conscious planning. But this cannot be said of the colonial policy of the Republic which appears to have been due to a political plan carefully studied and applied with persistence in the face of great difficulties (cf. (18) and (19), p. 25). German colonial policy was, of course, still more consciously and deliberately planned, with frank recognition of its economic nature and with the open support of financial and commercial interests. In internal policy the same characteristics of the English mind can easily be traced. The principles of democracy have never been clearly formulated and deliberately applied. The issues fought over have been particular changes in which only the historian can discern a steady tendency. The history of the Church of England also shows a quality essentially connected with empiricism, namely a dislike of pushing principles to their logical conclusions in face of the complexities of life. The dislike of the English for rigid principles and their distrust of abstractions is sometimes attributed by con-

* For numerous illustrations compare especially Boutmy (17), ch. IV.

tinental writers to a lack or weakness in the power of generalized thought. This seems absurd in view of the contribution of the English to science and philosophy. But it is true that in dealing with the practical problems of life the English mind prefers to proceed tentatively, by trial and error, and in this it appears to me to show a better and sounder sense of method than those who put their trust in dialectics.*

The second quality of the English mind, its individualism, can also be readily traced in the various spheres of the national life. It can be seen in the spirit of the English law which is a law of the liberty of the individual subject, in the strength of local government and resistance to centralization, in the stress laid by Puritanism on the autonomy of the individual and in a very widespread and deeply rooted impatience of compulsion and restraint. Continental writers, while stressing the individualistic tendencies of English institutions, have nevertheless also urged that this individualism has its limitations. Both Madariaga and Dibelius think that the tendency of English education and especially of the public schools and the universities has been to standardize behaviour and to repress the types that threaten to diverge from the norm. A recent writer, very friendly to England, has said that as compared with pre-Hitler Germany 'the English type in all classes lacks a certain touch of individualization' (21). I suspect, however, that these writers are impressed rather too much by a certain conventionality in the behaviour of some of the educated classes in England, which on closer analysis proves to be perfectly compatible with a plentiful variety and even eccentricity of character.

The individualism of the English is closely associated with a capacity for spontaneous organization, and indeed a great deal that is distinctive in English society rests on the power of

---

* Cf. the remarks of T. S. Eliot ((20), p. 352): 'The admission of inconsistencies, sometimes ridiculed as indifference to logic and coherence, of which the English mind is often accused, may be largely the admission of inconsistencies inherent in life itself and of the impossibility of overcoming them by the imposition of a uniformity greater than life will bear.' Cf. also the rather flattering account given by Madariaga ((10), p. 63).

combining an intense individualism with practical understanding of the needs of others. That these qualities are not peculiar to any particular social class in England can be seen from the enormous number of voluntary societies in England and, in particular, from the history of the trade unions, the cooperative movement and the Friendly Societies. I think Madariaga has laid his finger on a very important point when he stresses as a remarkable and typically English phenomenon what he calls 'collaboration in opposition' ((10), p. 22) and which he shows to be as important in the field of politics as in sport. With these qualities are associated also the capacity for collective deliberation, the toleration of divergent views and the considerateness shown to opponents, which are characteristic of so much of the social life of England. Social discipline is proved not to be incompatible with a respect for individual peculiarities and with freedom to criticize accepted and sanctioned views. The prestige of the law, for example, is not shaken in the least by the perpetual stream of satirical criticism directed against it. A French observer has said: 'There is no country where the judges, i.e. the persons whose duty it is to administer the law, criticize it with more irony, or ridicule it with more humour, and that from the Bench, in the presence of the litigants' ((17), p. 177). Equally illuminating is a comparison of the habits of debate or public discussion in England and other countries. I doubt whether any country excels England in the fundamental decency of public discussion, the urbanity and moderation which is shown to opponents and the care which is taken to keep out 'personalities' or imputations of bad motives to those from whom one happens to differ.* It remains to be added that

* Of German debates Müller-Freienfels writes: 'In hardly any other country of the world do political opponents so regard each other as moral scoundrels as in Germany, hardly anywhere else is political opposition so saturated with hatred as among ourselves. ... Just as two German scholars who differ in their opinion regarding the value of the Niebelungen manuscripts invariably despise one another morally, so it is in the field of politics' ((7), p. 144). 'In France', says Madariaga ((10), p. 158), ' a debate is a battle and arguments are loaded. Every pair of eyes look like the two barrels of a double-barrelled machine-gun turning at high speed, throwing

these qualities which I have stressed as exhibited in the public life of England are not independent but closely interwoven. The empirical habit of mind harmonizes well with the attitude of tolerance and respect for other persons which is implicit in individualism. It is in the fusion of these qualities with the tendency to spontaneous association which gives distinctive character to English institutions.

Strangely enough, individualism is a quality which authorities both German and non-German have taken to be deeply rooted in the German character. A distinguished student of comparative religion, Otto Pfleiderer, finds in the history of German Protestantism ample proof of an extreme individualism, of a tendency of the personality to isolate itself at once from the outer world and the community and to seek in its own being the connexion with the divine (22). The older descriptions of social life in Germany give a picture of people highly individual in their taste, unconventional, deliberately odd in their behaviour, blunt and rather brusque in their personal relations, stiff and reserved. In their political life this individualism is seen in a strong tendency to particularism and discord and an incapacity for wider unions except when they come under the influence of dominant leaders. Every German, said Bismarck, would rather have his own king. Their parliamentary history proves, as a recent commentator has pointed out, that every German would also like to have his own party. Their lack of political capacity seems to be the trait that has struck most observers. The individualism of the Germans thus differs from that of the English in not being accompanied or balanced by the capacity for spontaneous organization but requiring evidently organization based rather on some form of subordination.

Another quality generally ascribed to the Germans is strength of will. This is seen in economic life in their industry and in scientific work in the persistent *'laboriositas'* already noted by

---

ideas at the enemy with the utmost alacrity. Arguments, innuendoes, accusations, insults are hurled through the air like projectiles.'

Leibniz. There seem, however, to be certain characteristics of their thought and feeling which colour alike their will and their individualism. On the cognitive side the German mind seems often lacking in concreteness. Though the German works with abstractions, these do not seem to be reached by analysis of sense experience but rather by a sweep of imagination or fantasy. A German writer has characterized this tendency in the words: *'Die Eigenheit der deutschen Abstraktheit ist Begriffsphantastik'* ((7), p. 88). Their intellect is not inspired by a search for order and clarity. Their interest in system again is often not rooted in the need for order, not the product of a drive to classify and understand, but rather of an imaginative longing for grandiose architectural schemes. Hence an *esprit large et trouble* which with a certain profundity and comprehensiveness often combines a tendency to vagueness and obscurity. On the side of feeling the German writers speak of a depth and inner warmth (*Innigkeit, Wärme, Tiefe*), but they also point to a vagueness and indefiniteness which the non-German describes as sentimentality. This combination of cognitive and affective vagueness shapes the nature of the will which, though thorough and realistic in many ways, is also liable to be moved by vague and highly abstract ends. What the German calls his idealism, says Müller-Freienfels, is a devotion to fanciful abstractions. It is rooted in feeling and fantasy and tends to evade and even resist rational control or definition. No doubt this can be said also of other peoples, but it does seem to be true that Germans are more apt to be moved by large but vague ends, that their will, like their thought, is lacking in the sense of proportion or measure which is found in the English and the French.*

This account of the German as highly individualist and as led by vague and fanciful ideas, an account which has the authority

* Cf. Nietzsche's remark: 'As everything loves its symbol, so the German loves the clouds and all that is obscure, evolving, crepuscular, damp and shrouded; it seems to him that everything uncertain, undeveloped and growing is "deep" ' ((5), p. 198). Contrast Chateaubriand (23): *'Le ténébreux, l'embroussaillé, le vapoureux, le pénible me sont abominables.'*

not only of German writers but also of foreign observers, has of course to be brought into relation with another side of German life, with which at first it seems to stand in glaring contradiction. What of what is called German militarism, German docility, German thoroughness and attention to detail and method? Müller-Freienfels solves this problem by resorting to the mechanism of compensation and over-compensation. Afraid of the anarchy which his deep-rooted individualism would produce, the German is ready to accept the leadership of a strong personality; fearful of the conflicts which his powerful but indefinite strivings must generate, he has recourse to minute regulation and prescription of every detail of group life; aware of the dangers of his speculative fancy, he insists on exact method and painstaking investigation; to keep his feelings in check he cultivates hardness and reserve. These are all compensations, it is claimed, developed by the Germans in the course of a century-long struggle with their own nature, especially under the discipline inculcated under Prussian influence. The process of compensation on this view of the matter is largely unconscious and is by the Germans themselves regarded not as based on reasoned calculation of consequences but as irrational or suprarational. Hence what other people call militarism is not thought of as such by the Germans and what strikes others as slavish submissiveness is by them thought to be willing acceptance of constraint.

Müller-Freienfels appears to think that the traits of docility, thoroughness and discipline are secondary and not primary features of German character. It has, however, to be remembered that the notion of compensation is easy to invoke but hard to verify, and in any case, if the compensation is genuine it is likely to be deeply rooted in unconscious need, and consequently to be an integral element of character. Other writers give a different and perhaps more plausible account of the duality of the German character. Lacking in the power of spontaneous organization, which in the case of the English provides a balance to the forces of individualism, the Germans have only been able to achieve such unity as they have by authoritarian discipline. Realizing this need for regimentation they have consciously and unconsciously divided their lives into separate zones, a private zone of freedom and independence and a public zone of deliberate acceptance of constraint. Writing in 1893 Professor Richard M. Meyer tells us: 'The German frequently sadly disregarded political liberty, because he knew his liberty of thought to be safe from attack' ((14), p. 241). Dr A. Loewe tells us in a recent work that 'up to the present the German Philistine, even when most impressed by political authority, has always managed to maintain his personality in his own eyes. By a private interpretation of the universe he tried to give to the most banal life the consecration of supratemporal freedom' ((21), p. 25). Now that the Totalitarian regime has invaded even the personal zone of life it remains to be seen whether the individualist tendencies will have sufficient strength to assert themselves. It is clear that, for whatever reasons, the need for authority is deeply rooted in German life and that the relationship of inferior and superior pervades all spheres of activity. A prolonged period of education in other forms of organization will therefore be necessary before Germans are led to abandon the forms of order resting on authority and hierarchical subordination.* The view is often advanced that towards the end of the last century and the beginning of this century the Germans underwent a radical change of character which turned them from a nation of thinkers and dreamers into a nation of cool and hard realists. It seems more probable that with certain changes of aims the fundamental characteristics have remained unaltered. Especially noteworthy is the persistence of vague and cloudy aspirations and the admiration for the demonic, the heroic and the like. German *Realpolitik* and *Machtpolitik* are in many ways realistic and pursue perfectly definite and concrete aims, but equally the appeal which they make is essentially romantic. The same combination of definite aims with appeal to myth and fantasy is to be observed in much of the propaganda of the Nazis.

* This at any rate was the view of many German writers before the advent of Nazism. Cf. Müller-Freienfels ((7), p. 159).

III. THE FORMATION OF NATIONAL CHARACTER

Having given some examples of the character of nations as reflected in their collective life, I propose now to say something on the factors which contribute to its formation. This question has undoubtedly been greatly obscured by being entangled with the problem of race differences. I have discussed the relation between nation and race elsewhere (24, 25, 26), and here I desire to draw attention to some of the important points.

(a) The mental characteristics of the racial elements which have entered into the composition of the European elements are entirely unknown, and to explain national traits by reference to them is to explain the obscure by the more obscure. It is to be noticed that in recent anthropological work it has been found necessary to break up the three principal units, Nordic, Alpine and Mediterranean, into numerous subdivisions. Thus, for example, von Eickstedt has three subdivisions of the Nordic (27), Coon four types (28). The Alpine and Mediterranean groups are not in any sense unitary entities. The psychological descriptions that are given of these racial groups still lump them together, but it seems extremely unlikely that what is said of the mentality of any of these large aggregates can really apply to all its constituent groups.

(b) The theory that the existing distribution of racial traits is to be explained in terms of hypothetical pure races supposed to have intermingled in various proportions is coming to be abandoned by modern anthropologists.* If such pure races ever existed we certainly know nothing of their mental characters. The descriptions we have of the habits of Gauls and Teutons cannot be taken as descriptions of Alpines and Nordics, since by all accounts they were racially composite and the part played by race in the determination of *their* mental characters is just as complicated and insoluble as the part played by race in the formation of the character of the French and the Germans.

* Cf. especially Morant (29).

(c) There is a difficulty of a more general kind. It is the habit of those who explain national character in terms of race to refer highly complex institutions to specific innate tendencies. Mc-Dougall ((8), p. 223), for example, explains the prevalence of a centralized system of government in France mainly by the supposed intensity of the gregarious instinct in the Mediterranean and Alpine races. But from gregariousness to centralized government is surely a far cry. The evidence of all those who know the French character intimately is to suggest that the attitude of the French to the state is not that which would be expected from a spontaneous play of the social tendencies. Madariaga describes the state in France as something mechanical rather than organic. M. Paul Gaultier stresses the fundamental individualism of the French, their lack of discipline and social cohesion, and he even speaks of an instinctive opposition to the state ((30), p. 156). It is clear that if social institutions are to be referred to underlying psychological causes, use will have to be made of much more complex constellations than the instincts, and it seems highly probable that from very similar instinctive equipment very different forms of social grouping may arise.

(d) Any theory of national character must of course be able to account not only for the relatively permanent traits, but also for the changes that undoubtedly occur. On the racial hypothesis such changes are to be explained as due to various forms of racial changes brought about by emigration, immigration, conquest and social selection inside communities. An examination of the problems thus raised would require a lengthy treatise, but it may be worth while to give some brief illustration of the fundamental issues. As an example of explanation in terms of racial change due to war and immigration I may quote McDougall's assertion that the decline of the Greeks from the heights reached by them in the time of Pericles reflected a change in their mental qualities due to racial substitution brought about by wars, the slave trade and later by successive invasions of Slavs from the north. He goes so far as to commit himself to the statement that the modern Greek people is 'descended largely from Slav invaders and largely from the numerous and prolific slave population of the great age of Greece, but hardly at all from the men who made the greatness of that age' ((8), p. 249). Such explanations seem to suffer from two main defects, namely, the lack of adequate anthropological evidence and a failure to attend to negative instances. In the case of the Greeks it is to be remarked that McDougall's categorical assertions are not borne out by recent anthropological studies. Statements about the physical character of 'the Greeks' in general are of little value. If comparison is to be made with the Greeks of antiquity, care must be obviously taken that the reference is to the inhabitants of the same localities. It appears from recent investigations that when this is done the continuity of living Greeks with their ancestors of the ancient world is more striking than the opposite. Professor Coon ((28), p. 604) tells us that 'If one refers to the inhabitants of Attica during the sixth century, or to the Spartans of Leonidas, then the changes in these localities have probably not been nearly as great as that between the Germans of Tacitus and the living South Germans.' The explanation of cultural changes in terms of racial substitution thus rests in this case at any rate on slender foundations. Even more serious is the failure of such explanations to take into account negative instances, i.e. instances of significant cultural changes not accompanied by known racial changes. A case in point is that of the Romans. The periods of vigour from the fourth to the last century B.C., and the later brilliance of the Italians during the period from the eleventh to the sixteenth centuries A.D., have frequently been ascribed to the infusion of fresh blood. This explanation, however, fails completely to account for the later decline in the sixteenth century and the revival in the nineteenth century.* In the case of the Risorgimento the explanation is to be found in political factors connected with the re-establishment of contacts with Western civilization resulting from the temporary incorporation into the Napoleonic empire. But, if so, may not the earlier successes also have been largely shaped by social and political factors?

* Cf. the detailed examination of the facts by Prof. Toynbee ((31), pp. 16 seq.).

The problem of the effects of race mixture presents great difficulties. It has been claimed on biological grounds that the blending of allied races results in an increase of constitutional vigour and in a greater variety and variability of innate qualities. This may well be true, but the importance of these changes for cultural change is not forthwith to be assumed. We have to distinguish between the effects of race mixture on the genetic constitution of the resulting blend of peoples, and the effects of cultural stimulus and variability. The forces at work cannot be clearly isolated, yet the numerous cases of important cultural changes due to culture contact unaccompanied by race mixture on a big scale should make us hesitate to stress the purely genetic changes. No one, for example, would question the enormous influence exerted upon the political structure of England by the Norman Conquest, yet the invasion did not in any way modify the physical type of the English ((32), p. 82). Similarly, while the cultural effect of the Roman conquest on France was of decisive importance, the racial effect was negligible ((33), p. 157). An examination of the results of the contacts between European and non-European peoples is even more illuminating, since it at once becomes clear that the cultural effects are out of all proportion to the degree of racial admixture. It seems therefore highly probable that even in those cases where culture contact is accompanied by racial amalgamation the purely genetic effects of the mixture are not so important for the formation of national characteristics as the sociological effects of the stimulus due to contact with fresh elements of culture.

There remains the problem of the effects of social selection. By this is meant the influence exerted upon the genetic constitution of a people by the action of social forces. Thus for example long-continued differences in fertility between social groups may, if the groups differ in genetic qualities, result in a change in the character of the people as a whole due to the increasing recruitment of its population from the more fertile groups. Elaborate investigations have been conducted on these lines by the Anthroposociologists (Ammon (34), de Lapouge (35) and others). They claim to have shown among other things that Europe has undergone a process of 'denordicization' (*Entnordung*). This is supposed to have occurred through military selection (the Nordics being fighters and therefore tending to be killed off); through religious persecution (e.g. the emigration of Protestants); through urban selection (the Nordics being restless and enterprising and therefore attracted to the towns where they fail to reproduce themselves). I do not propose to discuss this particular view here. The evidence is considered by many competent authorities as insufficient to justify the formulation of general laws. It seems that there really has occurred an increase in brachycephaly, but the causes of this increase are disputed and some regard it as at least in part an environmental effect analogous to and accompanying the parallel increase in stature ((33), p. 278 and (28), pp. 10-11). In any case so far no one has succeeded in establishing any definite relation between broad-headedness and any mental quality, and the psychological effects of the increase in broad-headedness remains a matter of speculation. Another case frequently cited in this connexion is that of Spain, whose decline is attributed to negative selection resulting on the one hand from religious persecution, which killed off or drove out of the country individuals of independent mind and will, and, on the other, from the excessive multiplication of monastic orders which made celibates of large numbers of people presumably of superior ability. This argument suggested by Galton ((36), p. 344) was elaborated more fully by Fouillée ((4), pp. 158 seq.). The biological effects of clerical celibacy must be a matter of doubt, since many of the priests were only celibates in name and since there is no proof that the majority of the priests differed from the rest of the population in innate independence or ability. Fouillée himself doubts whether the biological effects of celibacy, even if combined with the graver influence of the persecutions and expulsions, could have been such as to produce a really vital change in the quality of the population. He lays greater stress on the wars of Charles V and particularly the American conquests which drained Spain of men endowed with energy and the spirit of enterprise, and he explains that to these biological factors must be added economic and moral causes which he discusses at length. Apart from these rather speculative arguments there is a certain amount of direct evidence of the selective action of immigration. It has been shown for example that the Poles who came to the United States during the nineteenth century and the beginning of the twentieth century differed in height, pigmentation and head-form from their own relatives who remained at home ((28), p. 8), and that they did not represent a cross-section of the entire Polish population. It does not follow, of course, that this selective immigration seriously altered the innate constitution of the Poles who remained in Poland.

It has also been alleged that the wholesale emigration from Ireland and Sweden to America has permanently affected the genetic constitution of these countries, but, so far as I know, there is no direct evidence of this change. The effects of urban selection have been studied in many countries since the question was raised by the Anthropo-sociologists, without however any stress on the racial aspect of the process.* Though none of these investigations are conclusive, it is highly probable that over long periods of time social forces may act selectively on the genetic constitution of a people, and conversely the genetic constitution may in turn influence the forms of social life. Yet even a little reflection is sufficient to show that the processes involved in social change differ radically from those involved in racial change and that vast changes can be brought about in society without parallel change in the inherited constitution.† To begin with what is acquired by one generation can be transmitted to the next without resort to the genetic mechanism of inheritance. This makes possible cumulative change on a vast scale. Further, there is not the same need for continuity as in genetic transmission, since even ideas which have been forgotten may again be revived after a long interval of time and exercise renewed influence. Furthermore, cooperative division of labour renders it possible for societies to achieve results amounting to specific changes without any change whatever in

* Cf. Coon (28), p. 8, for references.
† This was clearly pointed out by Huxley (37).

the genetic constitution of the component members. For these and many other reasons racial change and social change appear to differ radically in their nature, and it is not to be expected that they should follow parallel courses.

These considerations have an important bearing on the problem of social selection. A sort of selection is operative in society which has nothing to do with the substitution of one genetic type for another. This may be shown by a few examples. It has been argued by Pirenne (38) that each of the phases in the growth of capitalism in Western Europe was initiated by 'new men' who made their way by exceptional audacity and vigour. Is there any reason to believe that these men were 'mutations' suddenly called into being by the circumstances of the time? It is surely far more likely that these qualities were always present in the population and that sections of it which hitherto were denied opportunity were able to seize it by a change in the social conditions affecting commerce. Similarly present-day Germany is ruled by a group of people of distinctive mentality, but they are hardly like to be a fresh biological product. In different circumstances quite a different group may attain predominance and thus present to the world quite a different aspect of the German character. In short, the selection exercised by social forces need not operate by way of biological elimination or substitution. It operates rather by encouraging or inhibiting the expression of certain qualities and by determining their direction or mode of manifestation. A totalitarian regime may drive individuals of a certain endowment out of the country, and this may have some effect on the biological constitution of the stock. But in the main the hereditary qualities of peoples may well remain constant while changing circumstances bring different sides of the underlying character into play or give dominance to different elements of the population at different times. The process of adaptation is thus social rather than racial and, if the term 'selection' is to be used at all in this context, it must be given a meaning very different from that which it has in biology.

In summing up these arguments we must, I think, distinguish

between genetic qualities in general and those which are claimed to be racial traits. Since at present very little is known of the mental characteristics of races, we can obviously make very little use of them in accounting for national characteristics. But this is not to say that genetic qualities do not count. Unless we are prepared to deny the inheritance of mental characteristics we must regard it as highly probable that just as there are individual differences there are also group differences and that these play their part in shaping the collective life of groups. The difficulty is to determine exactly what their role is. The inherited constitution must in some sense put a limit to what can be achieved by social organization. If the latter puts too high a demand on the character of individuals it will not work, and, if a movement is forced by enthusiasts on a reluctant mass, it may come up against ineluctable predispositions which will in the end defeat it. Yet here again it must be remembered that the range of human potentialities is extraordinarily wide and that upon the same hereditary elements very different social structures may be built. There seems no warrant for assuming any such differences between national groups as would amount to an inherited incapacity of anyone for the arts and institutions achieved by another. We cannot infer from the incapacity hitherto displayed by any people to run democratic institutions that they must for ever remain so incapable. If, then, there is an inherited element in the character of nations of long standing they nevertheless retain considerable powers of adaptation and the limits of these powers cannot be determined with any accuracy from their previous history.

In view of the above considerations it would seem that the differences in the character of the European peoples are not in the main to be traced to variations in innate tendencies, but rather to variations in the ways in which these are expressed, balanced and directed. Even in referring to highly complex qualities of character like 'individualism', 'empiricism', 'collaboration in opposition', we cannot say that these qualities are either present or absent in a given people. There is, for example, a French individualism, an English individualism, and a German individualism. So again different peoples may successfully work the same institutions – but with a difference. To account for these differences we have to look to historical and social conditions and only in the last resort should we appeal to genetic variations. If for example we seek to ascertain the conditions which have given a definite tinge to the behaviour of British diplomacy, we have no need to appeal to unverifiable genetic factors. Far more illuminating is the attempt made by such writers as Bardoux (39) and Kantorowicz (1) to analyse the historical conditions in which that behaviour has taken shape, e.g. the geographical conditions which have given to British diplomacy a certain constancy of aim, the peculiarities of the English class structure which has put the conduct of foreign affairs in the hands of a class with special codes of behaviour, the feeling of security and confidence generated by the absence of the fear of war and fear of revolution which has formed the background of continental diplomacy. So again the peculiarities of the political individualism of the English are not traced with any probability to the supposed inborn qualities of the Saxon peasant. They are surely connected rather with the special conditions which prevented the growth of a centralized administration and encouraged the growth of local government, and of a legal system serving to protect the liberties of the individual.* In a certain sense no doubt the institutions of a people express in the long run the character of the people, but equally the character is formed by the institutions. The congruence of the different aspects of a nation's life in particular depends on the unity and continuity of its historical development. It has been remarked, for example, that in this respect there is a profound difference between England and Germany. In England there is a

* In a recent work (40), Profs. Buckland and McNair show the remarkable similarities that exist between the practical rules of the Roman Law and the Common Law, despite the difference in the fundamental conceptions on which the two systems rest. They attribute the similarity to a certain resemblance in the habits, the morale, the *Anschauungen* of the two nations and the difference in the conceptions to a difference in racial origin. It is difficult to see how such an hypothesis could ever be put to the test.

certain homogeneity of texture in the various manifestations of the national life, while in Germany religion, government and philosophy seem rather to diverge in their development. The explanation is surely that in England the early attainment of political unity facilitated the interaction of the various elements of the national life, while in Germany the conditions favoured the perpetuation not only of marked local variations but of more rigid distinctions between professions and social classes.*

I will now try to sum up briefly the general conclusions which emerge from the above survey. First, the study of national character is to be approached not through an investigation of individual differences in behaviour, but of the qualities manifested in the collective life of nations, their traditions and public policy. Secondly, the object of this study is to discover whether these manifestations of the collective life reveal the existence of relatively permanent and stable traits and dispositions and how far these form congruent systems. Thirdly, such studies as have so far been made indicate that although ultimately national character must be linked with the genetic qualities of the stock, these are highly plastic and susceptible of wide variation in their actual expression. Hence the national character is not something given once and for all, but something always in the making, moulding and being moulded by the circumstances in which nations find themselves.

* Cf. E. Barker (41), p. 235, and Dibelius (3), p. 154.

REFERENCES

1. Kantorowicz, Hermann, *The Spirit of British Policy*, 1931
2. Schucking, Levin L., *Der englische Volkscharakter*, 1915
3. Dibelius, W., *England*, 1923, English trans. 1930
4. Fouillée, Alfred, *Esquisse psychologique des peuples européens*, 1903
5. Nietzsche, *Beyond Good and Evil*, English trans. Helen Zimmern, 1907
6. Halbwachs, M., *Les causes du suicide*, 1930
7. Müller-Freienfels, R., *Psychologie des deutschen Menschen*, 2nd ed., 1930
8. McDougall, W., *The Group Mind*, 1920

9. McDougall, W., *National Welfare and National Decay*, 1921
10. Madariaga, S. de, *Englishmen, Frenchmen, Spaniards*, 1928
11. Fyfe, Hamilton, *The Illusion of National Character*, 1940
12. Stout, G. F., *Manual of Psychology*, 4th ed., 1929
13. Dixon, W. MacNeile, *The Englishman*, 1938
14. Meyer, Richard M., 'German character as reflected in national life and literature', *Int. J. Ethics*, III, 1892-3
15. Baldwin, S., *The Englishman*, 1940
16. Seligman, C. G., 'Psychology and racial differences', in *Psychology and Modern Problems*, ed. J. A. Hadfield, 1935
17. Boutmy, E., *The English People*, 1904
18. Fallot, E., *L'avenir colonial de la France*, 1901
19. Woolf, L., *Empire and Commerce in Africa*, 1920
20. Eliot, T. S., *Selected Essays*, 1932
21. Loewe, A., *The Price of Liberty*, 1937
22. Pfleiderer, Otto, 'The national traits of Germans as seen in their religion', *Int. J. Ethics*, III, 19, 1892-3
23. Chateaubriand, *Mémoires d'outre-tombe*, 1860
24. Ginsberg, M., *Sociology*, ch. III, 1934
25. Ginsberg, M., 'National character and national sentiments', in *Psychology and Modern Problems*, ed. J. A. Hadfield, 1935
26. Ginsberg, M., *Psychology of Society*, ch. VI, 1921
27. Eickstedt, E. von, *Rassenkunde und Rassengeschichte der Menschheit*, 1934.
28. Coon, C. S., *The Races of Europe*, 1939
29. Morant, *Journal of the Royal Anthropological Institute*, LXIX, 160, 1939
30. Gaultier, Paul, *L'âme française*, 1936
31. Toynbee, A. J., *A Study of History*, IV, 1939
32. Haddon, A. C., *The Races of Man*, 1924
33. Pittard, E., *Les races et l'histoire*, 1924
34. Ammon, O., *Gesellschaftsordnung und ihre natürlichen Grundlagen*, 1900
35. De Lapouge, G. V., *Race et milieu social*, 1909
36. Galton, F., *Hereditary Genius*, 2nd ed., 1925
37. Huxley, T. H., Prolegomena to the Romanes Lectures on *Evolution and Ethics*, sec. XIII, 1893
38. Pirenne, H., 'Les périodes de l'histoire sociale du capitalisme', *Bulletin de la classe des lettres, Académie Royale de Belgique*, no. 5, 1914
39. Bardoux, Jacques, *Angleterre et France: leurs politiques étrangères*, 1937
40. Buckland, W. W., and McNair, A.D., *Roman Law and Common Law*, 1936
41. Barker, E., *National Character*, 1927

6

Antisemitism*

THE term 'antisemitism' seems to have been used first by a German writer alleged to be of Jewish origin, Wilhelm Marr, in 1897 in a brochure entitled *Der Sieg des Judentums über das Germanentum*. It is clear from this pamphlet, as well as from the writings of the circle formed at that time, the Antisemiten Liga, that the word was intended to describe a movement directed not so much against the Jewish religion as against the race, nationality, and culture of the Jews, depicted as an Oriental group of Semites, sunk in materialism and seeking to dominate the world and especially the world of *Germanentum*. In the sense of an antagonism between 'Semites' and 'Aryans', antisemitism is thus a recent phenomenon and not applicable to hatred of the Jews in former epochs. The hatred itself is, however, very ancient. There are indeed writers who think that the anti-Jewish feelings in the ancient, medieval, and modern periods differ radically in their nature. But, in view of the fact that we can recognize in all periods an intermingling of the same elements, though in different proportions, religious antagonism, hatred of the stranger, national rivalry, economic competition, the resemblances are probably greater than the differences, and there is thus sufficient unity of character in anti-Jewish movements of different periods and areas to justify comparative study.

Is the attitude of hostility to Jews to be interpreted as a special case of phenomena familiar in the relations between groups? Is the treatment of the Jews simply one instance of the relation of minorities to dominant majorities? Is it just a case of the intolerance of strangers, or of the competitive struggle between groups?

* Paper read to the British Psychological Society, July 1943.

These are the questions which a broad survey of the facts suggests.

In approaching these questions it is necessary to make certain distinctions. We must distinguish first between the attitude of dislike for the Jews and the reasons which are given for it. The latter are of astonishing variety, ranging from the charges of predatory business habits, meanness, and aggressive pushfulness made by the man in the street to the elaborate racial theories of the academic antisemites. We must also, I think, distinguish different degrees of intensity of the feeling of hostility which may almost amount to a difference of kind. There is the mild dislike felt by many who have no personal experience of Jews at all and who have simply absorbed the attitudes prevalent in their circle. There is the paranoiac or paranoid hatred felt by others which is rationalized by theories of Jewish world power and influence and which the outside observer must regard as pathological in character.

The milder forms of antisemitism exhibit the characteristics which we are wont to group as prejudices. By this I do not mean to assert that the beliefs concerning Jews which are entertained by those who dislike them necessarily contain no grain of truth, but rather that these beliefs are of the nature of prejudgements, *Vorurteile*. Qualities are attributed to Jews not on the basis of direct experience, but rather because they are the qualities which the name Jew suggests, which one expects to find in Jews. The structure of the judgements on which these beliefs are founded is easy to disentangle. They are based on (i) *generalization* or the attribution to Jews in general of offensive qualities in fact noted in a few; (ii) *specification* or the labelling of certain qualities as specifically Jewish which are in fact common among many other people, e.g. vulgarity, pushfulness; (iii) *omission* or the tendency to overlook desirable qualities in the Jew, to regard them as exceptional when they cannot be ignored or at least to refuse to regard them as 'typical' when they have at least as much claim to be considered typical as the unfavourable qualities; (iv) *discrimination* or the tendency to condemn certain acts when committed by Jews which perhaps would not be noted or would be condoned when committed by others, e.g. when similar acts are condemned as sharp practice in the one case but regarded as a clever trick in the other, or when Jewish capital is depicted as destructive and Aryan capital as creative. There is finally (v) *calumny*, e.g. when Jews are charged with offences of which they are completely innocent, as in the various blood libels or the more modern stories of schemes of world domination.

With the mass of judgements thus built up are interwoven many others designed to make them more coherent and systematic. This again takes place in accordance with well-known psychological tendencies. There is in many people a desire to be able to claim rational grounds for their beliefs, especially when their cherished convictions meet with reasoned opposition. In this way beliefs which may have very little rational ground are supplemented by other beliefs formed *ad hoc* and constitute with them a system extremely difficult to shake. Familiar examples of this process can be given from the history of religious beliefs, where we often find that beliefs accepted on authority tend to be justified by further beliefs in the infallibility and complete reliability of the authorities.

The mass of beliefs concerning the supposed characteristics of the Jews is often accepted by Jews themselves. Jewish writers have drawn attention to the phenomenon and have spoken of Jewish antisemitism and even of 'self-hatred'. These terms are applied, not only to those who have left their people and turned into its bitter enemies, but to many others who consciously or unconsciously share the repugnance which non-Jews feel to Jews, or who, out of love for their people, are anxious to rid their people of the faults ascribed to them and who adopt in their criticisms many of the unwarranted generalizations about Jews current in the environment in which they have been brought up. The tendency towards the disparagement of one's own group is common in oppressed minorities. This is especially so in the case of the 'marginal' members, i.e. people who have come under the influence of other groups than the group in which they originate but are still deeply though often unconsciously attached to that group. In such cases the individual tends to adopt the hostility which he finds in his environment and uses it as a means for attaining liberation from his inner conflict (1).*

I have so far spoken of a mass of beliefs or judgements which have gathered round the name of the Jew and have indicated their logical structure. It is clear, however, that this body of beliefs would neither have persisted nor had any effective influence on behaviour if it were not linked with emotional drives due to underlying tension and conflict. The hostility to Jews is clearly a form of group rivalry. A vulgar *nouveau riche* Jew is not despised merely as an individual but as representative of Jews in general. Economic rivalry between Jews and non-Jews would cause no more bitterness than normal business competition between individuals if the Jew were not regarded as a 'stranger'. The fundamental problem is therefore why the Jew has remained a 'stranger' even in countries where he has been settled for a thousand years. This raises the further question: what sort of a group the Jews are. That they are not a race in any precise sense of the word is now generally admitted. Whether they are a nation or not depends to a large extent on the way we define 'nation'. I doubt whether a term that is applied to peoples of such differing social structure as, say, Belgium, Switzerland, Britain, the United States of America, is very useful in defining an entity whose status is so disputed as that of the Jews. The problem of Jewish nationhood becomes practically important only when discussing the desirability or possibility of giving the Jews independent political status in a country of their own. But whether they are a nation or not the Jews are certainly a body of people who feel bound to one another, to whatever historical factors this bond of union may be due. There are some who think that in ancient times the Jews were a nation, though even then the source of their unity was primarily religious in character, that with the dispersion the sense of nationality was lost, while that of religious unity remained; that modern Jewish nationalism is not the latest expression of an inner development, but the product of modern

* For such references see end of essay.

conditions. Modern Jewish nationalism is on this view European nationalism applied to the Jews, inspired and sustained by anti-semitism, in itself, in its modern form, a product of nationalism (2). Opposed to this view is the theory best represented by the well-known Hebrew writer Ahad Ha-am (3). He maintains that religion is only one of the ways in which the Jewish will to live has expressed itself. The Jews did not survive because of their religion; in order that they might survive, their religion developed in a certain way. It moved from polytheism to monotheism after the dispersion because there was need for a belief in a universal God ruling over all the nations. The stress which later Judaism laid on inner life and the rules which sought to regulate all spheres of the outer life became necessary to prevent the disintegration of the Jewish community. The theory that the Jews have a special mission to teach the peoples among whom they are dispersed the principles of ethical monotheism provided a convenient formula to those Jews who had adopted the culture of other peoples but could not quite rid themselves of their ancient attachment to their own people. The modern nationalist revival is on this view due to the realization that the emancipation of the Jews secured in modern times had not in fact solved the Jewish problem. In short, the Jewish will to live is deeper than any of its particular manifestations. The theory is given a biological flavour which raises doubts. It is difficult to believe that the attachment to a socially conditioned group like a people can be due to a specific instinct, genetically transmitted. But apart from this point, not, I think essential to the theory, there is more to be said for it than the opposed view which regards the Jews as nothing but a religious community. There can be no doubt that it is through religion that the Jews have survived as an entity, but the bond that held them together was always more than a religious bond, whether it was of the kind to constitute them a 'nation' or not. In the dispersion the Jews were certainly not political nationalists. They did not aim at establishing a separate political unit or even self-contained colonial settlements. They felt that they were bound to continue as a group within other political units and not themselves a political unit. The term 'nation' does not perhaps adequately describe the historical unity of the Jewish people, but neither does the term 'religious community'. They are an ethnic group with a structure which resembles in some respects the structure of other ethnic minorities, but with peculiarities which give them a character of their own.

To understand the nature of these peculiarities it would be necessary to survey the whole field of Jewish history, but there are a number of points which stand out fairly clearly. In the first place the dispersal of the Jews is world-wide. They are to be found as minorities small or large in all parts of the world, but nowhere have they a centre which can be called their own. Since there is a bond of union between the Jews of different countries, though this is not as effective in practice as their enemies suppose, the Jews of any one country, even though they be regarded as nationals of that country, are regarded also as members of a wider group – the Jewish people. In the second place, throughout the greater part of their history, whatever may be the case now or in the future, the Jews were not willing to lose their identity as a people. The driving power in this connexion was undoubtedly religion. It is fashionable now to explain all social phenomena in economic terms, but economic forces alone would long ago have broken up the unity of the Jewish people. After the collapse of Rome and during the period of the formation of the European peoples, there was nothing from the economic point of view to prevent the Jews from taking part in the general process of development and being absorbed in the social structures that were emerging. The root of Jewish isolation was the Jewish religion. In the ancient world the Jews stood for an imageless, non-mythological religion which was unintelligible and mysterious to the pagan peoples around them. In the Christian era they aroused the bitter hatred of the Christians, who could not understand their obstinate refusal to accept Christianity and who resented their arrogant belief in the superiority of Judaism. The strength of the Jewish faith was such that none of the forces making for assimilation were able to shake it. Whatever the explanation, it is an historical fact that the Jews were at no time moved to accept, in any numbers, the religion of the peoples among whom they lived, however ready they were to accept other elements of alien cultures. The distinctiveness and intensity of their faith strengthened the feeling of unity among the Jews, and they came to regard themselves and were regarded by others not merely as a religious community but as a people, a people moreover that 'dwells apart' and does not 'belong' to the peoples among whom is is dispersed. Jewish history thus presents the unusual phenomenon of a people living within other peoples and yet retaining its identity. Migration, dispersal, infiltration, conquest, are common enough, but it is rare for the incoming group to survive as a distict entity. It is difficult to account for this save by the strength of the faith in the Jewish religion as distinct and different from every other religion, a faith strengthened by persecution, upheld by a powerful religio-legal discipline, and producing or strengthening a bond of union which survives even among those over whom religion has lost its hold. Until the end of the eighteenth century the bulk of the Jews lived everywhere a life of their own, segregated in various degrees from the surrounding people by restrictive laws imposed from without and by the need for cohesion and solidarity felt within. The ghetto, it has well been said, was the land of a people without a land. Though the Jews had been Europeans since Roman times, they were everywhere regarded as strangers and wanderers, hated and despised, deprived of the legal rights which they had earlier enjoyed as Roman citizens, dependent on the whims of rapacious 'protectors'. Economic rivalry drove them out from most occupations save those despised or not desired by others. The feudal authorities drove them from the land and the burghers from trades and handicrafts. Thus the normal incorporation of the Jew within the community was made impossible. The image of the Jew as a parasite, living on the productive work of others, ever pushing himself into spheres to which he had no right, was created and added to the causes of hatred implanted by religious fanaticism. The suspicion of the stranger, economic rivalry, and religious fanaticism combined to form a fertile soil for other antagonisms and to provide an outlet for hate and aggression originating in causes not in themselves connected with Jews. It is a well-established generalization that in all countries where Jews have lived in any numbers there is a tendency for them to be blamed for any troubles that may arise. The isolation of the Jew was deepened by persecution and restrictive laws of various kinds, and, thus deepened, generated further antagonisms. The arguments between those who maintain that the hatred of the Jews is due to their obstinate refusal to assimilate with the peoples among whom they live and those who maintain that the hatred is the cause of Jewish particularism are very unreal. Isolation may have been originally due to inner needs, but discrimination tends to produce further defensive isolation, and this, in turn, encourages further discrimination.

Next in importance and closely connected with the wide range of the Jewish dispersion and the persistence of the will to survive as a people despite the dispersion is the character of Jewish migration. This is a subject that has never been adequately explored. The difference in cultural level between the country of origin and the country of settlement is of the greatest significance, and a thorough study would be of great value for the light it might throw on problems of culture contact in general. Here only a few points can be referred to. The Jewish immigrant brings with him differences in manners, speech, and so forth, and so keeps alive the notion of Jewish distinctiveness. The fact that migration may occur in recurrent waves produces a feeling of distance between the long-settled Jews and those of recent origin and at the same time hinders absorption. It is to be noted that in countries not subjected to waves of immigration, for example in Italy, the assimilation of the Jews proceeded apace. The economic factor is of great importance in this connexion. The immigrant is often accused of lowering the standard of life of the native worker. On the other hand, if he is ambitious and establishes himself in higher positions, he arouses jealousy and is regarded as a vulgar climber. Often he *is* a vulgar climber, and, in any case, he brings with him new ways of life and is apt to upset existing class align-ments. Group prejudice is then complicated by class prejudice.

The situation is often further complicated by the presence of other minorities. Of the conflicts thus arising there are several varieties. Illustrations may be found even in the world of anti-quity. Thus in Alexandria hatred of the Jews, to whom on the whole the Romans were friendly, was instigated by the Greeks, who worked out a pattern, later to be repeated with greater elaborateness, based on a combination of economic rivalry and religious antagonism. In the modern world the relations are of course far more complex. Only a few instances can here be given. In Czarist Russia the Jews lived on the whole in areas which though under the political domination of the Russians were not Russian in culture, e.g. Poland, Lithuania, White Russia. From the point of view of the possibilities of assimilation, the situation presented great difficulties. The attempt made now and again to Russify the Jews was bound to fail in view of the fact that the normal environment in which great masses of Jews lived was not Russian. On the other hand, the culture of the other subject populations was not such as to attract the Jews, and in fact ap-pears to have exercised very little influence on them. In the Aus-trian Empire the situation varied from case to case. In the German parts of Austria and also Hungary, the culture of the politically dominant group was the same as the culture of the masses of the people, and this facilitated Jewish absorption and assimilation. In other parts of Austria the Jews were torn between their attach-ment to German culture and the demands of the social environ-ment which was not German. The Jews thus frequently found themselves between the hammer and the anvil. If they sided with the politically dominant power, they were blamed by the oppressed peoples. If they sided with the latter, they were accused of encouraging revolution. Thus both cultural and political factors were frequently unfavourable to the assimilation of the Jews (4).

The distribution of occupations among Jews has, as is well known, certain peculiarities and is generally different from that which prevails among the peoples in whose midst they live. To see in the peculiarities of occupational structure a primary cause of anti-Jewish feeling seems to me to be unreasonable. This feeling already existed at a time when the occupational structure of the Jews differed little, if at all, from that of other peoples, and the hatred showed itself in fact in the persistent efforts to prevent the Jew from engaging in the productive occupations. There is good reason for the view that Jews, like other struggling minorities, have often been compelled to choose occupations neglected or despised by others or to invent new ones(5). The abnormalities of economic structure are thus an effect rather than a cause of antisemitism. Yet once produced, they hinder the normalization of Jewish social life and thus serve to foster antisemitic feelings (6).

In estimating the effect of the emancipation of the Jews which in West and Central Europe was attained by the middle of the eighteenth century, it is important to bear in mind the following points. Firstly, emancipation began in countries like France and England, where the number of Jews was small and the feeling against them was based on old memories rather than conflicts rooted in contemporary social conditions. Even so, it is maintained by many that antisemitism lingered among the masses, ready to be aroused in moments of national excitement. Secondly, in the areas where there were large Jewish populations, emancipation came much later and very frequently through external influence or intervention (Rumania, Congress of Berlin 1887; Algiers, Law of Crémieux; Minorities Treaties of 1919, etc.). With the exception of Soviet Russia, the Jews of Eastern and South-Eastern Europe owe their civic rights to foreign intervention, and emancipation took a form other than it would have done had it arisen from within. It should be remembered that in these areas the problem of Jewish-Gentile relations is far more complex than in Western Europe, owing to the large numbers involved and the difficulties arising out of the growing industrialization and the emergence of a non-Jewish middle class. The solution of the Jewish problem in these areas cannot be obtained merely by the granting of legal rights, but depends on general economic reconstruction designed to normalize Jewish relations and remove the economic sources of antagonism.

If we now bring together the points briefly discussed above, we may say that the primary source of anti-Jewish feeling is to be found in the conditions which led to the Jews being regarded as strangers, living in the midst of other peoples but not of them. Historically the determining factor was the uncompromising distinctiveness of Jewish monotheism. With the religious tensions thus generated there were soon associated other sources of group antagonism. Being regarded as strangers, the entry of the Jews into the economic life of other peoples was regarded as an unwarranted intrusion and economic competition assumed a character totally different from that between members of the same group. Persecution deepened his isolation and discrimination produced an economic structure which sharpened the sense of his peculiarity and distinctiveness. The isolation of the Jew began to be broken down with the emancipation about one hundred and fifty years ago, but this was achieved only in the areas where the number of Jews was small (except for the U.S.A.). In the areas of great Jewish density the Jews continued to live in communities of their own; the granting of civil rights is recent and in many instances was secured from above by governmental act and under the pressure of external influence. The waves of migration from these areas of great density kept alive the sense of the strangeness of the Jew even in the West and maintained the sense of community among the Jews in the world. His ubiquity and defencelessness made him a convenient object of aggression, and his situation was further complicated by the presence of other minorities themselves in conflict with the dominant authorities, the Jews in general never being strong enough to act as a united and self-contained group.

In dealing with more recent forms of antisemitism three further points have to be noted. These are the growth of nationalism; the emergence of new middle classes in Eastern and South-Eastern Europe, as a result of increasing urbanization and industrialization and the growth of official and governmental bureaucracies; and the deliberate use of antisemitism as a political weapon. For earlier periods, during which the nation-states were still in process of formation, a Jewish historian has put forward the hypothesis that there was a definite correlation between antisemitism and type of ethnic grouping. He tries to show that the position of the Jews has been most favourable in areas in which several ethnic groups were included, none being a dominant majority; least favourable in ethnically homogeneous states; and varying between the two extremes in states which included only part of a nationality. He thinks that up to the seventeenth century this law was operative practically without exception (7). Whatever may be thought of this interesting generalization, there can be no question that the revival of antisemitism in recent times is closely connected with the intensification of nationalist feeling. In Germany the revival of anti-Jewish feeling dates from the movement towards unification. In France antisemitism was fostered by the Integral Nationalists after her defeat in the Franco-Prussian War. In the empires of mixed nationalities the nationalists used the Jew as a buffer and scapegoat. The rise of new nationalities after the War of 1914–18 was in nearly all cases accompanied by antisemitic manifestations. On the other hand, in pre-war Britain and in America, where national antagonisms remained in the background, antisemitism found but little support. It is possible that the recent rise of antisemitism in the United States is connected with the emergence of a stronger sentiment of American nationality. Soviet Russia has shown great tolerance of national minorities, but whether this will continue when the vast conglomeration of ethnic groups of the U.S.S.R. has been welded into greater unity has been called in question.

Connected with the nationalist movements in Eastern Europe has been the rise of a native middle class. The growth of industry, the needs of the newly formed governments, the increasing urbanization have brought into being a new middle class apt to be resentful of the Jews who hitherto had fulfilled the role associated with the middle classes. Nearly everywhere in East and South-East Europe there grew up strong movements designed to oust the Jews from government employment and the professions and even to eliminate them from trade and industry. Strengthened by the German example, the view was gaining ground that the Jews must be driven from public and economic life, though the difficulties in which Jews found themselves had already reached an acute stage before the growth of National Socialism (8).

Finally, reference must be made to the deliberate use of antisemitism as a political weapon. The part played by antisemitism in Nazi and Fascist propaganda is familiar, but the fact that Jews provide a convenient and defenceless object on which discontent can be focused has long been known and utilized. The model is provided in the movement founded by Adolph Stöcker in 1878 and his Austrian counterparts. Stöcker first addressed himself to the workers, but getting a poor response he turned to the middle classes, and the party originally named the *Christlich Soziale Arbeiter Partei* was renamed the *Christlich Soziale Partei*. Christian principles were said to be endangered by liberal, democratic Judaism. Jews were attacked as being at once the mainspring of capitalism and of revolutionary Socialism, a line of attack which has since become very common. The Germans have found many imitators. Antisemitism, Bebel said, is the socialism of blockheads; it is also the anti-socialism of blockheads. The antisemites of Czarist Russia were already greatly influenced by German writers. Dubnow (9) has shown by an analysis of the relevant documents that the anti-Jewish agitation in Russia in the eighties was modelled on what was happening in Germany, and there is clear evidence to show that the Czarist government became more antisemitic as the revolutionary movement grew (10). The fact that the Jews can be so readily used as a scapegoat suggests the widespread existence of latent antisemitism among the masses. But this is not at all clearly established. Anti-Jewish risings are in general deliberately planned and organized and are in no sense 'spontaneous'.

The factors making for antisemitism can be generally paralleled from the history of the relations between other groups. But in the case of the Jews they appear in what is perhaps a unique combination, and they are intensified by the peculiarities of the Jewish position. Especially important in this connexion is the antiquity of the hostility towards Jews and the traditions which have gathered round it, and which are transmitted as a matter of course from generation to generation. Add the wide dispersal of the Jews, the migrations which they have been forced to make, involving continual disturbance of cultural standards and class alignments, the abnormalities of Jewish economic structure, themselves the product of antisemitism of the past, and the difficulties of adjustment in areas undergoing rapid economic change and liable to serious economic crises. Add furthermore the numerous factors making for the intensification of national feeling in modern times apt to lead to the view that all minorities are disruptive elements, and the phenomena of antisemitism will be seen in clearer light. It is important to bear in mind that in different areas or times different factors or combinations of factors may be at work, although certain common features recur with depressing regularity.

I want now to refer briefly to some recent theories of the causes of antisemitism. They fall broadly into two classes – those that appeal mainly to economic factors and those that rely chiefly on psychological explanations. The former is found mainly in Marxist or other socialist writings. They argue that antisemitism is a device of the capitalists to divert attention from the class struggle or a last desperate effort of the middle clases to escape the destruction with which they are threatened. Theories of this sort unquestionably find a great deal of support in historical fact, but as a general explanation they are subject to important qualifications. The Jew is apt to suffer not only in periods when proletarian revolutions are threatened, but whenever there is serious tension of any kind. This is particularly true of periods of national excitement, as during wars. The resurgence of antisemitism in recent times is closely related to the intensification of national feeling, and its explanation is therefore to be sought in the causes which have led to that intensification. It is to be noted further that antisemitic movements are not confined to periods of acute economic distress among the masses. Witness German 'scientific' antisemitism or the movement which sprang up in France in connexion with the Dreyfus affair. Finally, anti-semitism cuts across class divisions. The struggle is often between members of the same class, workers against workers, merchants against merchants, members of the professions against members of the professions. It is a struggle between ethnic groups rather than between social classes.

The psychological theories tend on the whole to make use of the concepts of psychopathology. Already in 1881 a Jewish writer in a well-known work entitled *Auto-Emancipation* put forward the view that antisemitism is an inherited phobia (11). This, he thinks, was developed in early times when the Jew – a landless stranger, without any roots anywhere, a wanderer among the nations – struck the imagination of the masses as a creature uncanny and demonic. This phobia has been, according to him, transmitted by heredity and has come to be part of the mental constitution of the non-Jew. As will be observed, the theory rests on doubtful genetics, since according to present-day theories of heredity it is difficult to see how such a fear could be genetically transmitted. More modern theories are mostly applications of psychoanalysis (12). According to these theories, the more obvious motives of group antagonism are not sufficient to account for the observable facts, and deeper causes of hostility must be involved, having their roots in primitive unconscious tendencies. These indeed find some other outlet within the group, and according to Freudian theory also in the formation of the moral conscience, but are most readily released when directed against members of an alien and potentially hostile 'out-group'. In relation to the members of his own group, the individual has perforce to repress his aggressive tendencies or to overcome them by identification or sublimation. The repression, however, is never complete, and the resulting conflicts are dealt with by the diversion of the hate impulses to an out-group. For various psychological and socio-logical reasons the Jew, it is argued, is a particularly apt target for displaced aggression, and for the same reasons rationalizations are easily provided and widely accepted. The theory deserves close study. To substantiate it, it would be necessary to show that there is some correspondence between the degree of repression of aggressive tendencies within the 'in-group' and the occurrence of anti-Jewish outbursts. This has so far not been seriously attempted.

A striking theory has recently been put forward by Freud (13) and, in a different form, independently, by Maurice Samuel (14). The essence of this theory is that the hatred of the Jew is at bottom a concealed hatred of Christianity.

We must not forget [says Freud] that all the peoples who now excel in the practice of antisemitism became Christian only in relatively recent times, sometimes forced to it by bloody compulsion. One might say that they are 'badly christened'; under the thin veneer of Christianity they have remained what their ancestors were, barbarically polytheistic. They have not yet overcome the grudge against the new religion which was forced on them, and they have projected it on to the source from which Christianity came to them. The fact that the Gospels tell a story which is enacted among Jews, and in truth treats only of Jews, facilitated such a projection. The hatred for Judaism is at bottom hatred for Christianity, and it is not surprising that in the German National-Socialist revolution this close connexion of the two monotheistic religions finds such clear expression in the hostile treatment of both.

Maurice Samuel, who develops his argument with a good deal of force, lays particular stress on what he calls the 'obsessional' character of many forms of antisemitism, the wild exaggeration of Jewish numbers, Jewish financial and political power, Jewish unity of purpose, and the ease with which currency is given to these exaggerations. He thinks that the hostility to Jews differs in character from the hostility and intolerance shown towards any other people, that it stands in no functional relation to the part actually played by Jews in economic and social life, that there is no sort of proportion between the so-called causes of antisemitism and the effects. Samuel's own explanation is that the horror of the Jew, the obsession of his ubiquity, subtlety, and persistence in crime is really a concealed attack on a set of ideas which in fact has the power to move the minds of men everywhere, the belief, namely, in universal love and an attempt to replace it by the principle of force as the regulator of human relations. Antisemitism is, in short, an attack on Judeo-Christian morality.

It is of Christ that the Nazi-Fascists are afraid; it is in *his* omnipotence that they believe; it is *him* that they are determined madly to obliterate. But the names of Christ and Christianity are too overwhelming, and the habit of submission to them too deeply ingrained after centuries and centuries of teaching. Therefore they must make their assault on those who were responsible for the birth and spread of Christianity. They must spit on the Jews as the Christ-killers because they long to spit on the Jews as the Christ-givers.

It is true, I think, that antisemitism in its recent manifestations is part of a more general attack on universalist and humanitarian ethics, and it is clear that the attacks on the Jews have been used to provide training in ruthlessness and violence. But the theories in the form briefly outlined above raise many doubts. To begin with, the 'obsessional' or perhaps more correctly the paranoiac character of many varieties of anti-Jewish behaviour need not be in any way connected with qualities actually possessed by Jews or with sets of beliefs of which Jews have become the symbol. They may be based on experiences which intrinsically have nothing to do with Jews, but which merely seize on Jews as convenient centres of hatred. When a paranoiac accuses judges of corruption, lawyers of being in the pay of his enemies, and imagines a conspiracy to prevent him from obtaining justice, the root of the trouble does not lie in the nature of the lawyers and the judges or the moral theories underlying legal justice. In short, in so far as antisemitism really exhibits paranoiac traits, the explanation would have to begin by an examination of the mental history of the individuals in question, and it is not very likely that one and the same set of causes would be operative in all cases. Secondly, I very much doubt whether the principles of universal morality have ever been so firmly rooted in the Western peoples that an attack on them could only be made in deeply disguised form. It has not proved difficult in practice to reconcile Christian ethical principles with war, intolerance, and violent persecution, and it is odd that at a time when Christianity is openly attacked, as it is by the Nazis, the attack on the ethics of love should have to be carefully concealed under the guise of an attack on Jews. Samuel himself notes that the Russian Communists, who, in his view, also repudiate the doctrine of 'non-force', have been able to condemn antisemitism just because, having openly rejected Christianity, they did not need the disguise of Jew-hatred. But if this is the right explanation, it is not clear why the Nazis needed antisemitism. Thirdly, it must be remembered that antisemitism is not confined to Christian countries. It existed in Arabic Spain and exists now in Moslem countries, not to speak of its manifestations in the Greco-Roman world. Finally, during the medieval period the persecution of the Jews often ceased with their conversion to Christianity, and it would require great subtlety to interpret such persecution as a concealed attack on 'true' Christianity. It is, of course, possible that recent antisemitism is something radically different from ancient or medieval antisemitism, but this, I think, has not been conclusively shown.

The psychoanalytic writers have rightly drawn attention to the part played by frustration and anxiety in generating hatred. Wherever there is widespread anxiety and a sense of insecurity and, in particular, a sense of injustice, the Jew is apt to furnish a convenient target for aggression. The causes making for such a widespread anxiety are largely social in character, the result of particular social and economic conditions. But in so far as they involve unconscious factors, psychoanalysis may help in throwing light on their nature, especially on the more intense forms of antisemitic reaction which are out of all proportion to the real character of the Jews and the part they actually play in social life. The milder forms of what may be called latent antisemitism appear to be traceable largely to traditionally transmitted anti-pathies. These can be roused to life in times of economic difficulty or intensification of national feeling, and occasionally still by a revival of religious fanaticism. The occurrence of anti-semitic outbursts is a symptom of social disorganization. From this point of view antisemitism is thus a problem, not only or even mainly for the Jews, but also for the peoples among whom they live.

REFERENCES

1. Stonequist, E. V., *The Marginal Man*, 1937
2. Mattuck, I., *What are the Jews?* 1939
3. Ahad Ha-am, *At the Parting of the Ways* (in Hebrew)
4. Kaufmann, J., *Strangers and Wanderers* and *Essays on the Troubles of our Times* (both in Hebrew, Tel Aviv, 1936). NOTE – I wish to express my sincere thanks for the help I have received from these most interesting contributions to the history and sociology of the Jews.
5. Bienenfeld, F. R., *Germans and Jews*, 1939
6. Ginsberg, M., 'The Jewish Problem', *Agenda*, Oct. 1942
7. Baron, S. W., *A Social and Religious History of the Jews*, 1937
8. Janowsky, O. I., *A People at Bay*, 1938
9. Dubnow, S., *Weltgeschichte des jüdischen Volkes*, 1930
10. Ruppin, A., *The Jews in the Modern World*, 1934
11. Pinsker, L., *Auto-Emancipation*, 1881
12. Graeber, I., and Britt, S. H. (ed.), *Jews in a Gentile World*, 1942, especially chs. V and VI
13. Freud, S., *Moses and Monotheism*, 1939
14. Samuel, M., *The Great Hatred*, 1941

7

The Life and Work of Edward Westermarck*

EDWARD WESTERMARCK was born in Helsingfors on 21 November 1862. His father was the University Bursar, Nils Christian Westermarck, whose family moved to Finland from Sweden during the first half of the eighteenth century. By temperament reserved and outwardly cold, he yet evidently took a warm interest in his son's scientific aspirations and gave him complete freedom in the choice of his career. His mother was the daughter of Alexander Blomquist, professor of the History of Learning and University Librarian. In contrast to his father, she had a sunny disposition which Westermarck in a great measure inherited. His memory of her was clearly dominated by a feeling of infinite devotion and affection. As a child Westermarck suffered from chronic catarrh complicated by asthma, and this prevented him from sharing in the normal active life of children of his own age and later from taking part in games and sports at school.

As an undergraduate Westermarck early developed an antipathy to German metaphysics which, he concluded, 'gave the impression of depth because it was so muddy.' He was, on the other hand, greatly attracted by the English Empiricists, where he found clearness and a sense of reality, and above all a readiness to test all hypotheses in the light of experience. In close connexion with his philosophical studies Westermarck was deeply interested in religious questions, and here he was greatly influenced by Spencer's *First Principles* and Mill's essays on religion which he read in a Swedish translation. He rapidly became an

* A lecture delivered at the London School of Economics. Cambridge, 1940.

agnostic and remained so for the rest of his life. In his later elaborate studies of religion there is to be detected, beneath the outwardly calm and detached exposition, a persistent mood of irritation and hostility. Yet in a deeper sense he was not without religious feeling. He retained throughout life a sense of the unfathomable mystery of the world and of the inherent limitations of human knowledge, but the only expression he found for his feeling was in music. Any attempt to embody it in a formulated creed was bound in his view to be tainted with anthropomorphism, and he even regarded all such efforts as blasphemous. His attitude to death and immortality was one of humble submission to the unknowable and acceptance of the inevitable, an attitude which again can hardly be described as irreligious.

The plan of writing a work on the origin and development of moral ideas came to Westermarck during the discussions at a philosophical society led by his teacher, Professor Thiodolf Rein, by whose candid and humble search for truth he was evidently deeply moved. The problem, however, on which he began to work was the limited one of the nature and origin of sexual modesty. He approached this along evolutionary lines. He made himself thoroughly familiar with the main principles of Darwinism and early saw that the theory of natural selection, especially in its application to instinct, was to prove of great importance in the study of social phenomena. He soon found that his problem raised the much wider question of the relations between the sexes and their historical development. He became interested in the hypothesis of primitive promiscuity, which Darwin took for granted, on the ground of the investigations made by Morgan, Lubbock, and McLennan, and at the age of twenty-five found it necessary to learn English in order to go back to the original authorities. He was soon convinced that the attempt to reconstruct the primitive forms of social institutions must lead to arbitrary conclusions unless their fundamental causes, i.e. their biological and psychological conditions, were first ascertained. In particular, we had, he thought, no right to assume the universal prevalence of any social phenomenon unless it could be shown that its causes were universally present and were not counteracted. He was thus led to the hypothesis that the family, consisting of father, mother, and children, being rooted in essential, biological conditions, already existed in primitive times, while the alleged causes, say, of group-marriage, or marriage by capture, were not such as to justify the belief in their universal prevalence at any stage of human civilization.

These general ideas gradually took shape in a plan to write a book on the history of marriage, and in 1887 he came to England in order to collect his material in the library of the British Museum, to him an island of bliss and a 'very temple as well'. Through Sully, with whom he formed an intimate friendship, he was introduced to intellectual circles in England. The book appeared with a preface by Wallace and had an immediate scientific success. The massive learning of the work so impressed reviewers that it was declared to be the 'earnest labour of the chief part of a life-time'. Later, Westermarck tells us, he came upon the belief that its author was a kind of patriarch, and twice he was taken for his own son. The publication of the book was in his own view the most momentous happening in his life. 'It has been said', he adds, 'that marriage has many thorns, but celibacy no roses. For my own part I would say that marriage has brought me many roses – and bachelorhood no thorns.'

The success of the book on marriage encouraged Westermarck to proceed with his plans of a much larger inquiry into the origin and development of moral ideas. It is clear that the main concepts took definite shape in his mind quite early in his career, but it took nearly eighteen years to carry out the task he had set himself. His work was interrupted by teaching duties at his university, where he was appointed Docent in 1890; but in 1893 he was awarded a scholarship which enabled him to go back to the British Museum and to Oxford, where he met Tylor and Marett. A further scholarship in 1897 gave him three years' quiet work, which he again spent in England. At the meetings of the Aristotelian Society he renewed his acquaintance with

English scholars, and it was here that he met Shand and became his warm friend. 'I have in great measure', he tells us, 'to thank my friend Shand for my conception of an English gentleman as seen at his best.'

In planning his work on the comparative study of Morals, Westermarck saw that it would be most useful to him to acquire first-hand knowledge of other cultures than our own. He intended to go to the East to study both civilized and savage races. He sailed, however, first to Morocco and, realizing the difficulties involved in getting to know even a single country, he never went farther. In the course of three decades he spent altogether nine years in Morocco, and the results of his labours were embodied in his trilogy on the customs and ideas of the Moors.*

In 1903 Westermarck again visited England to arrange for the publication of the first volume of his *Moral Ideas*. It was then that he first met Victor Branford, who invited his cooperation in a scheme for starting an English sociological society. Through Branford he made the acquaintance of J. Martin White, through whose generous benefaction the University of London was enabled to inaugurate the teaching of sociology, and later to establish professorships of sociology. As a Member of Parliament Martin White, it appears, came to the conclusion that it would be good for MPs to have a training in sociology, and his endowment was intended to provide facilities for such training. Under his benefaction Westermarck was appointed University Lecturer in Sociology for a period of three years, and during that period courses were also given by L. T. Hobhouse on Comparative Ethics and Comparative Psychology and by A. C. Haddon on Ethnology. In 1907 a permanent chair in sociology was endowed, and Hobhouse was appointed to it. At the same time Westermarck's Lectureship was converted into a chair with a five years' tenure. In 1912 the appointment was renewed for eighteen years more. Meanwhile Westermarck had been appointed to the chair of moral philosophy at Helsingfors and the

* Cf. *Ritual and Belief in Morocco; Marriage Ceremonies in Morocco; Wit and Wisdom in Morocco.*

two posts were held by him concurrently. For a number of years he devoted the first two terms to his work at Helsingfors, the summer term to the School of Economics, and the remaining summer months to his investigations in Morocco. In his scientific activities Westermarck adhered rigidly to the plans which he had formed when a young man. He lived long enough to realize these in his comprehensive works on the history of marriage, the origin and development of moral ideas, and on the ideas and customs of the Moors. On three occasions he took an active part in politics, namely, in organizing the International Address to the Czar on behalf of Finland, in the movement for its independence during the war of 1914-18 and in the Aaland campaign, and it is generally recognized that the services he thus rendered to his country were of the highest value. It is clear that the chief passion of his life was the pursuit of truth, and that he found his greatest happiness in those hours when he could work in peaceful solitude. Two other sources of happiness were given him – the love of nature and the experience of deep and enduring friendships. It is a great pleasure to those who knew and worked with Westermarck to have his own assurance that in the main he had achieved the goals which he had set to himself and that the sources of his happiness were not such as to run dry with advancing age. His capacity for the appreciation of beauty and for friendship grew no less with increasing years, and he continued with his scientific work right up to a few days before his death on 3 September 1939. There can be few people so justified as he was in declaring that if he had to live his life over again, he would on the whole follow the same path as he had in fact chosen.

In coming now to deal with Westermarck's work, I may best begin perhaps with his conception of the scope and methods of sociology. Sociology he defined as the science of social phenomena, and in this sense it was a collection of studies, including such disciplines as economics, politics, and the history of law. He himself was, however, most interested in developing that branch of sociology which he called the comparative study of social institutions, and the bulk of his work was devoted to this task. Social institution he defined as a social relationship regulated by society and sanctioned by it. The study of social institutions thus involves an account of the general nature of society and of the different forms in which it appears and of the sanctions and regulations employed by it. This is given in the *Origin and Development of Moral Ideas,* in which the forms of social regulations are studied in detail and analysed psychologically by reference to the fundamental emotions of approval and disapproval. The institution of marriage was dealt with in much greater detail in a number of works, in which it is examined both comparatively and in reference to the particular area of Morocco.

The method which he employed was in the main the comparative one. This aimed in the first place at a classification of the products of culture found among different peoples in different parts of the world; for example, the classification of religious beliefs and practices under the heading of animism, totemism, ancestor worship, polytheism, monotheism, or of marriage under the headings of marriage by capture, marriage by consideration, or monogamy, polygamy, polyandry, and group-marriage. From classification, he thought, we could move to causal explanation by a comparison of the circumstances common to a cultural phenomenon and those which could be shown to vary without corresponding variation in the phenomenon. Westermarck frequently uses the terms cause and origin interchangeably. By the cause of a social phenomenon he means in the first place the biological conditions determining it or at least giving it survival value. Thus the cause of marriage as an institution he finds in the need of prolonged marital and paternal protection. Such protection, he thought, was an indispensable condition of survival in the case of a species in which the number of the young is small, the period of infancy prolonged, and the supply of food such as to hinder a permanently gregarious mode of life. Through natural selection instincts would be developed impelling the male to stay with the female and the young and to care for them.

These instincts, together with the sex instinct, are at the root of the family as an institution. Under their impulsion it became the habit in primitive times for a man and a woman or several women to live together and to rear their offspring in common. The habit was sanctioned by custom and law, upheld by the tendency of members of the group to feel resentment against a man who forsook his mate and children. Of this set of relationships marriage is an integral part. As Westermarck puts it: marriage is rooted in the family rather than the family in marriage. Further, the instincts and sentiments which gave rise to the family are so deep-rooted that they are likely to preserve it, even though they may no longer be necessary for the survival of the race. In this example, which, I think, is typical of a good deal of Westermarck's work, causal explanation is in terms of the Darwinian theory of natural selection. In other cases the causes of social phenomena are sought in the motives which may be supposed to underlie them. Thus, in his study of human sacrifice, he argues that comparative investigation shows that human victims are offered in war, to avert or stop a famine or drought, to ward off perils from the sea, or to prevent the death of some particular person. This, he thinks, justifies the conclusion that human sacrifice is largely a method of life insurance, based on the idea of substitution.*

Two further points require elucidation. In the first place, Westermarck was not at all impressed by the objections raised against his views by the followers of Durkheim and others on the ground that social phenomena cannot be explained in terms of individual psychology. Who could deny, he argued, that even collective behaviour involves the actions of individuals? When we speak of the customs or religion of a people, we refer to something that the individual members of it have in common, and, in the last resort, they are the outcome of mental activity. Further, the force by which customs are maintained can only in the long run be understood in terms of an analysis of the moral consciousness, and he thinks himself justified in concluding that

* *Moral Ideas,* I, p. 440 seq.

this is ultimately based on the retributive emotions collectively felt and given a measure of generality and impartiality within a given community. In the study of particular social phenomena such as rites and ceremonies, Westermarck did not share the view held by Rivers that the task of disentangling the motives underlying them was hopeless. He thought that valuable information could be obtained, not so much from what natives say *about* their rites, as from what they say at the moment when they perform them, and he gives many examples of such interpretations from his own studies in Morocco.* Westermarck here perhaps over-simplifies the issue. He does not inquire into the various ways in which social forces react upon human motives by encouraging some and inhibiting others and by determining the manner in which they find expression. Unless this is done, it is difficult to account for the variations which Westermarck himself studies in the institutions and beliefs of mankind.

The second point that requires here to be mentioned relates to the use made by Westermarck of the theory of evolution. We have seen that in explaining social phenomena he was inclined to look for the biological conditions underlying them and to appeal to the theory of natural selection in accounting for the psychological make-up of man. He was not, however, interested in tracing stages of development, and in particular he repudiated in even his earliest writings the belief in the unilinear sequence of institutional stages. From the point of view of method, the reconstruction of the past, in the absence of direct historical evidence, stands on the same footing as the prediction of the future. In both cases it is necessary to know the cause of the phenomena and to ascertain whether they are likely to be operative in the period in question without being counteracted. Thus in dealing with the family Westermarck thinks we are justified in concluding that it existed already in primitive times, because the conditions necessitating it are then likely to have prevailed, and, further, that it is likely to persist in modern society, because the instincts and sentiments underlying it have

* Cf. 'Methods in social anthropology', *J.R.A.I.*, 1936.

become so deeply rooted that they will continue to demand satisfaction. The tracing of trends of change is likely to be misleading unless we are able at the same time to ascertain the causes of the changes. In the controversy between the diffusionists and the upholders of independent origination, Westermarck followed the lead of Tylor. Similarity in the cultural phenomena found among different peoples is to be ascribed 'sometimes to the like working of men's minds under like conditions, and sometimes it is a proof of blood relationship or of intercourse, direct or indirect, between the races among whom it is found.'*

In dealing with widespread or universal elements of culture, such as the right of property, punishment, the various forms of marriage, the rules of exogamy, and so forth, the diffusionist hypothesis seemed to him in the highest degree improbable. But he was quite prepared to resort to diffusion in dealing with particular problems, such as those which are connected with decorative art or with proverbs, and he gives examples from his own studies in Morocco.†

The greatest difficulty of the comparative method is due to the necessity under which it labours of detaching or isolating cultural phenomena from their context and the risk it thus runs of distorting their real character. Of this risk Westermarck was well aware, but he thought that analysis and comparison were essential to sociology as to other sciences, and that if due caution was observed, the difficulties inherent in the method could in a large measure be overcome

Passing now to the substance of Westermarck's work, I propose to confine attention to his theory of morals and to certain aspects of his study of marriage. In his moral theory Westermarck was profoundly influenced by Adam Smith, whose *Theory of Moral Sentiments* he considered as the most important contribution to moral psychology made by any British thinker,‡ and by the

* E. B. Tylor, *Researches into the Early History of Mankind* (1878), p. 5.
† Cf. 'Methods in social anthropology', *J.R.A.I.*, 1936, p. 226 seq.
‡ *Ethical Relativity*, p. 71.

theory of natural selection. Adam Smith had given an analysis of approval and disapproval in terms of sympathy. We approve of the feelings of another when we recognize that, if we or rather an impartial spectator were in the same situation, we should experience the same feelings, and we disapprove of them when on entering into the situation we cannot share those feelings. In his account of merit and demerit, Adam Smith had moreover laid special stress on the feelings of resentment and gratitude. According to him an action has merit if it is the approved object of gratitude and that has demerit which is the approved object of resentment. In other words, an act is meritorious if an impartial spectator can be expected to sympathize with the gratitude which it evokes, and, similarly, an act is to be condemned if the resentment aroused by it is likely to be shared by an impartial spectator. Westermarck's analysis starts with the emotions of gratitude and resentment, which he designates the retributive emotions and of which he gives a biological account in accordance with the theory of natural selection. He shows that gratitude or retributive kindly emotion has the tendency to retain a cause of pleasure, while resentment has the tendency to remove a cause of pain, and that these emotions are therefore both useful to the species. The difference in their prevalence is, he thinks, easily explained by the fact that living in groups is of advantage only to certain species and that even gregarious animals have many enemies but few friends. The retributive emotions are not however as such moral. They only become so if they acquire the three qualities of generality, disinterestedness, and impartiality. The disinterestedness is rendered possible by the presence in us of the power to sympathize with the feelings of others, and above all, by the altruistic sentiment which is an active disposition to promote the welfare of its object. The generality and impartiality of moral rules are due, he thinks, to the fact that they express not the emotions felt by isolated individuals, but those felt generally in a society in accordance with custom. Custom is general in its nature, i.e. it formulates what is expected from everyone in the same circumstances. Custom is also impersonal and impartial, i.e. is equally binding on all coming under the rule and under its influences there arises the feeling not so much that 'I must do this' as that 'this must be done.' Westermarck has been accused of arguing in a circle in maintaining that custom is the factor responsible for making the retributive emotions disinterested and impartial, while holding at the same time that custom is a moral rule only on account of the disapproval called forth by its breach.* But I am not sure that the charge can be sustained. A moral emotion is, I take it, in Westermarck's view, a public emotion, that is, one likely to be felt generally in a given community. Customary rules are in their origin generalization of emotional tendencies, but having come to be established in a given community they are upheld by the tendency of their violation to arouse disapproval whether or not the act in itself, i.e. apart from its being condemned by custom, would arouse emotions in particular individuals. The circle is thus not vicious.

Westermarck describes his theory as a form of ethical relativity, and it is important to inquire what precisely he understands by relativity and how far his view can be consistently maintained. The most general form in which he states his theory is that the predicates of all moral judgements are ultimately based on emotions. To say that an act is good or bad is to say that it is apt to give rise to the emotions of approval or disapproval, or perhaps a little more accurately, to refer the act to a class of acts which have come to be called good or bad because of their tendency to arouse these emotions. The concepts of good and of ought are in his view distinct and not deducible from one another. But he repudiates the claim that either is ultimate and unanalysable. The notion of goodness springs from the emotion of moral approval: that of duty from moral disapproval. Thus, to say that an act ought to be done implies that its omission has the tendency to arouse disapproval, and to say that it ought not to be done implies that its performance has

* Cf. Dewey, Anthropology and ethics, ch. III of *The Social Sciences*, ed. Ogburn and Goldenweiser, p. 28.

the tendency to call forth disapproval. It is because the ought-judgement has implicit in it the notion of a prohibition that the idea of duty has come to carry with it a suggestion of antagonism to natural inclination, and that philosophers have even tended to restrict the notion of duty to acts that result from a successful struggle against opposite inclination. In a similar way Westermarck gives an analysis of other terms used in morals, such as right, wrong, just, and unjust, merit, virtue, and vice. In all cases he thinks the qualities assigned to the subjects of moral judgements are generalizations derived from approval or disapproval and they indicate tendencies to arouse one or other of these emotions. The assertions made in ethical propositions are in this respect similar to the propositions asserting that something is fearful, lovable, wonderful, and the like. In short, what we are asserting is the presence of dynamic tendencies or the power of arousing certain emotions in the acts of which they are predicated. In this sense they may be true or false, since these tendencies are either present or absent in a given community. The approval or disapproval on the other hand being, in Westermarck's view, emotions, are not capable of being either true or false and to claim objective validity for them is therefore meaningless.

How far was Westermarck able to maintain this position consistently? To answer this question we must consider his views of the part played by reflection in the growth of the moral consciousness and his account of the variations of the moral judgements found in different societies. Since the higher emotions are stimulated by awareness of objects, they are bound to be affected by changes in knowledge. Thus our anger with a person who has told a lie may disappear or even change to approval when we discover that he acted from a desire to save life. In this way reflection has affected the emotions of approval and disapproval by revealing more fully the character of the objects which evoke them or by freeing them from associations which have gathered round them. A few illustrations may serve to make this clear. In the first place, we find gradually that indignation is properly directed only against acts deliberately intended to cause pain, and our anger dies when we realize that pain has been caused to us by an inanimate object or by a person acting unwillingly or in ignorance of the consequence of his acts. Historically this has been of the greatest importance in the changes that have come about in the infliction of punishment. Primitive codes, for example, fail to distinguish clearly between intentional and unintentional acts, and animals, children, and lunatics are treated as punishable even in modern times. Important changes are now occurring in the treatment of crime, partly as a result of growing insight into the psychology of the immature or the mentally unsound. In these cases the growth of thought has affected the moral emotions by deepening our knowledge of the nature of the subject of moral judgements, that is to say, the character of the agent. In the second place, there are aversions and sympathies which Westermarck, following Bain, calls 'disinterested' or 'sentimental', that is, likes and dislikes which are not based upon direct experience of pleasure or pain; as when we dislike persons who differ from us in taste, habit, or opinion. These antipathies have affected the moral consciousness by leading people to regard as wrong many acts which are merely unusual, new, or foreign. The morality of sexual relations in particular has, in Westermarck's view, been profoundly influenced by these 'sentimental' aversions. Examples are to be found in the condemnation, varying in intensity among different peoples, of auto-erotism and bestiality. They are regarded as immoral, not because they are known to cause harm, but because they inspire disgust. In the third place, religious or superstitious beliefs may affect our views of the nature of certain acts which then evoke our disapproval. In Westermarck's view the horror of homosexuality among the Hebrews, the Christians, and Zoroastrians is largely due to the fact that they associated it with the practices of infidels and therefore regarded it as a form of sacrilege. He argues that where no such religious influence has been operative, the moral attitude towards homosexual practices has been different and that in Christian Europe the growth of rationalism is bringing about important changes in the attitude of the law and of public opinion. Finally, many of our moral judgements are based, not on direct approval or disapproval of acts which are perceived to be the cause of pleasure or pain to others, but on sympathetic approval or resentment. In other words, we are inclined to get our resentments and approvals secondhand from those for whom we have a regard or who are in a position of authority. In this way, for example, punishment inflicted by society being regarded as an expression of the moral indignation of the community, may lead us to condemn an act which we should not otherwise regard as blameworthy. Acts which are in themselves harmless may thus, through ignorance, superstition, or prejudice, come to have opprobrium attached to them, and their condemnation becomes so deeply rooted in the moral tradition that no one ever thinks of inquiring into the original causes which led to their being regarded as immoral. In short, growing reflection may alter the direction of our emotions of approval and disapproval by revealing more fully the character of the agent, by dissipating superstitious beliefs which tend to endow acts with qualities which do not really belong to them, by revealing the existence of merely 'sentimental' sympathies and antipathies, and by challenging traditional morality to disclose the original causes which brought given rules of morality into being. Westermarck thinks that comparative study shows that in a measure moral ideas have in the course of social evolution become more 'enlightened' in all these respects, and that there is reason to believe that the influence of reflection upon moral judgements will steadily increase.

This account, Westermarck claims, is borne out by a study both of the differences and similarities that are found to exist in the moral judgements of different societies. With regard to the subjects of moral judgements, Westermarck concludes after a careful survey that in reflective morality moral approval and disapproval are felt with reference to persons on account of their conduct or to character conceived as the cause of their conduct. This is true in the main also of earlier and cruder phases of morality, though there is then no serious attempt to separate the external event from the will and there is an inclination to assume that the two always coincide. Hence, in part, the failure to distinguish clearly between intentional and unintentional acts and the ascription of blame or praise to agents whom the reflective mind cannot regard as strictly responsible. The fact that moral judgements are passed always on conduct and character is in harmony, Westermarck argues, with their origin in the retributive emotions. The latter are reactions towards a living being regarded as the cause of pleasure or pain, and they are not so regarded by the reflective mind unless they are taken to issue from the character or will of the agent considered as a continuous entity. Allowing then for differences in psychological knowledge, there is, according to Westermarck, no difference in principle between the moralities of different peoples regarding the subjects of moral judgements.

With regard to the content of moral rules, the result of Westermarck's elaborate study is to show that despite certain important differences there is a noteworthy similarity in the moral ideas of mankind. This similarity extends to the so-called uncivilized peoples.

When we examine the moral rules laid down by the customs of savage peoples, we find that they in very large measure resemble the rules of civilized nations. In every savage community homicide is prohibited by custom, and so is theft. Savages also regard charity as a duty and praise generosity as a virtue; indeed, their customs relating to mutual aid are often more exacting than our own and many of them are conspicuous for their avoidance of telling lies.

This similarity Westermarck explains as due ultimately to the fact that the emotions which the moral rules express are presumably similar in all groups of mankind. The differences which are found he attributes broadly to three causes, namely, differences in external circumstances which affect the consequences of otherwise similar acts and thereby their moral import, differences in knowledge of the nature and consequences of acts due very often to the influences of religious and magical beliefs, and finally differences in the strength and range of the altruistic sentiment which affect the range of persons to whom moral rules are held to apply. Examples of the operation of the first set of causes are to be found in the practice of infanticide, which is in the main due to the hardships of savage life; and the practice of killing aged parents, which is connected with deficiencies in the food supply and is inspired by the necessity of saving the young and vigorous and the humane intention of putting an end to prolonged and hopeless misery. Examples of the second set of causes are to be found in the different attitudes adopted by different peoples to suicide, which, according to Westermarck, have been greatly influenced by religious beliefs, such as the duty of absolute submission to the will of God or, as in the case of Christianity, the importance ascribed to the moment of death. Numerous other instances can readily be given from the varied taboos found among different peoples. The most important divergence in moral attitudes concerns the range of persons to whom moral rules are held to apply. Though the rules inculcating regard for life, property, truth, and the general well-being of a neighbour are found in all societies, they are held to be binding only in reference to members of the same group. The range is widened with the expansion of the social unit, but the distinction between the tribesman and the stranger survives even to-day, and the fact that morality is still largely group morality is seen in the survival of war and the precariousness of the rules supposed to control behaviour during war. Nevertheless, there has been a great advance in humanity with regard to the treatment of foreigners. Westermarck notes further that, so far as the teaching of the great moralists is concerned, the change from the savage attitude has been enormous. There is remarkable unanimity in this respect, in the teaching of all the higher religions. The doctrine of universal love is taught not only by Christianity but by Chinese thinkers, by the Buddhists and other Indian teachers, by the Greek philosophers, and the doctrine of a world citizenship was given definite content and historical importance by the Stoics. The most important cause of the extension of the range of moral rules has been the widening of the altruistic sentiment which has accompanied the increase in the size of social unit and the growth of intercourse between different societies. The change has been in the main due, according to Westermarck, to emotional rather than to cognitive factors. He argues further that variations in the range and intensity of the altruistic sentiment account also for the differences of moral opinion regarding the limits of the duty of self-sacrifice and the treatment of the lower animals.

We must now consider the bearing which this account of the part played by reflection in the growth of the moral judgement and of the variations of moral views among different peoples has upon the theory of ethical relativity. Westermarck himself notes that in so far as differences of moral opinion depend on differences of circumstances, or on knowledge or ignorance of facts, or on the influence of specific religious and magical beliefs, or on different degrees of reflection, they are perfectly compatible with the universal validity which is claimed for moral judgements.* Analogous differences of opinion may easily be shown to exist in other spheres of knowledge where no one would on their account call in question the possibility of establishing universally valid propositions. It may be added that moralists concerned to defend the claim to objective validity of moral truths have themselves explained the variety of opinion actually found, in terms which closely resemble the explanation given by Westermarck.† Westermarck, however, claims that there is an important class of differences in moral opinion illustrated by the differences in the range of persons to which moral rules are held to apply in different communities, which depend not on differences in knowledge but on differences of emotional dispositions, and he argues that variations of this sort are fatal to

* *Ethical Relativity*, p. 196.
† Cf. Dugald Stewart, *Collected Works*, vol. VI, p. 237, and Sidgwick, *Ethics of Green, Spencer, and Martineau*, p. 227.

the supposed universality of moral judgements. I cannot find his argument at all convincing. It rests on an unreal separation of feeling and thought. It is possible that without the power of sympathy the truths of universalist ethics could neither be discovered nor become effective in practice, but this throws no light at all on the nature of the truths once they are discovered. Just as certain feelings are only possible at a given level of rational development, so it may well be that certain thoughts or beliefs only emerge under certain emotional conditions. Certainly in grasping the essential relations between men, the power of imaginative identification, of entering fully into the situation of others, must be of the highest value, and perhaps this power only reaches its greatest intensity under the influence of the social feelings.

The difficulty here raised besets, I think, the whole of Westermarck's discussion of the part played by reason in morals. He assigns to intellectual factors very important functions, but he does not realize that he is giving them a claim to authority which is not compatible with his relativistic outlook. The statement, for example, that in the course of social evolution morality has become more 'enlightened' implies a value judgement which goes beyond his own emotional approval of certain of the changes that have occurred. It is indeed clear from Westermarck's account that the feelings of approval and disapproval are in themselves an insufficient guide to conduct. Apart from the 'sentimental' antipathies and sympathies whose origin is obscure, many other feelings have been implanted in man under conditions which no longer prevail and can therefore be no longer relied upon as a criterion of well-being. This appears to be the case in much of the morality of sexual relations, and Westermarck even feels justified in concluding that 'enlightened' people will probably come to look upon sexual acts as morally indifferent and as no 'proper object for punishment or moral censure' save in so far as they may involve injury to others. To be called wrong he says 'an act must be productive of other harm than the mere aversion it causes, provided that the agent has not in an indecent manner shocked anyone's feelings.'* But what is the meaning of the term 'proper' in this context? As a mere matter of biological or sociological fact the aversions which are indirectly attached to acts as a result of social suggestion or of magical and religious beliefs are as proper as the primary resentments, that is, those directed against the infliction of pain, since presumably they are also rooted in the tendencies of human nature. It would seem then that discriminating or enlightened reflection does not remain satisfied with merely ascertaining the actual or probable tendencies to approval or disapproval in given societies, but also seeks to criticize them in the light of a conception of what is deserving of approval or disapproval.

There is another difficulty in connexion with Westermarck's discussion of the relations between individual and social approval and disapproval. Sometimes he appears to suggest that for the emotion to be moral it is necessary that it should be 'public' or general in a given community. Yet he recognizes the importance of moral innovators and he even thinks that such moral progress as has occurred has been largely due to the example of such innovators and their efforts to raise public opinion to their own standard of right.† I do not think that Westermarck succeeds in overcoming this difficulty, which in one form or another besets all sociological theories of ethics. In one place he suggests that all that is required to give to the retributive emotions of the exceptional individuals moral character is that these emotions should possess the characteristics of disinterestedness and impartiality due to the social influence of custom, and in that case they may differ from public approval and disapproval either in intensity or with regard to the facts by which they are evoked. But surely this reference to the origin of impartiality is not very helpful. The value of the contributions of the moral innovators has often consisted, as Westermarck himself says, in showing that 'the apparent impartiality of public feelings is an illusion', and, what is equally important, in showing that rules which are impartially applied may themselves be unjust. Why should such

* *Future of Marriage*, p. 255.   † *Christianity and Morals*, p. 15.

contributions be regarded as 'progressive' or enlightened if the only criterion is public approval? In the end Westermarck has to appeal to an ideal society.

Even when standing alone, he (the moral dissenter) feels that his conviction is shared at least by an ideal society, by all those who see the matter as clearly as he does himself, and who are animated by equally wide sympathies, and an equally broad sense of justice. Thus the moral emotions remain to the last public emotions – if not in reality, then as an ideal.*

There is, however, in Westermarck's work no analysis of the concept of an ideal, and its use appears to introduce a value category for which it is difficult to find a place in his system.

Westermarck has defended his views with great vigour and lucidity, and has refuted many of the objections made to them convincingly. I have tried to look at his work, so to say, from within, and I do not find it quite self-consistent. Yet whatever criticisms may be made against his work regarded as a contribution to ethical philosophy, there can be no doubt of its value as a systematic and comprehensive sociological study of the moral ideas and customs of mankind. In this study he was a pioneer and he carried it out with an erudition, lucidity, and balance still unsurpassed.

Westermarck was led to his studies into the history of human marriage by his interest in the question of the origins of sexual modesty. The studies, however, came to cover the whole range of sexual relations and even in the later enlarged editions of the *History of Human Marriage*, only a single chapter is devoted to the question which initiated the whole inquiry, while in the first edition only a few lines are given to it. When it first appeared it was hailed everywhere as a scientific work of the highest importance. Of the later expanded edition I will quote the opinion of Havelock Ellis, with which I think most competent students would agree: 'In its extended and mature shape it stands out as a monumental achievement in the field of scientific sociology,

* *Moral Ideas*, vol. I, p. 123.

recalling the other great achievement of the same generation in an analogous field by Sir James Frazer, and with no other edifice of comparable magnitude in sight.'* Out of the vast range of topics dealt with by Westermarck the two that have attracted most attention are perhaps his explanation of the origin and significance of the rules of exogamy and his theory of the universality and primitive character of the family. As to the first, his view, which he defends with great learning and skill, is that the cause of all incest prohibitions is to be found in the want of inclination for and consequent aversion to sexual intercourse between persons who have lived together in close intimacy from childhood. He thinks that there may be a biological explanation of this disinclination. There is, he urges, strong evidence showing that exclusive and prolonged inbreeding tends to be injurious to the stock, and in accordance with the theory of natural selection it is probable that the sexual instinct has been moulded to meet the requirements of the species. The biological explanation is, however, only offered as a hypothesis, while the psychological facts which it is intended to elucidate are taken by him to be proved by common experience. Westermarck's theory has been accepted by many authorities, including Havelock Ellis. On reviewing the discussion of this whole question in recent literature I am not, however, convinced by his argument. The biological explanation certainly cannot be regarded as safely established, but without it I cannot see how Westermarck can explain the transformation from mere indifference to aversion which according to him has occurred. No doubt we have parallel cases of indifference turning into dislike but hardly into a deep-seated aversion comparable to that with which incest is regarded. The aversion may, indeed, be caused by the prohibition, but then the prohibition has to be accounted for.

With regard to his views on the family it will be recalled that when he began his work he was inclined to accept the hypothesis then widely held that primitive man lived in a state of promiscuity. He soon discovered, however, that there was no real

* *The Sociological Review*, January 1935, p. 94.

evidence for this hypothesis. He showed (i) that no known savage people either is or recently was living in such a state; (ii) that statements to the contrary from ancient writers are vague and untrustworthy; (iii) that in the case of people who have a form of group-marriage, the evidence suggests that it has arisen as a combination of polygyny with polyandry; (iv) that in the case of peoples alleged to have some kind of sex communism, in which several men have the right of access to several women, none of the women is properly married to more than one of the men and individual marriage subsists. Finally, he produces positive evidence that even among the food-gatherers and hunters, who might be supposed to live in conditions nearest to those in which primitive man lived, the family, consisting of parents and children, is a well-marked social unit. With regard to primitive man, he further argues, his general conclusion is strengthened by what is known of the social habits of the anthropoids, where the family unit, consisting of male, female or females, and young, has been shown to exist.

Westermarck's arguments both as regards the universality and the probably primitive character of the family have been widely accepted by anthropologists. Recently, however, his entire position has been fiercely attacked by Dr Briffault in a huge work of three volumes entitled *The Mothers*. Much to the amusement of those who knew Westermarck, he is depicted as a defender and upholder of moral theology, and, what is more serious, he is accused of distorting the evidence and of ignoring facts which do not fit in with his theories. Westermarck has written a lengthy rejoinder* to Dr Briffault, as he felt it 'a matter of honour with me to defend myself against false indictments that cast a stain on my character as a scientist and an honest seeker after truth'. He performs this task with a thoroughness which was to be expected, and no unbiased reader will have any doubt of his success. Dr Briffault's general position can only be stated here very briefly. He tries to show that the primitive human group was not the family nor an aggregation of families but the

* Cf. *Three Essays on Sex and Marriage.*

'motherhood', i.e. the biological group formed by the mother and her offspring, 'a group economically self-contained through the cooperation of brothers and sisters and one of which the sexual mate forms no partner.' The sexual instincts are, in his view, subordinate in primitive humanity to the deeper ties due to the maternal instincts and the bonds of sentiment connected with kinship. Nor is there a gregarious instinct as such. Gregariousness is derivative, being the effect of the offspring's dependence upon maternal protection. The group of mothers with their offspring form the clan, and the clan relationship is therefore more primitive than the family system of relationship. Individual marriage has an economic origin. Economic association between sexual partners has tended to establish individual sexual claims, and in the later stages of social development the betrothal of females has led to a retrospective restriction of sexual freedom and to the demand that the bride shall be a virgin. The paternal family begins to be important with the growth of private property, and the individual economic power of males and marriage acquires a social significance only when the paternal family has become a medium for the consolidation and transmission of private property. To establish his position Dr Briffault traverses the entire range of social anthropology, and at every point heatedly disputes Westermarck's interpretation of the evidence. He seeks to show that matrilocal marriage is a custom of 'almost universal distribution' in uncultured societies and that everywhere the paternal family has been preceded by the matrilocal family. He argues further that there is no known case of a primitive people insisting on prenuptial chastity except in societies which practise infant betrothal and marriage by purchase involving a high bride price; that there is no convincing evidence of the existence of monogamous institutions in any uncivilized peoples; that the existing cases of group-marriage and sex communism suggest that in their origin marriage regulations had no reference to individuals but to groups.

Anyone who takes the trouble of comparing Dr Briffault's

study and Westermarck's rejoinder will I think come to the conclusion that though the material used by both is often vague and ambiguous, Westermarck cannot rightly be charged with distorting the evidence in the interests of a preconceived theory, and those who knew him personally will only be strengthened in their admiration for his conspicuous candour and disinterestedness. It is obviously impossible here to examine the complicated problems raised in any detail. I have, however, in connexion with the work in which I collaborated with the late Professor Hobhouse,* had occasion to survey much of the evidence and will try to indicate my attitude to some of the points in this controversy. I can see no ground for believing that matrilineal descent everywhere preceded patrilineal descent. The evidence does not prove the maternal principle to be decidedly characteristic of the lowest culture, though it does suggest that the paternal principle becomes more prominent in the pastoral stage, while among agricultural peoples the two are nearly balanced. As to the precedence of the clan over the family, it appears that while the family is always found wherever the clan exists, there are cases of clanless tribes who nevertheless live in groups of families. Briffault's statements as to monogamy among primitive peoples are very sweeping. So far as the hunters and gatherers are concerned, it would seem on the evidence that monogamy is the prevailing practice, though not in most cases the strict rule. The evidence regarding prenuptial chastity is conflicting and extremely difficult to evaluate. But it does not seem to support the association alleged between marriage by purchase and prenuptial chastity; the most that can be said is that purchase tightens up a preexisting prohibition. The cases of alleged group-marriage and sexual communism are difficult to analyse, but on Dr Briffault's own showing there is in nearly every case some form of individual economic marriage alongside the relations which are permitted outside the narrow family. He has not, so far as I can see, produced any evidence of group-marriage in any strict sense, that

* *The Material Culture and Social Institutions of the Simpler Peoples*, by L. T. Hobhouse, G. C. Wheeler, and M. Ginsberg.

is, of a number of males married collectively and on equal terms to a group of females. In any event, I see no ground for believing that group-marriage was at any stage universal.

The last work in English to come from the pen of Westermarck is an impressive volume dealing with the influence of Christianity upon moral ideas and practices.* Here he restates the conclusions he had reached on the nature both of religion and morality, and considers in detail the effect that Christian teaching and practice has had on the institutions of the family, property, and economic organization, war and slavery, and the duties of regard for life and truth. In each of these spheres he produces an array of carefully sifted facts, and impressively challenges the claim so often made for Christianity that it has proved itself the highest ethical force in the history of man. Certain difficulties inherent, I think, in his outlook and method become here apparent. In accordance with his own relativistic ethics Westermarck should have confined his study of Christian morality to a record of the emotional responses of Christian societies to different classes of acts and of the feelings aroused in other societies by the behaviour of Christians. In fact, however, Westermarck does not impose this limitation upon himself, and his book abounds in value judgements for which general validity is claimed. A second difficulty arises from the fact that Westermarck's method does not enable us to disentangle and give due weight to the numerous factors involved in the history of civilization. If the advances in the direction of a more humane ethic cannot be attributed to Christianity alone, neither ought Christianity to be blamed for the backslidings, and there is much to be said for the view that often the most serious criticisms of Christianity have come from the Christians themselves. A parallel difficulty would, I think, be experienced by anyone who attempted to estimate the influence of rational thought on morals. Here too, alike in its failures and successes it would be difficult to disentangle what is due to thought as such, and what to the economic, political and religious factors with which it is interwoven. Despite

* *Christianity and Morals.*

these doubts, however, no one who reads the work can fail to be impressed by its massive erudition and the detachment with which a subject of profound emotional significance is here handled.

Westermarck has given a lively account of his work at the School of Economics and of his contacts with the students from all parts of the world who came to seek his guidance. Those who attended his seminars will always think of him with respect and affection and will recall his kindliness, his candour and tolerance, his singlemindedness in the pursuit of truth. In his own university in Finland he quite evidently exercised a profound influence. I should like to quote here a few words of appreciation from Eino Kaila, Professor in Theoretical Philosophy at Helsingfors University.

His greatest importance for many of his pupils lay, in my opinion, in the fact that he opened for us the world of English thought. For three centuries our scientific life had been completely under German dominance. Westermarck was the first, at least among the representatives of the philosophical faculties, to make himself thoroughly at home in the English language. This attitude of his became even more stimulating to us because he so splendidly developed the English tradition within the sphere of social philosophy. We admire in him equally the great scientist and the noble personality who devoted his whole life to those studies which are most essential to the advance of culture.*

Westermarck has on several occasions expressed his high appreciation of the contribution made by English thinkers to the study of society, but most emphatically perhaps on what must have been one of his last visits to this country. 'I am convinced,' he said, in concluding his Huxley Memorial Lecture given at the Royal Anthropological Institute in 1936, 'that there is no country in the world that can rival it in its achievements in social anthropology, whether pursued in the study or in the field, largely owing to its sterling qualities of lucidity and good sense.' English scholars will assuredly feel that of these qualities Westermarck's own work was a magnificent example.

* This comment was kindly sent to me by Westermarck's friend and pupil, Miss Agnes Dawson.

[8]

On the Diversity of Morals*

I SHOULD like to begin by referring briefly to the considerations which have influenced me in the choice of my subject. In the first place, it seemed to me that the variability of moral opinions was a highly fitting theme for a lecture devoted to the memory of T. H. Huxley. In the famous Romanes Lecture on *Evolution and Ethics*, delivered by him sixty years ago (Huxley 1893†), he showed, on the one hand, that the 'ethical process' could be conceived as a part of the general process of evolution, as part of the mechanism which nature employs to check or regulate the 'cosmic process'. He showed, on the other hand, that from our knowledge of the way in which moral codes may have evolved we can learn nothing about their validity; that we cannot move from the evolution of ethics to the ethics of evolution. This conclusion harmonizes very well with that which I propose to put before you, namely, that there is no necessary connexion between the diversity of morals and the relativity of ethics.

In the second place, I have been impressed by the increasing attention now being given by anthropologists – after a period of indifference – to ethical problems. Two sets of circumstances have, I think, contributed to this revival of interest, and both are highly relevant to my theme. Firstly, the fact that anthropologists are now often employed by governments and other agencies as advisers or consultants has made it very difficult for them to live up to the doctrine of ethical neutrality on which they, in common with other social scientists, used to pride themselves. It is becoming clear to them that in helping to shape policy they cannot confine themselves to a cold estimate of the consequences likely

* The Huxley Memorial Lecture, 1953.
† For such references see end of essay.

to follow from the various possible lines of action. They are bound, whether they like it or not, to take into consideration the worthiness of the ends to be pursued, and they soon find that ends and means cannot be dissevered and that it is not possible to abide by a division of labour which leaves the former to the statesman and the latter to the 'scientist'. In the second place, the attack on humanitarian values made by the Nazis has made the doctrines of ethical relativity, adopted more or less unreflectively by many anthropologists, emotionally untenable, and has forced them, as it has forced psychoanalysts and others who approach ethics from a naturalistic point of view, to examine their attitude to ethical problems afresh. Like other relativists they have to face the question whether it can really be the case that there is no rational way of deciding between the ethics of a Roosevelt and the ethics of a Hitler, and whether the moral indignation aroused by Nazi atrocities can really be intellectually on the same level as the contempt which the Nazis felt for what to them seemed the maudlin sentimentality of their opponents. 'It was', as Professor Robert Redfield tells us in a recent work (1953, pp. 145–6), 'easy to look with equal benevolence upon all sorts of value systems so long as the values were those of unimportant little people remote from our own concerns. But the equal benevolence is harder to maintain when one is asked to anthropologize the Nazis, or to help a Point Four administrator to decide what to do for those people he is committed to help.' The problem, in short, has to be faced whether the transition more or less unconsciously made from the fact that moral judgements vary to the doctrine that all moral judgments are relative, can be consistently maintained.

It is important to remember that historically the recognition of moral diversity has not always led thinkers to commit themselves to doctrines of ethical relativity. Thus Locke (1690), who was among the first to utilize anthropological data to illustrate the variability and contrariety of moral judgements, maintained that a science of morals was possible, possessed of the same certainty as mathematics. What he was interested in was to disprove the reality of 'innate moral principles'. To this end he tries to show that 'there is scarce that Principle of Morality to be named, or *Rule of Vertue* to be thought on (those only excepted, that are absolutely necessary to hold Society together, which commonly too are neglected betwixt distinct Societies) which is not, somewhere or other, *slighted* and condemned by the general Fashion of *whole Societies of men*' (*Essay* 1, iii, §10). But this did not mean that binding moral principles were not discoverable but only that they were not known innately. 'They lie not open as natural Characters ingraven on the Mind', and 'require Reasoning and Discourse, and some exercise of the Mind, to discover the Certainty of their Truth' (*Essay* 1, iii, § 1). Following this line of thought, it might be argued that the diversity of moral judgements affords no more proof of their subjectivity than the diversity of judgements regarding matters of fact throws any doubt on the possibility of valid scientific judgements about them.

The examples that Locke cites in support of his thesis are few and they have been repeatedly used ever since.* They are the killing of the aged and the sick and the exposure of infants. A much more elaborate compilation of varying moral codes is made from anthropological material by Herbert Spencer (1892, pp. 307–472). He, too, is concerned to disprove the theory of a universal moral sense. In harmony with his evolutionary theory he concludes that each society develops the kind of morals needed for its survival. We must accordingly expect a general correlation between social type and moral sentiments – a correlation which will be close in respect of conditions essential for survival, but less complete in matters such as temperance and chastity which need not directly interfere with the fundamental needs of social cooperation. The correlations are, however, not defined with any precision and, in any case, they are not employed by him to justify any extreme forms of ethical relativity. On the contrary, he thinks it possible to reach an 'Absolute Ethics', concerned with ascertaining

---

* His main authority is Melchissédec Thévenot's collection of travels, *Relations de divers voyages curieux*, of which some account is given in a chapter on the history of navigation prefixed to Churchill (1704, pp. lxxiv–lxxx).

necessary relations between actions and their consequences, and 'deducing from fundamental principles what conduct must be detrimental and what conduct must be beneficial' in an ideal society (Spencer 1892, 1, p. 58). From these principles Relative Ethics can derive in a more empirical manner the code applicable to actual societies.

From these and other cases that might be cited it is seen that there is no necessary connexion between the diversity and the relativity of morals. But before proceeding further, some definition of terms is needed. Ethical relativity may mean, in the first place, that moral value is relative to the subject asserting it or to the type of society in which it is commonly asserted. In both cases the implication is that there is no rational way of deciding between differing moral judgements and, indeed, that the distinction between true and false does not properly apply to them. But sometimes ethical relativity is used in another and very different sense to imply that what is right in one set of conditions may be wrong in another set of conditions, or to put it in another way, that in estimating the moral quality of an act the circumstances or situation in which it occurs must be taken into consideration. 'Relative' in this sense means related to surrounding conditions, and carries with it no necessary reference to subjectivity, or to the mental make-up of the person or persons judging. The two meanings are frequently confused when morality is said to be relative, and it will readily be seen that in so far as variations in moral judgement are due to differences in the circumstances or to differences in the moral import of acts under different circumstances, they cannot be used in support of ethical relativity in the sense of ethical subjectivity.

To determine the extent and the nature of diversity in moral judgements is a matter which presents great difficulties. Anthropologists seem usually to adopt Tylor's (1873, p. 706) minimum definition of morality as meaning 'a man's conformity to the customs (ἤθη, *mores*) of the society he belongs to.' But this is surely too narrow a definition. For morals must include not only the conventional code, but also the ideals which rise above the conventional and point to a good greater than has so far been achieved or required. Moreover, in all societies beyond the simplest and most homogeneous there is not one way of life but several ways of life which often conflict. In the moral system of Britain today there are many serious differences of opinion about fundamental moral issues. Thus some approve capital punishment, others condemn it. Some consider war between nations as a survival of barbarism and condemn it utterly; others distinguish between just and unjust wars. Some think that marriage should be indissoluble, others would grant divorce but differ on the grounds on which it might be allowed. Some approve of birth control, others think it abhorrent; and so forth. A similar situation is revealed every time any area or period is examined in detail. Morals never constitute closed systems, but contain divergent and conflicting elements derived from different sources, and they are liable to constant change by the action of rebels and innovators, the impact of outside forces and the slower processes of accretion and attrition. From this point of view it is a gross over-simplification to speak of 'the' morality of the Greeks, 'the' morality of the Romans or Egyptians, or of 'the' Christian or 'the' American way of life, as is often done in studies of comparative ethics.

It must be confessed that the encyclopedic surveys of morals attempted by such writers as Wundt (1912), Westermarck (1906), Hobhouse (1951), Sutherland (1898), Carveth Read (1909), and others are open to criticism along these lines. In their defence it should be remembered that they had not at their disposal the detailed monographs needed to give their conclusions a firmer foundation, and it is doubtful whether even now these exist in sufficient numbers to justify renewed attempts at a general synthesis. The reflections that I have to offer are in any event very tentative, and are based on what I have learnt from these writers and from the data that have been accumulated since their time. It seems to me that comparative study justifies the conclusion that the diversity in the actual content of morals is consistent with a measure of similarity in certain generic ethical relationships and with a certain unity of direction recognizable in the historical development of morality. Morality is universal in the formal sense that everywhere we find rules of conduct prescribing what is to be done or not to be done, or some conception of a good going beyond what is desired at the moment, in the light of which immediate impulse or desire is controlled. Behind this similarity of form there is considerable diversity of content. I would suggest that the variations may be provisionally grouped as follows:

1. Variations in the range of persons to whom moral rules are held to be applicable
2. Variations arising from differences of opinion or knowledge regarding the non-moral qualities of acts or their consequences
3. Variations due to the different moral import of the 'same' acts in different social situations and institutional contexts
4. Variations due to difference in emphasis or balance of the different elements in the moral life
5. Variations arising from the possibility of alternative ways of satisfying primary needs
6. Variations due to differences of moral insight and general level of development, moral and intellectual.

In what follows, I propose to give examples under each of these heads.

Firstly, there seems to be general agreement that within the primary group there is everywhere what Tylor called a 'natural solidarity', i.e., a measure of mutual forbearance, helpfulness and trust. Elementary duties, positive and negative, arising out of this solidarity are thus found to be everywhere recognized. On the other hand, the rules do not apply outside the group. As Tylor (1881, p. 412) pointed out, 'a man knew his duty to his neighbour, but all men were not his neighbours', or, as T. H. Green (1883, p. 220) later put it, 'It is not the sense of duty to a neighbour, but the practical answer to the question, "Who is my neighbour?" that has varied.' Tylor (1881, p. 413) remarks that 'In this simple contrast between one's own people and strangers, the student will find a clue to the thought of right and wrong running through ancient history, and slowly passing into a larger and nobler view. Some, indeed, like Boas (1929, p. 219) are led by these facts to deny the reality of any fundamental change in moral ideas. All that has happened, it is asserted, is that the same fundamental duties have been gradually extended to larger groups. But this hardly does justice to the history of moral universalism and especially to the ideas of equality and the intrinsic value of the individual as such. The quantitative extension of moral rules to wider groups is parallel with a change in the conception of the human person himself. It was a startling thing to say that free men and slaves have a common nature: *natura communis est.* This was not obvious to Aristotle and I think that A. J. Carlyle (1927, p. 8) was right in asserting, with reference to Cicero's summary of the principle of equality, that 'There is no change in political theory so startling in its completeness as the change from the theory of Aristotle' to a passage such as this.* So again, 'Thou shalt love thy neighbour as thyself' is in itself sufficiently remote from the conventional, but it must have come with a shock of surprise to be told that this includes the enemy and the stranger: 'Thou shalt not abhor an Edomite; for he is thy brother' (Deut. xxiii, 7), or to hear the words of the Buddhist teacher: 'For never in this world does hatred cease by hatred; hatred ceases by love; this is always its nature' (see Davids 1920, p. 128), or the words of Jesus: 'Love your enemies' (Matt. x, 44; Luke vi, 27). The work of the modern mind has been to link the moral universalism of

* The passage in question is as follows: 'For no single thing is so like another, so exactly its counterpart, as all of us are to one another. Nay, if bad habits and false beliefs did not twist the weaker minds and turn them in whatever direction they are inclined, no one would be so like his own self as all men would be like all others. And so, however we may define man, a single definition will apply to all. . . . For those creatures who have received the gift of reason from Nature have also received right reason, and therefore they have also received the gift of Law, which is right reason applied to command and prohibition. And if they have received Law, they have received Justice also. Now all men have received reason; therefore all men have received Justice' (*De legibus*, I, x, § 29, I, xii, § 33, Keyes ed., 1928, pp. 329, 333).

the spiritual religions with the philosophical idea of the essential rights of human beings and to find the appropriate institutional expression for equality and freedom. This vast and tortuous movement has involved not only an extension of sympathy but a deepened insight into the fundamental human relations. I agree with Hobhouse (1927, p. 186) that it is not true to say that there have been no discoveries in the ethical field. The notion of equality before the law in the sense of the impartial application of rules and in the sense of the equality of rights themselves, the various efforts that have been made to define rights and to universalize them, and the experiments that have been tried out to reconcile freedom with order represent achievements which should rank high in the history of thought. The embodiment of these ideals in a world order, overriding differences of race, nationality or class, is the work of the future. But that real progress has been made in this direction cannot be denied and the change in scale involves, it seems to me, a qualitative change in the moral consciousness.

The second group of moral variations comprises all those differences which are connected with the growth of knowledge or changes of opinion about the nature of acts and their consequences. Thus in our own time we find that the discovery of new facts gives rise to the application of recognized duties to situations hitherto not known as coming within their scope. For example, the discovery of the part played by microbes in generating disease extends our obligations of cleanliness and hygiene. Again, the Christian attitude to birth control may be changed by new knowledge of the conditions affecting maternal and infant health, or of the laws of heredity and the eugenic considerations arising therefrom, or by a fuller realization of the economic aspects of population policy. Another example may be given from the attitude to vaccination which may vary according to the answer given to the question whether vaccination does or does not prevent smallpox. In these and similar cases the moral differences depend mainly on differences of opinion about the facts and not about fundamental moral principles. In other instances the changes in moral outlook may be deeper in nature and give rise to genuine moral divergences difficult to resolve. The growth of psychological insight into the nature of personality has, for example, deeply affected our views of responsibility and this change, in turn, has been connected with real differences of opinion regarding the ethical basis of punishment, which will no doubt for long remain a matter of dispute.

Especially important in this connexion is the influence of religious beliefs. That this can be exercised in very different ways for both good and ill has been very fully shown by Westermarck and by Lecky among others. Here only a few examples can be given. The moral attitude to suicide was deeply affected by Catholic teaching, which brought it under the category of murder, and even declared it to be the worst form of murder. The act was considered as a particularly heinous defiance of God's will, aggravated by the fact that the individual deprives himself of opportunity to expiate it by repentance. Lecky points out that the influence of Catholicism was seconded by Muhammadanism, which on this as on many other points, borrowed its teaching from the Christian Church and even intensified it. Theological doctrines concerning the duties of resignation, the penal nature of death and the destinies of the soul thus brought about an attitude to suicide markedly different from that which prevailed in the non-Christian world. The treatment of the insane affords another instance of the influence of religious and magical beliefs on moral attitudes. Thousands were burnt as witches or heretics or else treated as criminals. In Europe it was not until the eighteenth century that their treatment began seriously to be humanized. We must agree with Westermarck (1906, 1, p. 274) that 'whatever share indifference to human suffering may have had in all these atrocities and all this misery, it is likely that thoughtlessness, superstition and ignorance have had a much larger share.'

The history of religious persecution affords another very interesting example. Leaving aside social and political factors, there can be no doubt that the doctrine of the guilt of error and of its infectious nature, together with the doctrine of the infallibility of the Church, served to justify acts of persecution which now seem the gravest moral aberration. In this case, as Lecky points out, a moral inference was drawn from propositions now unacceptable, but then assumed as theologically beyond doubt, namely that to hold certain beliefs is not only a heinous crime but one which by infection is liable to cause the eternal damnation of others. Granted these propositions, there was no moral difficulty in drawing the conclusion that the heretic should be put to death. The effect of the dogma of infallibility was to stifle and to pervert moral insight. The fact, however, that moral insight can be perverted no more establishes the impossibility of genuine insight in the sphere of morals, than the fact that such dogmas as infallibility were once unquestioned shows the impossibility of valid thought in other spheres of knowledge.

In the third group that I have distinguished I include variations attributable to differences in the general framework of life as between different peoples or periods of time, or within the same social system to differences in circumstances, which may give a different moral import to what at first sight appear to be the 'same' acts. In comparing moral codes we are apt to look for such rules as 'no fraud', 'no lying', 'no sexual excess', 'no aggression', 'no parental neglect', and the like. But it is obvious that such rules cannot be defined with precision or applied in practice without reference to context or situation. What is theft in one system of property, for example, will not be such in another. Such rules refer to the direct tendency of a class of acts considered in abstraction or isolation. When applied to a complex situation allowance has to be made for other tendencies which come under other rules. Thus to attack first is 'aggression' in peaceful conditions, but 'self-defence' to ward off suspected violence; to speak falsely to an invalid is not 'lying' if deemed necessary to avoid dangerous shock, and so forth. In these and similar cases we recognize, as we say, that 'circumstances alter cases.' But we are apt to forget this in comparing different peoples. Thus infanticide and senicide are 'murder' in our own society but may not be so regarded in the circumstances of primitive life. What is 'usury' at certain levels of economic development is 'legitimate interest' at another. So again self-redress is condemned in societies which possess a system of public justice but may be considered a duty where there is no regular public machinery for obtaining redress. In all such cases apparently similar acts have a different moral import if considered in their context.* It should be added that there is often a lag in development, so that practices persist despite changes in the circumstances. Adam Smith quotes in this connexion the case of infanticide, which continued to be tolerated in Greece at a time when there was no longer any real justification for it, and he complains that philosophers instead of condemning it, went out of their way to find plausible reasons for it. 'When custom can give sanction to so dreadful a violation of humanity', he adds (Smith 1853, p. 305), 'we may well imagine that there is scarce any particular practice so gross which it cannot authorize.'

I come now to the variations which arise from a difference in the emphasis placed on different elements in the good life or the urgency of different duties. In essentials the moral systems of the world show striking similarities. A list of virtues or duties drawn up by a Buddhist would not differ very greatly from one drawn up by a Christian, a Confucianist, a Muhammadan, or a Jew. Formally all the ethico-religious systems are universalist in scope, and their insistence on sincerity and the inward nature of virtue implies that for them goodness consists in doing what is right because it is believed to be right. But the formal resemblance is deceptive. The universalism is never thoroughgoing and is variously limited. Doing right because it is believed to be right may mean in one case because it is the will of God and that will may well be considered inscrutable; or it may mean because of the love of God, or because of the love of men, not so much because they are worthy of it, but because they are the objects of divine love and ennobled by the Incarnation; or again for

* This was pointed out very clearly by Dugald Stewart (1828, 1, p. 237).

prudential reasons because it would lead to beatitude in this or another world.

In content there are differences of balance or stress. Self-control may deviate into asceticism; the search for inward peace may lead to detachment from and contempt for the things of this world; the stress on love may mean that insufficient attention is given to justice; personal salvation may be sought at the expense of social well-being. Above all, moral systems differ enormously in the clarity with which they distinguish between ethical rules proper and ritual or ceremonial rules. The tendency of sacerdotalism is to invade all spheres of life and to turn every action into a rite. The effect is to blur moral distinctions, to substitute observance for moral discrimination and thus to encourage the growth of the arbitrary or rationally unfounded elements in the moral life. It is a mistake to think that in these respects the line of division is between east and west. There are similar divisions within each religion. In all there are to be found mystics and moralists, sticklers for the letter and for the spirit of the law, partisans of action and of contemplation. It should be remembered that it was Aristotle who thought that the greatest and most perfect happiness was to be found in a life of contemplation. On the other hand, it is in the *Gita* that we are told that action is superior to inaction and that the doctrine of speculation and the doctrine of action form but one science (see Janet 1884, p. 340).

In many instances the difference in emphasis can be readily explained. The duty of charity, for example, loses its primacy in an age in which the abolition of poverty by organized effort has become possible. The giving of charity to individuals may then even come to be deprecated as likely to divert attention from the need of a radical reconstruction of the system of property. In other instances the emphasis on particular virtues presents puzzling problems. It is difficult for us to understand the hold which the cult of virginity had over the mind of Christians in the fourth and fifth centuries, or why virginity came, as Harnack (1897, p. 128) tells us, to be considered 'the specifically Christian virtue, and the essence of all virtues'. Or consider an example of lesser importance: *'Above all things,* my brethren, swear not.' If, as Lecky (1899, p. 49), from whom I take this example, points out, this refers to the use of oaths in common conversation, 'how remote from modern ideas is the place assigned to this vice, which perhaps affects human happiness as little as any other that can be mentioned', and how interesting the fact that 'the vice to which this supremacy of enormity is attributed continued to be prevalent during the ages when theological influences were most powerful, and has in all good society faded away in simple obedience to a turn of fashion which proscribes it as ungentlemanly!' In our own day it is not always very easy to account for the remarkable variations in the depth of reaction of different types of offence against the moral code. The intensity with which we condemn 'unnatural' lust, fraud, treachery, pride, cruelty does not seem to be at all closely related to the degree of evil which the reflective conscience would find in each of these cases. Little attention seems hitherto to have been given by students of comparative morals to problems of this sort (Taylor 1930, 1, p. 194).

I come now to a further group of variations in morals which, I suggest, may be due to the fact that first order values may be combined in different ways to constitute second order values and that the same values may be thought to be attainable in different ways. Of this type of variations, sex morals afford interesting examples. In modern Western societies a number of values are implicitly or explicitly appealed to in justifying the monogamous family and the rules of sex morals associated with it. They include at least the following: the association of sex with enduring companionship and the fusion of sex with tenderness, the enhancement of the parental relationship through the common interest in the well-being and love of their children, the value to children of a stable affection and the feeling of security engendered thereby, the recognition of the partners as each an end in himself, and the value consequently attached to a form of union based on reciprocity and freed from possessiveness. These values are held to justify the monogamous family and the restrictions on extra-marital relations associated with it. In other societies, however, the primary values involved may well be recognized but in different combinations or clusters. 'Indeed, in Bantu society', we are told (Culwick 1942, p. 36), 'physical attraction, affection and companionship usually follow quite different channels, a man desiring his wife, loving his sister and seeking companionship among his male relations and friends.' Among the Bemba, Dr Audrey Richards (1940, p. 23) tells us, 'the pattern of married relations is one of economic and sex partnership, not of close companionship. In fact intimacy between husband and wife is laughed at.' So again we are apt to assume that the mental and physical well-being of children is best secured in the narrow unit of the Western family. But it may well be that children are no worse off in the extended family familiar in other societies, and, indeed, that they are better prepared to face the loss of the parents or their separation, if they are equally at home in a variety of houses and are protected and educated by a large circle of relatives. It is not even clear that the principle that individuals should always be treated as ends and never merely as means, necessarily and in all circumstances involves monogamy, as Kant and his followers think. Everything depends upon the way in which the rights or claims of the partners are balanced. In certain conditions polygamy may not be incompatible with reciprocity of rights, while in other conditions monogamy may fail to assure real equality.

If these considerations are borne in mind, it would appear that some of the variations in sex morals do not rest upon any radical differences in what I have called first order valuations. There need be no disagreement about the values of affection or companionship or the well-being of children, though there may well be different views about the way in which these values may be combined or about the regulations needed to achieve them. In the matter of pre-marital sexual relations it has been suggested (Crawley 1910, p. 480) that in checking early sexual indulgence 'a certain ideal seems to be unconsciously aimed at ... the prolongation of the period of growth', especially of the intellectual faculties. Very little seems to be known, however, of the relation between enforced retardation of the sexual life and general growth. Freud (1930, p. 74) has suggested that, psychologically, the efforts of society to repress sexual expression in children are intelligible if we remember that the control of sexual behaviour in the adult would have no chance of success if not begun in childhood. Freud, however, is obviously thinking of modern Western societies. In other societies the condemnation of pre-nuptial relations is by no means universal, but, as far as I know, there is no satisfactory explanation of the variations in this res-pect. So again, there seems to be no agreement about the rationale of the prohibitions of sexual relations or marriage between near kin. The explanations vary from those which appeal to the need of suppressing quarrels about sex within the family circle (Ben-tham, Ogden ed. 1931, p. 217) to those which resort to a deeply-rooted feeling of incompatibility between sexual intimacy and family relations of affection and respect (Montesquieu, Neu-mann ed. 1949, p. 282; Lotze 1885, p. 71; Hobhouse 1951, p. 146; Malinowski 1927, p. 251; Radcliffe-Brown 1950, p. 70). The lines of demarcation are very variously drawn, though it seems that the nearer we get to the closest relationships the more we approach a certain degree of uniformity (cf. Sutherland 1898, 11, p. 149).

Our discussion so far suggests that amidst variations moral codes everywhere exhibit striking similarities in essentials. There are no societies without rules of conduct backed by the general approval of the members. There are none which do not regard that which contributes to the needs and survival of the group as good, none which do not condemn conduct interfering with the satisfaction of common needs and threatening the stability of social relations. Indeed, the similarities are so great that they have led many investigators to doubt whether a case can be made out for moral development. Not to go back as far as Buckle, anthropologists like Boas (1929, p. 219) have argued, as we have noted above, that there has been no evolution of moral ideas, but only changes in conduct brought about by the enlargement of the group and an increasing social control. Others, slightly more cautious, would say that if there have been changes in moral ideas they have been such as naturally resulted from changes in the level or degree of complexity of conduct, connected with the enlargement of the area of human intercourse and the multiplication of contacts among people previously separated. In other words, it is argued that if there has been moral development at all, this has been brought about for the most part, not by distinctively moral causes, but rather by intellectual changes or by changes in economic and political conditions which have necessitated an extension of the scope of previous moral concepts and thereby led also to some change in their content (cf. Dewey 1927).

In dealing with arguments of this sort, the practical difficulty of isolating the distinctively moral factor in social development must be admitted. Everything concerned with the satisfaction of human needs and the ordering of human relations comes within the scope of morals which must therefore be affected by the general advance in knowledge and the problems set to it by changes in social relations. From this point of view the history of morals is part of the general theme of the changes in human culture. Yet, does not the argument cut both ways, can we not recognize the operation of moral factors in intellectual development itself? It was the moral attitude to authority and tradition that limited freedom of inquiry in the Middle Ages. Equally, the self-sacrifice and determination with which at the beginning of the modern epoch scientists defied authority implied a moral change in the attitude to truth (cf. Lange 1925, iii, pp. 246-7). No doubt the intellectual virtues were recognized in the ancient world, but the full moral implications of the search for truth – disinterestedness, self-criticism, respect for evidence and the determination to follow it wherever it leads however unpalatable the conclusions – were not realized until the modern period. Again the combination of the scientific outlook with the humanitarian spirit has brought into prominence the conception of rational self-determination and inspired the belief that man can by taking thought shape the course of future development. This has led to the recognition of a new duty – consideration for posterity. As Bury (1920, p. 347) points out, this extension of the moral code, though not much discussed in ethical treatises, has in late years been obtaining recognition in practice. It would be very difficult indeed to determine what in all this movement to-wards self-determination is intellectual and what moral. In short, new knowledge and new circumstances may help to generate new ethical demands, and on the other hand, ethical advance may be a factor in the growth of new knowledge.

It seems to me beyond dispute that despite a certain similarity in what may be called elementary rights and obligations moral codes differ very widely in the clarity with which the rights and obligations are conceived, the sanctions by which they are up-held and the area of conduct which they cover. In all these respects we may distinguish levels of development and in doing so we cannot escape value judgements, we cannot help regarding some as better than others. Whatever may be the case in dealing with other forms of social development, to describe moral deve-lopment is to evaluate.

As an example, let us consider briefly certain aspects of the history of the idea of justice and its concrete embodiments. There are certain common elements recognizable throughout. Its cen-tral core is the exclusion of arbitrariness and especially of arbitrary power. It takes shape first in the negative injunction not to hurt or obstruct others, and it moves slowly towards the task of securing an equitable or non-arbitrary distribution of the con-ditions required for the satisfaction of common needs. It is early recognized that 'justice is a kind of equality.' To exclude arbit-rariness, it is necessary to have rules and to apply them imparti-ally. 'Regard him whom thou knowest as him whom thou knowest not' is a maxim inculcated in ancient Egypt. In Deutero-nomy (i. 17) we are told, 'Ye shall not respect persons in judge-ment; but ye shall hear the small as well as the great'; and, it may be noted, this is said to apply to the stranger within the gate. The principle of the equal application of the laws among citizens is clearly recognized in Greek jurisprudence, and becomes an axiom of all legal systems. Yet impartiality in the administration of law involves neither universality nor equity. Early codes distinguish sharply between members and strangers and within the community there arise gradations of rights shading into rightlessness. The notion of impartiality before the law does not of itself suffice to decide what kind of rules should be thus impartially applied.

To carry the notion of equality in the sense of fairness further, it is necessary to specify a body of rights and obligations and this cannot be done without some reference to the ends of action. In the notion of a right or a duty, rule and end have to be combined. Rights are generalized claims to the conditions required for the realization of some good, e.g., the satisfaction of a need, the fulfilment of a capacity. They thus imply some conception of wellbeing. In the early formulations, however, the content of this conception remains vague. 'To give each man his due' and 'to hurt no one' are formulae for which wide assent may be claimed, but there are great differences in defining what is a man's due and what constitutes a hurt, and the definition will be deeply affected by distinctions of status. The Golden Rule, which is found in both its negative and positive form in most of the higher religions, carries the notion of fairness somewhat further. Yet it is generally considered by philosophers to be imprecise. It is not true to say that we ought to do to others only what we think it right for them to do to us, for there may be differences in the circumstances – and even in the natures of two individuals, A and B, which would make it wrong for A to treat B in the way in which it is right for B to treat A. The 'other' may not be satisfied with what we would want in his place, and what he wants may not be good for him or for the world. The real problem in equitable relations is to know what differences between individuals are relevant and what irrelevant in dealing with claims to differential treatment.

The problem is seen clearly by Aristotle (*Politics* III, xii, §1) in his discussion of distributive justice. Justice requires that 'persons who are equal should have assigned to them equal things' (Barker ed. 1946, p. 129). But equals in what? Clearly, he says, certain differences are irrelevant. People who have the advantage of a better complexion or greater stature are not thereby entitled to a greater share in political rights. Yet he thought that birth and wealth were relevant considerations and he saw no incongruity in this. The doctrine of the natural equality of men as taught by Stoics fared no better. It took two thousand years before it was applied explicitly to slavery, and it is still denied in the actual relations of many of the white peoples towards the coloured. It took as long to recognize that differences of sex have nothing to do with political rights.

The further development of the idea of justice or equity from the point of view from which I am considering it here, seems to have involved two things. Firstly, the notion of proportionate equality or as it may also be called the principle of relevant differences has been slowly extended from political to social and economic rights. Secondly, the notion of rights has been, so to say, socialized. There has been a movement from the conception of rights as inhering in individuals and limiting the law to a conception of rights as defining social relations and of law as based on rights so defined. In both respects the task is far from accomplished. Thus, for example, in the matter of economic rights it is generally recognized that inequalities of ownership or income require justification in terms of some relevant difference. But though the principle of a minimum is widely accepted, opinions differ whether distribution above the minimum should be proportionate to need, effort or productivity. Furthermore, the individualist conception of rights survives in the claims put forward for 'free enterprise' and in the attitude to such claims as the right to work. In its application to the relations between states the conception of rights is still largely in what may be called an 'individualist' phase. The 'rights of nations' are still interpreted as inherent in each nation or state independently of the rest, instead of being regarded as defining the relations in which states can live together in an international community.

So again, though the principle of the 'equality of states' is widely appealed to, very little has been done to define it in terms of what I have called relevant differences, either in reference to political rights, such as representation in international organs, or in reference to economic rights, e.g., migration or the distribution of raw materials.*

The trends here briefly indicated are suggested, of course, by the history of Western thought. Their influence, however, can be traced to all parts of the world, as can perhaps most easily be seen from a study of the contributions submitted by the non-European members of the Symposium on Human Rights organized by U.N.E.S.C.O. (1949). Everywhere the concern is ultimately with the liberation of personality and the equalization of the conditions under which different personalities may develop. Everywhere the problem is what can be done by organized effort to assure equal freedom in a common life. The answers differ in the way the different elements are balanced and according to the views taken of the means to be adopted, but they all move within a range of very similar ideas and they rest upon very similar scales of value.

Reviewing the movement as a whole, some will conclude that the essential principles of equity have always been known and that there has been no substantial development. Others will find irreducible variety. But surely there is identity as well as difference in the movement from the simpler rules of reciprocity of the pre-literate societies, the Golden Rule of the spiritual religions, and the doctrine of Natural Law, to the systematic efforts made in the modern period to define the rights of man and to universalize them. Despite constant change we can trace a certain persistent content and the modifications represent a true development; they bring out more fully something that was already suggested at an earlier stage. In this sense there is truth in the theory of Natural Law with varied content. There is a principle of growth recognizable in its varied manifestations.

We must now consider what bearing this survey of the diver-

* For further discussion see Ginsberg (1947, pp. 258 ff.).

sity of morals has upon theories of ethical relativity or, as the American anthropologists call it, cultural relativism. So far as I can see, ethical relativity is supported by two main arguments. The first is based on an analysis of the cognitive status of judgements of value and obligation. These are said to be 'emotive' rather than descriptive; they express not a characteristic of acts, but an attitude towards them favourable or unfavourable. 'This action is right' means 'I am favourably disposed towards actions of this type.' Now, it is argued, it is either true or not that certain individuals tend to have emotions, desires or attitudes in relation to certain classes of acts. But the desires, attitudes or emotions themselves cannot be either true or false; they are non-rational, and the question whether they are valid or not cannot arise. In one form or another, theories of this sort are now being widely discussed. I do not propose to examine them in detail. They seem to me to take an unduly narrow view of the range of valid experience. It is mere dogma to assert that no intuitions are important save those which have a sensory orgin or that verification is limited to the sphere of 'fact'. There is no doubt that moral experience contains elements of feeling and impulse, and without these moral judgements would be powerless to affect action. The question is whether there can be such things as rational impulses or rational acts of will, whether reason can play a role in clarifying and systematizing the ends of action, and this question is not to be dismissed at the outset by epistemological assumptions about the sphere of truth.

The second argument is based on the diversity or variability of moral judgements. If we all agreed about values, says Russell, we might hold that we know them by intuition. But disagreements in this field are much more frequent, he thinks, than in the case, say, of colours, and there is no way of convincing the moral deviant as there is of convincing the colour-blind person, that he lacks a power of discrimination which most men possess. Since there is no way of deciding by argument or evidence, the difference must be 'one of tastes not one as to the objective truth' (Russell 1935, p. 238).

Russell does not follow up this argument by an inquiry into the nature and extent of the observable differences of moral opinion or into the possibility of applying to moral judgements the same sort of criteria as are applied in dealing with judgements of sense perception, such as consistency, freedom from contradiction, and possible systematization. It is interesting to note, as we have seen, that neither Locke nor Spencer saw any necessary connexion between the diversity and the subjectivity of moral judgements but thought on the contrary that a science of ethics was possible. Dugald Stewart (1828, I, pp. 171 ff.) and later Lecky (1869, I, pp. 100 ff.), with a much greater command of the historical data, tried to show that if allowance is made for differences in knowledge of the nature and consequences of acts, differences of circumstances and historical conditions, the variations in moral sentiments and opinions are not such as to rule out the possibility of objectively valid moral judgements. Westermarck, himself a supporter of ethical relativity, has shown that in so far as differences of moral opinion depend on knowledge or ignorance of facts, on specific religious or superstitious beliefs, on differences in the conditions of life, and on what he calls 'different degrees of reflection,' they are not incompatible with the claim that universally valid moral principles are discoverable; though he believes that some of the differences, e.g. those concerned with the range of persons to whom moral rules are held to apply, confirm his view of the subjective nature of moral judgements (Westermarck 1932, p. 196).

Let us now see whether any light is thrown on this problem by the classification of variations in moral opinion that I have suggested above. The variations in my second, third, and fifth groups lend no support to the relativist view. They turn not upon any difference of moral principle but upon the application of the same moral principles to different situations, whether due to changes in circumstances or to changes in knowledge of the non-moral qualities of acts; or in the case of the fifth group, on the fact that primary moral requirements may be satisfied in different ways, or through different social institutions.

The remaining classes of variations, on the other hand, point to genuinely moral differences. In dealing with them, it should be pointed out that on the assumption that universally valid moral principles are discoverable such differences are to be expected. It would be very strange if a Congo pygmy, whose experience of social relations is limited to a group of about thirty or forty individuals, living in conditions of isolation, had the same insight into the nature and conditions of freedom as a modern European, or if a Trobriand philosopher – were one such to arise – showed the same skill in analysing the rules of reciprocity he finds in his society as that shown by Sidgwick in disentangling the moral axioms implicit in the common-sense morality of our own day. It is not a question of innate differences in intellectual faculty, but of the range and experience and knowledge and command of method, which must tell in dealing with moral as with other matters.

The variations included in my first group, namely those connected with the expansion of the range of persons to whom moral rules are held to apply, were held by Westermarck to support his view of the emotional nature of moral judgements. This expansion cannot in his view be attributed to any process of reasoning or refinement of moral insight, but to a widening of the altruistic sentiment due to the expansion of the social unit and the increasing intercourse between different societies. There can be no doubt, I think, that sympathy, in the sense of imaginative identification with others, has played an important part in the growth of moral universalism. Sympathy, however, is not a matter of feeling only but requires imagination, the power of seeing oneself in the place of the other and recognizing that the other is a person like oneself, and therefore includes a cognitive element. In any case, moral universalism cannot depend on kindliness or benevolence, which, I suppose, is psychologically always limited and discriminatory. One cannot love anybody and everybody with the same intensity, but one can recognize that there are certain things to which men are entitled whether we love them or not. This is a matter of moral intuition, which, however, can be deepened by enlargement of experience and increased insight into the essentials of human relations.

Next, it is not to be denied that opinions differ about the comparative worth of different goods or about their relations to each other. But this is to be expected. Our moral knowledge is not derived by deduction from some single certain principle. It grows with the growth of our moral experience and insight into the grounds of our choices and preferences, approvals and disapprovals. We learn slowly about human needs and capacities and the values attaching to their satisfaction or fulfilment. We certainly have not solved the problem of the comparability or commensurability of moral values. But this does not justify the conclusion that there are no standards of value or that our preferences are arbitrary or dependent on individual or racial constitution.

Finally, there are the variations in morals due to differences in the general level of mental development. The concept of levels of moral development is extremely vague and I shall try later to give it some precision. Here I confine myself to some observations on the relations between intellectual and moral development. Westermarck (1932, p. 215) was of the opinion that, compared with the progress of scientific knowledge, the changes of moral ideas appeared very small, and he gave as the reason for this that 'the changes of moral ideas have been no discoveries at all but have only been due to the more or less varying reactions of the moral emotions.' I wonder how psychology, anthropology, sociology, and political science would fare if judged by a similar test. The question is important because moral judgements necessarily contain factual components, and it may quite well be that advance in ethical thought has been hindered by the comparative failure of the social sciences to throw light on the relevant facts.

It is true that gifted seers have in the past penetrated to some of the essentials of man's moral nature by direct insight or intuition and may do so again in the future. But their maxims are, as we have seen, imprecise and require to be corrected and systematized, and this cannot be done without more pedestrian inquiry into human needs and the laws of social interaction. That ye love one another' will not solve the problems of war or economic depression; it may not even suffice to enable people to understand one another. The really difficult problems are those in which facts and values are interwoven. We may agree that to use violence against others is *pro tanto* evil, but this will not help us to determine the limits within which force may be rightly used. To do this we need to know whether the ends sought *can* be attained by force and cannot be attained in any other way. This leads to further inquiries into the efficiency of the appeal to reason, the indirect effects of repression, the importance of freedom for social cooperation. Very often in political morality the most perplexing problems are those which arise from the fact that the ends we set ourselves change in the process of their realization, and are apt to be distorted or perverted by the means used in attaining them. In dealing with questions of this sort, it is extremely difficult to isolate the purely moral factors, and further progress depends as much on fuller grasp or more refined analysis of the relevant facts as upon improved moral insight. In popular morality differences of attitude are often rooted in ignorance and distortion both of the relevant facts and the values and in confusions between them. Examples can readily be found in the attitudes towards race equality or sex equality. In both cases it is as difficult to obtain agreement about the facts as about the values.

The conclusions that emerge from this survey of the main types of variations in moral opinion and sentiment may be now briefly summarized. Firstly, morality is universal in the sense that everywhere we find a recognition, implicit or explicit, that conduct has to be controlled or guided by reference to principle. Secondly, in content moral systems vary greatly but the variations are far from arbitrary. The recognition that there must be rules does not suffice to tell us what the rules should be. These are arrived at slowly and gropingly and embody judgements of good and evil, ultimately traceable to primary experiences of value. These judgements are made at very different levels of insight and experience. The primary valuations may be combined in various ways to form higher order valuations and different peoples may find different ways of achieving similar ends. Hence it is not at all surprising that there should be considerable variation in the content of morals. But, thirdly, there is evidence of development in the sense of growth of insight into the nature and conditions of well-being made possible by a wider experience of human needs and capacities and of the conditions of social co-operation. Especially important in this connexion is the discovery of methods of reflection and analysis. This has made possible efforts at systematization and a measure of self-criticism and self-direction which are almost completely absent in the earlier phases of the history of morals. It follows from these considerations that in comparing different moral systems we should have, firstly, to elicit the primary experiences of value on which they are based. Since these relate to basic human needs, bodily and mental, they would probably be found much the same everywhere. We should have, secondly, to inquire how these primary values are combined to form higher order values and how these are embodied in the institutional framework. Here we should expect to find, and easily do find, much variation. Thirdly, in considering these variations we cannot but recognize differences of level. I doubt whether anybody seriously believes that all cultures are 'equally valid'. The question is what we mean by differences of level.

I think that the above discussion throws some light on the direction in which an answer is to be sought. It points to a number of characteristics which we probably have in mind obscurely in estimating differences of level.

To begin with, moral systems differ in the range or area of persons who come within the scope of the common good. As far as doctrine is concerned, the decisive step is taken by the higher religions which at their best are all universalist in outlook. The injunction to love all men, however, rarely means all men; and in any case, the general goodwill does not pervade the specific rules of behaviour, which are always limited in range of application. The rise of what may be called an international conscience as distinguished from a vague philanthropy, it has been well said, is a new thing on the earth (cf. Muirhead 1932, p. 307). The extent to which universalism has entered into the working codes of morality is therefore a good indication of the level of moral development.

In the second place, moral systems differ widely in the range or comprehensiveness of the experience which they embody. Morality changes with growing knowledge of human needs and capacities and experience of conflicts and their adjustment. Especially varied is the history of the way in which men learn to balance control and spontaneity, self-denial and self-fulfilment, personal good and social good, and in the adventurousness they show in the search for new values. In this connexion it is difficult, as we have seen, to isolate knowledge of fact from moral insight. But I do not see how anyone can deny that in both fields there has been advance both in range and depth of experience.

In the third place, moral codes differ in the extent to which the principles underlying them are brought to light, and in the degree of coherence and systematic connectedness between the parts. The study of any system of morals always reveals inconsistencies and contradictions, as is shown for example by Sidgwick's (1907, pp. 337 ff.) analysis of the 'commonsense morality' of his day. Philosophers, of course, have given a good deal of attention to the general principles of morals. But the disrepute into which 'casuistry' has fallen has brought it about that little attention is given to the 'middle principles' and to the ways in which these are applied to the detail of life. The result is that the systematization of morals compares very unfavourably with that achieved in the sphere of law. In this respect, too, there must be differences between different systems of morals.

A fourth point in defining level of development is the differentiation of morals from religion and law. The way in which the sphere of law is demarcated from the sphere of morals is of special importance, since it involves an answer to the question, what can be left to the individual and what requires enforcement by the machinery of the law. The extent to which societies resort to coercion seems to me to be perhaps the best general index of the level of moral development.

Finally, moral systems may be judged by the extent to which they permit or encourage self-criticism and self-direction. In the more complex societies social forces are deliberately manipulated and change is consciously directed. Hence, from the ethical point of view, the part that is played by objective and disinterested thought in the shaping of public policy is of the greatest importance. Could we but find a way of estimating the influence of changes in moral outlook upon legislation in different societies, we should have an important index of the level of development.

In all this I have assumed a rationalist ethic. The tests that I have employed – comprehensiveness, systematic connexion, articulation of principles and assumptions, objectivity, and disinterestedness – are tests of rationality in general. They would no doubt be considered inappropriate by those who consider that morality is outside the domain of reason. Those who take this view would, however, have to dismiss the concept of levels of development as devoid of meaning.

Relativist theories are at their weakest in dealing with change and development. They hover between moral nihilism and complete *Gleichschaltung*, and in order to escape they invariably resort sooner or later to principles to which on their assumptions they are not entitled. Those who think that moral judgements express attitudes, emotions, or desires tend to be individualistic in their approach, though, as they point out, there are many desires or attitudes which are common to all the members of a group, and may even be universal. When desires conflict, however, the decision rests with the individual. He need not necessarily decide in accordance with the prevailing norms. Thus Russell (1949, p. 109) insists that 'If a man seriously desires to live the best life that is open to him, he must learn to be critical of the tribal customs and tribal beliefs that are generally accepted among his neighbours.' On what basis he is to criticize is not clear. From the way in which Russell handles particular social problems, as distinguished from the logical analysis of moral

Judgements, it is clear, however, that he does not really believe that desires are beyond the domain of reason. Thus, for example, in dealing with sex ethics he explains that the morality which he advocates does not consist in telling people to do what they like. 'There has to be consistency in life; there has to be continuous effort directed to ends that are not immediately beneficial and not at every moment attractive; there has to be consideration for others; and there should be certain standards of rectitude' (Russell 1929, p. 243). A rationalist need hardly ask for more.

It is sometimes thought that a solution of this problem may be found in the principle of 'equal freedom'. Each person, it is assumed, prefers to conduct his life as he chooses. If, however, people were willing to concede an equal right to other people each to conduct his own life as he chooses we should have a higher order principle – i.e., a preference for freedom of preference – which could be appealed to quite independently of the content of particular desires or preferences. This, however, not only begs the question, but is quite insufficient in practice. Though each person may prefer to live his life as he chooses – and there are many who prefer others to decide for them – it is certainly not true that each is prepared to give equal freedom to others, and I do not see how on relativist grounds anyone can be refuted who prefers to coerce those who differ from him. But even if the principle of equal preference were accepted, it would soon prove insufficient. No individual can give equal weight to all his desires, and to decide between them, he has to consider and compare the values of the objects desired. Similarly, disputes between individuals cannot be decided intelligently without discussing what the dispute is about, apart from the desire of each to have his own way. People may agree not to interfere with each other, but they have to decide what constitutes interference, and this is not possible without some conception of a common good or general well-being.

While for the individualists it is man, the individual, who is the measure, for cultural relativists it is society that is the measure: morality consists in conformity with group-norms. But here again principles are allowed to creep in which go beyond the prevailing norms, or else the court of appeal is not the actual but an ideal group. An interesting example is provided by the theory of cultural relativism advocated by Professor Herskovits (1948, pp. 76-7). Cultural relativism, he says, 'is a philosophy which, in recognizing the values set up by every society to guide its own life, lays stress on the dignity inherent in every body of custom, and on the need for tolerance of conventions though they may differ from one's own.' The lesson this philosophy teaches is that of mutual respect: 'Emphasis on the worth of many ways of life, not one, is an affirmation of the values in each culture.'* The principle is admirable, though it requires careful definition. But it certainly does not follow from cultural relativism. From the fact that each people believes in the validity of its own values, it does not follow that it believes in the values of other peoples, or in the principle that differing value systems all deserve of respect. It is far more likely that each will claim superior excellence for itself. The principle of respect for other cultures can only be binding within the cultures that accept it and cannot consistently with relativist theory claim general validity. Even so, the difficulty reappears. For even within such cultures, there is no general or widespread agreement about the values of other cultures, and to claim validity for the principle is therefore, on relativist assumptions, only to express the preference of a particular philosopher.

Relativists generally stress the great diversity of morals. Yet the similarity is far greater. Westermarck – himself, be it noted, a relativist – concluded on the basis of his elaborate survey that 'the moral rules laid down by the customs of savage peoples ... in a very large measure resemble the rules of civilized nations' (Westermarck 1932, p. 197), and, so far as I can judge, later anthropological work strongly confirms his conclusion. The higher religions converge in their teaching of the inward nature of morality and the universality of love and its obligations. The

* For criticism of this view see Bidney (1953, pp. 689–94).

philosophers, after the manner of their trade, emphasize their differences from each other.* But in their accounts of the good for man they move within a restricted circle of ideas – happiness, wisdom, virtue, fulfilment. These are, except on superficial analysis, interrelated, and taking large stretches of social life. none can be attained or maintained without the others. It is the rationalist assumption, at any rate, that these elements of the good life are combinable, and one of the aims of a rationalist ethic is to reduce as much as possible the physical and social conditions that separate them.

Yet, as we have seen, the differences of views are no less real. There are different opinions about the comparative worth of different goods, or on their order of priority in different circumstances, including the comparative disvalue of different evils, different views about the relations between freedom and control, and between the requirements of personality and the common life. It is not always easy to see whether, in dealing with these problems in the form in which they arise in our own day, it is deeper moral insight or fresh moral principles that are required, or a more consistent application of known moral principles and fuller knowledge of the relevant facts. Thus in connexion with the institution of property, it may well be that the differences of opinion arise not so much from disagreement about the principles of distributive justice, as from our ignorance of the psychology of motivation and of the effects of the different possible ways of reducing inequality upon the total productivity. In the case of the moral attitude to war, the divergence of views cuts deeper; for here we are faced with a choice of evils and certainty in such a matter is hard to come by.

In conclusion, I should like to make a few further comments on the notion of levels of moral development. In connexion with the first of the criteria that I suggested, above, namely the expansion of the range of the persons to whom moral rules are held to apply, it should be remembered that the test is not intended to be purely quantitative. It is not only a question of the number of

* For a brief review see Read (1909, pp. 21 ff.).

persons belonging to other groups than one's own who come within the scope of the rules, but also of the kind of consideration that is given to their needs and claims. This can be estimated not only by the degree of readiness to respond to the cry of distress anywhere in the world, but by changes in the moral character of political relations, e.g., in the attitude to the 'right' of conquest, in the willingness to resort to arbitration in case of disputes, or to bear in mind the needs of would-be migrants in considering laws restricting immigration.

The test of coherence and systematic connectedness has to be applied in conjunction with the test of comprehensiveness. For a system may be internally coherent and yet clash with other systems. In such a case the conflict can only be resolved within a wider system which includes and reconciles the claims and interests of both systems.

The test of differentiation of morals from religion and law may raise doubts. As regards religion, I have in mind mainly the distinction between moral rules and ritual rules, which as far as I can see has everywhere been connected with deepening of moral insight. As to law, the important point is the emergence of the distinction between inward and outward sanctions. Systems in which law, religion, and morals are fused tend to regulate every detail of life and thus to leave little scope to individual initiative.

Finally, the part played by objective and disinterested thought in the shaping of policy and the remoulding of institutions is a test which in a sense includes all the others. For objective thought necessarily involves appeal to the test of comprehensiveness, systematic connexion, and articulation of principles and assumptions, and cannot proceed far without self-criticism and the ability to distinguish between subjective and objective factors of belief. The value of a moral system depends not only on the clarity and objectivity of the concepts it uses, but on the extent to which objective and disinterested thought is allowed to influence conduct in the various spheres of economic and political life. Judged in this way, there are unmistakable differences of level as between the pre-literate societies and the societies of the ancient and modern world, and as between the different societies within the modern world. The concept of levels of development involves a distinction between higher and lower and it is the higher that decide that they are the higher. But this, I fear, cannot be helped.

REFERENCES

Barker, Ernest (ed.), 1946, *The Politics of Aristotle*, trans. with Introduction, Notes and Appendices by Ernest Barker (Oxford: Clarendon Press)

Bidney, David, 1953, 'The concept of value in modern anthropology', in *Anthropology Today*, ed. A. L. Kroeber, pp. 682-99 (Chicago: University of Chicago Press)

Boas, Franz, 1929, *Anthropology and Modern Life* (London: Allen & Unwin)

Bury, J. B., 1920, *The Idea of Progress* (London: Macmillan)

Carlyle, Sir R. W. and A. J., 1927, *A History of Mediaeval Political Theory in the West*, 6 vols. (1903–36), 1 (2nd ed., 1927), by A. J. Carlyle (Edinburgh and London: Blackwood)

Churchill, Awnsham and John (eds.), 1704, *A Collection of Voyages and Travels*. (1st ser.) (London: Churchill)

Crawley, A. E., 1910, 'Chastity (Introduction)', *Encyclopaedia of Religion and Ethics*, ed. James Hastings, 12 vols. (1908–21), III, pp. 474–90 (Edinburgh: Clark)

Culwick, A. T., 1942, *Good Out of Africa*, Rhodes-Livingstone Pap., no. 8 (Livingstone, N. Rhodesia: Rhodes-Livingstone Institute)

Davids, T. W. Rhys, 1920, *Buddhism*, new. ed. (1st 1877) (London: Macmillan)

Dewey, John, 1927, 'Anthropology and ethics', in *The Social Sciences and Their Interrelations*, eds. William Fielding Ogburn and A. A. Goldenweiser, pp. 24-36 (Boston, Mass.: Houghton Mifflin)

Freud, Sigmund, 1930, *Civilization and its Discontents*, Int. Psycho-Anal. Lib., no. 17, trans. by Joan Riviere of *Das Unbehagen in der Kultur* (Wien, 1929) (London: Hogarth Press and Institute of Psycho-Analysis)

Ginsberg, Morris, 1947, *Reason and Unreason in Society: Essays in*

Sociology and Social Philosophy, Publ. Lond. Sch. Econ., New Gen. Ser., no. 1 (London: Longmans)

Green, Thomas Hill, 1883, *Prolegomena to Ethics*, ed. A. C. Bradley (Oxford: Clarendon Press)

Harnack, Adolph von, 1897, *History of Dogma*, 7 vols. (1894–9), III, trans. from 3rd German ed. (1894) by James Miller, Theol. Trans. Lib. (London: Williams and Norgate)

Herskovits, Melville J., 1948, *Man and His Works: The Science of Cultural Anthropology* (New York: Knopf)

Hobhouse, L. T., 1927, *Development and Purpose*, new (2nd) ed. rev. (1st 1913) (London: Macmillan)

Hobhouse, L. T., 1951, *Morals in Evolution*, 7th ed. (1st 1906) with new Introduction by Morris Ginsberg (London: Chapman and Hall)

Huxley, Thomas H., 1893, *Evolution and Ethics* (Romanes Lecture, 1893), reissued in *Collected Essays*, 1893–4 (London: Macmillan)

Janet, Paul, 1884, *The Theory of Morals*, trans. Mary Chapman (Edinburgh: Clark)

Keyes, Clinton Walter (ed.), 1928, *Cicero: De republica, De legibus*, ed. with English trans. and Introductions by Clinton Walter Keyes, Loeb Class. Lib. (London: Heinemann)

Lange, Friedrich Albert, 1925, *The History of Materialism*, trans. (1881) Ernest Chester Thomas, 3rd ed. with Introduction by Bertrand Russell, Int. Lib. Psychol. (London: Kegan Paul)

Lecky, William Edward Hartpole, 1869, *History of European Morals from Augustus to Charlemagne* (London: Longmans)

Lecky, William Edward Hartpole, 1899, *The Map of Life: Conduct and Character* (London: Longmans)

Locke, John, 1690, *An Essay Concerning Human Understanding* (London: Thomas Bassett)

Lotze, Herman, 1885, *Outlines of Practical Philosophy*, trans. by G. T. Ladd of *Grundzüge der praktischen Philosophie* (2nd ed., Leipzig, 1884) (Boston, Mass.: Ginn)

Malinowski, Bronislaw, 1927, *Sex and Repression in Savage Society*, Int. Lib. Psychol. (London: Kegan Paul)

Muirhead, J. H., 1932, *Elements of Ethics*, 4th ed. (1st 1892) (London: Murray)

Neumann, Franz (ed.), 1949, *The Spirit of the Laws* by Charles de Secondat, Baron de Montesquieu (1st ed., Genève, 1748) trans.

(1751, rev. J. V. Prichard 1878) J. Nugent, ed. Franz Neumann, Hafner Lib. Class., no. 9 (New York: Hafner)

Ogden, C. K. (ed.), 1931, *The Theory of Legislation* by Jeremy Bentham, trans. (1864) from French of Etienne Dumont by Richard (properly Robert) Hildreth, ed. with Introduction and Notes by C. K. Ogden, Int. Lib. Psychol. (London: Kegan Paul)

Radcliffe-Brown, A. R., 1950, Introduction to *African Systems of Kinship and Marriage*, eds. A. R. Radcliffe-Brown and C. Daryll Forde, pp. 1-85 (London: Oxford University Press for International African Institute)

Read, Carveth, 1909, *Natural and Social Morals* (London: Black)

Redfield, Robert, 1953, *The Primitive World and its Transformations* (Messenger Lectures, 1952) (Ithaca, N.Y.: Cornell University Press)

Richards, Audrey I., 1940, *Bemba Marriage and Present Economic Conditions*, Rhodes-Livingstone Pap., no. 4 (Livingstone, N. Rhodesia: Rhodes-Livingstone Institute)

Russell, Bertrand, 1929, *Marriage and Morals* (London: Allen and Unwin)

Russell, Bertrand, 1935, *Religion and Science*, Home Univ. Lib. (London: Thornton Butterworth)

Russell, Bertrand, 1949, *Authority and the Individual* (Reith Lectures, 1948-9) (London: Allen & Unwin)

Sidgwick, Henry, 1907, *The Methods of Ethics*, 7th ed. (1st 1874) (London: Macmillan)

Smith, Adam, 1853, *The Theory of Moral Sentiments*, new. ed. (1st 1759) with Memoir of Author by Dugald Stewart, Bohn's Stand. Lib. (London: Bohn)

Spencer, Herbert, 1892-3, *The Principles of Ethics* (London: Williams and Norgate)

Stewart, Dugald, 1828, *The Philosophy of the Active and Moral Powers of Man* (*Collected Works*, ed. Sir William Hamilton) (Edinburgh: Black)

Sutherland, Alexander, 1898, *The Origin and Growth of the Moral Instinct* (London: Longmans)

Taylor, Alfred Edward, 1930, *The Faith of a Moralist*, ser. 1 and 11 (Gifford Lectures, 1926-8) (London: Macmillan)

Tylor, Edward B., 1873, 'Primitive society', part 1, *Contemporary Rev.* 21, pp. 701-18

Tylor, Edward B., 1881, *Anthropology* (London: Macmillan)

UNESCO (ed.), 1949, *Human Rights: Comments and Interpretations*, Introduction by Jacques Maritain (London and New York: Allen and Wingate)

Westermarck, Edward, 1906, *The Origin and Development of the Moral Ideas* (London: Macmillan)

Westermarck, Edward, 1932, *Ethical Relativity*, Int. Lib. Psychol. (London: Kegan Paul)

Wundt, Wilhelm, 1912, *Ethik*, 4th ed. (1st 1886) (Stuttgart: Enke)

9

Reason and Experience in Ethics*

THE subject I have chosen for my address is closely related to the problems which occupied Comte's attention throughout his life. With Comte I believe that ethics has to be firmly rooted in our knowledge of human nature and human history, and, like him, I believe that the concept of the growth of *humanitas* – of man's humanity to man – is of fundamental importance in the interpretation of morality. At the same time I take a somewhat different view from that of Comte as to the relations between the empirical and the rational elements in theory and practice, and I believe, further, that the concepts or categories that ethics requires are *sui generis* and not reducible without remainder to those employed in psychology or sociology.

I should like to begin by dwelling a little on Comte's way of handling ethical problems. Ethics, it will be remembered, is not given a separate place among the six fundamental sciences in Comte's earlier writings. But this is not really surprising. In a sense the whole of his work is ethical in character and inspiration. Of Spinoza, Novalis has said that he was a God-intoxicated man. Of Comte we may say, with J. S. Mill, that he was a morality-intoxicated man, 'that with him every question is one of morality, and that no motive but that of morality is permitted.'† In the later writings this is formally recognized, ethics being placed at the head of the hierarchy of the sciences and indeed regarded as *'la science par excellence'*, at once the most comprehensive and the most useful.‡

Following the requirements of the positivist method, Comte finds a basis for ethics in the science preceding it in the hierarchy,

---

* Auguste Comte Memorial Trust Lecture, 1956.
† *Auguste Comte and Positivism*, p. 140.
‡ *Catéchisme Positiviste*, 1852, *Deuxième Entretien*.

namely biology, or as we should now say, psychology. Man, in his view, is incorrectly defined as a rational animal. The preponderating power in human behaviour belongs not to the intellect but to the instincts and emotions. The intellect can of itself prescribe no ends of action. It has no energy of its own and is moved to action only by the instincts. All it can do is to help us to choose the best means to any ends that we wish to achieve. Furthermore, the egoistic, or self-regarding, instincts are much more powerful than the social or other-regarding. Nevertheless, in the course of history the altruistic tendencies gain ground, strengthened by the greater command which the intellect gives man over his passions and the increasing insight which it makes possible into the needs of others. The fundamental law of human evolution consists according to Comte in the 'growing ascendancy of our humanity over our animality, brought about by a double process, namely the increase in the power of the intellect over the instincts and of the other-regarding instincts over the self-regarding'. From all this Comte concludes that altruism – the principle 'live for others' – is the basic principle of morals. In adopting it men will be furthering the order which a study of human development discloses as the dominant trend of human history. If it be asked why we should trouble to seek that which would in any case be reached spontaneously, the answer is that this spontaneous order is liable to various disturbances, and that these can to some extent be controlled by deliberate intervention. It is part of Comte's doctrine that the greater the complexity of any order, the more does it admit of modification. Social phenomena, being the most complex of all, are not only most easily liable to perturbations, but also the most open to rational control. His theory is thus not completely deterministic. Within limits much can be done to change the speed and intensity of social processes. Positive knowledge of the laws of social life would therefore enable us to control human development, just as knowledge of the laws of physical science gives us power to control natural forces. The function of a positivist ethic is to systematize and to bring into consciousness ends which have been working themselves out unconsciously in the course of man's struggle with the forces of nature.

It will be seen that in arguing thus Comte lays himself open to the criticism which, as we shall see, Hume made of all systems of morality, namely that they move imperceptibly from statements of what is, or is not, to statements of what ought, or ought not, to be. If Comte's account of mental functions be accepted, the intellect has nothing to say about the ends of action. It can only act as the *'ministre'* of the natural propensities. It is true that Hume's famous maxim: 'Reason is and ought to be the slave of the passions, and can never pretend to any other office than to serve and obey them' is restated by Comte in a manner which gives reason a somewhat higher status. *'L'esprit doit être le ministre du cœur, mais jamais son esclave.'* The question remains whether this 'ought' is a deliverance of the intellect or of the heart. Possibly this dichotomy would not be accepted by Comte. He suggests that if we were more intelligent, we should also be more moral, and if we were more moral, we should also be more intelligent. His point is that positive knowledge would bring home to men the intimate connexions which bind them to each other and to the whole, and so would strengthen the altruistic feelings. There is truth in this, but we need hardly to be reminded that positive knowledge can be used also in the service of selfish ends. If, then, as Comte seems to think, the intellect is of itself asocial and amoral, there is no rational ground for preferring the benevolent to the selfish affections. In any event benevolence cannot be the whole of morality. Comte notes that 'we can only desire for others that which we desire for ourselves.' But if this 'can' is to be translated into 'ought', does not then the question arise of what we ought to desire for ourselves? Butler pointed out that 'People may love themselves with the most entire and unbounded affection, and yet be extremely miserable.'* So it may be suggested that the love of others, though of the greatest importance in overcoming selfish exclusiveness, will not of itself solve the problems of social life.

* *Works*, vol. II, p. 190.

Both in regard to self and others, we need to know what objects are by their nature adapted to afford satisfaction, and on what principles the means to afford such satisfaction are to be distributed. If there is to be an intelligent desire for the well-being of others, we need to know the nature of the values that constitute such well-being.

It may well be that in his approach to ethical problems Comte sinned against his own method. The important thing in positivism is the refusal to rely on purely dialectical or, as Comte put it, metaphysical, arguments. Concepts, so the positivist insists, should be continually referred back to the experiences which they interpret. Their value lies in their power to relate or connect the different parts of the empirical order. They have no validity independently of all reference to experience. From this I think it follows that we are not entitled to impose limitations on the range of experience in advance. It may well be that there are different sorts of experience, including aesthetic and moral experiences, referring to contents other than those we call 'facts'. The analysis of experience leads us to distinguish between judgements of facts and judgements of norms or values. If so, the function of positivism in morals is not to reduce morals to facts, but to insist that value judgements should be treated 'positively', i.e. referred back to the experience in which they are rooted, with the understanding that none should be treated as above criticism or as requiring no corroboration or support from other experiences. It is a condition of 'positivity' in moral inquiries to distinguish between judgements of fact and judgements of value. It is no mark of positivity to deny at the outset the reality of the experiences which are the basis of value judgements. These distinctions are blurred in Comte's treatment, as they are also in more recent forms of positivism.

It is not my task here to attempt any general estimate of Comte's achievement. I share fully the admiration felt for his great effort at sincere and constructive thinking by Mill, Morley, George Eliot, Spencer, Bridges, Hobhouse, and, more recently, Gilbert Murray. I have pointed to some difficulties I find in his ethical views, but these in no way diminish the importance of his contribution. It is true, as he urges, that morality is the result of a long process of development, that it has its roots in human nature. It is true that morality is self-authenticated and self-justified, and in need of no supernatural sanction. It is true that benevolence and sympathy are essential to morality, even if they do not exhaust its entire nature. It is true that to serve mankind is a worthy ideal, even if humanity be no god. Finally, whatever view we form of the theoretical coherence of his system, there can be no doubt of the great part he played in the humanitarian movement. I should like to cite in this connexion the verdict of Whitehead, which I have quoted elsewhere.[*] In discussing the intellectual movements led by Bentham and Comte he says: 'Most of what has been practically effective, in morals, in religion, or in political theory, from their day to this has derived strength from one or other of these men.'[†]

I can now return to my central theme which is concerned with the relations between the empirical and the rational elements in ethical theory. Unfortunately the words 'reason', 'rationalist', 'rational', like the word 'positivism', are highly ambiguous and emotion-laden. In religious discussions 'rationalism' has come to be contrasted with rationality. Rationality is, so to say, logically neutral; it signifies the submission of beliefs to the test of reason without prejudice to the outcome. Rationalism, on the other hand, has a polemical implication. It is used as a war-cry by those who attack theological dogma in the name of reason[‡] and as a term of reproach by the defenders of religious beliefs. To the latter rationalism signifies not the use of reason but the use of pseudo-reason – crude, unimaginative, lacking in real insight. On both sides the usage is vague and it would hardly be profitable to explore it further.

[*] Cf. my *Essays in Sociology and Social Philosophy* (Heinemann, 1947), vol. I, ch. XIII.

[†] *Adventures of Ideas*, p. 46.

[‡] 'Rationalism is the mental habit of using reason for the destruction of religious belief' (A. W. Benn, *The History of English Rationalism in the Nineteenth Century*, 1906, vol. I, p. 4).

The terminology is far from clear even in the more technical philosophical discussions. The term 'rationalist' is sometimes used to refer to thinkers, if any such there be, who believe that the world can be made intelligible by 'pure' reason without resort to experience. In less extreme form it also includes those who think that the human mind is possessed of or can discover certain necessary and universal principles in the light of which the data of experience can be organized. There are differences of opinion as to the nature of these principles. Some, following Kant, regard them as transcendental, that is implicit in experience, applicable only to what is experienced, but not themselves derived from experience. Others leave the question of the nature of these principles open, but still believe that they can be used in synthesizing the data supplied by experience. By contrast the term empiricist is used to refer to those who with varying degrees of consistency derive all principles, including first principles, from experience, this being frequently considered as in the last resort sensory in character.

The matter is further complicated by the use of yet other terms, namely intuitional or intuitionalist. These terms also have many different meanings, but they have something in common. They refer to forms of knowledge taken to be immediate, direct, and self-evident. It is usual to distinguish between perceptual and rational intuitions, according as the object apprehended is a sensory particular or a general principle, such as an axiom. But in either case, the apprehension is supposed to be unmediated, neither requiring, nor permitting of, proof. When rationalism is contrasted with intuitionism, I take it that the rationalist point of view is based on an unwillingness to rely on self-evidence as a test of truth. The feeling of certitude is, for the rationalist, no guarantee of certainty. Hence he refuses to take the self-evident as an isolated datum and insists that it should be subject to criticism and correction in the light of other judgements or other products of experience and thought.

These distinctions reappear in the history of ethical theory. Here too there have been rationalists, intuitionists, and empiricists, in much the same sense as in the theory of knowledge. The empiricist finds the data of moral experience in feelings of approval and disapproval, or in desires, or in attitudes. Thereupon may follow either psychological analysis of the ways in which these are built up into more complex constellations, or else an inductive inquiry may be undertaken to discover the common features in the objects or activities that call them forth, or the two procedures may be combined as, for example, in the work of Hume. The intuitionist approach appeals to a direct and immediate apprehension, as contrasted with mediate, discursive, or argumentative knowledge. The apprehension may refer to a particular situation, as in the various forms of the Moral Sense schools, or to general principles, as in the case of the rational intuitionists. In either case the experience is supposed to yield a sort of insight, whose deliverances are evident in themselves and independent of each other.

The varieties of ethical rationalism are much more difficult to characterize. They have, perhaps, this in common, that they all maintain (a) that ethical statements claim to be valid, i.e. are subject to rational tests, and (b) that the knowledge of right and wrong has conative force, i.e. is capable of influencing, if not necessarily determining, action. In further analysis it may be convenient to make use of the classification of ethical theories into those which start from the concept of good, value, or end, and those which stress the concept of obligation, rule, or law. Thus there may be a rationalism of ends or a rationalism of principles. There are, of course, links of connexion between the two conceptions, but they represent, nevertheless, different ways of looking at the general problem of morality.

As far as the value theories are concerned rationalists maintain that reason helps us in arriving at right judgements about ends as well as means and that its function is not exhausted in finding the best means to ends otherwise determined. The opposite view has the support of Aristotle among the ancients, and of Hume among the moderns, and many psychologists in recent times have taken it for granted that reason has nothing to do with the choice of ends. Nevertheless, this restriction of the role of reason has very little in its favour. It is true that in our daily activities we take many ends as given, and are concerned only to find the best means to them. But even on a prudential level, we have to compare different inclinations with one another or with more inclusive interests. On the moral level qualitative differences between ends become all-important. We soon find that we know very little about the nature of many of the ends we value. Thus we value freedom. But it is not a meaningless question to ask why, or rather what it is in freedom that we value. A good many of our difficulties arise from the failure to distinguish between ends desired for their own sake and ends whose value is instrumental. You may say that all men seek happiness, but as the moralists of all ages have informed us they frequently look for it in activities wherein it is not to be found. Given an agreed end, we often have to consider whether it is worth the cost. In other cases we have to choose between different goods or, what is even more difficult, between greater and lesser evils. Again, we may have to inquire whether different ends are compatible, whether, for example, liberty is compatible with equality, or liberty in one sphere with liberty in another. Surely these are matters for sensitive insight and methodical scrutiny. In reply, it will be said that what is intended is not that we do not reflect about ends, but that our reflections about them can never terminate in demonstration, that our doubts about them cannot be resolved by the same sort of inquiry as we undertake in deliberating about means. In this there is some truth, but it does not justify the assertion that ends fall outside the scope of reason.

It remains to be added that those who hold that reason has nothing to do with the choice of ends may have a rationalism of their own. A good example is to be found in Lord Russell's ethical theory as recently expounded by him. Though he thinks that the ends of action are given by desire, and that the basis of moral judgements is to be found in emotions of approval and disapproval and the feeling of enjoyment, he claims, nevertheless, that it is possible to build up a theory of ethical propositions 'which are true (or false) in the same sense as if they were propositions of science'.*

In theories which stress the conception of rule or law rather than that of good or end, rationalism also appears in different forms. The most important example is still that presented in Kant's ethical theory. His procedure consists essentially in an analysis of moral experience designed to bring out the presuppositions which make it possible, or in other words to discover the *a priori* elements in morality. Whether Kant applied his own method consistently has been much disputed. It has been argued that in drawing a sharp distinction at the outset between inclination or desire on the one hand, and will and the practical reason on the other, and further in insisting on the moral irrelevance of the consequences of acts, he has not elicited his principles from, but rather imposed them upon, experience.

But Kantian exegesis is notoriously difficult. It may well be that what he was trying to do was not to extrude desire, but rather to provide a principle for choosing among different desires. What is of abiding importance in his contribution is the insistence that in deciding what we may rightly will, we must take into consideration what others besides ourselves may will, and that this concern for others is in principle universally applicable to all men as 'ends in themselves'.

Thus interpreted, the Kantian ethics has its points of contact with other forms of rationalism, which start from a different view of the relations between desire and the practical reason, and which seek to avoid the suggestion that the practical reason is independent of the desires and rules over them, so to say, from above. In these other forms of rationalism the conceptions of rule and end are combined and considered in their mutual relations. The principles of morals are conceived as determining the conditions in which ends ought to be pursued or avoided, and the ways in which the means to human well-being should

* *Human Society in Ethics and Politics*, 1954, p. 116.

be distributed among different persons. The task of a rational ethic is to elicit these principles from our moral experience and to define and clarify them.

The term 'reason' is unfortunately still used in many different senses. Sometimes it is taken, as it was by Hume, to cover the whole range of cognition. Sometimes it is restricted to the drawing of inferences from propositions taken as established, sometimes to the *a priori* element in knowledge, or to the knowledge of what is universal and necessary. It is not always distinguished from intelligence which in its turn is vaguely defined. There seems, however, to be a growing agreement among psychologists to use 'intelligence' for the capacity of apprehending relations between characteristics, especially relations not immediately obvious to direct perception. The term 'practical' intelligence might then be used to cover apprehensions of relations in the sphere of conduct, e.g. relations of ends to each other or between means and ends. The term 'practical reason' has been traditionally used by philosophers for reason in its application to moral conduct. By Kant, however, it is distinguished from the 'understanding' as being concerned with the unconditional or absolute, and in this special sense it is used by him both in reference to the speculative and practical spheres. The trouble with all this is that we tend to reify these abstractions and to pit them against other abstractions such as the conative tendencies. The important thing for the rationalist is to insist that it is the whole man who thinks, wills, and acts, and that there are many desires or volitions which are only possible at a certain level of cognitive development. The rationalist attitude carries with it two further implications. One is that reason has a directive or normative function, in other words, that it is capable of integrating the data of sense to yield valid knowledge, and that in the sphere of action it has the power and authority to evaluate and guide or direct. The second implication is that reason is common to all men, that both in the sphere of theory and of practice other experiences besides our own must be considered and that where there is disagreement there is something in each man to which appeal can be made in the hope of arriving at a solution acceptable to all.

Critics of rationalism have for the most part relied on arguments developed with great force by Hume. Their main drift is summed up by Hume in a famous passage:

> In every system of morality which I have hitherto met with, I have always remarked that the author proceeds for some time in the ordinary way of reasoning, and establishes the being of a God, or makes observations concerning human affairs: when of a sudden I am surprised to find, that instead of the usual copulation of propositions, *is* or *is not*, I meet with no proposition that is not connected with an *ought* or *ought not*. The change is imperceptible, but it is, however, of the last consequence. For as this *ought* or *ought not* expresses some new relation or affirmation, 'tis necessary that it should be observed and explained, and at the same time, that a reason should be given, for what seems altogether inconceivable, how this new relation can be a deduction from others which are entirely different from it.*

A similar point is made by H. Poincaré:

> If the premisses of a syllogism are both in the indicative, the conclusion also will be in the indicative. For a conclusion to be in the imperative, it is necessary for at least one of the premisses to be in the imperative. Now the principles of science are always in the indicative. . . . It follows that however subtly a dialectician can play with his principles, combine them or reshuffle them as he may, whatever he gets out of them will be in the indicative. He will never obtain a proposition which says: 'do this', or 'do not do that'; that is a proposition confirmed or contradicted by morality.†

These arguments have been restated by others in many forms and with no less vigour. But as directed against a rationalist approach to ethical problems they do not appear to be formidable. There are four points I should like to make about them. Firstly, it is true that the moral cannot be derived from the non-moral, and that 'practical conclusions' cannot be drawn except from 'practical premisses'. But, secondly, this so far from

* *Treatise*, III, pt. I, i.   † *Dernières Pensées*, 1913, p. 225.

being denied, is what is asserted by rationalists. They begin by distinguishing between judgements of fact and judgements of value, and insist that moral experience has its own distinctive and irreducible characteristics. The task of rational inquiry is not to create morality or derive the moral from the non-moral, but to examine the moral judgements that it finds, to elicit the assumptions latent in them and the categories employed by them and to discover whether any fundamental principles can be formulated whereby actual morality might be made more coherent and systematic. Thirdly, although moral judgements cannot be reduced to judgements of fact, a knowledge of the relevant facts is of the greatest importance for the study of morality. We need fuller knowledge than we possess of human needs and potentialities and in particular of the ways in which the means to their fulfilment, including the modes of distribution, are likely to affect the ends and ideals aimed at. Finally, morality must be considered as undergoing development both in the individual and the whole human race. This development is highly diversified, and in its course both the excellences and the weaknesses and corruptions of human nature become manifest. If the rationalist case is to be sustained, it must be possible to distinguish between higher and lower forms of development in accordance with rationally acceptable criteria. In what follows I propose to discuss these points a little more fully.

It may be remarked to begin with that, in accusing all previous moral systems as deducing moral relations from relations entirely different from them, Hume overstated his case. His charges hardly apply, for example, to Aristotle or Spinoza. In different ways both these thinkers held that there was an intimate connexion between conation and cognition, and that every stage in the development of the mind has its proper quality of feeling and desire, and that there was such a thing as rational desire. This, I think, is also the lesson of modern comparative psychology. But if reason can penetrate the field of desires, then moral relations do not have to be traced back to relations 'entirely different from them'. They arise in the course of the transformation of man's animal nature brought about through the correlated growth at once of his passions and of his intelligence.

However strong Hume's case was in relation to his predecessors, his strictures have no relevance at all as against such a rationalism as that of Kant. Obviously Kant was not deducing the moral from the non-moral. He starts with the experience of moral obligation as a given fact, and tries to discover its presuppositions and underlying principles, just as in dealing with knowledge generally he does not doubt that there is such a thing as valid knowledge and is concerned to bring out the *a priori* conditions which make it possible. As he explains in the Preface to the *Critique of the Practical Reason*, 'it is not the business of the philosopher to invent new rules of conduct, as if the whole world before him was ignorant of what duty was and waited for him to discover it.' But he adds: 'Whoever knows of what importance to a mathematician a *formula* is which defines accurately what is to be done to work a problem will not think that a formula is insignificant and useless which does the same for all duty in general.'* Pareto was fond of pointing out that while people of different civilizations or regions or philosophies conformed to much the same rules, the explanations they offered for the rules differed widely. 'A Chinese, a Moslem, a Calvinist, a Catholic, a Kantian, a Hegelian, a Materialist, all refrain from stealing; but each gives a different explanation for his conduct.'† It followed, he thought, that the explanations were mere 'derivations'. But this misconceives the function of ethical theories. The theories do not create the norms which they set out to explain. They are inferred from the particulars shown to exemplify the norms and can have no greater truth than these. If, indeed, we found that an ethical theory led to conclusions which did not encourage truth and honesty, or advocated selfish indulgence at the cost of public good, we should suspect that there was something wrong with the theory rather than the maxims inculcating honesty and public service.

But if value judgements are self-justifying and not reducible to

* Abbot's translation, p. 93.
† *The Mind and Society*, ed. A. Livingston, vol. III, p. 897.

or deducible from judgements of facts, it does not follow that a knowledge of the relevant facts is not of the greatest importance in the study of morality. On the contrary, many of the central problems of morals turn upon questions of fact, and this remains true, I think, whatever view be accepted of the logical character of what may be called the primary or first-order judgements of value or obligation. If actions are judged by their tendency to promote an end or ends, then a knowledge of the conditions in which such end or ends can be attained is of vital importance. If the quality of an action is supposed to be known by direct intuition, or by reference to a rule intuitively known to be binding, then a detailed knowledge of the situation is still needed, since every concrete situation will reveal different qualities and may come under different and possibly conflicting rules. Clearly what is ethically obligatory must be psychologically and sociologically possible. There cannot be principles of morality irrespective of the condition of human nature, as it is or might be.

Moral maxims are sometimes stated in the form of statements of fact. Such is the Buddhist teaching: hatred does not cease by hatred, but by love alone. But this passes readily into the injunction: 'Let a man overcome anger by love, let him overcome evil by good.' In Spinoza's *Ethics*, prop. XLVI, the injunction to repay hatred with love is supported or 'proved' by an appeal to psychology. 'Hatred', we are told, 'is increased by reciprocated hatred and, on the contrary, can be demolished by love in such a way that hatred is transformed into love.' Hence 'he who lives under the guidance of reason will endeavour to repay another's hatred with love, that is nobleness.' There is a similar intermingling of psychology and ethics in such maxims as 'Force is no remedy', 'Evil cannot be overcome by evil', 'Love cannot be commanded'. In these cases moral intuition depends upon and presupposes an intuitive grasp of human relations which, on occasion, is later confirmed by the more pedestrian methods of scientific observation and analysis.

Descending from these heights to the ordinary or everyday rules of morality we find that the facts involved are taken for granted.

Maxims such as those which are given in the Decalogue or similar tables lay down the elementary conditions of group-survival
easily seen as such. Examined in detail, however, they are seen to
presuppose a particular set of institutions. 'Thou shalt not steal'
means 'thou shalt not violate the laws of property.' The prohibition of adultery presupposes the family institution based on marriage. When these institutions themselves are challenged the facts
required are no longer readily available and philosophers begin
to dispute about their 'true' ends or functions. Thus, for example,
private property, i.e. some power of exclusive control over things,
is defended or justified on the ground that it is a necessary condition for the growth of personality. Stated generally this is plausible. But how much property is so necessary, and what degree of
control? Neither the psychologist nor the sociologist can answer
this question.

An interesting example of the difficulties involved is to be found
in the way philosophers have handled the problem of sexual purity
or chastity. The need for a sociological and psychological basis
is most evident in the Utilitarian approach. Sidgwick, for example,
finds two grounds for current sexual morality: 'the maintenance
of a certain social order, believed to be most conducive to the pros-
perous continuance of the human race; and secondly, the protection of habits of feeling believed to be most generally important
to their perfection or happiness'. But he notes with great candour
that these beliefs are a mere *anticipatio mentis* awaiting empirical
verification. We have not sufficient sociological knowledge to show
what amount of sexual licence is incompatible with the maintenance of the population in quantity and quality. Nor do we know
to what extent the 'lower' kind of sexual regulations are likely to
interfere with the development of the 'higher'. Elsewhere he suggests that as far as legislation is concerned restrictions on the free
union of the sexes should be considered from a single point of
view: 'in respect, that is, of their tendency to secure the provision,
control and training of children until they are old enough to become ordinary members of an individualistic community.'* The

* *Elements of Politics*, 1897, p. 57.

end aimed at being the maintenance of such permanent unions as are necessary for the proper rearing and training of children, the fundamental rule is that which directly secures conjugal fidelity. Other rules can be deduced from this requirement. If marriage is to be adequately protected, all extra-nuptial intercourse of the sexes must be condemned; otherwise men would not have adequate motives to incur the restraints and burdens which marriage entails and the young would form habits of feeling and conduct which would unfit them for marriage.* While for Western societies there may be sufficient evidence of a rough empirical kind to justify these assertions, we cannot pretend that either psychology or sociology is sufficiently advanced to enable us to decide what sort of regulations are most likely to serve the ends in question.

The intuitionist approach to the problem of sexual morality seems at first sight to dismiss all reference to consequences as irrelevant. The decisive argument according to Dean Inge, for example, is 'that sexual transgressions defile the soul'.† If this is not merely another way of saying that defilements defile, the implication must be that extra-nuptial relations are a hindrance to the development of the higher faculties of the mind. If so, it becomes a question of fact what kind of sexual 'irregularities' have this effect, and in what degree. Similar remarks apply to the position of the Ideal Utilitarians such as Rashdall. According to him the prohibition of sexual indulgence outside the monogamous family can be stated in the form of a judgement as to the ultimate value of an end. 'It is a state of feeling which is pronounced to be of intrinsic value – a state of feeling which the clearest moral insight and highest spiritual experience of the race have decided to be incompatible with sexual indulgence outside a relatively permanent monogamous marriage.'‡ Rashdall's statement can be extended to include other intrinsic values linked with monogamous marriage. Among these are the following: the association of

* *Methods of Ethics*, 1890, pp. 329, 448.
† *Christian Ethics and Modern Problems*, 1931, p. 95.
‡ *Theory of Good and Evil*, 1924, vol. I, p. 197.

sexual satisfaction with enduring companionship and tender relations, the enhancement of the parental bond through common
interest in the well-being and love of the children, the value to
children of a stable affection and the feeling of security engendered thereby, the recognition of the partners as each an end in
himself, and the value attached to a form of union based on reciprocity and freed from possessiveness. These values are held in
Western societies to justify monogamous marriage and the restrictions on extra-nuptial relations associated with it. Whether in
other societies or under different conditions the same values might
be otherwise satisfied, and to what extent they are actually satisfied in Western societies, are evidently matters for psychological
and sociological inquiry.

The importance of exact study of the factual components of
ethical judgements becomes obvious when we consider practical
questions about which men disagree. Ignorance or distortion of
the relevant facts frequently results in false value judgements,
while, conversely, ingrained and uncritically accepted value judgements as frequently lead to distortion of the facts. Conspicuous
examples are disagreements about sex or race equality. These are
of special interest because there is some evidence which suggests
that psychological and biological inquiries into the nature of sex
and race differences and more particularly into the relative importance of hereditary and environmental factors are having some influence on public opinion and the shaping of policy. I am not
suggesting that ethical differences would necessarily all disappear
when the relevant facts are better known. But I have no doubt
that the area of disagreement would be reduced and that, at the
very least, there would be a better chance of discovering what
the disagreements are about.

It seems then that the function of reason in morals can be stated
partly in terms favoured by Hume himself. According to him the
office of reason in morals is twofold: 'either when it excites a
passion by informing us of the existence of something which is a
proper object of it; or when it discovers the connexion of causes
and effects, so as to afford us means of exerting any passion.' These

two would cover what I have called the factual components of moral judgements. But there is a third which Hume refused to admit, which concerns the value-components proper, namely to discover the inner structure of ideals, their relations to each other, and the degree to which they are liable to be affected by the means used to attain them. The relations thus discovered are not deducible from the facts. They may be none the less 'real', in the sense of being apprehended by moral insight, clarified by analytic reflection and generalized by intuitive induction, much in the same way as relations within the field of sensory experience are judged to be real when they satisfy the tests of rational investigation required in that domain.

I come now to what from the rationalist point of view presents the greatest difficulty, namely the fact that moral codes differ, and that the feeling of obligation can and does attach itself to much that cannot justify itself when brought to the test of reason. In order to meet this difficulty it is necessary to study the actual development of morality and to inquire whether, behind the diversity of codes, general principles are discoverable which are implicit in all of them and which come increasingly to be recognized as universally binding. Such a study of development, it should be observed, does not commit us in advance to any such metaphysical view as that of Hegel or T. H. Green, who regard development as the manifestation or unfolding of a spirit who eternally 'is all which the human spirit is capable of becoming'.* It does not seem to be necessary to assume that the ends to which mankind is tending are already realized in their fullness in the mind of God, or even that any mind is in possession of an idea of a completed morality. Empirically regarded, development does not suggest the working out of a completed idea. It looks rather like a series of groping efforts towards ends which change in character in the process of their realization. What the ends are can only be discovered, as Green himself saw, through an analysis of existing usage and law. This is not to say that morality is nothing but a residuum from the past. On the contrary it is continually under-

* T. H. Green, *Prolegomena to Ethics*, 1884, p. 198.

going change, and in this change reason contributes its part, as it itself grows and develops in and by the material that experience provides.

The lines of moral development have been traced in considerable detail in the encyclopedic surveys of Hobhouse, Westermarck, and Wundt. Their results are largely congruent, despite an initial difference of philosophical outlook. They agree, I think, in stressing the growing importance of the reflective or rational element in morality. They show how moral judgements have gained in detachment, generality, and impartiality, and how rational standards have slowly but increasingly taken the place of magical fears, blind aversions and approvals.

Following their lead I have elsewhere examined the conception of levels of moral development and have suggested criteria which we probably have in mind when we distinguish differences of level.* Moral systems may, I think, be compared on the basis of the following five closely related but distinguishable criteria, namely differentiation or the emergence of a distinctively moral attitude, universalization of moral judgements, scope or comprehensiveness of moral experience, systematic connectedness and articulation of principles, and capacity for self-criticism and self-direction.

By differentiation I understand the process through which there emerges the notion that goodness is self-sustained and independent of external sanctions. This is not to be identified with the notion of duty for duty's sake. There is moral goodness also in the love of truth for its own sake, or in kindly feeling, or in the steady effort to lessen the sum of human suffering. The process of differentiation can be followed in the complicated history of the relations between morality, religion, and law. Leaving aside the simpler, we can see that among the more highly developed peoples moral rules tend increasingly to free themselves from religious sanctions and to claim autonomy. In modern thought ethics come to claim not only independence from theology but

---

* 'On the diversity of morals', *Essays in Sociology and Social Philosophy*, vol. I, ch. VII.

even primacy. So far from being based on divine authority, moral and other values come to be regarded as data constituting the most important evidence for the reality of the divine. Formerly no one hesitated to correct a moral judgement by a religious text. In our own day religion itself is weighed in the balance of the ethical judgement, and to show that a religious creed is incompatible with the demands of justice would tend to throw doubt not on the morality but on the creed.

The growth of a distinctively moral attitude was greatly facilitated by the distinction that came to be drawn between ritual rules and moral rules. This distinction between ceremonial performances expected by Gods and actions which are thought to affect the well-being of human beings seems everywhere to have been connected with a deepening at once of moral and religious insight. The history of the struggle thus arising is familiar to us in the case of Judaism and Christianity, but analogous developments can be observed in other religions. In India, for example, ritualism has for long predominated, but according to Indian observers significant changes are now occurring.* In Muhammadanism tremendous importance is attached to ceremonial observances. But from time to time rigid formalism has called forth protests from minds with deeper moral insight.†

Whether the emergence of the distinction between ceremonial holiness and moral purity is to be regarded as a contribution of morals to religion, or conversely a contribution of religion to morals, is a question I will not pursue. It remains that as a result an inward morality of character and intention slowly takes the place of a merely conformist morality of outward performance. Traces of this change can be found as far back as the Egypt of the Middle Kingdom. 'More acceptable is the nature of one just of heart than the ox of him who doeth iniquity' – a really notable anticipation of the saying in the *Mahabarata*, 'If a man be intemperate or lustful, of what use his penance, of what use his sacri-

---

* Aiyer, Sir Siraswami, *The Evolution of Hindu Moral Ideas*, 1935, p. 181.
† Ameer Ali (Syed), *The Ethics of Islam*; R. Levy, *The Sociology of Islam*, 1933, vol. II, ch. II.

fice',* or of the 'I will have mercy and not sacrifice' of the Hebrew prophet. The emancipation of ethics from theology and the emphasis on inward sanctions may also be followed in the history of Chinese life and thought, and, in another form, in Buddhism.

On the legal side, the secularization of the law may have contributed to the differentiation of morals by removing from the category of criminal or punishable actions matters of belief, such as atheism, heresy, or schism, or the non-performance of religious rites as well as, for example, certain sexual offences. The important thing from the angle of moral differentiation is the emergence of a distinction between a sphere of acts whose value depends on their being freely performed and a sphere which it is felt cannot be safely left to individual choice. The level of moral development, from this point of view, depends upon where the line is drawn between the sphere of law and the sphere of morals, and upon the nature of the sanctions by which moral and legal rules are upheld. Systems in which law, religion, and morals are fused tend to regulate every detail of life and thus to leave little scope for individual initiative.

In the second place, moral systems differ in the extent to which moral judgements are universalized. This can most easily be seen by determining the range of persons to whom moral rules are held to apply. Elementary duties, arising out of what Tylor called 'natural solidarity', are found everywhere. But the rules in earlier stages do not apply outside the group and the group itself may be very restricted. With the increase in the size of groups the range widens, but, unfortunately, distinctions arise within it. There emerge different moralities for the classes within society, and different loyalties on the basis of subordination replace the rudimentary equality or reciprocity of the earlier phases. On the whole, however, there is a widening of the sympathies, a growth of altruism, as Comte showed, and a recognition that, in principle, moral rules are universal in scope.

In theory the decisive step is taken by the moral codes associated with the higher religions. Tenets of universal love have been

* E. W. Hopkins, *The Ethics of India*, 1924, p. 235.

laid down by Chinese, Hindu, Buddhist, Jewish, Stoic, Christian, and Muhammadan teachers. Quite apart from obvious limitations in practical application it is, however, difficult to determine how far universalism went even in intention. Confucian writers, for example, inculcate benevolence to mankind in general. But from the nature of their historical position, it is hardly likely that they had the whole of mankind in mind. Even in the Christian world the unity of mankind often meant the unity of Christian mankind. It is not until the modern period that the effort is made to give concrete expression to the conception of a law binding all mankind and applicable to man as man. Group-morality persists in all moral systems, but with variations in extent and degree. On the whole, the notion that moral rules are universalizable gains ground and arbitrary differentiation comes increasingly under attack.

Thirdly, moral systems differ in comprehensiveness. By this is meant not the range of persons to whom the rules are applicable, just discussed, but rather the scope of the needs and values to which the moral consciousness is sensitive. Thus at different times and among different peoples there are wide variations in the scope of loyalty, courage, benevolence, or truthfulness or respect for self and others. The higher systems find room for spontaneity and control, self-fulfilment and self-denial, personal and social good. Richer in content, they are more sensitive and differentiated in response. They vary greatly in the way they deal with conflicting claims and diverse interests, their openness to new values and their attitude to the rebel and innovator.

The fourth criterion is the degree of coherence or systematic connectedness and the extent to which the underlying principles are made explicit and articulate. Every known moral system contains a mixture of elements of varying consistency and coherence. Witness the mingling of intimidation and correction, retribution and reparation, in each of the penal codes of the world, or the difficulty of eliciting or formulating the ethical principles inherent in the property systems, or the methods of determining rewards for services. Contradictions and incompatibilities invariably come to light as soon as any effort is made to disentangle the principles underlying the working code. Systematic connectedness and articulation of principles are thus mutually dependent.

The importance of systematic connectedness may be easily overstressed. Philosophers have been in search of a final good or *summum bonum* to which all other ends are subordinate, or a single rule or principle from which the detailed particulars of morality can be deduced, or at least to which they can be related. It is questionable whether such unification is logically required. I have a good deal of sympathy with J. S. Mill's criticism of Comte in this connexion. To Mill, Comte's effort after system seemed to be the result of an original mental twist very common, he thought, in French thinkers, 'of an inordinate desire for unity'.

That all perfection consists in unity, Comte apparently considers to be a maxim which no sane man thinks of questioning. It never seems to enter into his conceptions that anyone could object *ab initio*, and ask, why this universal systematizing, systematizing, systematizing? Why is it necessary that all human life should point but to one object, and be cultivated into a system of means to a single end?*

The history of morality discloses a plurality of ideals and there seems little reason for thinking they are reducible to unity. This is not to deny the importance of coherence and consistency. Perhaps what ethics needs is a principle analogous to what J. M. Keynes has called the *Principle of Limited Independent Variety*. In its application to scientific investigation this principle requires 'that the objects in the field, over which generalizations extend, do not have an infinite number of independent qualities, that, in other words, their characteristics, however numerous, cohere together in groups of invariable connexion, which are finite in number.'† So it may be that in a given way or form of life not every combination of rules is possible. Societies are not organisms, but they have sufficient organic character to necessitate a measure

* *Auguste Comte and Positivism*, p. 141.
† *A Treatise on Probability*, p. 256.

293

of consistency and mutual support among their parts. In this way, for example, the rules governing the relations between the members of a family are closely linked with the rules governing the distribution of property, and the ideals relating to the one institution have to be accommodated to the ideals relating to the other. But this does not preclude a great deal of variety within any one form or way of life, or as between different ways of life.

To survey the various efforts at systematization would be to undertake an encyclopedic task. Here I am only concerned with salient points. In the early stages of development, morality is unreflective. The rules imposed by custom are accepted as binding, and it does not occur to anyone to question their validity. To the anthropologist the various rules may seem to be functionally interconnected. But the connexion is not present to the people concerned and there is no attempt to discover underlying principles. In the higher stages systematization is most easily seen in the growth of legal systems, which in part, at any rate, reflect the growing moral sense of the community. Apart from the work of the lawyers, we find in most societies a succession of teachers and prophets who, from time to time, draw up lists of virtues and duties, or – and this is more important – formulate an ideal morality in the light of which the current code is examined and found to be wanting.

These lists show great similarities. The enumeration of virtues and vices given by St Paul, for example, can easily be paralleled from Hindu and Buddhist writings. Of greater interest, from the point of view of systematization, are the occasional attempts to formulate principles stating what is thought to be fundamental or superordinate to the mass of rules constituting the codes of morals. There is, for example, a summary of the Law which is given in the *Talmud* several times with some variations:

Moses gave 613 commandments; David reduced them to eleven (Psalm xv), Isaiah to six (xxxiii. 15), Micah summed them up in three, viz., to do justly, to love mercy and to walk humbly with thy God, and Isaiah again in two: keep ye judgment and do righteousness. The great Hillel answering a prospective proselyte compressed the Law into the commandment: do not to another what is hateful to thyself. All the rest is commentary.*

Similarly, in Buddhist writings we meet with summaries giving a kind of résumé of what has been previously expounded in various codes. For example, in the Psalms of the Early Buddhists we find the following stanzas:

To refrain from killing living beings, to covet no man's wealth, to speak the truth, to give with timely generosity according to one's means, to quench lustful desires, to be reverent towards spiritual teachers, to be compassionate towards all creatures, this is the path of good men, this is the law that is in accord with all the codes, this is the universal law.†

Often in summaries of this kind the intention is to emphasize the distinction between moral principles and ritual rules and to relegate the latter to a subordinate position. In some, however, this distinction is not made. Muhammadan authorities, for example, distinguish five categories of acts: compulsory (thou shalt), recommended (thou shouldst), permitted (thou mayest), disapproved (thou oughtest not), and prohibited (thou shalt not). Included under the first are worship, almsgiving, fasting, and pilgrimage. The classification is interesting, but there seems to be no disposition to seek for a philosophical basis for the grouping. Arguments are founded rather on texts accepted as authoritative beyond dispute.‡

Systematization and articulation of principles are, of course, the explicit aim of philosophic ethics. Here we are interested in the role assigned to reason and experience. If we adopt the classification of theories into those based mainly on the concept of good or value, and those based mainly on the concept of rule or law, we can distinguish monistic and pluralistic varieties. Thus there is a monism or pluralism of ends, according as the search is for a single or all-embracing end or value, or for a number of

* Cf. I. Mattuck, *Jewish Ethics*, 1953, p. 44.
† Cf. E. W. Hopkins, *The Ethics of India*, p. 253.
‡ Cf. H. A. B. Gibb, 'Law and Religion in Islam', in *Judaism and Christianity*, ed. E. I. J. Rosenthal, 1938, vol. III, ch. VII.

specific, though related goods or values. Similarly, there are theories which seek to formulate a supreme law of human action and others which distinguish a plurality of duties, each based on a specific principle.

As an example of a monism of ends, we may take Utilitarianism. In this the link with experience is closest. No one can read Hume's *Inquiry* or Sidgwick's *Method of Ethics* without realizing the plausibility of the view that there is an important connexion between the characteristics of acts considered good and their tendency to promote happiness. Sidgwick, in particular, makes a powerful case for the view that Utilitarianism represents in systematic form the sort of principles for the regulation of conduct, which are imperfectly and inchoately grasped in common-sense morality and towards which the course of history has tended. Of special interest is his suggestion that variations in moral codes are in part to be ascribed to variations in the real or perceived effects on general happiness of actions prescribed or forbidden by the codes.

Unfortunately, hedonistic Utilitarians were led by their psychological theories to consider happiness too much in abstraction from the activities in which it is found, or from what Sidgwick himself calls the sources of happiness. The separation of happiness from the experiences which it tones or qualifies makes it difficult to distinguish kinds of happiness, a distinction which, in developed moral experience, we certainly make. Once the separation or abstraction is avoided, we are led to admit a plurality of ends. Sidgwick rightly stresses the vacillations and inconsistencies of ordinary morality. But these, I think, are more intelligible on the hypothesis of a plurality of ends than on the hypothesis of a single or all-embracing end. On the former hypothesis, variations and vacillations can be explained, in part at least, as due to different combinations of the ends of action or to clashes between, or to a different ranking of ends, and possibly also to the fact that the same ends may among different peoples be served by different rules or institutions. Variations in the rules pertaining to marriage, for example, or in duties to the kindred as compared with other groups, can be made intelligible in these ways. That happiness as estimated by hedonic tone is the only good contemplated in such rules has not been shown and is far from being self-evident.

In his discussion of justice, Sidgwick allows that the principle of seeking the greatest happiness on the whole has to be supplemented by a principle of the just or right distribution of this happiness. This principle he takes to be that of equality, on the ground that it must be reasonable to treat anyone in the same way as any other, if there be no reason apparent for treating him differently.* This seems to suggest that equal distribution is just in itself, irrespective of whether it makes for greater happiness on the whole. Elsewhere he suggests that as far as the distribution of the means of happiness is concerned, equality is likely to promote general happiness, not only because men have a disinterested aversion to unreason, but still more because they have an aversion to any kind of inferiority to others, which is much intensified when the inferiority seems unreasonable.† If so, it would seem to follow that men attach value to reasonableness and disvalue to inferiority.

Despite all the criticism to which Utilitarianism has been subjected, it is plain that it represents a valuable strain in moral experience. It has focused attention on the removal of known evils and on the importance of investigating the conditions upon which human happiness and misery depend. It has rendered great service by insisting on the need for a reasoned ethical basis for political reform and demanding that human feelings receive equal recognition wheresoever and in whomsoever found. Perhaps its greatest contribution lay not so much in what it enjoins, as in what it excludes: that no course of action should be approved which sacrifices the interests of one section of the community to another. This criterion would retain its value, even though it cannot be claimed – and no prudent Utilitarian ever has claimed – that it exhausts the entire field of morals.‡

* *Methods*, bk. IV, ch. I.   † *Elements of Politics*, p. 44.
‡ Cf. R. Adamson, *The Development of Modern Philosophy*, 1893, vol. II, ch. VI; T. H. Green, *Prolegomena*, bk. IV, ch. IV.

The attempt to formulate a supreme principle of morals does not appear to have been more successful than the attempt to find a supreme end of action. The nearest approach, I suppose, is to be found in Kantian ethics. Philosophers now generally recognize that the formulae that Kant gives of the Categorical Imperative contain something of abiding value. They bring out again the importance of impartiality in human relations, especially impartiality as between ourselves and others. On the other hand, the claim that the formulae give a complete analysis of rationality in action cannot be sustained. What they assert is that there are moral principles, and that these principles are universal, in the sense that they govern all cases coming under them. But in the nature of the case they cannot say what these principles are. Furthermore, rationality does not seem to be rightly identified with universalizability. This can be seen from the analogous case of truth. If particular judgements had no truth quality, they could not be made true by being universalized. Similarly, if actions had no moral quality in themselves, they would not acquire that quality by being universalized. If there is rationality in action, then reason must penetrate into the ends or purposes themselves and, if necessary, modify them and adjust them to each other. But this cannot be done without considering the nature of the objects desired or willed – a task which Kant's view of the relations between desire and the practical reason precluded him from undertaking.

In the *Metaphysik der Sitten* he sums up his teaching in the injunction: promote perfection in yourself, and happiness in others. But both perfection and happiness are indeterminate without a statement of the activities through which they are to be attained. We can only be happy in something and we can seek perfection only in realizing our powers. Those who take the view that man's rational nature manifests itself not only in his cognitive but also in his other powers will therefore be led to inquire whether there are values other than the exercise of reason which are possible constituents of a personality rationally directed.

This brings us to what I have called pluralist theories of the good. The discussion of what is to be included in a list of intrinsic goods has caused much dissension among philosophers. Put on the whole there is probably more agreement about these matters than about most other problems in metaphysics. The following excellences would, I think, be included: the exercise of the creative faculties, cognitive and aesthetic, in getting to know what is true and making what is beautiful; the enjoyment and appreciation of knowledge and beauty or loveliness in nature and art; the satisfaction of the impulses of affection and love; certain personal qualities, such as serenity or peace; freedom in the active exercise of our faculties. In addition there are the various moral virtues, for example the habits or dispositions which are inherent in the pursuit of ideals, such as detachment, disinterestedness, self-knowledge in the pursuit of truth; patience, steadfastness, selflessness needed for love at its best; self-respect, respect for others, loyalty, the readiness to forgo one's own good when it would bring with it pain and suffering for others, the willingness to give and take, and other qualities needed for group life.

Pleasure or happiness is sometimes given as an additional good, or even as *the* good. But this, as we have seen, involves an undue abstraction. For pleasure we should write pleasant experience, for happiness fulfilment and enjoyment of vital capacity. The value of virtue is often overstressed by moralists, no doubt because, of all goods, it is least an object of spontaneous desire. It is hard to acquire and the learning of it, as Aristotle notes, is often contrary to pleasure. Those who have learnt it agree that it is fairer and more gracious than aught else. But you would hardly think so from the look on their faces. Those who preach virtue have themselves noted that the worship of it is favourable to self-mortification, pride, and bitterness.*

It is odd that bodily fitness and health are so rarely included among the intrinsic goods. Can it be that bodily health is considered as having value only as a means to the goods of the mind? But, metaphysics apart, it is not obvious that the body is only

* Cf. Carveth Read, *Natural and Social Morals*, 1909, ch. II.

the tool or instrument of the mind. A more probable reason for the exclusion of bodily health from among the intrinsic goods is probably to be found in the ascetic tendencies of some of the higher religions. Indulgence in 'sensual' pleasures is said to endanger the 'higher' or spiritual goods; the tyranny of the body has therefore to be resisted. Of the tyranny of the mind we do not hear so often.

The values so far enumerated are not peculiar to Western ethical thought. Hindu philosophers, for example, distinguish four ends of human action: Dharma (duty or virtue), Artha (wealth), Kama (pleasure or happiness), and Moksa (salvation or emancipation). Of these Dharma and Artha are regarded not as ends in themselves, but as means to Kama and Moksa. Moksa, the highest end, is considered negatively as the extinction of suffering and unhappiness and positively as a condition of unalloyed bliss. The term Kama indicates the pleasures or happiness derived from contact with the external world. It is said to include not only the pleasures of the senses, but also all the pleasures derived from the exercise of the intellectual faculties as well as those of aesthetic appreciation. Moksa can only be reached after severe discipline culminating in the identification of the self with the Atman or spirit of the whole universe. Dharma is secondary to Moksa, though in later writings the performance of duty for its own sake is enjoined.*

The part played by renunciation in the attainment of the final end is variously interpreted. Often the severely ascetic view predominates, but in later thought there is a strong tendency to interpret the teaching of the *Gita* and of *Manu* in a more positive manner. What stands in the way of the ideal is not activity or response to the demands of social life, but excessive attachment to the pleasures of the senses. The *Gita* does not teach insensibility or emotional indifference; on the contrary emphasis is laid on the development of kindly feelings and instincts of humanity, love, compassion, benevolence, charity. To master the emotions and not be mastered by them, to discharge one's duties without

* Aiyer, op. cit., p. 154.

an eye to personal advantage or reward, and so attain to serenity and repose of mind – these are said to be the essentials of the good life. The attitude of mind is thus not unlike that inculcated by the Stoics.

Of the attempts to systematize obligations or duties on pluralist lines, I can only give a few examples. Westermarck has adopted a classification into six groups: (i) rules relating to acts, forbearances, or omissions which directly concern the interests of other men, their life or bodily integrity, their freedom, honour or property, and so on; (ii) rules relating to acts which chiefly concern a man's own welfare, e.g. temperance, asceticism, suicide; (iii) rules relating to sexual relations, which partly coincide and partly differ from those included in the first two groups; (iv) rules relating to conduct towards the lower animals; (v) rules relating to conduct towards the dead; (vi) rules relating to conduct towards beings regarded as supernatural.* This scheme has great merits. It enables Westermarck to bring together in systematic form a vast body of data derived from the whole field of comparative morals. It enables him also to bring out the directions in which there has been moral progress, or as he put it, morality has become more 'reflective' and 'enlightened'.

Another sociological classification is that suggested by Durkheim.† He distinguishes two main groups: (i) rules arising out of membership of a group, e.g. the family, the professions or corporations, the state; (ii) duties which are independent of particular groupings, e.g. respect for the life, property, and honour of persons, irrespective of whether they belong to one's own group. He argues that the rules which regulate conduct in the different spheres of life, e.g. the domestic, the professional, the political, do not form a unified system deducible from a single principle. Furthermore, the moralities prevailing in the different spheres do not keep pace in their development and, on examination, reveal different degrees of coherence and consistency. Durkheim himself has made effective use of this classification in the recently

* *Origin and Development of Moral Ideas*, I, p. 328.
† *Leçons de Sociologie*, 1950.

published *Leçons de Sociologie.* The idea that moral rules should be studied in relation to different types of social groupings and their institutions seems to me to be very helpful and capable of wide application.

It is interesting to compare Westermarck's scheme with that adopted by Sir David Ross.* If we leave out the religious or ritual duties, the resemblance is striking. The duties of fidelity, requital, reparation, justice (in the sense of equitable distribution), beneficence and non-maleficence or non-injury can be seen from Westermarck's survey to be very widely recognized, though in different forms, alike in the primitive as in the civilized world. Even the duty of self-improvement is anticipated on the primitive level in the notions of self-regard and self-respect. Unlike Westermarck, however, Sir David claims that the duties he enumerates are intuitively certain and self-evident. Considering the different forms in which these duties appear, his arguments do not strike me as convincing. The duty of justice, for example, is said to rest on the general principle that we should produce as much good as possible, and this includes the distribution of happiness between people according to merit. But the conception of merit is highly complex and variable, and lacks the determinateness which one expects in self-evident positions. It cannot, for example, be everyone's duty to see to it that offences which have escaped the law should not go unpunished or to arrange that every fine deed is rewarded by a suitable dose of happiness. Similarly, the notion of non-injury has to be defined in reference to the conceptions that prevail in different societies of what constitutes the physical and mental integrity of the individual. In these and other cases moral rules should not be considered in isolation, but by reference to the institutional framework of which they form a part.

Further progress in the systematization of morals seems to me to depend on an extension of comparative studies. What is needed is an application of the method used by Sidgwick in his analysis of the common-sense morality of our society to other peoples and periods. This is a field in which philosophical ethics

* *The Right and the Good,* 1930.

can benefit greatly by cooperation with the students of comparative law, comparative religion, and comparative institutions.

I turn now to my fifth criterion of moral development, namely capacity for self-criticism and self-direction. What I have in mind is not only the conscious efforts of philosophers to clarify and systematize moral ideas and beliefs, but the extent to which impartial investigation of the facts and critical scrutiny of the ends to be pursued is allowed to shape public policy. Of special importance in this context is the fact that students of legal systems have come to recognize that legal decisions rest on unconscious assumptions of an ethical and political nature, and that, if legislation is to be rational, these assumptions must be made explicit and openly formulated. That the recognition of this need has passed from the philosophers to judges and administrators is an important factor in the rationalization of public policy. Professor W. Friedmann in his survey of the relations between legal theory, social ideals, and legal practice, notes a 'very definite swing of the pendulum from judicial contempt for that "vague jurisprudence sometimes attractively styled Justice between Man and Man" or "well-meaning sloppiness of thought" to an attitude much more reminiscent of Lord Mansfield', and he cites in this connexion several recent pronouncements by eminent contemporary judges to illustrate this change in outlook.* I should like to quote the following as an example:

Law is not an end in itself. . . . It has to justify itself by its ability to serve the ends of government, that is to help to promote the ordered existence of the nation and the good life of the people (Lord Wright, in University of Toronto *Legal Journal* (1941), pp. 271–2).

The development I have in mind may be further illustrated by a shift of attention from private to public morals, by a movement from commutative justice, or justice as a sort of equivalence of exchange between individuals, to distributive justice, conceived as a cooperative provision of the conditions of well-being, defined by a communal standard. In the field of international relations a

---

* W. Friedmann, *Legal Theory*, 1944, p. 275.

noteworthy example of the tendencies here referred to is to be seen in the public recognition of the duty of governments to come to the aid of 'underdeveloped' nations in their efforts to raise their standards of life. Another example is the more explicit recognition of a duty to posterity. Both these developments indicate advance as judged by the second criterion, namely that of universalization, since they constitute an extension of the duty of beneficence. But they also satisfy the fifth of my criteria, since they show the impact of ethical ideals on large-scale social policy.

It is to be noted that advance as estimated by one of the criteria I have distinguished does not necessarily imply advance in the direction of the others. Thus a system may be internally coherent, but narrow and exclusive, and thus fail in universality. Again, a system may be comprehensive in the sense of covering a wide variety of needs and interests, but rely on coercion and other external sanctions, and thus fail to satisfy the criterion of differentiation, as defined above. On the other hand, self-criticism and self-direction are likely to be associated with coherence and articulation of principles, and to satisfy also the tests of universality and comprehensiveness. Thus the value of a moral system on the whole depends on the coherence and consistency of the concepts it uses, the extent to which self-critical and disinterested thought, both in reference to facts and values, is allowed to pervade conduct in the various spheres of economic and political life, and on the way in which the line is drawn between the spheres of internal and external sanctions, that is, the spheres left to the individual and the spheres which are held to call for social control.

I must now try to draw together the main threads of my argument. The conclusions to which I have been led by my survey may be briefly stated in the following way.

Morality is mainly concerned with human helpfulness, with the removal or mitigation of evil, especially of pain and suffering, the provision and fair distribution of the means to well-being, and of opportunities for the pursuit of what is excellent. It is, I think, implicit in morality that all human beings have the capacity for suffering and enjoying and for forming ideals, that is, of conceiving of ends having intrinsic worth or value.

The formation of ideals is an expression of man's rational nature. Idealization is not confined to the moral consciousness, but is characteristic of all exercise of reason, whether theoretical or practical. It involves the power of detaching the contents of thought, perception, or desire from the temporary conditions of their actual occurrence and of recombining them, with the aid of constructive imagination, into new wholes. In the case of moral ideals there occurs a specially intimate blending of feeling, striving, and knowing. Their formation involves insight into the possibilities open to human nature, constructive imagination, going beyond what has actually been experienced to a prevision of what might be, an emotional commitment or concern for the ends envisaged. These functions are not to be assigned to separate faculties. It is one and the same self that knows, feels, and wills. There are emotions and strivings that are only possible at certain levels of cognition, just as there are thoughts which are only possible at certain levels of emotional intensity.*

But if man is one he also is many. The various parts or elements of his nature are unequally developed, with resulting conflict and disharmony. This is the basis of the dualism of human nature on which moralists dwell, which they represent as an opposition between the flesh and the spirit, animality and humanity, passion and reason. But human nature is multiple rather than dual. The elements of which it is composed are not separate faculties. The facts are better expressed with the aid of the concept of development as a process tending towards unity or integration. Each level has its own quality of striving, feeling, and cognition. Hume was right when he said it was misleading to talk of a conflict between reason and passion. Not, however, because, as he thought, reason was powerless to exert any influence, but because the conflict is not between 'reason' and the passions, but sometimes between partial systems within the self and the more organized

* Compare the saying of Vauvenargues: 'Les grandes pensées viennent du cœur.'

parts of the self, and sometimes between a relatively dissociated impulse and the rest of the personality.

There is conflict not only between the parts of the self but also between individuals and society. From the point of view of the individual the problem of the moral life is to introduce order into the chaos of warring impulses and turbulent desires. In this struggle he is helped by the rules which he finds in his society. These are not of his making and they come to him, as it were, from without. No doubt in their origin they can be traced to the needs of individuals. But the process of their formation is very complex, involving countless interactions of interests and counter-interests. They are of necessity general and undiscriminating, indifferent to individual peculiarities. Moreover, as societies become more differentiated, the needs of 'the' community tend to be identified with the needs of a dominant group or section, and the order established by them may not meet the needs of the rest of the society. The legal system and the moral outlook justifying it may then be repressive instead of liberative. Without committing ourselves to Freud's view of an inherent antagonism between culture and happiness, we must grant that in complex societies the individual may, in submitting to the demands made upon him by the prevailing code, fail to satisfy his deepest needs.

These divisions within the self and within society are important in considering the relations between good and duty, end and rule. In dealing with obligation, it is necessary to distinguish between the sense or feeling of obligation which may be due to habit, suggestion, or social pressure, and the rational constraint analogous to the relation in which we stand towards all that is or is taken to be objective. The coercive or binding element in moral obligation is sometimes explained in terms of the command-obedience relationship. But a command, whether it emanates from God, society, or ourselves, has to be justified, and the justification cannot lie in the mere *fiat* of anyone's will. There is no doubt an element of value in the virtue of submission or abnegation. But to emphasize this element is to ignore the other, and possibly the more important, of liberation and fulfilment. What the moral judgement asserts is the superiority of a given mode of life or action to any other that conflicts with it. It seems to me that the concept of an ideal comes nearest to expressing the nature of this claim to superiority. For the ideal stands before us as something desirable, though not necessarily desired, as something which may involve abnegation or renunciation, but which none the less is also a fulfilment of our nature. What gives the ideals worth or value is specific to each ideal, the bloom and vigour of health, the beauty and orderliness of truth, the delicacy and sensitiveness of reciprocal affection, the greatness and nobility of self-sacrifice. Each ideal generates its own norms and makes its own demands. The element of obligatoriness varies from ideal to ideal. It is not everybody's duty to devote himself to the pursuit of science or art, or to seek for the beauty of perfect love. Perhaps we ought to distinguish between the obligatory and super-obligatory, and to confine the concept of duty to the minimum of morality, that is, the avoidance of evil and the securing of the necessary conditions of a common life. We feel admiration for those who set themselves a lofty ideal, but we do not blame them if they fail to reach its summits.

A survey of ideals shows that they are rooted in basic human needs and capacities. These needs fall into well-marked, though not separable, groups, the needs of the body, the needs of the mind, the needs of social intercourse. The ideals arise in connexion with these major ends, and in their advanced form they are interrelated. The ideal of bodily health, for example, cannot be separated from the ideal of mental health, and many would think that if we had fuller knowledge of their nature and conditions, we should have the answers to the principal questions of ethics. It is worth noting that while the subject's own feelings are important as criteria of health, they have, from a scientific point of view, to be evaluated by reference to more objective criteria of efficiency or adequate performance of function. When these criteria, in turn, are examined, it soon becomes clear that they raise fundamental questions of the nature of the ends in relation to which efficiency or adequacy of performance is judged. Medicine and ethics then have to meet. Even a cursory study of the attempts to define health and disease will show that they cannot go far without reference to some concept of well-being, individual and social.*

Other basic needs give rise to their own ideals, for example, the need to know the world generates the ideal of truth, the need for mutual response inspires the ideal of love at its best, the needs of social cooperation slowly lead to the ideal of justice. The norms regulating the ideals are defined by disciplines especially devoted to them, logic in the case of truth, aesthetics in the case of beauty. But these norms have moral quality in so far as they involve control of immediate impulse and the cultivation of qualities of character needed for their fulfilment. These are the virtues or excellences of character, e.g. in the case of truth, detachment, disinterestedness; in the case of the social ideals, generosity of thought and feeling, sensitiveness to suffering and unhappiness, loyalty and steadfastness.

The relation of virtue to rule is not always the same. In some cases the virtues consist in enduring dispositions or habits of obedience to rules. Thus veracity is the habit of telling the truth. In others they consist rather in a certain strain of fineness shown not in conformity to rule, but in a differentiated and sensitive response to the situation, e.g. compassion, kindliness. In general, the virtues are features of larger patterns of conduct, and to judge them we have to consider them in relation to the ends or values which they serve or qualify.

It follows from these considerations that the function of reason in relation to the ideals is threefold: to clarify and define them, to show their relations to each other, and to discover the conditions, inner and outer, upon which they depend for their realization. Much of this work of inquiry is factual, and requires the aid of the social and natural sciences. The philosopher is concerned with the ideals themselves and with the ways or forms of

* See Aubrey Lewis, 'Health as a social concept', *British Journal of Sociology*, June 1953.

life in which they have been variously graded and combined. The rationalist assumption is that such comparison and evaluation of the forms of life are logically possible, and that, despite the diversity of moral codes, general principles are discoverable which are implicit in all of them, and which come to be recognized as universally binding in the course of development.

It is important to distinguish between principles of high generality, which state the formal character of morality, without reference to specific ends or values, and principles which necessarily involve reference to such ends. An example of the former is the Kantian categorical imperative: 'Act on principles which you would see universally adopted.' Very similar is Sidgwick's axiom of justice: 'Whatever action any of us judges to be right for himself, he implicitly judges to be right for all similar persons in similar circumstances.' A corresponding proposition stating what ought to be done *to* – not by – different individuals is Clarke's rule of equity: 'Whatever I judge reasonable or unreasonable that another should do for me, that, by the same judgement I declare reasonable or unreasonable that I should *in like case* do for him'; which, as Sidgwick shows, is the Golden Rule more precisely stated. Mention must also be made of Sidgwick's principles of prudence and benevolence, which may be briefly summed up in the statement that it is irrational to prefer the present to the future, merely because it is nearer, and ourselves to others merely because we are ourselves. Reason requires that like things should be treated alike, and different things differently. Hence in so far as *A* and *B* are alike, the good of each is of like value. These principles do not prescribe any end as good. They are formal principles applicable to whatever ends may be considered good.

If to these principles we add the further assertion that all men are capable of enjoying and suffering, of happiness and misery, of morality and membership of a common society, we have the essential elements in the principle of equality. This enjoins that all men are equally entitled to be considered, that no one should be simply ignored or have his claims overridden; and that every difference in treatment requires justification in terms of some relevant difference in the grounds on which the claims are made. These principles are again purely formal, applicable to all claims whatever. The difficulty in applying these principles lies in deciding what is and what is not a relevant difference, and this cannot be done without reference to the specific content of the various rights and duties. Thus society may recognize a right to education. But, when a certain minimum has been assured for all, we should not think it right to provide higher education without reference to ability or interest. In the case of political rights, democracies have adopted the principle of 'one man, one vote', in the interest of securing general participation and in the absence of any agreed method of estimating differences in political capacity. But though this is accepted, *faute de mieux*, in respect of the right to choose representatives, no one would suggest that those chosen from among them to form the government should be elected indiscriminately, e.g. by lot, without any reference to fitness.

The difficulty of deciding what differences are relevant is perhaps greatest in dealing with 'economic rights'. The right to minimum conditions of subsistence is now widely recognized. But there is no agreement as to the distribution of property or the reward of services, above the minimum. The problem is much too difficult for brief treatment and, in any case, I do not feel competent to deal with the very complicated economic issues involved. But I will venture a few comments on points relevant to my main argument. 'Arithmetic' equality has few defenders.* If the principle of proportionate equality is to be adopted, the question arises whether distribution is to be proportionate to needs, ability, productivity, or effort. All these have been defended. But apart from difficulties of measurement, none is free from objection on ethical grounds. A very persuasive case, for example, was made for the claims of 'effort' by Lowes Dickinson a

* There are, it seems, forces at work in Western societies making for uniformity in the wage structure. But how much in this movement is to be attributed to ideas of equity is very uncertain.

generation ago.* But it is not at all obvious that a person who finds his task difficult and irksome should have a higher remuneration than one who performs it with ease and pleasure. The notion of desert or merit is particularly perplexing in this context. If merit means intrinsic worth or value, it might be argued that as such it is its own reward, and that at any rate there can be no proportion between it and external conditions. They are not in *pari materia*. Even if the principle of distribution according to merit could be defended on ethical grounds, its administration would require an amount of wisdom and humanity hardly likely to be generally available.

I would like to suggest a somewhat different approach to this difficult problem. Firstly, it is fitting that individuals should have the means to well-being, and this not as reward, but as necessary conditions. In so far as these conditions can be secured by social effort, individuals may be said to have a 'right' to them. It follows, secondly, that there is a correlative duty, the duty of work, that is to play one's part in the task of providing the means of well-being. Thirdly, functional needs, that is, needs arising out of one's work, may differ and these differences may justify differential awards. Fourthly, more general needs have to be considered, e.g. opportunities to pursue worthwhile objects. These two kinds of needs may point in different directions. Those who pursue occupations least worth doing for their own sake may be entitled to claim special facilities in compensation. Finally, since distribution depends on production, an equitable scale would have to take into consideration the bearing of the principle adopted on the total available for distribution. Thus an additional ground for differentiation may be found in the necessity to provide an incentive to effort, with a view to maximize production.

The practical difficulties remain, of course. There is no reliable method of estimating the differentials that follow from the application of the above principles. We cannot know in advance of experience what conditions are needed, say, by an artist, a philosopher, a bishop, a lawyer, a coal-miner, a road-sweeper, to enable

* *Justice and Liberty*, 1908.

them to make the most of their capacities for good, and at the same time to induce them to put out their best efforts in the performance of their specific functions. In the end, it would appear that in democratic societies we have to rely on the forces of supply and demand. The problem is, therefore, whether a scale so based can be operated in a manner to satisfy the demands of equity.

To bring about a state of affairs in which the scale of equity would tend to coincide with the scale of supply and demand, the following conditions would seem to be necessary, though they may not be sufficient. Firstly, there must be a widening of the access to education, in order to secure initial equality of opportunity in the choice of occupations. Secondly, a system of education is required likely to maintain a high level of intelligence and taste, and so generate and sustain a demand for and interest in the 'higher' kinds of work. Thirdly, it is desirable that there should be a change in the prestige value of occupations. Finally, ways must be found to prevent powerful industrial or professional organizations from obtaining special privileges for their members, not justified by the above principles. Granted conditions of equal social opportunity, there would be a stronger tendency than now for people to choose their work in accordance with their interest and capacity, and this is not only likely to conduce to greater well-being, but may be an important factor also in enhancing productivity. On the other hand, less agreeable work would have to be given sufficient differential advantage to overcome the resistance to engage in it. In general, differentials have to be justified by showing that they are required, either in the interests of efficiency, or as necessary conditions of well-being, and, in any case, they ought not to be of a magnitude likely to endanger the minimum to which all are entitled.

Here I must leave this matter. It is clear that further analysis would have to deal with the ethical basis of property, and with the formidable problems of the relation of the state to industry. My object has been only to illustrate the distinction between principles of high generality, such as the general principle which excludes arbitrariness and insists that like cases should be treated in like manner, and the middle principles which attempt to define what constitutes arbitrariness in a given context. It is in this field of middle principles that knowledge of the ways in which institutions affect the individuals concerned, directly or indirectly, is of vital importance, and in which ethics most needs the cooperation of the social sciences.

The middle principles of morals and the body of rights and duties, deducible from them, lend themselves to comparative study in the light of the criteria of moral development I have suggested above. This can most easily be seen in the history of the concepts of rights. Thus, the 'rights of man' have been slowly universalized, that is, applied to ever wider ranges of persons, and arbitrary differences, such as those based on sex, religion, and colour have been greatly reduced. Judged by the test of comprehensiveness, it can be shown that rights have been extended from the political to the economic, cultural, and social spheres. Applying the test of differentiation, different systems may be compared by inquiring whether and how far they distinguish between moral and legal rights, and by what sanctions these are supported. From the angle of systematization and articulation of principles, we can follow the movement from the simple rules of reciprocity, which we find in the simplest societies, to the Golden Rule of the higher religions, the doctrine of Natural Law and the systematic efforts made in the modern world to define the rights of man and to obtain universal recognition for them. Finally, the growth of self-criticism and self-direction may be traced in the increasing use made of fact-finding inquiries in the shaping of policy, the efforts to base legislation upon an articulate conception of well-being and, in recent times, to find concrete expression for the idea of human rights in the sphere of international relations.

In reviewing the development of ethical theories, we cannot help being overcome by a certain feeling of despondency. The advances made seem so small when viewed in relation to the terrifying problems facing mankind. Has there been a failure of ethical insight? Some will say that the fundamental principles of morals are simple and have always been known – that we should wish well to others, that hatred is evil, that we should rid ourselves of envy and greed. Or is it the lack of agreement about what I have called the middle principles of morals, combined with the growing scale and complexity of the problems and our ignorance of the forces at work, that is the source of our failure? Or is it that knowledge is not enough, that evil is not entirely due to ignorance?

Yet the grounds of hope remain. The problems facing humanity are of old standing. But they undergo continuous change, and in the character of the change there is evidence of real progress.

10

Psychoanalysis and Ethics*

I

THE contribution of Psychoanalysis to ethics may be considered from three points of view. We may enquire, in the first place, what light analytic theory throws on the natural history of morals, that is the ways in which moral rules and moral sentiments are formed and developed in the individual and the group. We may ask next whether Psychoanalysis can, from its own resources, provide the basis for an ethical theory or a set of standards or principles in the light of which existing moral codes can be criticized or evaluated. Finally, there is the question how far the insight into human nature acquired through the exploration of the unconscious elements in the human mind can help us in releasing the energies of man and removing the obstacles that hinder the realization of his ideals, whatever may be their ultimate source.

I propose to confine myself to the first and second of these questions. I do so not because I consider the third less important. On the contrary it may well be the most important. The reason for this self-imposed limitation is that a satisfactory treatment would necessitate a detailed study of case histories and should not properly be undertaken by anyone who, like myself, has no personal experience of analytic procedure. The problems raised in the first two questions are not always clearly distinguished by psychoanalytic writers and some would deny that there is such a thing as ethical theory other than the psychology of morals. Freud himself tells us that it is not the object of his investigations to provide an ethic, still less a *Weltanschauung*. Such activities, he says, may be left to philosophers who avowedly 'find it impossible

* The forty-third Conway Memorial Lecture, delivered at Conway Hall on 25 April 1952.

315

to make their journey through life without a Baedeker of that kind to tell them about everything.'* Professor Flugel, in his very thorough and searching examination of the ethical aspects of Psychoanalysis, distinguishes between questions of origin and questions of validity, and he is of the opinion that the problem of ultimate or intrinsic value is one for ethics and not psychology. Despite these disclaimers, however, the impression is conveyed, perhaps unwittingly, that a fuller knowledge of the psychology of motivation will render philosophic ethics unnecessary, and this despite the fact that assumptions are made about the nature of value judgements which certainly require philosophical justification. Thus Freud has no hesitation in asserting, despite his professed modesty in these matters, that value judgements are ultimately determined by desires and are in fact illusionary in character.† Similarly there are many passages in Professor Flugel's book which suggest that he favours a 'naturalistic' view of moral judgements, as, for example when he argues that moral judgements are 'orectic', i.e., expressions of feelings, desires or wishes, and that reason is concerned with the means but not the ends of action. These are views which, of course, have a respectable philosophical tradition. I do not wish to prejudge the issue. But it is important to bear in mind that the problems thus raised are philosophical rather than psychological and that sooner or later they must be squarely faced as such.

Psychological theories of morals tend on the whole to be relativistic in outlook. For if moral judgements are considered to be expressions of desires or emotions there will be a tendency to stress the fact that they vary from one individual or group to another. From this the conclusion is readily drawn that they are not subject to rational tests, and, indeed, that the distinction between true and false does not properly apply to them. It is interesting to note, however, that recently several attempts have been made by psychoanalysts to move away from at least the more extreme forms of relativism. Thus Dr Erich Fromm tries to show

* *Inhibitions, Symptoms and Anxiety*, p. 29.
† *Civilization and its Discontents*, p. 143.

316

that it is possible on empirical grounds to distinguish between 'genuine' and 'fictitious' ideals – 'a difference as fundamental as that between truth and falsehood', and that the test is not subjective attractiveness but is to be found in the objective conditions of mental life.* From another point of view, Dr Money-Kyrle tries to escape relativism by a redefinition of the 'normal' which he seeks to identify with the rational. In both these cases and in others the revulsion against relativism is to be traced to the impact of Nazism which made ethical relativism emotionally untenable. The question had to be faced whether it could really be the case that when Nazis say it is good and fitting to torture Jews and we say it is abominable the difference is one of personal taste only. The test of 'adjustment to the environment' which would come naturally to a psychotherapist clearly failed. As judged by this test, the Nazi could be as 'good' as the democrat, so long as both were equally conditioned to fit into the environment favoured by their societies. Could it be that the real crime of the Nazis was their inefficiency, that is their failure to adopt the means likely to achieve the ends they set themselves? If this is rejected as morally repugnant, it would follow that moral judgements relate not merely to the means but also to the ends of action or else that the repudiation of the Nazi mode of life is emotional only and has no rational foundation. Questions of this sort troubled the minds of all who favoured ethical relativism. But they were felt with special acuteness by psychoanalysts, who realized that they had to re-examine their conception of what constitutes mental health, and that this could not be done without raising the problem of the validity of the criteria implicit in the ethical codes prevailing in different societies. The answers that have been given reveal a tacit reluctance to abandon ethical relativism combined with or qualified by a hope that objective or universal standards of the 'normal' or the 'healthy' can be derived from the data furnished by empirical psychology. In this respect the claims made by recent writers are bolder than anything to

---

* *Escape from Freedom*, p. 266.

be found in Freud's work. With what success we have now to inquire.

II

A striking feature of Freud's treatment of morals is his preoccupation with the sense of guilt. In this respect he differs markedly from the philosophers, who with the exception of Plato and Kant give little attention to moral evil. For analogy we have to go to the doctrine of original sin, and it is interesting to note that theologians have themselves noted the affinity between their doctrine and Freud's. The theme forms the centre of Freud's *Totem and Taboo* where morality is represented as a reaction-formation against the evil inherent in man. As is well known, he connects it with the early Oedipus situation in the primal horde, the incestuous desires of the band of brothers, the murder of the father, the subsequent remorse and identification with him. Social organization and moral restrictions are all traced back to this sequence of events. The bond which holds the group together is complicity in a common crime; religion is rooted in the sense of guilt and the consequent remorse; and morality is 'based partly on the necessities of society, and partly on the expiation which this sense of guilt demands'.*

Freud's reconstruction of primeval society was based on the views of Atkinson and Lang and on Robertson Smith's interpretation of the totem feast, and as it is not now accepted by anthropologists, the matter need not here be pursued further. Freud, however, never abandoned it, as is evident from one of his latest writings.† It retains its importance, I think, for two reasons. Firstly, it is taken by Freud as providing an explanation of 'ambivalence', that is the coincidence of love and hate towards the same object, a concept essential to psychoanalytic theory. Secondly, it survives in Freud's deep-rooted belief in the existence of an inherited sense of guilt, transmitted in some way not further explained, through racial heredity. If this is taken seriously, it would involve the assumption of a group-mind, or a psyche

* p. 238.   † *Moses and Monotheism.*

318

of the mass as Freud calls it, in which mental processes occur analogous to those that occur in the mind of the individual, or else the possibility of the inheritance of acquired characters.

In the later writings the account that is given of the sense of guilt is not necessarily connected with these biological or anthropological theories and is compatible with the assumption that the individual starts his life as neither moral nor immoral but as amoral. The child acquires his morality from his environment. The formation of the 'conscience' consists essentially in a process whereby the external authority of the father or of father-substitutes is transformed into an inner authority. It is described both by Freud and by his followers in terms of the distinctions they draw between the id, the ego and the super-ego. Throughout, emphasis is laid on the negative or repressive aspects of morality, the 'Thou shalt not' of the moral codes. This is no doubt partly due to the fact that in therapeutic treatment analysts are struck with the great severity of the conscience, often resulting in cruel self-humiliation and self-torture. To account for this, appeal is made to the part played by the aggressive tendencies in the formation of the super-ego. In incorporating the authority of the father into his own self the child also incorporates the aggression imputed to the father as the source of frustration, and, at the same time, the child turns the aggression which he feels towards the father, but which he has to repress, against himself. The conscience thus contains a double dose of aggression, the aggression of the father and that towards the father. To this redoubled aggression is attributed the rigour and severity of the conscience, often going beyond the actual severity of the father; it explains the fact that the individual can be harsher towards himself than his parents ever were. The tensions of the conscience are, on this view, due not merely to the discomfort of resisting the pressure of habits inculcated by the group, but result from the fact that every time we refrain from meeting frustration by aggression, the aggression is turned against ourselves. The tension is felt as the sense of guilt, in essentials the result of a struggle between the ego and the super-ego. It may be noted in passing that one of the functions of religion is to relieve this tension by the promise of salvation and inward peace.

Freud repudiates the charge frequently made against him that he ignores the more positive aspects of the moral life.

It is no part of our intention [he says] to deny the nobility of human nature, nor have we ever done anything to disparage its value. On the contrary, I show you not only the evil wishes which are censored, but also the censorship which suppresses them and makes them unrecognizable. We dwell upon the evil in human beings with the greater emphasis only because others deny it, thereby making the mental life of mankind not indeed better, but incomprehensible. If we give up the one-sided ethical valuation then we are surer to find the truer formula for the relation of evil to good in human nature.*

It remains that the side of the moral life which is concerned with what is positively worthwhile receives scanty treatment. What there is, is couched in terms of the theory of sublimation, and the formation of the ego-ideal. Sublimation seems to be closely related to the process of identification, though in some of the later essays there are suggestions that it might be due also to the independent work of the ego, among whose functions is included that of introducing unity and harmony into the mental life. On the whole, however, what Freud has to say about the nature of ideals is brought within the framework of the theory of the libido. The love of ideals is in fact reduced to self-love or 'narcissism'. A portion of the libido is directed to ourselves, but some of it goes to ourselves not as we are but as we should like to be, in other words, to our ego-ideal. Now the ego-ideal is built up by identification with the father or father-substitute, and in the course of identification these are idealized, and we ascribe to them qualities which would make them worthy of our love. The root of the idealization, however, is narcissism or self-love. 'The object serves as a substitute for some unattained ego-ideal of our own. We love it on account of the perfection which we have striven to search for in our own ego and which we should now like to procure

* *Introductory Lectures to Psycho-Analysis*, p. 128.

in this roundabout way, as a means of satisfying our narcissism.'*
It will be seen that this leaves the problem of the root of idealism
unresolved, since nothing further is said of the reasons which
make us seek our own perfection. Furthermore, I find it difficult
to believe that the love of ideals can be reduced to self-love. Why
should there not be other things and qualities which are loved
directly and for their own sake and not as parts of the self? Behind this assumption there seems to be a lingering attachment to
the theory of psychological hedonism, the theory that desire is
always for pleasure to the subject or self.

The value of the psychoanalytic contribution to the natural
history of morals does not, I think, depend upon whether or not
these particular theories will prove acceptable. It is to be found
to a far greater extent in the wealth of material which analytic
experience has brought to light, showing the enormous part
played by unconscious factors in the formation of the moral
sentiments. No doubt the fact that in the censure which we direct
against ourselves and against others, repressed impulses and
desires find an outlet, has long been known.† Again self-deception
and sophistication are processes which have been frequently described by novelists, and to some extent by moral psychologists,
long before the days of Psychoanalysis. But no one has shown so
clearly as the analysts how infinitely varied are the distortions to
which the conscience is subject, or disclosed in greater detail the
extent to which the processes may be concealed from the agent
himself. Psychoanalysis has further thrown a flood of light on the
fact that the knowledge of good is so frequently dissociated from

* *Group Psychology and the Psychology of the Ego*, p. 74.
† Professor Laird quotes in this connexion the following passages from
King Lear: 'Look with thine ears: see how yond justice rails upon yond
simple thief. Hark in thine ear: change places; and, handy-dandy, which
is the justice, which is the thief? . . .'
    'Thou rascally beadle, hold thy bloody hand!
    Why dost thou lash that whore? Strip thine own back;
    Thou hotly lust'st to use her in that kind
    For which thou whipp'st her . . .'
A Study in Moral Theory, p. 151.

the will to good, the fact so vividly described by St Paul: 'That which I do I allow not; for what I would, that I do not; but what I hate that I do ... the good that I would I do not, but the evil which I would not, that I do.'* Psychoanalysis can perhaps also help to explain the very remarkable variations in the emotional depth of the response to different types of offence against the moral code. The intensity with which we condemn 'unnatural' lust, fraud, treachery, pride, cruelty, does not seem to be at all closely related to the degree of evil which the reflective conscience would find in each of these vices. Traditional moral psychology seems to have paid little attention to problems of this sort.‡

The central weakness of Freudian moral psychology lies, I think, in its failure to deal adequately with the nature of moral obligation, and this in turn is due to the obscurity which surrounds the treatment of the relation between the cognitive and emotional components of the conscience. Obligation, it seems, consists in submission to authority, whether internal or external. The emotional basis is in either case fear, that is fear of punishment or of losing the love of those around us, or of our aggression towards those whom we love. The attitude towards ourselves when the moral sanctions have been internalized retains all the characteristics it had when the authority was external. Nothing is said of the possibility in the advanced levels of moral development of self-imposed rules, or of respect for principles of conduct rationally accepted as binding. The conscience, I would suggest, is a system of emotional dispositions or 'sentiments', or rather a cluster of such sentiments of varying degrees of unity, which have gathered round our beliefs or judgements concerning right and wrong. The emotional components and the rational level of the judgements vary greatly in the different clusters or systems. There is not in fact one conscience, but an indefinite plurality of consciences, each with its own degree of emotional intensity and intellectual grasp. A man may be highly 'conscientious' in his commercial dealings, but not in controlling his appetites; another may have rigid standards of sexual morality but very flexible ones

* Romans vii, 15–19.   † Cf. A. E. Taylor, *The Faith of a Moralist*, p.194.

in matters of business relations or professional morality. 'I ought' may mean to one 'my social circle expects this of me'; to another 'God expects it of me'; to yet another 'I expect it of myself.' The degree of 'internalization of authority' may differ widely from case to case in the same person and in different persons. The extent to which this internalization occurs can easily be exaggerated. For many individuals even in advanced societies a great deal of morality remains prudential and conventional. People like to believe that their conscience is their own, but in this they are easily deceived. Nevertheless the whole of morality is not 'borrowed' morality. In morals as in other matters people do not live by taking in each others' washing. At some point we have to assume direct value judgements which are slowly clarified by experience and reflection. On this psychoanalytic theory seems to have very little to say.

Furthermore, the account given of the way in which the individual moves from a stage in which authority is external to that in which it becomes an inward monitor is, I think, open to objection. The transition is said to be effected through identification with the father, whereby his authority is incorporated into the self. It seems to me, however, that this process of internalization and individualization owes at least as much to our experience with equals with whom we have to establish a *modus vivendi*. It is through such experience that people come to make their own rules, and these may often be at variance with the rules that have come to them from superior authority. Another important factor is contact between different groups which brings to light conflicting moral standards between which the individual has to choose. In this context the psychoanalysts have tended to treat the family too much in isolation from the larger group, and this has led them to underestimate the part played by social factors in the moral life, and almost completely to ignore the forces, rational and other, making for change and development.

III

We have now to deal with the question whether psychoanalytic theory can provide the basis for a rational ethic. The morality so far discussed is super-ego morality. Its basis is the authority of the father or father-substitute internalized. If all the rules of morals come to us from without as commands, is there any rational method for choosing between them? We have seen that Freud himself nowhere claims to have worked out a rational ethic, yet in various places in his writings he holds out hopes for such an enterprise. In general, he has great faith in the power of rational inquiry. He dismisses subjectivist or relativist views of knowledge as 'intellectual nihilism'.* Though our knowledge of nature is affected by the structure of the mind, this does not make knowledge necessarily subjective, since the structure of the mind itself can be scientifically investigated, and the errors arising out of subjective factors allowed for. The theory of Psychoanalysis, so often accused of exaggerating the strength of the non-rational elements in human nature, rests in fact on the assumption that these are subject to rational control. The function of analysis is to extend the area of conscious control by bringing what was unconscious into consciousness, to ensure, as we are told, that 'where id was there shall ego be.' The ultimate ideal is the 'primacy of reason' and on the moral side, 'the brotherhood of man and the reduction of suffering'.† An ethic of this sort, it is suggested, requires another foundation than that of religion.‡ Only hints are given, however, where such a foundation is to be sought for. It is suggested, for example, that a scientific ethic might play a therapeutic role analogous to that which the physician plays in dealing with neuroses in the individual. The analyst frequently finds that he has to do battle with the individual's conscience, which is often excessively severe and makes demands which he cannot possibly fulfil and which threaten his happiness. What Freud calls the 'cultural super-ego' as represented, for example, in the ethical injunctions of the higher religions, calls for similar therapy. They set up standards too high for human nature and are therefore easily defeated by those who take a more realistic

* *New Introductory Lectures*, p. 224.
† *The Future of an Illusion*, p. 93.
‡ *New Introductory Lectures on Psycho-Analysis*, p. 215.

view. Thus the command to love your neighbour as yourself is no defence against human aggressiveness. 'Such a grandiose inflation of love only lowers its value and cannot remove the evil.' It is not clear, however, by what principles such an examination of idealistic codes is to be guided. The analogy with individual therapy breaks down. In dealing with the individual, the analyst assumes a 'normal' environment and considers behaviour as neurotic which is in conflict with it. No such standard is available for societies, since there exists no scientific, comparative study of the pathology of civilizations, and we therefore cannot tell what is normal and what pathological.

Despite the lack of comparative data Freud has ventured on a general statement of the role of repression in the history of culture. Our civilization, he argued already in his early papers, is in the main founded on the suppression of instincts.* The theme is developed more fully in his sombre essay on the Malaise of Culture.† Both the libidinal and the aggressive tendencies have to be repressed if civilization is to flourish. Sexual energy has to be diverted from its original object to make possible the formation of wider groups and to keep them together. This is one of the reasons for the rules and regulations by which all known societies seek to control the sexual relations of their members. Another reason is to be found in the fact that love is needed to control hate. The aggressive impulses which, in Freud's view, are an ineradicable and primary element in human nature, could destroy mankind if left to work themselves out. To control them, aim-inhibited sexual energy has had to be used. The process involves the building up of the super-ego by the aid of which aggression is turned inwards and prevented from expressing itself directly. Following this line of thought Freud might have said with Buddha that 'hatred does not cease by hatred; by love alone is hate destroyed.' Freud, however, does not share the hope held out by the spiritual

---

* *'Civilized' Sexual Morality and Modern Nervousness*, 1908. *Collected Papers* II.

† *Das Unbehagen in der Kultur*, 1930. English translation, *Civilization and its Discontents*.

religions of the ultimate triumph of love. Eros is pitted against Thanatos and the antagonism between them will in all probability never be overcome.

In urging that the growth of civilization depends on the control or repression of fundamental instinctive drives Freud is saying what, in their different ways, the moralists of all ages have said. From the point of view of ethical theory the important problem is whether it is possible to elicit from his teaching any principles for determining the limits of this inevitable repression or any standards for estimating the loss and gain involved. As regards 'civilized' sexual morality his discussion in the early papers at least is tentative and inconclusive. It is possible, he allows, to maintain that the cultural gains derived from sexual restraint outweigh its manifestly injurious results. But he finds himself unable to balance gain and loss with any precision. And he ends by saying that as judged by individual happiness it is very doubtful whether the sacrifices demanded can be justified – so long, at least, as we are 'still so insufficiently purged of hedonism as to include a certain degree of individual happiness among the aims of our cultural development'.* As regards the effect of sexual restraint on cultural activities, Freud's conclusions are equally tentative. He does not, of course, claim to have undertaken any comparative study of moral codes from this point of view. But on the basis of his own personal impressions he believes that 'the relation between possible sublimation and indispensable sexual activity naturally varies very much in different persons, and indeed with the various kinds of occupation.' He does not support the view that 'sexual abstinence helps to shape energetic self-reliant men of action, or original thinkers, bold pioneers and reformers; far more often it produces "good" weaklings who later become lost in the crowd that tend to follow painfully the initiative of strong characters.'† In the end it emerges that while Freud

* *Sexual Morality and Nervousness*, 1908. *Collected Papers*, II, p. 99.

† Dr J. D. Unwin has produced an elaborate argument to show that in primitive societies there is a definite relation between sexual continence and degree of cultural advance (*Sex and Culture*, 1934). But the criteria

is convinced that the code of sexual morality in Western societies urgently needs to be reformed, he is not prepared as a physician to come forward with definite proposals. This was not to be expected. But the discussion throws light on the sort of ethical theory that Freud might have developed, had he chosen to pursue the matter further. It is clear that the ethical criteria to which he appeals in criticizing existing moral codes are individual happiness and cultural advance. Furthermore, he realizes that we have not the knowledge that would be necessary for any accurate application of these criteria, and he is obviously disturbed by the fact that gains in one direction are often countered by loss in the other.

In the later writings the problem thus raised reappears in another form. Freud finds that there is a certain antagonism between the growth of culture and the development of the individual. The antagonism results, in the first place, from the struggle between Eros and Thanatos. The aim of cultural development is the unification of all mankind. This can only be achieved by a repression of aggression. But every time we control our aggression, it turns against the self. The result is an increasing tension between the ego and the super-ego which is felt as a sense of guilt. It seems to be assumed that the larger the group, the greater the difficulty of achieving libidinal unity and the greater the cost in human happiness. The progress of mankind can only be achieved at the expense of an intensification of the sense of guilt 'until perhaps it

---

which he uses both for cultural condition and sexual regulation are very vague and the evidence he adduces is not sufficient to justify a generalization so far-reaching. (Cf. my review of this book in *Nature*, vol. CXXXV, p. 205, 1935.) Westermarck, who made a very comprehensive survey of the available information, concludes that there is no relation between the toleration of unchastity and the degree of culture, and that on the contrary chastity is more respected in the lowest tribes than in the higher ones. In *The Material Culture and Social Institutions of the Simpler Peoples* (1915), L. T. Hobhouse, G. C. Wheeler and the present writer found that the evidence was not sufficient to establish a universal association between sexual regulation and cultural grade as judged by economic criteria.

may swell to a magnitude that individuals can hardly support.'* No wonder that Freud thought the sense of guilt constituted the most important problem in the evolution of culture.

In the second place, there is, according to Freud, not only this irreconcilable conflict between the life and death instincts but a fissure within the libido itself, which from the ethical point of view is at least as important. The growth of the individual is shaped by the pleasure principle, that is by the desire of the individual for his own happiness. No doubt he can only attain this through membership in a community. But this condition is sometimes represented by Freud as a sort of unfortunate necessity, as something he would be better without. For culture, as we have seen, is necessarily restrictive of the individual; it demands instinctual renunciation. There is thus, as Freud says,† dissension in the camp of the libido itself, a struggle between the striving for happiness and the impulse towards union with others. Freud asserts that this contest will ultimately be resolved in the case of the individual and perhaps also in the future of civilization. But unfortunately the theme is not further developed.

The ethical theory that Freud's discussion suggests is one of enlightened self-interest, that is self-interest purged of unconscious distortions, fears and anxieties not rooted in the objective situation. What such self-interest would require can only emerge after therapeutic analysis both of the individuals and societies. But it is difficult to believe that psychology will ever by itself solve the fundamental problems of human relations, or in the Freudian terminology, the problem of the right apportionment of libidinal attachment as between self and other 'objects'. A theory of ethics which rests on the assumption that in dealing justly with others the individual can after all secure his own happiness has all the air of an 'illusion' which, from the Freudian point of view, should be relegated to the infantile stages of the development of morality.

It is, I think, remarkable that while Freud and his followers have so much to say about love, they pay hardly any attention

* *Civilization and its Discontents*, p. 116.   † ibid., p. 136.

to justice. The only reference I can find is in Freud's *Group Psychology and the Psychology of the Ego*. 'Social justice', we are told, 'means that we deny ourselves many things so that others may have to do without them as well, or what is the same thing, may not be able to ask for them.' The demand for equality among the members of a group is said to be rooted in the jealousy aroused against those who would monopolize the love of the leader, just as their sense of community rests on their common renunciation of his exclusive love. This reduction of humanity and justice to envy and jealousy is somewhat mitigated by his interpretation of Eros as a force working for unity and harmony. But the two sides of his theory, ultimately due to the vagueness and ambiguity of the concept of the libido, are nowhere satisfactorily brought into relation, and on the whole the 'egoistic' trend in his thought predominates. It is difficult to see how such a conception of human nature can ever provide the basis for a rational ethic.

The most important problems of ethics centre round the theory of justice and in dealing with it Psychoanalysis is, I think, at its weakest. I see no reason, from the purely psychological side, for accepting the Freudian view of the origins of the sense of justice. Neither in the history of the individual or of civilization can this be shown to be rooted predominantly in the desire that no one shall fare better than ourselves. It owes at least as much to the power of sympathy, that is the power of entering in imagination into the situation of another and seeing it as though it were our own. Above all there is a rational element in it which the Freudian analysis completely ignores. The core of justice is the demand for equality and this is based at bottom on the rejection of arbitrariness, the recognition that individuals ought not to be treated differently unless a reasonable ground can be given for so treating them. I can see no ground for regarding this demand as merely emotional. If I say that 'one man's good is of as much intrinsic worth as the like good of another,' I certainly do not mean that 'the emotion which I experience in knowing that one man is benefited or injured is the same as that which I should experience in the case of any other.' This latter statement would be manifestly untrue in many instances but the recognition of its falsity has no bearing on the truth or falsity of my recognition of the principle of equality as binding on me. The difficulties in the theory of equality begin to emerge when we try to think out the grounds which justify differential treatment. On these again psychology may throw some light, but in the end value judgements have to be made, which, though ineffectual if lacking in emotional warmth, do not depend for their validity on the strength of the emotional response.

In sum, the issue that psychoanalytic theories of ethics have to face is that with which all naturalistic ethics are confronted. The problem is whether moral judgements express desires, strivings or emotions, or whether they go beyond what is actually desired to what *ought* to be desired. It seems to me that psychoanalysts suffer from what might be called an 'ought phobia'. They show too great an anxiety to explain the 'ought' away, and they tend to pass from the indicative to the imperative mood without realizing the implications of the transition. Thus, for example, Profesor Flugel in his very illuminating study of the psychological basis of morals is in search of an ethic purged of anger and aggression and one that would make its appeal to reason. Yet reason is, in his view, concerned with means and not with ends, which in the last resort are set by 'orexis' or desire. The moral criterion which is finally adopted, however, clearly goes beyond what individuals actually desire to what they ought to desire, or, if you like, to what they would desire if they were rational. This criterion is the free and spontaneous expression of the instincts in so far as this is compatible with harmony not only in the individual but in society. Is this ideal then 'orectic' or cognitive? Again when we are told that increasing sociality and increasing individualization are complementary aspects of moral evolution, is this a statement of fact or of what ought to be fact? We have seen that according to Freud the conflict between individual and social development is far from being resolved, and Professor Flugel also points out that the compromise which has to be effected between socialization and individualization remains one of the most acute problems of modern democracy.* To set up social harmony as an ideal is to describe a form of life held to be desirable, not one which is necessarily desired. If the test is to be found in what people actually desire, the impulses making for discord may prove more powerful, or no less powerful, than those making for harmony. Despite a good deal that is attractive in Professor Flugel's exposition I feel that in the end he leaves undefined the relation between the striving and the cognitive elements in the moral judgement. He says that in a scientific handling of human relations 'we must substitute a cognitive and psychological approach for an emotional and a moral one.'† But this, I think, would be not to explain morality, but to explain it away.

IV

I turn now to the views of Erich Fromm, which in important respects involve a departure from Freudian theory. In the first place, his conception of human nature is not as individualistic, or asocial, as he takes Freud's to be. He has a different conception of both the love and hate elements in the human mind. Man is fundamentally social in that he needs to be related to others, to escape aloneness, to belong or to be needed. Destructiveness on the other hand is the result of a baulking of vitality, not an inherent or primary need to hurt or destroy. In the second place, he distinguishes more radically than the Freudians between what he calls an 'authoritarian' conscience and a 'humanistic' conscience. The former is the voice of an internalized external authority, the super-ego of Freudian theory. The latter is not 'the internalized voice of an authority we are eager to please and are afraid of displeasing; it is our own voice, present in every human being and independent of external rewards and sanctions.'‡ It is the expression of our true selves', 'the reaction of our total personality to its proper functioning or disfunctioning'. It bids us develop fully and harmoniously, that is 'to realize ourselves, to become what we potentially are'.

* *Man, Morals and Society*, p. 253.   † *Man, Morals and Society*, p. 255.
‡ *Man for Himself*, p. 158.

Here we are back full circle to theories long familiar to philosophers, but now claiming to be derived from empirical psychology. While there is a great deal that is very helpful in Fromm's analysis of the conditions of harmonious development, he does not seem to succeed any better than the Freudians in making the transition from what is or may be to what ought to be. To say that we should aim at becoming what we potentially are is not illuminating, since we are potentially evil as well as good and what we need is a criterion for distinguishing between them. The appeal to the 'real' or 'true' self is purely verbal, since the real self is not the self as it is but as it ought to be. Furthermore, the formula of self-realization leaves out of consideration the central problem of ethics – that of the relation between self and others. In the end, it is not any form of self-fulfilment that is desirable, but only that which is compatible with the fulfilment of others. Clearly such an end goes far beyond what any particular individuals actually desire, and it may require them to abandon or sacrifice a good deal of what they so desire. The philosophical problem of the principles of justice thus remains. It seems to me that writers like Fromm and Karen Horney are too optimistic in assuming that these can be discovered by 'listening to ourselves'. What we may thus hear may not be very enlightening. The conditions of social harmony have to be discovered; they will not follow automatically from the striving towards self-realization, even if each individual is 'true to himself'.

V

An interesting approach to the ethical aspects of Psychoanalysis is to be found in the various attempts that have been made to clarify the concept of a 'normal' mind. It soon becomes clear that from the point of view of mental health the 'normal' is not equivalent to the 'well adjusted'. Adjustment is a relation between the individual and his environment, and it is obvious that not every environment is equally likely to elicit what is best in the minds it moulds. The best adjusters, say, to a criminal environment are not necessarily the healthiest. If we value individuality and spontaneity we should have to regard the individual who conforms most fully to the pattern of a totalitarian society as unhealthy. The criterion of efficiency, in the sense of effective use of capacities, is equally unhelpful. A selfishly prudent person may be successful in achieving his own ends to the detriment of others. 'Social efficiency' is again relative to the standards prevalent for the time being and, as judged by them, the finest and those most sensitive to new values would have to be called 'abnormal'.* Again in periods of rapid changes in the social structure the individual who shapes his conduct in accordance with standards developed in periods of greater stability may have to carry a burden too heavy for mental peace. In such circumstances the 'well adjusted' person may well be the exception and not the rule.

Considerations such as these suggest that the normal and the abnormal cannot be fruitfully defined in terms of conformity with, or departure from, current standards.† From the point of view of psychoanalytic theory we have to consider not only the fact of deviation but its causal background. Dr H. J. Wegrocki has suggested that the differentia of abnormality is to be found in 'the tendency to choose a type of reaction which represents an escape from a conflict-producing situation instead of a facing of the problem'.‡ This may serve well enough, I imagine, provided the notion of 'escape' can be defined in a manner which would make it include all the symptoms that psychopathologists use in identifying neuroses. But in its broader applications the charge of 'escapism' can easily be levelled against anything that we do not happen to approve. Those who think that radical social reforms can only be brought about by inward psychological changes will regard all those who put their faith in external institutional

* 'Nor must we overlook the fact that the greatest ethical reformers, prophets and heroes were certainly neurotics, and that ethics has been furthered by them' (Pfister, *Some Applications of Psycho-Analysis*, p. 229). It is not clear to me by what tests they are adjudged 'neurotic'.

† Except, of course, in dealing with gross pathological deviations.

‡ 'A critique of cultural and statistical concepts of abnormality', *Journal of Abnormal and Social Psychology*, vol. 34, 1939.

changes as 'escapists', and conversely. Similarly the pacifist and his opponent may well accuse each other of running away from the facts and not 'facing reality'.

An important attempt to arrive at an objective standard of normality has been made by Dr Ernest Jones in his paper on 'The concept of the normal'.* In effect, if I have understood him rightly, he gives a psychoanalytic version of the Aristotelian doctrine of the mean, with the analyst playing the part of the 'phronimos'. If the individual could through analysis be purged of his unconscious fear, hate, and guilt, his potentialities would have the chance of developing in due proportion. In his relations with others he would then show neither the excessive friendliness which may mask an unresolved sadism, nor the insensitiveness which may be a defence against a love of which he is afraid. He will thus avoid the kind of selfishness which is a form of 'secondary narcissism' and the sort of self-sacrifice which is rooted in unconscious guilt. Having inner security, he will meet frustration and hostility calmly and fearlessly. Freed from unconscious guilt he will develop the capacity for happiness, that is a combination of the capacity for enjoyment with self-content. He will have the inner freedom which will result from the removal of undue repressions and the barriers that impede the flow of energy between the conscious and unconscious levels of the mind.

Clearly this describes an ideal rather than an existing state of affairs. To the question whether a normal mind thus defined exists, Dr Jones replies 'definitely in the negative'. He adds that we are only in the early stages of learning about the conditions in which the standard laid down can be attained. From the point of view of ethical theory the problem is whether Dr Jones is describing what people actually desire or what in his view they ought to desire. On his own showing people are in fact torn between love and hate, between gratification and repression, between the super-ego actuated by guilt based on fear and the super-ego actuated by affection. To say that as a result of analysis the ethics of affection will be shown to be superior to the ethics of authority

* *International Journal of Psycho-Analysis*, vol. XXIII, 1942.

is to say that the former ought to prevail over the latter; it is a value judgement and not an assertion of psychological fact. Furthermore, we are told very little about the contents of an ethic of love. It is not to be taken for granted that love, even if 'desexualized', will suffice to solve the problems of human relations.* There will remain the difficulties of choice and the grading of values. We cannot and ought not to love everything in ourselves and in others indiscriminately. The principle of universal love, taken by itself, might easily lead to the position of philosophical anarchism, that everyone should be allowed to do what he wills. If it is urged that to do so would result in the majority of people not getting what they want, we are brought back to the real task of social ethics which is to discover the principles of distributive justice and the limits with which constraint may rightly be used to ensure their being carried into effect. To this task psychology may contribute much of importance, but is hardly likely to have the last word.

Dr Jones makes the interesting observation that 'analysed people, including psychoanalysts, differ surprisingly little from unanalysed people in the use of their intelligence. . . .' They show greater tolerance, he tells us, in sexual and religious matters, but in other spheres, e.g., in dealing with the relative merits of capitalism or communism or the problems of class structure or international relations, they continue to be extensively influenced by the distorting effects of unconscious complexes. He goes on to suggest that if the analytic technique were applied to the convictions men hold in relation to all these problems, we should gain knowledge that would aid us in the study of normality.†

* Of course, if you begin by putting all the virtues into love you can take them out again. Cf. St Augustine: Temperance is love keeping itself uncontaminated for its object; Fortitude is love readily enduring all for the beloved's sake; Justice is love serving only the beloved and therefore rightly governing; Prudence is love sagaciously choosing the things that help her and rejecting the things that hinder (De Moribus, I, 15, 25, 1841; translation of passage as given by Sidgwick, Outlines of the History of Ethics, p. 132, 5th ed., 1925).

† loc. cit., p. 4.

This suggestion has been elaborated and carried further by Dr Money-Kyrle, who by its aid arrives at a definition of the normal which identifies it with the rational.* A desire is rational according to Dr Money-Kyrle if all the beliefs that influence it are true. Presumably all the beliefs are true if they represent accurately the qualities of the objects desired, or the appropriateness of the means used to attain these objects. On the other hand, the desires themselves cannot be either true or false, rational or irrational. The chain of means and ends cannot of course go on indefinitely. There are, however, no ultimate or irreducible desires until we reach the most primitive desires of all, such as 'the hedonic impulse to avoid painful and seek pleasurable experiences'. This, of course, is the sort of theory that has long been familiar to philosophers in various forms. What psychoanalytic theory adds is to stress the part played by unconscious factors in influencing beliefs. A desire is rational if these have been brought to consciousness and accepted only if shown to be true.

The distinction drawn by Dr Ernest Jones between a super-ego actuated by guilt based on fear and a super-ego actuated by affection reappears here in the form of a distinction between the 'authoritarian' and the 'humanistic' character. In the former moral behaviour is predominantly shaped by the fear of punishment; in the latter, by the fear of injuring or disappointing something that is loved. Moral behaviour is defined as behaviour dictated by a sense of guilt. But while in the authoritarian character the sense of guilt is based on what, following Dr Melanie Klein, Dr Money-Kyrle calls the 'persecutory position', in the humanitarian this gives place to the 'depressive position', sorrow at having injured something loved. It is claimed that as a result of analysis a patient gets rid of his irrational fears and thus of his authoritarian morality. But as he gains increasing knowledge of himself he has an 'emphatic understanding of his fellows and can neither injure nor neglect them without distress – or what is the same thing, without depressive guilt'. It is not clear whether this new form of guilt is just a feeling of depression or a recogni-

* *Psycho-Analysis and Politics*, 1951.

tion of wrong, nor whether the whole of the 'ego morality' is exhausted in the unwillingness of the agent to injure or neglect his fellows. Be this as it may, the conclusion is drawn that since the transformation is effected through increasing knowledge or insight, we may say that to be normal, to be rational and to be humanistic are one and the same thing. In this way, Dr Money-Kyrle argues, ethics can be given a scientific basis and thus escape the relativism which, as he explains, he finds emotionally intolerable.

The weakness of this line of argument is revealed when we ask, why be rational or normal? The only answer that can be given, we are told, is that there is in us a desire for truth.* The question then arises as to the status of this desire. So far as I can see it is not one of the primitive or irreducible desires, since hedonically truth is far from being what we always want. But even if it were, it would be only one desire among others which conflict with it, and as between ultimate desires there is according to this view no rational way of deciding. We are thus left with a non-rational desire for rationality. It is not easy to see how this escapes relativism.

Dr Money-Kyrle argues that it is possible on the evidence provided by Psychoanalysis to define the 'good' state, and to decide rationally between the rival political theories now clamouring for our allegiance. The 'good' state is, in short, the one that provides the most favourable opportunities for the development of the 'normal' or 'humanist' character in its citizens. If the non-humanist disagrees, we can show him that his beliefs are rooted in a character dominated by irrational anxieties within himself and that, if he submitted himself to analysis, he would be freed from their domination, his character would become more humanistic and his political views would be correspondingly transformed. I do not know whether this argument is purely hypothetical, or whether it has been empirically verified by actual analysis of representative samples of the different political parties. But in any case Dr Money-Kyrle wins his battles too easily. A very complex inquiry would be needed to determine to what extent political

* ibid., p. 87.

theories differ about the ends of social life or about the means. That Tories want freedom without welfare, Socialists welfare without freedom, and Communists neither freedom nor welfare are statements that each might make about the other, but hardly about themselves. Psychoanalysis can no doubt help in clarifying the ends of conduct relatively to the means needed to realize them. But I do not see how it can decide rationally which theories are 'right' and which 'wrong', if it starts from the assumption that the distinction between true and false does not apply to the ends of desire. All that can be said on this assumption is that some prefer one political theory and some another.* In this context the communists are on sounder ground when they urge, in agreement with many non-communist philosophers, that ends and means are dialectically interdependent and that in any evaluation they must be considered together. If so, we should be led to a different view of what constitutes rationality in action from that which seems to be favoured by psychoanalysts. We should in fact be searching for principles guiding desire and recognized as rightly guiding them. No doubt Psychoanalysis gives powerful support to the doctrine that force is no remedy and that repression takes its revenge by generating fresh conflicts. In doing so it is in harmony with certain aspects of liberal political theory. But liberal thought has long ago recognized also that liberty rests on restraint, a principle again supported by what Psychoanalysis has to teach us concerning the functions of repression in the development of the mind. The problem both in the case of the individual and of society is to determine the limits of coercion and the spheres within which it may be properly used. It is at this point that political theories diverge and I do not see why we should expect Psychoanalysis to clear away the formidable difficulties which these theories have to face.

* I think Bertrand Russell is more candid in dealing with a similar question. In an account he gives of an imaginary dialogue between Nietzsche and Buddha, he admits that in the end the issue cannot be decided by an appeal to facts, but only by an appeal to the emotions. (*A History of Western Philosophy*, pp. 799–800.)

VI

It follows, I think, from the above survey that the attempts that have been made to derive an ethical theory from Psychoanalysis have not so far proved successful. Psychoanalysis, it seems to me, is not necessarily committed to any particular theory, and is compatible with very different theories of the logical character of moral judgements. Its business as a therapy is to break down the barriers between the unconscious and the conscious levels of the mind and in this way to expand the area of conscious control. But it is not to be assumed that when an individual has become more fully aware of the impulses by which he has been influenced he will necessarily have discovered the right principles of conduct. That would only follow on the assumption of a natural moral sense which needs only to be freed from the obstructions to which it has been subjected to be enabled to see at once what is right and what is wrong in human relations. Psychoanalysts are of course as entitled as anyone else to subscribe to a naturalistic theory of morals, but I cannot see that such a theory derives special support from the teaching of Psychoanalysis.

The predilection shown by psychoanalytic writers for the view that moral judgements are 'orectic', that is expressions of desire or striving, is, I think, traceable to two sources. Firstly psychoanalysts have never freed themselves from the doctrine of psychological hedonism, despite the criticisms directed against it by moral philosophers. They tend to interpret Freud's 'pleasure principle' as implying that impulses have for their sole object the pursuit of pleasure and the avoidance of pain. From psychological hedonism they pass in a manner familiar in the history of philosophy to ethical hedonism, in other words from the assertion that men seek pleasure or happiness to the assertion that happiness is their good. The appeal to the 'real self' also lends itself to a species of naturalism amounting to the assertion that the good is what satisfies the self or what would satisfy it, if it knew its 'true' nature.

In the second place, I suggest that the predilection for the view that moral judgements are rooted in desire or striving may be a sort of defensive reaction against the authoritarian element in morals. In their flight from the 'ought' psychoanalysts overlook the distinction between moral obligation and self-coercion. This is encouraged by the fact that the moral law is often regarded as a sort of command. But strictly the relation of command-obedience is inter-personal, and it is only by analogy that it is extended to the self. A man cannot really 'obey' himself or such an abstraction as a general principle. It is no doubt the case that moral judgements claim to possess authority, but this is only another way of saying that they claim to be true. It is psychologically convenient to speak of recalcitrant impulse struggling against reason or of conflicts between impulses. But all this has little bearing on the problem of the logical validity of moral judgements. Constraint and validity are not inter-changeable terms.

On the empirical side Psychoanalysis can, I think, make important contributions to the study of morality mainly in two directions. It can help, in the first place, by building up what might be called a comparative moral pathology. It would be of the greatest interest to the moralist to know what changes are brought about by analysis in, say, a Muhammadan, a Buddhist, or a Communist living in their own setting. The analysis of representatives of these creeds in other than their own environment is another matter, the issues being complicated by the influence on the individual of conflicting moral codes. Data of this sort would provide valuable material for the study of the causes making for variation in moral codes and they would facilitate the task of their critical evaluation.

In the second place, Psychoanalysis can contribute towards the clarification of moral experience by ridding it of the magical elements that have gathered around it and purging it of fear and anger. An example of what I have in mind is to be found in the persistent influence of the emotional demand for retribution on the criminal law and on the philosophical theories of the ethical basis of punishment. The movement in recent psychoanalytic writings towards a 'humanist' ethics is clearly in this direction. But though an ethic based on love is vastly superior to one based on obedience, it will not suffice to solve the complex problems of human relations, even in small groups, and still less in the 'great society'. The demands of love generate conflicts of their own. There are fissures, as Freud saw, within the libido itself. To overcome them we need more than goodwill. Neither in theory nor in practice can love replace justice.

11

The Nature of Responsibility*

I SHOULD like to begin by expressing my sense of the great
honour which The Clarke Hall Fellowship have done me by in-
viting me to give the Clarke Hall lecture this year. Unlike most
of my predecessors in the series I have had no first-hand experience of penal procedure or of the psychological treatment of
delinquency. I imagine that in suggesting the subject of this
lecture and asking me to deal with it the Committee of the Fellowship may have wished to draw attention to the ethical and
sociological aspects of the problem of responsibility, and I can
only hope that such reflections as I can offer may serve this purpose and have some bearing also on the practical problems of
penal administration and reform.

Legal responsibility is frequently defined as a liability to punishment and, similarly, moral responsibility as liability to moral
blame (or, presumably, praise). Such definitions are, I think,
from the ethical point of view misleading. They suggest that
moral obligations depend on external sanctions and that there is
an intrinsic and necessary connexion between guilt and punishment. But it may well be that moral obligations and legal obligations, in so far as they have a moral basis, are self-justified and
independent of the praise or blame of others; and that while
just punishment involves responsibility, responsibility does not
necessarily involve punishment.

To avoid begging these important questions, I propose to begin
by considering responsibility and punishment independently and
then to inquire how they are connected. In ordinary usage, to
be responsible means, firstly, to be capable of discharging a duty.
It means, secondly, to be liable to be called to account, to be

* The thirteenth Clarke Hall Lecture, May 1953.

answerable. Religious writers regard responsibility as answerableness to God. In ethical discussions it is often considered as 'answerableness to one's own conscience'. This, however, is metaphorical. It implies that the self consists of two beings, one of whom is responsible to the other. Strictly to be answerable to one's conscience means no more than to recognize a duty to do something or to refrain, or to recognize that one ought to have done something or refrained. When we say that a person takes on responsibility we mean that he takes on duties to act without detailed guidance from others. To be responsible *for* others means either to have duties towards them, as when a parent is said to be responsible for the well-being of his children, or it may mean to be held accountable for what they do, as when a parent is responsible for the debts of his children. The notion of accountability is also implied in the use of such a phrase as 'responsible government'; but here the stress is on the contrast with autocratic government. Responsible government is government in which those who govern know that they may be called upon to render account of their actions, and are ready and willing to do so. In all these senses there seems to be three elements: causation, obligation, accountability. We impute responsibility to a person for an act of which he is the cause or author. Second, the act in question is one which is governed by rules, legal or moral. Third, the person is accountable in the sense that in consequence of the act it may be his duty to perform other acts by way of rectification or reparation.

To impute an act to any person is to say that he is its origin and cause. This means, firstly, that no one is responsible for the acts of others. It means, in the second place, that the agent is the cause not in the sense of containing within himself the whole sum of conditions resulting in the event, but only that without his act the event would not have occurred. Thus the causes of a criminal act may include factors in the social environment not due to the individual and over which he has no control and for which he is therefore not responsible. But he is responsible for his part in the chain of causation which is decisive in bringing about the event. In the third place, only that in an event is imputable which results from a voluntary act. We do not hold a man responsible for what he does in ignorance or under compulsion or when his mentality is such that he is incapable of forming any intent at all. Voluntary action implies prevision. A man is responsible only for those consequences of his act which were foreseen by him or could have been foreseen. If you sell a gun to a man who subsequently uses it to commit murder, or if you help him to find his way to the scene of the crime, you cannot be accused of complicity unless there is reason to believe that you knew the intentions of the murderer. Responsibility involves not only intent but also the presence of an obligation to do or refrain of which the agent is aware or ought to be aware. The agent must know not only the physical quality of his acts or consequences, but also their moral or legal qualities, i.e., their conformity or lack of conformity with the legal or moral rules under which they come. Finally, the agent is accountable for his acts in two senses of the word. He is accountable to someone, but even if there is no one to call him to account, he is still accountable in the moral sense that it is his duty to make reparation or in any other way to restore the situation he has disturbed.

It follows that a person is responsible for acts (i) which he performs with intention or choice, where alternatives are possible, (ii) when he knows the nature of the acts and the consequences likely to follow from them, (iii) when he knows that the acts are governed by a law (legal or moral) binding on himself. Responsibility thus implies freedom. By freedom in this context I mean the power or the ability to form a judgement of the relative goodness or badness of the alternatives possible and of acting in accordance with that judgement. Freedom involves two elements, cognitive and affective. The agent must be capable of forming a judgement of right or wrong, and knowledge of it must have sufficient emotional warmth and drive to enable him to act in accordance with it. Thus where the affective and cognitive elements are dissociated, or to the extent that they are dissociated, there is a corresponding restriction of freedom in the sense here relevant. Responsibility and freedom are correlative, and since there are degrees of freedom, it follows that there are degrees of responsibility.

I cannot attempt here to settle the ancient controversy between the determinists and the indeterminists. But I will ask you to consider whether anyone seriously doubts that a man can be influenced in his action by the judgement he forms of the consequences of his acts and of the relative value or worth of the alternatives open to him. We make such judgements every day, and we do so more or less impartially, that is with greater or lesser freedom from bias. The freedom that is required as a minimum condition of moral accountability is the ability to make an impartial estimate of the relative worth of the alternatives open to me and of acting accordingly. If I am not capable of any measure of impartiality, if I am unable to know what I am doing, or whether what I am doing is right or wrong; or again if having such knowledge I have not the emotional or conative energy to act in accordance with it, then I am neither free nor responsible.

If it be maintained that a man's judgements are themselves completely determined, that he cannot help making the judgements he makes, the answer is that this would make nonsense of all knowledge. For if all judgements were causally necessitated, they would all be on the same level and it would be impossible to distinguish some as true and others as false. Sense and nonsense would all be equally necessitated. The whole notion of going by the evidence would lose all its meaning, if in forming a judgement we were completely unable to resist the violence of present desires, the effects of past habits, the persistence of ancient prejudices or the forces of the unconscious. There would be no sense in arguing about determinism or indeterminism if all our arguments were rigidly determined in advance. If we admit that we can sometimes eliminate bias, that we can sometimes act on the basis of a judgement we form of the facts and of the relative value of the alternatives between which we have to choose, we have the minimum freedom required for moral accountability or responsibility. It should be added that the power of making impartial judgements is one that can be developed by practice and weakened by neglect. If so, we are responsible for making the best of this power.

These conclusions are not, I think, in any way shaken by the psychology of the unconscious. Psychoanalysis is sometimes regarded as completely deterministic and as denying the efficacy of the rational powers of the mind. But if the conscious personality were unable to govern our actions, psychotherapy would be impossible. The object of psychotherapy, I take it, is to break down the barriers between the conscious and the unconscious, to enable the patient to face realities, to be honest with himself, to see himself as he is and not to blame others for his troubles, in short, to become a responsible person. The whole procedure would be futile, if it was assumed at the outset that the patient could not be helped to help himself.

As an example consider a case of 'compulsive' stealing as reported by Alexander and Staub.* This was a case of a highly intelligent girl who was brought to court for stealing a cheap edition of *Faust*, dresses which she could not wear and for which she had no use, and simple pictures presenting a mother and child, while other apparently more valuable pictures failed to interest her. She was completely unable to explain to herself why she stole these things. Analysis showed that the acts of stealing, and the aggressive feelings which accompanied them, were of the nature of substitutive gratifications or compensations for deprivation of parental love and the frustration of her desire to have a child. The case is thus interpreted as a transition between criminality and a neurosis of the compulsive type. The treatment which in this case was successful consisted in bringing the unconscious motives to light and thus enabling her to control her impulses and to learn to seek gratification in real life instead of living on the substitutive gratifications of a neurotic. The treatment thus consists in enabling the patient to know what she is doing and to control her actions in the light of her knowledge.

* *The Criminal, the Judge, and the Public*, pp. 108 seq.

This implies freedom and responsibility, as I have defined them, i.e., the capacity to act in accordance with one's knowledge of the nature of the act and its consequences and the obligations attaching to such knowledge.

We have now to consider the relation of responsibility to reward and punishment. Obligations are self-justifying and self-authenticated, not indeed when taken in isolation, but when they are considered as contributing to an order of life thought to be good and binding on the whole. They are thus independent of praise or blame, reward and punishment. The function of punishment is to protect society and that of reward to stimulate endeavour. In both cases the appeal is to non-moral motives, though in favourable circumstances they may have indirect moral value as aids in the formation of character. We come up here against the difficult problem of the retributive element in reward and punishment. In 1874 Sidgwick expressed the view that the notion that justice requires pain to be inflicted upon a man, even if no further benefit results either to himself or to others from the pain, was one that was gradually passing away from the moral consciousness of educated persons in most advanced communities.* It appears, however, that in this he was too sanguine. The retributive theory retains its vitality and comes up again and again in various guises. A subtle defence of it was made in the first Clarke Hall Lecture by the late Archbishop Temple. In the main he follows English Hegelians, especially Bosanquet. 'Retributive punishment', he says, 'even in brutally vindictive forms, does at least treat its victims as persons and moral agents and has thus an ethical superiority to mere deterrence or to a merely medicinal treatment aiming at reformation.' The moral justification of penal action is, he thinks, that by its means the community dissociates itself from the criminal act and expresses its repudiation of the crime. The matter is, however, not pursued in detail. He does not show why this repudiation must take the form of the infliction of pain over and above that involved in public trial and condemnation, nor does he

* *Methods of Ethics*, p. 281.

inquire whether the notion of equivalence which is inherent in retribution can be given an intelligible meaning. Here I am concerned only with the relation between punishment and responsibility and would like to urge that as a basis for penal action administered by courts of law retribution cannot possibly be adjusted to degree of responsibility. Responsibility, as we have seen, involves causation, knowledge of right and wrong and sufficient integration of knowledge and affect to enable the agent to act in accordance with what he knows. These are all matters of degree and they cannot be determined with any precision. It is quite impossible to estimate how much in the effect is to be attributed to the individual and how much to the social setting within which he acts. It is impossible for the observer to ascertain whether the individual could have acted otherwise than he did. Nor can the punishment inflicted be apportioned to the guilt. We may indeed rightly wish that the offender should suffer, in the sense that he should realize what he has done. But this is an inward and spiritual process which punishment inflicted by society cannot ensure. Metaphysically, retribution may or may not be an integral part of the moral order of the universe. It is not something which can be safely entrusted to human hands. 'Vengeance is mine,' saith the Lord. This means, we may add with Bernard Shaw, 'it is not the Lord Chief Justice's.'

We are on surer ground when we consider the relation between responsibility and the protective and deterrent aspects of punishment. For if responsibility implies the ability to be influenced in one's action by the knowledge of its consequences, the certainty of detection and punishment adds an additional motive which may sway the balance. How far people are in fact restrained by a knowledge of legal penalties and their regular infliction is a matter which permits of empirical investigation. Bentham laid down the principle that the degree of punishment ought to be sufficient to deter and not more than sufficient. In practice this is far from being adhered to, partly because other motives than deterrence enter into punishment, and partly because we have no precise knowledge of the deterrent effects of different degrees of punishment. That the knowledge of legal penalties does in fact in many cases act as a deterrent can hardly be seriously disputed. Normal, law-abiding people will forget to light their bicycle lamps after dark in country lanes if they have no reason to fear that they will be caught. The efficiency of the Factory Acts relating to the protection of workers against accidents varies directly with the number and vigilance of the inspectorate. In these, as in graver offences, what counts is not the severity of the punishment but the certainty of detection and conviction. On the other hand, it is clear that punishments frequently fail to deter and this presents a difficult problem. We have moved a long way since it was thought that even animals could be deterred from crime by exemplary punishment. According to the Zend Avesta a dog that killed a sheep or wounded a man was ordered to have its right ear cut off at the first offence, its left ear at the second offence, its right leg at the third, and so on. In the year 1595 the City Court of Leyden sentenced a dog that had killed a man to be hanged and to remain hanging on the gallows 'to the deterring of all other dogs'.* That executions in public were effective deterrents was widely believed. 'In extreme cases it was usual for the court to direct the murderer after execution to be hung upon a gibbet in chains near the place where the crime was committed, with the intention of thereby deterring others from capital offences, and in order that the body might all the longer serve this purpose it was saturated with tar before it was hung in chains. The popularity which mutilation as a punishment enjoyed during the Middle Ages was largely due to the opinion that a "malefactor miserably living was a more striking example of justice, than one put to death at once." '†

Such behaviour strikes us now as at once horrible and absurd. Yet we still have capital punishment for murder, though it is by no means certain that as a deterrent it is more effective than other forms of punishment or that its abolition would lead to an increase of murders; we still consider attempted suicide as a

* Kenny, *Outline of Criminal Law*, p. 45.
† Westermarck, *Origin and Development of Moral Ideas*, vol. I, p. 192.

crime, though there is no evidence that its punishment is likely to deter others who may be inclined to kill themselves; we still get repeated demands for flogging as a punishment, though long experience has proved it to be ineffective; we still deal with habitual criminals in the unfounded hope that they will be deterred from future crime by repeated imprisonment. Clearly our attitude to punishment as a deterrent is full of ambiguities and inconsistencies. These considerations have an important bearing upon the nature of responsibility. If responsibility consists in the ability to be influenced in one's behaviour by an adequate motive, including the motive based on the anticipation of legal penalties, it would follow that persons incapable of being affected by the threat of punishment are so far irresponsible and that in their case punishment considered solely as a deterrent cannot be justified.

The need of protecting society suggests different considerations. It is obvious that society has to be protected against the non-responsible as much as or more than against the responsible. But in the case of the non-responsible, punishment is irrelevant: the important thing is to keep them out of the way of doing further harm. This is recognized in the law relating to lunatics in the case of murder, and in the provisions for dealing with mental deficiency in the case of offences which would be punishable in adults with imprisonment or in children by being sent to an approved school. I take it that the Acts dealing with these matters are not primarily penal but protective of the individuals concerned and of society; they are not concerned to punish the offender but to provide for segregation and treatment. We thus come up against the problem of how we are to draw the line between those acts which call for punitive measures and those which call for non-punitive ones, by whom the line is to be drawn and at what point. These are the issues hotly debated by lawyers and psychiatrists. Being neither a lawyer nor a psychiatrist, what I have to say can only be very tentative.

There is, I think, a growing consensus of opinion that retributive justice is not the concern of the law. Quite apart from the philosophical difficulties which retributive theories of justice have had to face, it has come to be recognized that the machinery of the law is unequal to the task of moral assessment, that it can neither determine degree of causality and guilt, nor the just apportionment of the one to the other. Nevertheless in practice judges and magistrates do take into consideration the mental state of the offender and, quite aside from insanity, use discretion in mitigation of sentence on the ground of mental abnormality. It is not clear whether in doing so they are guided by a lingering attachment to notions of retribution, and so still try to fit the penalty to the crime, or whether their aim is deterrence and the protection of society. The principles involved are far from clear and appear to be receiving less attention in current discussion than the questions arising in connexion with legal insanity. The experience which will no doubt be gained under the new Criminal Justice Act (1948) which provides for mental treatment, under probation, of persons guilty of crime, whose mental condition is relevant to their guilt, though neither insane nor defectives, should be valuable in this context.

I find similar ambiguities in the controversy relating to the distinction between 'treatment' and punishment. In a sense, of course, any measures ordered by a court involving restrictions of freedom to make treatment possible constitute punishment. But if punishment other than this inevitable interference with the individual is advocated, the question arises what its object is taken to be. If the punishment is considered as itself a part of the remedial treatment, it has to be shown that it can act in this way. If the object is to deter, the punishment inflicted may produce consequences incompatible with reform; it may, for example, as Dr Pearce has pointed out,* 'turn a neurotic delinquent into a hardened criminal, or at least stamp his pattern of thought with anti-social tendencies, which medical and psychological treatment might have permanently cured'. On the other hand, deterrent punishment may be justified on the ground of its effect on others. Conflicting considerations are thus involved between which it is difficult to strike a balance.

* *Juvenile Delinquency*, p. 242.

The resolution of these and kindred difficulties must depend upon further progress in psychiatry and in the accurate classification of types of crime. It would be extremely helpful if psychiatrists could give us a fuller account than, to the best of my knowledge, they have so far given, of the degree of freedom which is attributable to the various types of neuroses, especially those akin or tending to criminal behaviour. We must not be browbeaten by words like determinism. The problem is how rigid is the barrier between the conscious and the unconscious elements of the mind. If the separation were complete, the unconscious would be strictly inaccessible, and, from the point of view of the ego or conscious self, uncontrollable. So long as there is a link between the conscious and the unconscious there is a measure of freedom and a corresponding measure of responsibility. Freud is quoted as saying that a man is responsible even for his dreams, i.e., for his unconscious wishes. How could this be if the conscious and the unconscious were completely isolated? What we need to know is the degree of isolation in the various forms of neurosis and of criminality in so far as it is akin to neurosis; or in plain words, to what extent the persons concerned bring their troubles upon themselves and what they can do to help themselves. Only then will it become possible to define the scope of responsibility and to clarify the concept of 'limited responsibility'.

Estimates differ very widely of the proportion of criminals who are neurotic or akin to neurotic. Alexander and Staub say that in their view only a very small proportion will be found to be normal. According to Henderson and Gillespie at least ten to fifteen per cent of criminals are mentally disordered or defective. This is not likely to be an overestimate. Indeed, according to Mr Binney,* 'of the ordinary Assize Court calendar, the persons found unfit to plead, criminal lunatics, mental defectives, women guilty of infanticide and persons who have attempted suicides, by themselves almost make up this percentage.' As to the rest, there are no reliable statistics, nor indeed adequate

* *Crime and Abnormality*, p. 145.

definitions. An illustration may be given from the case of sexual offenders. These constitute a sizeable proportion of those dealt with in Assize Courts. But under sexual offences are included cases of young men who are prosecuted for having girls between the ages of thirteen and sixteen, who have anticipated the date of marriage with girls whom they love, and others who cannot be assumed to be mentally abnormal. Reviewing the evidence Mr Binney concludes that perhaps about a third of those charged with sexual offences may be considered as in some degree abnormal.* Others will no doubt give a different estimate. Similar difficulties arise in connexion with many other types of crime. On present information I do not see how it is possible to decide between those who, like Alexander and Staub, conclude that the number of neurotic criminals is very great† and those who, like Mr Binney, think that 'a large number of those who commit crimes are certainly not abnormal in any way.'‡

It thus appears that though there can be no justification for the extreme view sometimes put forward that all criminals are pathological, a considerable proportion are. It follows that the administration of justice requires the fullest knowledge available of the mental condition of the offender, and consequently the machinery for examination and treatment. This is of course to some extent already recognized in law and more widely in informed public opinion. The criteria of criminal responsibility are, however, still obscure and will only be clarified with further progress in the classification of crimes and their relation to mental abnormalities. The legal definitions concentrate almost entirely on the cognitive aspects of responsibility. They are designed to establish whether the offender knew what he was doing and that what he was doing was wrong. But, as I have argued above, responsibility involves more than knowledge. There must also be the capacity or power to act in accordance with such knowledge. This involves an integration of cognition with emotional or conative tendencies, and if this integration is lacking or impaired, behaviour will be correspondingly affected.

* op. cit., p. 163.   † op. cit., p. 146.   ‡ op. cit., p. 146

Since the cognitive and conative capacities vary independently, and each capacity shows a very wide range of variation, we must expect that the degree of integration achieved will also vary widely in different individuals. Thus some individuals may be well aware that what they are about to do is forbidden by the law, but may lack the emotional organization required for control. These resemble Aristotle's 'incontinent' man, who knows what is good and does what is bad. Others may have an excess of moral sensitivity which, however, does not prevent them from doing wrong. Such are the depressives who are tortured by a sense of guilt, showing itself in bitter self-torture and self-denunciation, but who nevertheless may be indifferent to their ordinary duties and who may be driven to serious acts of aggression. Leaving aside the extreme types included in insanities and mental defects, there are endless varieties of self-deception, conscious and unconscious, endless gradations in the power of self-regulation and, therefore, of responsibility. These gradations of responsibility are of the greatest interest to the moral psychologist. It remains that the law cannot 'consider too nicely'. It must assume that most people who come before it are capable of the minimum amount of self-control to enable them to observe the rules of society and it cannot take into account individual differences in the capacity for self-regulation. Nevertheless we are not entitled to assume that the proportion of cases in regard to which psychological investigation is desirable is as small as used to be thought, and opinion seems to be moving in the direction of 'individualization', to some extent before conviction and, to a greater extent, after conviction. Much has already been done to this end and more is still to come.

So far as I can see the argument against individualization is two-fold. The first is based on the necessarily impersonal character of judicial procedure just referred to. This precludes attention to individual differences and, in the interests of the Rule of Law, courts may be chary of allowing exceptions, or, if they allow them, insist that they should be narrowly defined. No one familiar with the history of legal procedure will dismiss an argument of this kind lightly. Yet suggestions have been put forward which go some way to meet the difficulties. These are based on the idea that the stages in which criminal proceedings are at present divided might be differentiated still further in respect of method and personnel. The first stage would be restricted to the inquiry whether a man has committed a specific transgression of a specific law and should be left largely in its present form. The second stage would be concerned with sentence and treatment and would be in the hands of a specially constituted treatment tribunal, made up of the judge who conducts the trial and assisted by experts who might include psychiatrists and educationists and whose decisions would be implemented in various ways according to the special needs of the individual cases.

The second objection to individualization is of a more radical nature, though closely connected with the first. It is argued that a tribunal, given the power not merely of exacting a specific penalty but of controlling and remodelling the whole life of a man, might easily constitute a threat to the hard-won liberties of the subject. Indeed, in certain circumstances it might make the administration of justice more ruthless than under existing systems and enable it to invade areas of life and conduct which now escape legal control. These dangers are obvious enough in an era of concentration camps. Yet in democratically minded countries with long practice in the art of curbing arbitrary power, it ought not to be beyond the wit of man to devise the necessary safeguards.

I am not competent to pursue this discussion in greater detail.* My object in referring to it is to draw attention to the growing recognition of the need to carry to its logical conclusions the line of differentiation already pursued in dealing with the insane, the mentally defective and, more recently, some other forms of mental abnormality. The difficulties that arise are due mainly to the absence of any agreed classification of types of crime and of the mental and social conditions relevant to them. It is safe to conclude that as our knowledge grows there will be greater readiness

* Cf. Sir Walter Moberly, *Responsibility*, Riddell Memorial Lectures, 1951.

to accept specialized methods of ascertainment and treatment.

The movement towards differentiation and the shift from purely punitive to protective and remedial measures is bound to be powerfully influenced by the experience gained as a result of the legislation relating to juvenile offenders. Differentiation by age is after all only a rough and ready method of allowing for individual differences. The age limits differ from country to country and there seems no scientific reason behind the variations. In England a child cannot be charged with an offence until he is eight years old and he cannot act with *mens rea* until he is fourteen, unless this is rebutted on proof of malice. In other countries the lower limit is higher, ranging from nine to fourteen. The French Penal Code formerly allowed some discretion. A person under sixteen was not punished if it could be shown that he acted *sans discernement*, and if he acted with discernment, his punishment was mitigated in accordance with a fixed scale. Under the German Juvenile Court Act of 1923 children under fourteen were entirely exempt from criminal responsibility and young persons between the ages of fourteen and eighteen were not punishable, if at the time of the offence they were unable to understand the unlawfulness of their behaviour or incapable of acting in accordance with such understanding. Westermarck cites examples from other legal systems which take age into consideration in mitigation of sentence, the upper limit varying from sixteen to twenty-one. It is interesting to note that an ancient Chinese code assimilates youth and old age in this context. Offenders of ages not more than seven nor less than ninety were not punishable except for treason or rebellion; those not more than ten nor less than eighty were recommended for mercy for capital offences other than treason, and there were other mitigations for those not more than fifteen nor less than seventy. In regard to the young the tendency in most legal systems seems to be to raise the age of responsibility, though in this country the suggestion has been made that the lower limit of eight is too high. The problem in regard to the lower limit is to balance the rights and responsibilities of parents to look after their children in their own way and the need of protecting children against vicious or apathetic parents. As to the upper limit the line seems to be drawn quite arbitrarily. This may be unavoidable, but sooner or later the question will be raised whether classification by age is the best way of taking individual differences into account, and in this way as in others the experience of juvenile courts may continue to exert an invigorating influence on the entire system of criminal justice.*

Legal discussions of responsibility have tended to concentrate on the contrast between full responsibility and non-responsibility. This may be due to the fact that these discussions have generally been conducted in connexion with the McNaughten Rules, which define the conditions in which insanity may be used as a defence for those charged with murder. Perhaps one of the most important effects of the legislation relating to juvenile deliquency and the experience gained in administering it has been to draw attention to the reality of degrees of responsibility and to lay stress on the value of non-punitive methods in dealing with cases of immature or impaired responsibility. The ideas implicit in this movement are capable of wider application and this is being slowly realized in law and in opinion. Their full implications will only be grasped when we have a more accurate classification of types of adult crime and are able to relate them to the mental conditions determining them and to estimate the effect upon them of the various forms of deterrent punishment. It may well be that in the case of many crimes punishments may not only act as deterrents, but help to create a state of mind in the offender and in others in which the offence comes to be looked upon as wrong in itself. In graver cases and especially those in which mental abnormality is involved, punishment may not only fail to cure but may effectively prevent a cure. What proportion of these should be handed over to non-penal

* Cf. Westermarck, *Origin and Development of Moral Ideas*, I, pp. 265 seq.; Fauçonnet, *La Responsabilité*, ch. I; H. Mannheim, *The Dilemma of Penal Reform*, p. 195.

agencies for education and treatment and at what point in penal procedure the discrimination is to be made and by whom is a matter on which at present opinion is still very divided.

What is the bearing of all this on the nature of responsibility? We are apt to be led astray, I think, if the problem is approached primarily in relation to crime. This leads us to think of responsibility as liability to punishment. But liability to punishment assumes responsibility as a prior condition. Strictly, responsibility is the obligation attaching to the knowledge that one's voluntary acts have been or may be effective in conditioning subsequent events.* This obligation subsists, on any rational view of ethics, whether or not its abrogation is to be followed by punishment or condemnation. The *sense* of obligation is another matter. This may be variously conditioned, for example, by habit, by the desire for conformity, by fear and by rational acceptance. Legal systems make use of all these forces in varying degrees. They are all provided with sanctions which in the last resort may involve physical coercion. But in any moral evaluation of legal systems we judge them among other things by the extent to which they rely on the threat of force, and the degree in which appeal is made to intelligent will and loyalty, the recognition of mutual needs and an active interest in a common good. From this point of view the contraction of the area of coercion and the fear of coercion is not a contraction of the area of responsibility. On the contrary the less we rely on fear the more we have to depend on a positive sense of obligation and the rational acceptance of duty.

In relation to crime, responsibility may be considered from two points of view, namely from that of society and that of the individual. Society is involved in so far as social factors contribute to the causes of crime. Whilst we must insist that the individual is in large measure self-determining and must be held accountable for what without his action would not come about, it remains that he is enmeshed in a chain of causation which constricts his powers of self-direction. That action is not completely shaped by

* Cf. F. R. Tennant, *The Concept of Sin*, ch. VII.

outward circumstances is clear from the fact that persons living in similar environments nevertheless behave differently. People respond selectively to their environment and in varying degrees create their own environment. If poverty or overcrowding or broken homes are among the causes of crime, it is nevertheless the case that the bulk of the poor are not criminals and those coming from broken homes are not necessarily delinquent. It remains that the rate of crime differs with social conditions. The evidence suggests that the aetiology of crime is highly complex. It does not depend on any single factor but on varying combinations of numerous factors, individual and social. The frequency of these combinations depends upon social conditions. It follows that in so far as society brings these conditions about it is responsible for them and ought so far as possible to remove or alter them. Social causation carries with it social responsibility.

This involves, in the first place, the duty of promoting and encouraging the scientific study of the causes of crime and of enabling those who are concerned in the framing of the law and its administration to keep in touch with advancing knowledge. The greater the progress towards 'individualization', the greater the need for trained personnel; in incompetent hands individualization will tend to become mechanical, erratic and arbitrary. To deal with the problem fully would involve us in an examination of the relation between legal and social studies for which this is not the place. The question of training is especially important in relation to magistrates who are appointed to juvenile courts. As Mr John Watson points out, 'Magistrates in the juvenile courts have it in their power to make or mar lives; for no matter how devoted the probation officer, how skilled the psychiatrist, how highly trained the staff of the approved school, the work of the experts is of little avail, if the decision of the bench is the wrong one.'*

In the second place, society has the duty of creating the conditions likely to favour the growth of a strong sense of responsibility in its members. And, of course, it has the duty of protecting

* *The Child and the Magistrate*, p. 195.

itself against the destructive elements in its midst. In dealing with them society recognizes the duty of doing its best for the offender so far as this is compatible with the common safety. At this point it comes up against the problem of responsibility from the point of view of the individual, since what society does with the offender depends upon the degree of responsibility imputed to him. It is now widely recognized, as we have seen, that the law must take into account not only the gravity of the offence but also the character and personality of the offender. But the consequences following from this principle are not clearly sorted out either in theory or in practice. The difficulty is due, as I have pointed out above, to the persistence of the retributive element in the criminal law, our ignorance of the effectiveness of punishment as a deterrent and the lack of agreement regarding the part that punishment can play in reform.

It is sometimes maintained that a complete theory of punishment must combine all three aspects, the retributive, deterrent and reformative. But in fact they clash and are often irreconcilable. It is argued that retribution leads to reform when the offender realizes that he has been justly punished. But this begs the question; for it assumes that there is a morally just punishment legally determinable. Or is it enough that the offender should think the punishment just, whether in truth it be so or not? Psychoanalysts tells us that in the case of 'compulsive' crimes punishment can neither cure nor deter, and on more general grounds we are bound to be sceptical of any method which pretends to combine reform with punishment, at any rate in the case of adults. It is very doubtful, to say the least, whether prison life can ever provide the conditions needed for genuine moral improvement, or in the case of the mentally affected, for effective psychiatric treatment. In the end we cannot but conclude that punishment has hardly been a successful institution, and it is very doubtful whether it can be made so. At best it is a mechanical and dangerous means of protection. It may be unavoidable, but in its incidence upon different persons it can hardly help being inequitable and, if it is to be used as a means of reform, it requires an amount of wisdom and humanity but rarely available. The kinds of punishment that have hitherto been tried have failed to secure reform and, in the case of the graver crimes, even to deter. When this is more widely recognized we shall cease to rely much on punishment for the maintenance of order. Dangerous criminals will have to be segregated. For the rest, society will concentrate on removing the conditions which encourage crime and on the best means of ensuring a widely diffused sense of responsibility independent of punishment.

[12]

Ethical Relativity and Political Theory*

IT is a curious and disconcerting fact that theories of ethical relativity have been used to justify both totalitarianism and democracy. The logical positivists who incline towards relativism in ethics have been accused of encouraging moral nihilism and thus providing a basis for fascism. On the other hand, writers like Kelsen, Radbruch and others both in England and America have argued that the real justification for democracy lies in the idea of toleration, and this implies, in their view, an empirical and relativist outlook both in the theory of knowledge and in ethics; while the authoritarian attitude finds its natural support in what is described as an 'absolutist' view of knowledge and morals. It is this somewhat paradoxical situation that I would like to consider.

Historically there seems to be little justification for either claim. The defenders of democracy have not, on the whole, been ethical relativists. The philosophical radicals in England, for example, were adherents of an empirical theory of knowledge and no doubt they claimed to base their ethical theory on the basis of experience. But they cannot be called ethical relativists, since they certainly sought to establish general principles of conduct which were to be the basis alike of moral and legal rules. They believed in democracy because they believed it to be the form of government most likely to conduce to general happiness. Neither Green, nor Hobhouse, nor Mill, who must be regarded as the best exponents of liberal thought in England, can by any stretch of imagination be considered ethical relativists. On the other hand,

* A guest-lecture delivered at the Hebrew University, Jerusalem, 7 May 1950.

it would not be difficult to point to philosophers who favoured a 'Positivist' view of knowledge and morals who were on the side of absolutism in their political views. Such, for example, were Auguste Comte and Hobbes. Again, while it is true that much in Nazi and Fascist literature employs the language of ethical relativism, it is equally true that those who originated logical positivism in its modern form and their supporters in England and America are very far from being adherents of totalitarianism. It thus becomes clear even on a cursory survey that the relations involved must be more complex than appears at first sight and that if a fruitful analysis is to be conducted, it is essential to define more closely what is to be understood in this context by ethical relativism or positivism, on the one hand, and democracy and totalitarianism on the other.

For the purpose of this discussion I should like to distinguish two forms of ethical relativism, which may be called sociological and psychological. By sociological relativism I mean the theory that moral rules are statements which assert that within a given group there is a general tendency for classes of acts to arouse reactions of approval or disapproval. Such statements are either true or false in the sense that it is either the case or not the case that the approval or disapproval will be generally aroused. On the other hand, the approval or disapproval themselves cannot, according to some supporters of this view, be either true or false, since this distinction is regarded as inapplicable to feelings or emotions. The theory is relativist in the sense that morals are tied to the group, so that different groups have different moralities and there is no common standard by which they can be judged. The group in question according to the Nazi writers is the *Volk* or racial community. According to Marxist writers the group is the dominant class, but each class has its own morality and between them there is conflict. The main difficulty in defining this type of theory is that it has never been worked out in any detail. The moralities of different peoples are alleged to differ, but no one has ever set out how precisely they differ, or defined the boundaries of the groups which are to be compared. Are we to say, for example, that there is a European or Western morality, or is there a Teutonic, an Anglo-Saxon, a French, an Italian and a Spanish morality? Similarly we may ask how many class-moralities there are, how exactly do they differ and to what extent do they interpenetrate?

It is easy to see that sociological relativism can easly be used to support totalitarian policy. For, if morals come from the group and enjoin attachment to the group, this can be readily interpreted in a sense which would leave little or nothing to individual autonomy. Nevertheless, sociological relativism and totalitarianism are not necessarily connected. Thus for example Durkheim, who certainly holds a group theory of morality, is anxious to defend the notion of individual rights and to find room in his theory for the autonomy of the individual. The root of the matter lies in the answer to the question how what the group requires is to be ascertained. In Durkheim's view this cannot be done merely by yielding to the pressure of group opinion. It is a matter for scientific inquiry into the needs of society. Durkheim in the long run believes in the autonomy of reason, and reason is exercised by individuals. On the other hand, in the Nazi theories reason is decried. Values are the expression of the vital impulses of the race and are above reason. The interpreters of the values are the leaders or creative minds of the race and the rest have to accept their edicts as binding. The validity which these claim is absolute within the group or racial community and not a matter of individual preference. Between this kind of group-morality and totalitarianism there is thus a close link. The masses are not asked what they want; they are told what they ought to want by the self-appointed interpreters of group values.

Of the theories of what I have called psychological relativism it is not easy to find a precise formulation. They claim generally that moral judgements are emotive rather than descriptive. Moral judgements express not a characteristic of acts but an attitude towards them favourable or unfavourable. 'This action is right' means 'I am favourably disposed towards an action of this type; I give myself and others leave to do it should similar circumstances arise.' These theories start with the individual and with the group, since clearly only individuals can have emotions, or likes and dislikes. Lord Russell, who is one of the strongest supporters of this theory, is very far from holding that the individual must always conform: 'If a man seriously desires to live the best life open to him, he must learn to be critical of the tribal customs and tribal beliefs that are generally accepted among his neighbours.'* On what basis he is to critcize is, however, not clear. Strictly it would seem any desire, if felt with sufficient strength, will generate its own morality. Lord Russell believes that an impersonal or universal morality is possible because human desires are in fact more general and less selfish than many moralists imagine. It is the business of 'wise institutions', he argues, to encourage such a universal morality, to create conditions in which self-interest and the interest of society can be harmonized.† 'Wise' presumably means such as Russell would approve. But to persuade others of what is wise it is necessary to appeal to their emotions and not to their reason – a curiously monopolistic sense of the word 'wise'.

The example of Lord Russell shows that there is no necessary link between ethical relativism or subjectivism and totalitarianism. On the face of it, moral subjectivism is more naturally linked with individualism or even anarchism. Lord Russell himself likes freedom, creativeness, universal love and sympathy, while, certainly, hosts of Nazi and fascist writers would dismiss all these as the fear-ridden impulses of weaklings and degenerates. Whether freedom or coercion is to be the basis of the political organization would depend on the presence or absence of the corresponding desires in those who decide policy and on the extent of their capacity to imbue others with similar desires or emotions. In *gleichgeschaltete* communities common desires would be inculcated and morality would be the same for all. On the other hand, in differentiated and diversified com-

* *Authority and the Individual*, p. 109.
† *Religion and Science*, p. 241.

munities there would be more scope for individual peculiarity and moral originality or eccentricity. But there is nothing in the theory of moral relativism which could be logically used to justify either type of society. Strictly speaking the term 'justify', if used in an ethical sense, would have no meaning. The term could have only 'ideological' value as pretending to give a rational ground for what in fact is no more than individual desire or preference.

Is there then no connexion at all between moral relativism and totalitarianism? I think there is, but the connexion is psychological and sociological rather than logical. This raises the general problem of the influence exercised by philosophical theories on political and social development. There are some who attribute a great deal of power to the thought of philosophers, while others regard theories as the passive product of circumstances, and as reflecting rather than shaping the course of events. This is the sort of question upon which a great deal has been written and it would not be profitable to pursue it further in general terms. I assume that the relation is one of reciprocal interaction, that philosophers tend to make explicit and to give form to tendencies which seek embodiment, but in doing so they give these tendencies greater strength than they might otherwise possess.* In the case before us, it would be absurd to blame philosophers for generating moral nihilism, but it remains that in giving it theoretical form they encourage its growth. Lord Russell has formulated a general principle which is of interest in this connexion.

A philosophy [he says], developed in a politically advanced country which is, in its birthplace, little more than a clarification and systematization of prevalent opinion, may become elsewhere a source of revolutionary ardour and, ultimately, of actual revolution. It is mainly through theories that the maxims regulating the policy of advanced countries become known to less advanced countries. In the advanced

---

* To this audience it is not necessary to stress the power of an ideal, held with passion. 'If you believe it, it is no dream,' you were told. You did believe it, and it is no dream.

countries, practice inspires theory; in the others theory inspires practice.*

It is, I think, probable that the theories of moral relativism will be used as a basis for moral nihilism not only in the countries in which they have been formulated, but also and with even more devastating effect when transplanted in other countries whether advanced or not.

The real danger of these theories is that they remove the problem of values from the sphere of reason. In their mildest form they reflect a failure of nerve, a method of running away from the difficult task of tackling the problem of fairness and equity in human relations. At worst they provide those who resort to coercion and violence with an ideology which gives them a moral sanction, while at the same time undermining the moral foundations of those who favour justice and freedom. Philosophers can hardly be blamed for the abuse of their theories, but they are not entirely free from responsibility, especially if, as I think is the case, these theories are not really consistent with what is best in the positivist spirit. What is important in positivism is a sceptical attitude towards metaphysical assumptions and the insistence that all inductions must rest on observation of facts. Neither of these requirements is satisfied, so far as I can see, by the ethical theory of the logical positivists. It assumes without investigation that only those categories are of scientific importance which are employed in ordering sensory experience and it makes no attempt to examine systematically the data provided by the comparative study of morals. That only statements relating to what are called 'facts' permit of the distinction between true and false is mere dogma. On the factual side, we are continually told that the variability of moral codes is so extensive as to preclude any hope of our ever reaching any generally acceptable body of moral principles.

If we all agreed [says Lord Russell], we might hold that we know values by intuition. We cannot *prove*, to a colour-blind man, that grass

* *A History of Western Philosophy*, p. 624.

is green and not red. But there are various ways of proving to him that he lacks a power of discrimination which most men possess, whereas in the case of values there are no such ways, and disagreements are much more frequent than in the case of colours. . . . Hence, the conclusion is forced on us that the difference is one of tastes, not one as to any objective truth.*

One would expect that such a statement would be substantiated by an inquiry into the extent and nature of the divergences in moral outlook and into the possible reasons for such divergence. It is always possible, for example, that differences arise to a considerable extent from ignorance of facts and from confusion between questions of fact and questions of values, and that when these confusions have been cleared up, the differences in value judgements proper might conceivably turn out to be no greater than those which are found in other spheres of knowledge.† These are matters which require prolonged investigations and the positivists of all people have no right to assume that they know enough about them to justify the very sweeping conclusions they claim to have established in the analysis of ethical judgements.

The use made of ethical relativity by the totalitarians differs from case to case. The Fascists, as represented by Mussolini at any rate, cannot really be said to hold a particular theory of morals, unless the rejection of all theories can be designated a theory. They consider all moral and political theories as ideologies which everyone is free to create for himself and impose on others if he can. In practice, of course, this does not mean 'everyone' but only the leader, and there is nothing to check or control his ever-changing intuitions. The Nazi writers too appeal to intuition, but in their case this is linked with the theory of the race as the ultimate source of all values and the leader as its exponent or interpreter. The Nazi view is more clearly a form of group-relativism than the Fascist; but in both cases reason is dethroned, the interests of the nation or race are put above all

* *Religion and Science*, p. 238.

† Especially if allowance is made for differences due to differences in the general level of knowledge.

moral laws. Ultimately therefore there is no criterion other than the arbitrary intuitions of the leader.

Marxist morality is more complex. There are, it would seem, two moralities – a universal morality which will become operative when class antagonisms have disappeared, and an 'interim' morality which is functionally related to the class struggle. During this period each class has its own morality based on its own needs, and what is called general morality is in fact the morality of the dominant class, disguised by an ideology which serves to impose it on the other classes. In a period of revolution the morality is that necessitated by war, and this 'justifies' any measures required by revolutionary tactics and strategy and recognizes no limits above those needed to maintain the morale of the working classes. The condemnation of violence is 'counter-revolutionary' and is merely the ideology of the exploiting classes. There is a certain inconsistency in the Marxist attitude to bourgeois morality. Strictly speaking, this cannot be 'condemned' in the period of the class struggle, except in an 'ideological' sense, since during this period there are no common moral standards. In fact, however, Marxists have it both ways. They appeal to the ethics of the interim morality in defending the actions of the revolutionaries and the ethics of the morality of the future in judging the actions of their opponents. This use of a dual morality is, of course, not peculiar to Marxists. But here the fissure between the two codes is so deep as to endanger the whole substance of morality.

It will be seen that relativist ethics can be put to very different uses. This is to be expected. For if moral judgements express nothing but individual or group desires or preferences, the content of morals will vary with the interpretation of these desires or preferences. From the theoretical point of view we should expect some account of the method by which these needs or desires can be ascertained and how these are related to the working moral codes. But beyond vague generalities this is not forthcoming. There is no real attempt to discover in what ways the moral codes of the different groups differ from one another, or how far they are reconcilable. The function of reason is restricted to the investigation of the means used in the attainment of ends. The ends themselves are not open to rational scrutiny and where there is a conflict of ends wisdom stands helpless. In the Marxist view it is recognized that ends and means are dialectically related, from which it should follow that reason is capable of dealing not only with means but also with ends. But this promising deduction is of little importance. All reasoning in moral and social matters is classbound and, until the age of proletarian knowledge is reached, is subject to no tests other than those imposed by revolutionary tactics and strategy. The possibility of a rational harmonization of conflicting interests is ruled out so long as the class struggle continues. If my analysis is right, it follows that the different forms of totalitarianism have this in common: they all involve the subordination of ethics to politics and the removal of morals from the sphere of reason. Theories of ethical relativity are therefore congenial to them, even though the logical connexion is slender. In Marxist teminology, ethical relativity provides totalitarianism with just the ideology which it needs.

Ethical relativity has been used as a basis not only for totalitarianism but also for democracy. Democracy, it is argued, implies that there is no such thing as absolute knowledge, that no one has a monopoly of truth; from which it is deduced that everyone is entitled to be heard and that coercion should only be employed when it has been accepted as necessary by at least the majority of those concerned. This, however, implies that there is at least one ethical principle which may be taken to be assured, the principle namely that where there is disagreement force ought not to be employed and that the majority is entitled to impose its will on the rest. If moral judgements are subjective and express nothing but individual group preferences, I do not see how anyone can be refuted who prefers to coerce those who differ from him. No doubt ethical relativism is compatible with democracy, but it is equally compatible with anarchism or absolutism, according to the emotional make-up of the individuals or groups concerned and their power of persuading or coercing others. From the psychological point of view also it may be questioned whether the best preparation for respecting the opinions or wishes of others is to doubt your own. Toleration and self-doubt by no means always go together; and not infrequently the fanatical persecutor is a person who hunts his own doubt in the doubt of others.

If democracy is to be justified, we need a surer foundation than ethical relativity. This indeed is a truism since if moral judgements are emotive or express the demands of groups, the term 'justify' has no meaning other than 'persuade or coerce'. In rejecting ethical relativism we are thus insisting that there is such a thing as a rational justification of democratic policy. This is not to claim infallibility. Moral reasoning, like reasoning in other spheres, is probable reasoning and open to correction in the light of wider experience or deepened insight. But it is nevertheless incumbent on us to form the best judgement that we can of what is good and then act on it. Our first problem is to define what we are to mean by democracy in this context. This is a question on which a good deal of time can be wasted. If we take it that, as popularly used, the word 'democracy' means 'a government of the whole people by the majority, generally through representatives, elected nowadays by a secret ballot of the adult population'* our problem is on what grounds such a form of government is held to be better than others. I will not attempt to survey the various answers that have been given to this question. I think the most promising line of approach is to say that democracy in this formal sense is considered good because on the whole it is the best device for securing certain elements of social justice. If the device is so used that it does not attain this purpose, then a democracy may be bad. Some people would say that in that case it is not a democracy, but this is a matter of words. What is important is to consider what are the elements of social justice which constitute the ultimate ground of appeal. It seems to me they are two: first, equality, and second, freedom with its

* Cf. E. F. Carritt, *Ethical and Political Thinking*, p. 150.

correlative, individual responsibility. Equality in this context means two things: first, equality of consideration and, secondly, the exclusion of arbitrariness. The first requires that everyone is entitled to be considered, to have his claim heard; the second means that differences in treatment require as their justification some relevant difference in the ground on which the claim is put forward. The justification for this principle is, I think, rooted in the nature of rational procedure. To proceed rationally involves at least two requirements: first, to treat like cases in like manner and to insist on justification for differential treatment; second, not to impose principles from without, but rather to seek to elicit them from experience by a process of mutual correction and systematization. To suppress an experience unheard is to eliminate what may be a valuable contribution to the common stock. Hence freedom of discussion and freedom of election. Inherent in government by discussion is decision by majority. The difficulty, of course, is to operate this device in a manner which will satisfy the above requirements. Free elections may fail to give expression to divergent views, and majority decisions may ignore or override rather than integrate opposed opinions. The theme is well-worn and need not be further pursued here, but it is clear that in practice formal democracy may lack the moral authority which our principles demand. Equality and freedom are closely connected. The function of free institutions is to encourage variety and spontaneity and to minimize the abuses arising out of inequalities in power. Compulsion may be required for both purposes, firstly, to secure the resources necessary for a full life and, secondly, to prevent interference by the strong with the weak.

It is sometimes thought that the notion of liberty does not involve any particular conception of the content of good, that, on the contrary, it is based on the contention that everyone knows best what his own good is and the important thing is that the individual should be free to pursue whatever ends he chooses, provided he does not interfere with the like freedom of other persons to pursue their own ends in their own way.* But

* F. Knight, *Freedom and Reform*, p. 53.

this is unworkable. To give freedom any concrete meaning it is necessary to define a body of rights and to devise means of balancing them when they conflict. Now rights are claims to the conditions of a good life and must vary with our conception of the good and our command of the conditions necessary to attain it. In particular the rightful use of coercion must turn upon the nature of the ends aimed at, that is on the question how far they *can* be attained by force without distortion and moral pauperization. In short, the idea of liberty cannot be profitably discussed without considering its relation to the intrinsic values of individual personality and without an analysis of the relations between the individual and society. It is certainly not enough to say that anyone is free to do what he likes provided he does not interfere with the like freedom of others. Every claim may have to be considered not only in relation to the like claims of others, but to the entire system of liberties. This, in turn, cannot be done without some conception of a common good, that is a form or way of life in the light of which the various values are graded and arranged in an order of priority and importance. There are, no doubt, principles of justice which can be formulated without reference to the content of the good. Such are, for example, the principles designed to secure equality of consideration and the exclusion of arbitrariness. But it is easy to see that they cannot be applied mechanically. For what is arbitrary or not cannot be decided without some criterion of relevance, and this involves consideration of the particular values involved, such as the satisfaction of needs in some order of importance, or the stimulus of effort, or fulfilment of human potentialities. Similarly the problem of the relation between freedom and coercion cannot be resolved without taking into consideration the nature of the ends to be secured and the effects likely to be produced on the character of those affected. In this connexion, as in others, the good and the just cannot be fruitfully considered in isolation from each other.

In the last resort, then, the best defence of democracy is that on the whole it is a form of government most likely to secure equality and freedom. Freedom, it should be added, is closely connected with responsibility, that is the knowledge of values and the power of acting in accordance with that knowledge. Democracy, if it is to attain these objects, must be representative and responsible government; that is, based on the alert and active consent of the governed and a widely diffused and informed sense of values and a strong feeling of accountability on the part of those to whom power is entrusted and on whom it is exercised. If these requirements are not satisfied, formal democracy, in the sense of majority rule, will lack the moral basis which alone can give it authority.

To base democracy on ethical relativity is then to say that equality and freedom are not principles which can be rationally defended but generalized desires or attitudes which happen to be felt by defenders of democracy but not by others. Now impulses and feelings are undoubtedly important elements in the moral life, since without them moral judgements would be powerless to affect action. The question is whether there are such things as rational impulses, that is impulses which stand the test of critical scrutiny. I find it difficult to believe that the striving for justice, for example, has no basis in reason or cannot be subjected to rational tests. The view that moral judgements are illusory is usually defended on two grounds. Firstly, it is argued, moral judgements confuse assertions of a certain kind of fact – the fact, namely, that certain individuals tend to experience emotions or desires in relation to certain classes of acts – with assertions of a non-factual kind, e.g., that certain classes of acts have value or disvalue, ought or ought not to be done. These latter, it is then argued are not susceptible of empirical verification and the distinction between true and false does not properly apply to them. This is further strengthened by a second consideration which emphasizes the great variability of moral judgements and the difficulty of reaching agreement about them. Neither of these grounds seems to me to be valid. It is mere dogma to assume that no intuitions are important save those which have a sensory origin or that experience is limited to what is called 'fact'. As to the variability of moral judgement, it is admitted by some relativists, such as Westermarck, that in many instances psychological and sociological reasons can be given which account for the variations and that these are compatible with the claim that universally valid moral judgements are discoverable.* I suggest that the problem of the cause of the variations in moral insight and in particular of the part played by ignorance or distortion of the relevant facts and the confusions of factual assertions with moral assertions proper deserves and requires much fuller investigation than it has received. If we consider, for example, the variations in attitude towards the equality of the sexes or of races it will soon become apparent that the distortions of the relevant facts are as difficult to remove as the divergence in moral outlook. In neither respect have we the right to abandon the task of rational inquiry. Similarly, the drive to punish crime has deep psychological roots and has expressed itself in many different forms, but this does not mean that one treatment of criminals is as good as another or that the problem is one of arbitrary choice or preference. From the fact that people differ either about facts or values and that it is difficult to get them to agree about either, we are not entitled to conclude that true judgements are unattainable without exploring the nature of the differences and the psychological and sociological factors which stand in the way of their removal.

The problem thus suggested is of especial importance today. We are told by politicians and theologians alike that behind political conflicts there lie fundamental differences in moral outlook. The 'realists', on the other hand, tell us that morality has nothing to do with the matter, that the struggle is for power and not for moral ends. Yet the rival powers all speak in the name of morals and it is this more than anything else that is responsible for the widespread moral scepticism of our age. Nevertheless the fact that moral principles can be distorted ideologically and used to justify rival causes does not prove that there are no moral principles. Ideological distortions are well nigh as common and

* Cf. *Ethical Relativity*, p. 196.

375

as difficult to dispel in the realm of facts as in the realm of values. It is interesting in this connexion to consider the differences in outlook that exist within the rival groups and not only those between them. The erstwhile communists who have recently discovered that their god has failed them were firm adherents of equality and freedom. They were willing for a time to sacrifice the one in favour of the other, in the hope that ultimately both would be secured. They have now learnt that what once seemed to them the only way to bring about economic and social equality as distinct from political equality has entailed such terrible disasters that the attempted cure has been worse than the disease, and have consequently returned to the democratic fold. Their conversion does not turn upon a change of moral principle but is the result of what experience has taught them of the consequences inevitably resulting from dictatorial methods. I suspect that in many other cases, too, political differences do not rest on differences regarding fundamental moral principles, but in so far as they have a moral basis at all, on differences in moral sensitiveness, imagination and sympathy. The liberal, unlike the totalitarian, is persuaded that it is not beyond the wit of man to devise methods for harmonizing conflicting interests without resort to violence. Experience has taught him that radical changes can be brought about with the consent of those concerned and that, if other methods are used, there is grave danger of the means defeating the end and of replacing one kind of tyranny by another. He knows that power won by violence tends to grow by what it feeds on and, eventually, to be sought for its own sake without reference to the end originally pursued. The totalitarian has no such scruples. The very loftiness of the ideals which he sets himself removes them from the sphere of reality, with the result that the means become all important and are pursued fanatically without any consideration of their effect upon the end. The difference between the liberal and the totalitarian is thus a problem for the sociology rather than the logic of morals. This, however, is not to say that the fundamental principles of morals are established beyond doubt. Even if, as may be the case, there is wide agreement about the ultimate ends of conduct, there are certainly different conceptions of the general form or way of life in accordance with which the ends are graded or balanced. Further, we often lack the secondary principles or *axiomata media* for making the transition from the ultimate ends to the details of life. In the absence of these mediating links, it is easy for lofty principles to remain on a safe level of abstraction or to be used in justification of contradictory policies. The moral perplexity is increased by confusions between questions of fact and questions of values and by the difficulty of foreseeing the consequences of human interactions, especially in large-scale societies. From this point of view ethical thought stands to gain from the development of the social sciences. The deeper our knowledge of human needs and potentialities and of the laws of social interaction, the greater is the chance of increased insight into the nature of ideals. Theories of ethical relativity have proved utterly sterile in dealing with the problems of our age. The positive spirit is another matter. To it we owe the impetus to seek a basis for morality in human experience and to regard ideals, not as patterns laid up in heaven, but as rooted in fundamental needs and attainable by rational effort.

Index

Adamson, R., *The Development of Modern Philosophy*, 297
Aiyer, Sir Siraswami, *The Evolution of Hindu Moral Ideas*, 290, 300
Alexander, S., 28–30
Beauty and other Forms of Value, 53
Alexander, F., and Staub, B., *The Criminal, the Judge, and the Public*, 346, 352–3
Ali, Ameer (Syed), *The Ethics of Islam*, 290
Ammon, O., 14, 182
Gesellschaftsordnung und ihre natürlichen Grundlagen, 189
Aristotle, 241, 246, 277, 282, 354
Politics, 252
Ashton, T. S.
Eighteenth Century, The, 158n.
Industrial Revolution, The, 155n.
Atkinson, J. J., 318
Augustine, St, *De Moribus*, 335

Bach, J. S., 170
Baer, K. E. von, 130
Bagehot, W., *Physics and Politics*, 74
Baillie, J., *The Belief in Progress*, 78n., 80, 126
Baker, E., 188n.
Baldwin, S., 170n.
Englishman, The, 189
Bardoux, Jacques, 187
Angleterre et France: leurs politiques étrangères, 189
Barker, E., 66, 253
National Character, 189
Politics of Aristotle, The, 267
Barnes, E. W., *Religion amid Turmoil*, 81n.
Baron, S. W., *A Social and Religious History of the Jews*, 208
Bartlett, F. C., and others (eds.), *The Study of Society*, 7n.
Bateson, W., *Biological Fact and the Structure of Society*, 105, 126
Bebel, A., 202
Becker, C. L., *The Heavenly City of the Eighteenth-Century Philosophers*, 126
Benn, A. W., *The History of English Rationalism in the Nineteenth Century*, 275n.
Bentham, Jeremy, 249, 275
Theory of Legislation, The, 269
Bergson, H., 31–2

Deux Sources de la Morale et de la Religion, Les, 53
Bevan, Edwyn, *The Kingdom of God and History*, 77
Bible, The, 241, 251, 285, 294, 322, 348
Bidney, David, 264n.
'Concept of value in modern anthropology, The', 267
Bienenfeld, F. R., *Germans and Jews*, 208
Binney, C., *Crime and Abnormality*, 352–3
Bismarck, O. von, 143, 175
Bloch, M., 134
Historian's Craft, The, 133n., 154
Blomquist, A., 209
Boas, Franz, 241, 249
Anthropology and Modern Life, 267
Bosanquet, B., 160, 347
Philosophical Theory of the State, The, 69
Bouglé, C., 12
Idées Égalitaires, Les, 53
Boutmy, E., 172n.
English People, The, 189
Bowden, W., *Industrial Society in England towards the End of the Eighteenth Century*, 146n.
Bradley, A. C., 268
Bradley, F. H., 77
Branford, Victor, 212
Bridges, G. H., 274
Briffault, R., *The Mothers*, 230–32
Britt, S. H., 208
Broad, C. D., *The Mind and its Place in Nature*, 91, 126, 156
Bryce, Lord, 52
Bücher, 47
Buckland, W. W., and McNair, A. D., *Roman Law and Common Law*, 187n., 189
Buckle, H. T., 117, 249
Introduction to the History of Civilization in England, 126
Bury, J. B., 78, 87, 251
Idea of Progress, The, 76, 79, 126, 267
Butler, Joseph, *Works*, 273
Butterfield, H., *Christianity and History*, 156–7

Cabanis, P. J. G., 83
Carli, F., 13
Carlyle, A. J., 241, 267
Carlyle, Sir R. W. and A. J., *A History of Mediaeval Political Theory in the West*, 267

Carr, E. H., *A History of Soviet Russia*, 158
Carr-Saunders, A. M., 13
Population Problem, The, 53, 132n.
World Population, 139n.
Carritt, E. F., *Ethical and Political Thinking*, 67n., 371n.
Chapman, Mary, 268
Chateaubriand, F. R., 176n.
Mémoires d'outre-tombe, 189
Childe, V. Gordon, 41n.
Man Makes Himself, 53
Most Ancient East, The, 111n., 126
Social Evolution, 126
Churchill, Awnsham and John (eds.), *A Collection of Voyages and Travels*, 237, 267
Cicero, 241
Clapham, J., *A Concise Economic History of Britain*, 140n.
Clarke, Samuel, 309
Clemenceau, G., 170
Cohen, M. R.
Meaning of Human History, The, 126
Reason and Nature, 155n.
Collingwood, R. G., 130
Idea of History, The, 126
Comte, Auguste, 8, 47, 82, 84, 87–97, 131, 159, 271–5, 291, 293, 363
Catéchisme Positiviste, 271
Cours de Philosophie Positive, 84, 88, 126
Condorcet, M. J. N. C. de, 71, 73, 82–4, 86, 110, 119
Esquisse d'un tableau historique des progrès de l'esprit humain, 87, 126
Conrad, J. 162
Coon, C. S., 181, 184n.
Races of Europe, The, 189
Cournot, A. A., 146–8
Considérations sur la marche des idées, 146–7
De l'enchaînement des idées fondamentales dans les sciences et dans l'histoire, 147
Crawley, A. E., 248
'Chastity', 267
Cuenot, L.
Science et Loi, 156n.
Culwick, A. T., 248
Good Out of Africa, 267

Darwin, Charles, 37, 101, 210
Origin of Species, 37, 102
Davids, T. W. Rhys, 241
Buddhism, 267
Dawson, Agnes, 234n.
Dawson, C., *Progress and Religion*, 126
Delvaille, J., *Essai sur l'histoire de l'idée de progrès jusqu'à la fin du 18ème siècle*, 126
Dewey, John, 250
'Anthropology and ethics', 219n.

Dibelius, W., 173, 188n.
England, 188
Dickinson, Lowes, *Justice and Liberty*, 310–11
Dilthey, W., 130, 153
Dixon, W. MacNeile, *The Englishman*, 189
Dodd, C. H., *History and the Gospel*, 77, 126
Dubnow, S., 202
Weltgeschichte des jüdischen Volkes, 208
Dumont, Etienne, 269
Dürer, A., 170
Durkheim, E., 8–10, 12, 45, 49, 52, 59, 131, 158, 215
De la Division du Travail Social, 53
Leçons de Sociologie, 301–2
Règles de la méthode sociologique, 159

Ehrlich, E., 24n., 25
Fundamental Principles of the Sociology of Law, 53
Eickstedt, E. von, 179
Rassenkunde und Rassengeschichte der Menschheit, 189
Eliot, George, 274
Eliot, T. S., 173n.
Selected Essays, 189
Ellis, Havelock, 228–9
Emerson, R. W., 170
Engels, F., 99–100, 160
Anti-Dühring, 119, 126, 160–61

Fallot, E., *L'avenir colonial de la France*, 189
Fauçonnet, A., *La Responsabilité*, 357
Fisher, H. A. L., *History of Europe*, 134
Flint, R., *The Philosophy of History*, 126
Flugel, O., 91, 316, 330
Man, Morals and Society, 331
Forde, C. Daryll, 269
Fouillée, A., 163, 166, 169, 183
Esquisse psychologique des peuples européens, 188
Frazer, Sir James, 229
'Condorcet on human progress', 126
Freeman, E. A., 52
Comparative Politics, 53
Freud, S., 34, 205, 249, 306, 318–21, 324–9, 339, 352
Civilization and its Discontents, 267, 316, 325, 328
'Civilized' Sexual Morality and Modern Nervousness', 325, 326
Future of an Illusion, The, 324
Group Psychology and the Psychology of the Ego, 321, 329
Inhibitions, Symptoms and Anxiety, 316
Introductory Lectures to Psycho-Analysis, 320
Moses and Monotheism, 208, 318
New Introductory Lectures on Psycho-Analysis, 324

Friedmann, W., *Introduction to Legal Theory*, 110n., 303
Froissart, 170
Fromm, E. 34n., 331–2
  Autorität und Familie, 53
  Escape from Freedom, 316–17
  Man for Himself, 331
Fyfe, Hamilton, *The Illusion of National Character*, 189

Galileo Galilei, 91
Galton, F., 183
  Hereditary Genius, 189
Gaultier, Paul, 180
  L'âme française, 189
Gibb, H. A. B., 'Law and Religion in Islam', 295n.
Gillespie (Henderson and), 352
Ginsberg, M., 232n., 254n.
  'Causality in the social sciences', 53
  'Conventions, social', 53
  Essays in Sociology and Social Philosophy, 275n., 289
  'Jewish Problem, The', 208
  'National character and national sentiments', 189
  Psychology of Society, 189
  Reason and Unreason in Society, 57n., 126, 267–8
  'Recent tendencies in sociology', 53
  Sociology, 53, 189
Gobineau, J. A. de, 21
Goldenweiser, A., 55, 219n.
Graeber, I., and Britt, S. H. (ed.), *Jews in a Gentile World*, 208
Green, T. H., 59, 66, 240, 362
  Prolegomena to Ethics, 268, 288
Guizot, F., 89

Ha-am, Ahad, 194
  At the Parting of the Ways, 208
Haddon, A. C., 212
  Races of Man, The, 189
Halbwachs, M., 165n.
  Causes du suicide, Les, 59, 188
Harnack, Adolph von, 246
  History of Dogma, 268
Hastings, James (ed.), *Encyclopaedia of Religion and Ethics*, 267
Hayek, F. A., 59, 61, 123–4
  'Facts of the social sciences, The', 60
  Individualism: True and False, 60
  'Scientism and the study of society', 123n.
Hazard, P., *La pensée européenne au 18ème siècle*, 126
Hecker, J. F., *Russian Sociology*, 55
Hegel, G. W. F., 82, 96–8, 288
  Lectures on the Philosophy of History, 97, 126
Henderson (and Gillespie), 352
Herder, J. G. von, 71, 83–5

Ideas of the Philosophy of the History of Humanity, 75
Herskovits, Melville J., 264
  Man and His Works: The Science of Cultural Anthropology, 268
Hildreth, R., 269
Hitler, Adolf, 236
Hobbes, T., 58, 363
Hobhouse, L. T., 10, 36, 45, 47, 49, 50, 59, 66, 80, 102, 212, 232, 239, 242, 249, 274, 289, 362
  'Comparative Ethics', 53
  Development and Purpose, 127, 268
  Elements of Social Justice, 67
  Metaphysical Theory of the State, The, 64n.
  Morals in Evolution, 54, 127, 268
  Social Development, 54, 64n., 123n., 127
Hobhouse, L. T., Wheeler, G. C., and Ginsberg M., *The Material Culture and Social Institutions of the Simpler Peoples*, 232, 327n.
Hobson, J. A., 66
Hopkins, E. W., *The Ethics of India*, 116–17n., 291, 295n.
Horney, Karen, 332
Hubert, R., 24n.
  'Croyance morale et règle juridique', 54
  Science Sociales dans l'Encyclopédie, Les, 85n., 127
Hume, David, 27, 29, 150, 273, 277, 280, 282–3, 287–8
  Inquiry concerning Human Understanding, An, 296
  Treatise of Human Nature, A, 281
Husserl, E., 11
  'Phenomenology', 54
Hutcheson, 27
Huxley, J. S., 42
  Evolutionary Ethics, 81n., 127
  'Natural selection and evolutionary progress', 54
Huxley, T. H., 104, 184n.
  Evolution and Ethics, 127, 189, 235, 268

Inge, W. R., 77, 78
  Christian Ethics and Modern Problems, 286
  Idea of Progress, The, 77, 79–80, 127

Janet, P., 246
  Histoire de la Science Politique, 86, 127
  Theory of Morals, The, 268
Janowsky, O. I., *A People at Bay*, 208
Jaspers, K., 63n.
Javary, A., 85
  De l'Idée de Progrès, 71, 127
Jones, Ernest, 336
  'The concept of the normal', 334–5
Jones, Sir William, 37, 101
Joseph, W. H. B., *An Introduction to Logic*, 152n.

Kaila, Eino, 234
Kant, I., 31, 71, 74, 81, 83–5, 98, 248,
    276, 279, 280, 283, 298, 318
  Critique of the Practical Reason, 283
  *Idee zur einer allgemeinen Geschichte in
    weltbürgerlicher Absicht*, 127
  Metaphysik der Sitten, 298
  Principles of Politics, 127
  *Über den Gemeinspruch: Das mag in der
    Theorie richtig sein*, 127
  Werke, 85n.
Kantorowicz, H., 187
  Spirit of British Policy, The, 188
Kaufmann, J.
  Essays on the Troubles of our Times, 208
  Strangers and Wanderers, 208
Kelsen, H., 362
Kenny, C. S., *Outline of Criminal Law*, 349
Kepler, J., 85
Keyes, C. W. (ed.), *Cicero: De republica,
  De legibus*, 268
Keynes, J. M., *A Treatise on Probability*,
  293
Klein, Melanie, 336
Knight, Frank H., *Freedom and Reform*,
  60, 137, 372
Kroeber, A. L., 267
Kulischer, E. and A., *Kriegs- und
  Wanderzüge: Weltgeschichte als
  Völkerbewegung*, 13, 54

Ladd, G. T., 268
Laird, J., *A Study in Moral Theory*, 321
Lang, A., 318
Lange, F. A., 250
  History of Materialism, The, 268
Lapouge, G. V. de, 14, 182
  Race et milieu social, 189
Lassalle, F., 149
Lecky, W. E. Hartpole, 243, 247, 256
  *History of European Morals from
    Augustus to Charlemagne*, 268
  *Map of Life, The: Conduct and
    Character*, 268
Leibniz, G. W., 176
Lenin, V. I., 146
Lessing, G. E., *The Education of the
  Human Race*, 75, 127
Levy, R., *The Sociology of Islam*, 290
Lewis, Arthur, *The Theory of Economic
  Growth*, 143n.
Lewis, Aubrey, 'Health as a social
  concept', 308
Lindsay, Lord, 66, 69
  'Individualism', 69
Locke, John, 236–7, 256
  *Essay Concerning Human Understanding,
    An*, 268
Lockwood, W. W., *The Economic
  Development of Japan*, 143
Loewe, A., 178
  Price of Liberty, The, 189

Lotze, H., 249
  Mikrokosmus, 127
  Outlines of Practical Philosophy, 268
Lubbock, 210

McDougall, W., 166, 180–81
  Group Mind, The, 188
  National Welfare and National Decay, 189
MacIver, R. M., 15n., 17–19, 21
  Community, 64n.
  Society, 19, 54
McLennan, J. F., 210
McNair, A. D. (Buckland, W. W., and)
  Roman Law and Common Law, 187n.,
    189
Madariaga, S. de, 166, 168, 173–4,
    175n., 180
  Englishmen, Frenchmen, Spaniards, 189
Maine, Sir Henry, 109
Malinowsky, Bronislaw, 249
  Sex and Repression in Savage Society, 268
Mannheim, H., *The Dilemma of Penal
  Reform*, 357n.
Mansfield, Lord, 303
Marett, 211
Maritain, Jacques, 270
Marr, Wilhelm, 190
Marshal, T. H., 'Revision in economic
  history', 132
Marshall, A., *Principles of Economics*, 54
Marvin, F. S. (ed.), *Progress and
  History*, 127
Marx, Karl, 82, 98–9, 120
  Das Kapital, 99, 101, 127
Mattuck, I.
  Jewish Ethics, 295
  What are the Jews?, 208
Meillet, A., *Les Langues dans l'Europe
  Nouvelle*, 54, 101n.
Meyer, Richard M., 178
  'German character as reflected in
    national life and literature', 189
Mills, J. S., 47, 66, 87, 209, 271, 274,
    293, 362
  Auguste Comte and Positivism, 87, 127,
    271, 293
Miller, J., 268
Moberley, Sir Walter, *Responsibility*,
    355n.
Money-Kyrle, R., 317
  Psycho-Analysis and Politics, 336–7
Montandon, G., 21
  Traité d'Ethnologie Culturelle, 54
Montesquieu, Baron de, 249
  Spirit of Laws, The, 268
Morant, G. M., 179n., 189, 210
Morgan, C. Lloyd, 45, 104–5
  Emergent Evolution, 54
Morley, J., 274
  'Essays on Condorcet and Turgot', 127
Muirhead, J. H., 261
  Elements of Ethics, 268

Müller-Freienfels, R., 174n., 176, 177, 178n.
  Psychologie des deutschen Menschen, 188
Murray, Gilbert, 274
Mussolini, Benito, 368
Myrdal, G., *An American Dilemma*, 155n.

Needham, J., *Integrative Levels*, 105, 127
Neumann, Franz, 249
  (ed.), *Spirit of Laws, The*, 268–9
Newton, Sir Isaac, 85, 91
Niebuhr, R.
  Faith and History, 78, 127
Nietzsche, F. W., 164n., 176n.
  Beyond Good and Evil, 188
Novalis, 271
Nugent, J., 269

Ogburn, W. F., and Goldenweiser, A.
  (eds.), *The Social Sciences and their
  Interrelations*, 55, 219n., 267
Ogden, C. K., 249
  (ed.), *Theory of Legislation, The*, 269

Pareto, V., 14, 79, 145
  Mind and Society, The, 54, 127, 283
Pearce, J. W. D., *Juvenile Delinquency*, 351
Pearl, 139
Pfister, O., *Some Applications of
  Psycho-Analysis*, 333
Pfleiderer, Otto, 175
  'National traits of Germans as seen
  in their religion, The', 189
Picavet, Fr., *Les Idéologues*, 83n., 127
Pinsker, L., *Auto-Emancipation*, 208
Pirenne, H., 14, 48, 141, 185
  History of Europe, 142n., 147, 160n.
  *Périodes de l'histoire sociale du
  capitalisme, Les*, 145–6, 189
Pittard, E., *Les races et l'histoire*, 189
Plato, 318
Plucknett, T. F. T., *A Concise History of
  the Common Law*, 145n.
Poincaré, H., *Dernières Pensées*, 281
Poor Law Commissioners' Report 1834, 152n.
Prichard, J. V., 269
Proudhon, P. J., *Philosophie du Progrès*, 127

Radbruch, G., 362
Radcliffe-Brown, A. R., 249
  *African Systems of Kinship and
  Marriage*, 269
Ranke, L. von, 130
Rashdall, H., *Theory of Good and Evil*,
  286
Read, Carveth, 36, 239, 265n.
  Natural and Social Morals, 54, 269, 299
Redfield, Robert, 236
  *Primitive World and its
  Transformations, The*, 269
Reeve, Henry, 57
Rein, Thiodolf, 210

Renouvier, C. B., 44, 73, 120
  Essais de Critique Générale, 74, 127
Richards, Audrey, 248
  *Bemba Marriage and Present
  Economic Conditions*, 269
Rickert, H., 130, 153
  Kulturwissenschaft und Naturwissenschaft,
  130
Rivers, 216
Riviere, Joan, 267
Robbins, L., *Nature and Significance of
  Economic Science*, 54
Robinson, G. T., *Rural Russia under the
  Old Regime*, 141n.
Roosevelt, F. D., 236
Rosenthal, E. I. J. (ed.) *Judaism and
  Christianity*, 295n.
Ross, W. D., 35
  Right and the Good, The, 54, 302
Ruppin, A., *The Jews in the Modern
  World*, 208
Russell, Bertrand, 255–6, 262–3, 268,
  278, 365–8
  Authority and the Individual, 269, 365
  History of Western Philosophy, A., 338n.,
  367
  Human Society in Ethics and Politics, 279
  Marriage and Morals, 269
  Power, 132
  Religion and Science, 269, 365, 368

Samuel, Maurice, 205–7
  Great Hatred, The, 208
Sapir, E., *Language*, 157n.
Schmoller, 47
Schucking, Levin L., 163
  Englische Volkscharakter, Der, 188
*Sciences Sociales en France, Les:
  Enseignement et Recherches*, 55
Sée, H., 52
Seligman, C. G., 170
  'Psychology and racial differences', 189
Shakespeare, William, 170
Shand, A., 212
Shaw, G. B., 348
Sidgwick, H., 25, 257, 261, 302, 309
  Development of European Polity, 52
  Elements of Politics, The, 54, 285, 297
  *Ethics of Green, Spencer, and
  Martineau*, 225n.
  Methods of Ethics, The, 269, 286,
  296–7, 347
  Outlines of the History of Ethics, 335n.
Simpson, G. G., *The Meaning of
  Evolution*, 106, 127
Smith, Adam, 27–9, 33, 218, 245
  Theory of Moral Sentiment, The, 217, 269
Smith, Robertson, 318
Smuts, J. C., 45n., 105
  Holism and Evolution, 54
*Social Sciences, The: Their Relations in
  Theory and Teaching*, 55

Söderblom, N., 'Ages of the World', 76n.
Sombart, 52
Sorel, G., *Les Illusions du Progrès*, 127
Sorokin, P. A.
  Contemporary Sociological Theories, 54
  Society, Culture and Personality, 127
Spencer, H., 48, 52, 87, 131, 142, 237–8, 256, 274
  First Principles, 209
  Principles of Ethics, The, 269
  Principles of Sociology, The, 54, 73, 127
  Study of Society, The, 131–2, 143
Spengler, O., 79, 111
  Decline of the West, The, 127
Spiller, G. G., 35n.
  Origin and Nature of Man, The, 54
Spinoza, B., 271, 282
  Ethics, 284
Staub, B. (Alexander, F., and), *The Criminal, the Judge, and the Public*, 346, 352–3
Stewart, Dugald, 245n., 256, 269
  Collected Works, 225n., 269
  Philosophy of the Active and Moral Powers of Man, The, 269
Stöcker, Adolph, 202
Stonequist, E. V., *The Marginal Man*, 208
Stout, G. F., 168
  Manual of Psychology, 189
Sully, J., 211
Sutherland, A., 239, 249
  Origin and Growth of the Moral Instinct, The, 269

Tacitus, 165, 181
Talmud, The, 294
Taylor, A. E., 247
  Faith of a Moralist, The, 269, 322n.
Temple, Archbishop, 347
Tennant, F. R., *The Concept of Sin*, 358n.
Thévenot, Melchissédec, *Relations de divers voyages curieux*, 237n.
Thomas, E. C., 268
Thurnwald, R. (ed.), *Soziologie von Heute*, 55
Tocqueville, A. de, *De la Démocratie en Amérique*, 57, 73, 127
Tönnies, F., 15–18, 21
  Einführung in die Soziologie, 54
  Einleitung, 17n.
Toynbee, A. J., 13, 21, 41, 80, 181n.
  Civilization on Trial, 80, 113–15, 127
  Study of History, A, 54, 189
Trevelyan, G. M., *History of England*, 152n., 153, 160n.
Troeltsch, E., 130, 134, 153
Turgot, A. N. J., 71, 83
  Oeuvres, avec biographie et notes par G. Schelle, 128

Tylor, E. B., 38, 101, 211, 217, 238, 240, 291
  Anthropology, 270
  'Primitive Society', 269
  Researches into the Early History of Mankind, 217n.

UNESCO (ed.), *Human Rights: Comments and Interpretations*, 270
Unwin, J. D., *Sex and Culture*, 326n.

Vauvenargues, L. de, 305n.
Vierkandt, A., *Gesellschaftslehre*, 11, 54
Voltaire, F., *Essai sur les Moeurs et l'Esprit des Nations*, 128

Wallace, A. F., 211
Watson, John, *The Child and the Magistrate*, 359
Weber, A., 111
  Prinzipien der Geschichts- und Kultur-Soziologie, 128
Weber, Max, 61, 110
Wegrocki, H. J., 'A critique of cultural and statistical concepts of abnormality', 333
Westermarck, E., 28–9, 35–6, 52, 89, 209–34, 239, 243, 256–8, 264, 289, 302, 327n., 356
  Christianity and Morals, 227, 233
  Ethical Relativity, 54, 217, 225, 270, 375
  Future of Marriage, 227
  History of Human Marriage, 228
  Marriage Ceremonies in Morocco, 212
  'Methods in social anthropology', 216n., 217n.
  Moral Ideas, 212, 215, 228
  Origin and Development of Moral Ideas, 54, 214, 270, 301, 349, 357n.
  Ritual and Belief in Morocco, 212
  Three Essays on Sex and Marriage, 230
  Wit and Wisdom in Morocco, 212
Westermarck, N. C., 209
Wheeler, G. C., 232n.
Wheeler, W. M., 45
  Emergent Evolution and the Development of Societies, 55
White, J. Martin, 212
Whitehead, A. N., 94, 275
  Adventures of Ideas, 275
  Religion in the Making, 113, 116n., 128
  Science and the Modern World, 90, 113, 114, 128
Wiese, L. von, 11, 18–19
  Allgemeine Soziologie, 55
Windelband, W., 130
  Introduction to Philosophy, An, 128
Woolf, L., *Empire and Commerce in Africa*, 189
Wright, Lord, 303
Wundt, W., 45, 239, 289
  Ethik, 270